REDEEMING THE SOUTH

The Fred W. Morrison
Series in Southern Studies

PAUL HARVEY

Redeeming the South

Religious Cultures
and Racial Identities
among Southern
Baptists, 1865–1925

The

University

of

North

Carolina

Press

Chapel Hill
and London

Library of Congress
Cataloging-in-Publication Data
Harvey, Paul, 1961–
Redeeming the South: Religious Cultures
and Racial Identities among Southern
Baptists, 1865–1925 / by Paul Harvey.
p. cm. — (The Fred W. Morrison series in
Southern studies)
ISBN 0-8078-2324-4 (cloth: alk. paper).
ISBN 0-8078-4634-1 (pbk.: alk. paper)
1. Baptists—Southern States—History
—19th century. 2. Baptists—Southern
States—History—20th century. 3. Afro-
American Baptists—Southern States—
History—19th century. 4. Afro-American
Baptists—Southern States—History—
20th century. 5. Southern States—Race
relations. 6. Southern States—Church
history—19th century. 7. Southern
States—Church history—20th century.
8. Southern Baptist Convention—History.
9. National Baptist Convention of the
United States of America—History.
I. Title. II. Series.
BX6241.H37   1997   96-32882
286'.175'089—dc20   CIP

01 00 99 98 97   5 4 3 2 1

For my parents,
William Gipson and
Willie Maude Harvey,
two Southern Baptists
who have lived out the
best of their tradition

CONTENTS

ACKNOWLEDGMENTS

I am deeply indebted to the libraries and archivists who made my research both possible and fruitful, including the following: the North Carolina Baptist Historical Commission in the Smith-Reynolds Library, Wake Forest University; the Records Room of the Foreign Mission Board of the Southern Baptist Convention; the Howard University Library; the American Baptist Historical Society Library, Rochester, New York; and the Boyce Library at the Southern Baptist Theological Seminary, Louisville, Kentucky. Interlibrary loan personnel at the University of California at Berkeley, Valparaiso University, Belmont University, and The Colorado College expedited an inordinate number of requests with efficiency. My deepest debt is to the Southern Baptist Historical Library and Archives in Nashville, Tennessee. The librarians and archivists there provided me with a research home, ferreted out obscure documents from the depths of their vaults, searched out places for me to live, directed me to the closest lunch bargains, and endured my overdue book lapses. For all this and more, thanks go to Bill Sumners, Pat Brown, Mary Jo Driscoll, Lynn May, and Charles DeWeese.

My research was also made possible by grants and fellowships that allowed me extended time for travel to numerous archives and libraries. At the University of California at Berkeley the Max Farand Fund afforded me two travel grants, and the Humanities Research Grant funded a separate research outing, which provided invaluable information for this work. After completing the dissertation on which this book is based, the Louisville Institute provided summer research monies that kick-started the process of revising it into a book. I thank James Lewis, Dorothy Bass, and the members of the Louisville Institute Grant committee for their encouragement. A National Endowment for the Humanities Seminar directed by Charles Reagan Wilson at the University of Mississippi allowed me to test out many ideas. From 1993–95 the Lilly Fellows Program in Humanities and the Arts at Valparaiso University generously provided me with a two-year teaching postdoctoral fellowship. Final revisions on the manuscript were funded by a grant from the Pew Program in Religion and American History at Yale University, whose directors, Harry "Skip" Stout and Jon Butler have provided a tremendous resource for younger scholars in the field of American religious history. At the University of North Carolina Press, David Perry has been a constant source of encouragement, and Mary Caviness was a model copyeditor.

The University of California at Berkeley provided me with an intellectual and social environment that encouraged, sustained, and excited me during years of graduate study. I am most indebted to Mabel Lee and Jane Stalhut, who shepherded me through the treacherous UC bureaucracy. Jim Gregory, the second reader of the original manuscript, knew when to challenge me to do better and when to provide encouragement and support. This book is much better for his careful attention to it. My interest in the history of the South was sparked originally by Leon F. Litwack. Over the years, he has provided the kind of professional guidance and personal warmth that epitomizes the ideal of a mentor and friend.

My list of personal acknowledgments is long, and I hope my friends and colleagues will understand if I simply list their names here: Michele Fontaine, Glennys Young, Nicky Gullace, and the other denizens of 2800 Garber; Ron Yanosky, Mark Shulman, Lynne Stiles, Zhao Xiaojian, Burt Peretti, and numerous other friends and colleagues at Berkeley; Anita Tien, a friend during some trying times; Carol Neel, Liz Feder, Mark Johnson, Peter Blasenheim, and the other members of the History Department of The Colorado College; Buzz Berg, Keith Schoppa, Michael Caldwell, Nandini Bhattacharya, Jon Pahl, and other colleagues at Valparaiso University; Arlin Meyer, Mark Schwehn, Pamela Corpron Parker, and others in the Lilly Fellows Program at Valparaiso (the Chicago weather nearly turned me into an icicle, but the warmth of my fellow fellows at Valpo sustained me for those two years); John Boles, Bill Leonard, Samuel Hill Jr., Beth Schweiger, Daniel Stowell, Yvonne Chireau, Laurie Maffly-Kipp, Patrick Rael, and other professional colleagues who have read and critiqued portions of this work at conferences and in other settings; and the members of the Young Scholars in American Religion seminar group at the Center for the Study of Religion and American Culture in Indianapolis, who continue to delight me with their ideas, wit, and support.

Over the last several years Stephanie Paulsell has graced my life with her friendship. Best of all, she served as the minister at my marriage to Susan Nishida Harvey, who is my best friend, my fiercest editor, my mentor in the art of living, my deepest love.

REDEEMING THE SOUTH

Southern Baptists and Southern Religious History

Southern historians have searched for a central theme to bring together the difficult contradictions of the southern past—in particular, the paradox of slavery and freedom. Scholarship on religion in the American South, however, has engaged in little argument on the topic. The central theme of southern religious history in scholarly works remains the rise of evangelicalism, symbolized in the term "Bible Belt" and expressed institutionally in the numerical and cultural dominance of Baptist and Methodist churches. According to this view, the focused moment of salvation has constituted the bedrock of southern religious belief and practice. This evangelical individualism stifled any social ethic, leaving southern churches captive to racism and a dogmatic literalist theology.[1]

Musicians and novelists of the South have recognized the centrality of evangelical Protestantism in a region "haunted by God." William Faulkner, hardly renowned for adherence to evangelical morality, nevertheless acknowledged how he "assimilated" the regional religious tradition, how he "took that in without even knowing it. It's just there. It has nothing to do with how much I might believe or disbelieve—it's just there."[2]

But an overly simple and static use of the concept of evangelicalism hides the diversity of southern religious life. Thomas Dixon Sr. was a conservative Baptist minister in North Carolina. His son Thomas Dixon Jr. also pastored in Baptist churches but branched off into Shakespearean theater and authored the novels *The Leopard's Spots* and *The Clansman*, graphic classics of the popular cul-

I

ture of American racism. The later adaptation of these works into "Birth of the Nation," the 1915 technological wonder of the film world, provided Dixon (and director D. W. Griffith) with a canvas painted with grotesque white supremacist visions of a unified nation. Yet the junior Dixon also served as an advocate of the social gospel, a movement anathematized by many southern evangelicals. His brother, Amzi Clarence Dixon, helped to organize the emerging Fundamentalist movement of the early twentieth century and abhorred Thomas's popular works of fiction as much as Thomas poked fun at Amzi's stuffy theology. The Dixon family of North Carolina illuminates some of the diverse varieties of southern evangelicalism.[3]

In the 1890s, many southern Baptist* parishioners heard weekly homilies espousing conformity to a private, domestic evangelicalism and warning of the dangers of radical ideologies such as Populism. At the same time, rural congregants might hear fiery sermons that condemned the plutocrats and "social parasites" of the era. Rural Baptists of the era typically met in a one-room structure in the countryside in congregations of one hundred or fewer, heard a part-time bivocational minister at monthly meetings, and concentrated their religious expression on overcoming sin and achieving salvation. Meanwhile, inside the impressive structure of the First Baptist Church of Atlanta, a congregation of several hundred experienced an ordered and decorous service. The concept of southern evangelicalism thus explains everything and nothing at the same time.[4]

The static use of this paradigm also obscures the dynamic function of black churches in the postbellum era. Booker T. Washington, a black Baptist layperson, found himself appointed as the designated race spokesman after his famous "Atlanta Compromise" speech in 1895, in which he had advised black Americans to "cast down" their buckets where they were—the South. In the minds of white listeners he seemed to accept second-class citizenship for African Americans. Washington found many supporters within the National Baptist Convention, an organization created in the same year of Washington's speech. But the black Baptist church also nourished figures such as Sutton Griggs, a minister, educator, and novelist from Texas who formulated an early form of Afrocentrism, and Nannie Burroughs, a woman

---

*In this book I use the lowercase "s" in southern Baptist rather than the more conventional uppercase "S" because the former better signifies that "southern" refers to region rather than to any one particular Baptist group. Conventionally, the term "Southern Baptist" refers to those affiliated with the Southern Baptist Convention. Because the SBC in the time period covered in this book was all white and did not include *all* white Baptists in the South, the lowercase is more accurate. The majority of black Baptists, after all, were "southern" also. When a racial qualifier is needed, it will be provided in the text.

who lashed out unflinchingly at racial hypocrisies while fiercely defending middle-class ideals and the rights of African Americans to aspire to them. After Reconstruction these churches rarely challenged the southern racial order in an overt way, providing instead a means of survival for a beleaguered community. This response in itself constituted a rebuke to a southern social order that mercilessly attacked the essential humanity of black people.[5]

The growth of Baptist churches from small outposts of radically democratic plain-folk religion in the mid-eighteenth century into conservative and culturally dominant institutions in the twentieth century illustrates one of the most impressive evolutions of American religious and southern cultural history. The story up to 1865 has been told well for both whites and blacks. The saga of the sixty-year period after the Civil War still lacks a narrative that interprets the black and white Baptist experience in the South within the central themes of American cultural history. This book defines "southern religion" as a biracial and bicultural phenomenon, an understanding much further advanced among scholars of antebellum southern culture than of postbellum southern life. In hearing the combined story of southern Baptists, white and black, we may better understand the broadest themes of southern cultural history from the Civil War to the 1920s.[6] By 1910, about 40 percent of white churchgoers and 60 percent of black churchgoers in the South were Baptists. Most of these nearly five million southern Baptists worshiped in churches associated with the Southern Baptist Convention (white) or the National Baptist Convention (black). In the twentieth century, the Southern Baptist Convention (SBC) became the largest Protestant denomination in America, while the National Baptist Convention (NBC) grew to be the largest black religious organization in the world. Both conventions expanded their influence into outside areas, but until the 1920s the great majority of constituent churches for both groups remained in the South. Churches not affiliated with the SBC or NBC usually were connected to Primitive Baptist groups, who rejected larger denominational structures and mission endeavors. Primitive Baptists, concentrated in Appalachia and in up-country regions of the South, made up just over 10 percent of Baptists. Numerous other groups—Regulars, Old Regulars, Independent, Two-Seeds-in-the-Spirit, and so on—made up a rich tapestry of Baptists in Appalachia. Their religious expressions, lovingly described in Deborah McCauley's work, *Appalachian Mountain Religion*, made up an alternative subculture from the mainstream Baptist expressions that form the primary emphasis of this book.[7]

Historians now understand southern Baptists as part of the mainstream rather than the exotic fringes of American religious and cultural history,

Evangelical Protestantism ordered the lives of millions of common folk in the South long after its central role in other parts of the country had been diminished. The southern evangelical emphasis on direct, immediate, and vibrantly emotional contact with God has given the South its distinctive religious coloration. This emphasis on experience remains firmly in the center rather than on the fringes of religious expression in the region.

Historians also have explored thoroughly the argument that southern churches languished in "cultural captivity." White southern churches rarely sought to overturn the southern social and racial hierarchy but rather reinforced and even defined it. In this sense they remained in bondage to southern culture, at least according to traditional definitions of this term. The cultural captivity thesis highlights the moral failings of white southern religion, as it was originally designed to do. But the argument fails to place southern religious history in a bicultural context. Based on studies of white churches and denominational organizations, the model ignores the presence and agency of black churches. It could just as easily be said, moreover, that southern culture fell captive to southern religion. But which "southern religion" and which "southern culture"? Would it be the southern religion of Thomas Dixon Sr., or his son, the famous novelist Thomas Dixon Jr., or Dixon's fundamentalist brother, Amzi Clarence Dixon? Would it be the southern religion of Martin Luther King Jr.'s father, or of Ned Cobb, the black cotton farmer and activist in the Sharecropper's Union in Alabama? By singularizing the terms southern religion and southern culture, the argument overlooks the multilayered nature of religious and cultural interactions.

Beyond the cultural captivity thesis, there remain deeper questions about the relationship of southern Baptists and southern cultures. Anthropologists have explained how religion provides mythological underpinnings for particular cultures, while it also allows dissident groups a chance to formulate alternative visions for a new order. When this idea is applied to southern religion, it is possible to replace the "captivity" metaphor altogether and use instead anthropological notions of religion and culture as inextricably intertwined. Southern culture has been identified closely with decentralized, localistic, traditionalist patterns of life and with highly persistent cultures. Well into the twentieth century, southern folk remained intensely defensive of local norms and reluctant to break from entrenched practices. They found in both their white and black Baptist churches a powerful theological and ecclesiastical tradition—congregational independence—that taught that God had sanctioned local men and women to run their own spiritual affairs and implied that they were meant to control their own destinies. The fierce localism of southern Baptist churches, the tenacity of rural religious practices, and the conflict between these practices and the centralizing desires of denominational reformers and Progressive Era activists suggest a fresh way to look at the relation of southern religion and southern culture. This same congregational control allowed black Baptists to nourish a unique religious culture that, though politically subdued during the early twentieth century and relentlessly criticized by both white and black Baptist denominationalists, was a wellspring from which flowed later movements for freedom.

The various meanings of the term "Baptist democracy" derived from the polity of congregational independence developed by English Baptists and Anabaptists in Europe during the early years of Puritanism. English Baptists preached the doctrines of the absolute necessity of a "regenerate membership" in true church congregations, adult baptism by immersion, the illegitimacy of any religious authority above the conscience of the individual believer or the local congregation, and the evils inherent in state-supported religion. The role (if any) of man's free will in earning salvation divided congregations and soon differentiated the Calvinist "Particular" Baptists from the "General" Baptists, so named because of their belief that God had extended the opportunity of salvation to mankind in general. But Baptists of various theological leanings and differing shades of Calvinism concurred on the necessity of individual salvation prior to church membership and the independence of local congregations from the dictates of outside authority.

In America, the Baptist faith originally spread from Connecticut and Rhode Island, where Roger Williams and other settlers in the mid-seventeenth century transplanted English Baptist ideas and were excluded from Puritan towns for their radical beliefs about the autonomy of individual souls. In the 1750s and 1760s a growing sect of Separate Baptists arose in the backcountry of Virginia, while in Charleston the "Regular" Baptists, who preached a less harshly Calvinist theology, spread through the South Carolina low country. The pioneering missionary efforts of Shubal Stearns and Daniel Marshall sparked the growth of the Baptist faith in North Carolina. These men had become evangelicals during the Great Awakening in Connecticut and later moved south to evangelize in the Piedmont region of North Carolina. The congregations they formed in North Carolina soon branched out. Early Baptists in the region formed their first association (groupings of churches in local areas who met together for worship and advice) in the 1750s. In the 1760s and 1770s, Separate Baptist congregations in Virginia and the Carolinas grew rapidly. By the 1780s the Baptist insistence on the "wall of separation" between church and state influenced framers of the Constitution to enshrine the principle in the founding document of the new nation.[8]

The religious culture of Baptists in the Colonial and Revolutionary era South developed within the context of eighteenth-century revivalism. Southern believers cultivated a democratic evangelicalism with an emphasis on communal emotionalism and a conscious self-denial of worldly goods together with a significant bent toward acquiring wealth in the form of land. The evangelicals defined "sin" as personal behavior (for example, gambling, horse racing, fashionable dressing, dueling) that, for the gentry, signified honor. Southern pietists, many of whom lived at the margins of their society, found in enthusiastic religion and plain living the elements of a common consciousness. Their ethic also provided a theology of discipline, savings, and acquisition as well as a polity of patriarchal authority for men on the move in the early-nineteenth-century South.[9]

As Baptist churches and associations grew numerically and geographically in the early nineteenth century, evangelical activists laid the groundwork for the system of benevolent ventures that would blanket the country in the nineteenth century. In 1814 the first national convention of Baptists met, attracting both northerners and southerners. This meeting inspired the formation of a number of voluntary societies that collected funds from interested individuals and churches for projects of religious benevolence. The most important of these for this study was the American Baptist Home Mission Society, organized in 1832, which played a central role in work among the freedpeople.

Slavery split the nation in 1861. Twenty years previously, it already had ruptured nearly every American denomination and fractured Baptist benevolent societies along sectional lines. Mainline northern Baptists, mostly antislavery but also antiabolitionist, tried unsuccessfully to mediate the conflict between abolitionists and proslavery southern Baptists. The division grew bitter in the early 1840s, when northerners contested the appointment of slaveholders as home missionaries. In 1844, southerners demanded a policy statement from northern Baptists engaged in home mission work. The northerners replied, "One thing is certain: we can never be a party to any arrangement which would imply approbation of slavery." Deeply angered by this action and impressed with their duty to evangelize more actively in their own region, white southern Baptists convened in Augusta, Georgia, and organized the Southern Baptist Convention (SBC).[10]

Rather than organizing discrete societies for separate benevolences, as had formerly been the practice among Baptist groups, the founders of the SBC formed a single denomination with the power to appoint boards to oversee separate missionary programs. Membership was limited to individuals, churches, and associations that made specific contributions to the denomination. In fact, the "convention" itself existed, in a legal sense, only during the time of the biannual (and later annual) meeting. In this way, though the SBC benefited from the central control of benevolent endeavors, it still held no power over individual churches, since each congregation could opt whether or not to cooperate with the central body. Those attending the meetings of the SBC were dubbed "messengers" rather than "delegates" because they were said to be presenting "messages" from their local churches and associations, not acting as delegates with specific instructions.[11]

By the Civil War, prominent ministers and congregations in the region claimed a status of respectability far removed from their humble beginnings in the Colonial era. In the older southeastern states, especially in Virginia and North Carolina, state conventions erected colleges for ministerial education, established and edited religious newspapers, and raised money for architecturally impressive churches in important southern cities. Hundreds of local associations, formed when ministers and laypeople from various churches in a particular region met together for mutual counsel, advised churches on important matters of discipline and doctrine. Associations allowed for congregational independence while also providing some guidance by informally resolving disputes between churches on questions of doctrine. Churches were not required to follow the dictates of associations, but these regional bodies nevertheless held the power to "break fellowship" with congregations that violated doctrinal or behavioral standards. Associations could also withhold funds for ministerial support, student scholarships, church building construction, and other endeavors. Regional and state Baptist conventions supported a variety of educational institutions where young men trained for the ministry. The work of missionaries, who established thousands of churches in the South, and the support of educational institutions of both the secondary and collegiate level, proved the most enduring contributions of white state Baptist organizations.[12]

The march from the popular enthusiasms of the eighteenth century to the denominational respectability of the nineteenth engendered resentments in much of the rural South, particularly in the newly settled areas of the Southwest. Just as southeastern Baptists formed a self-conscious establishment, Baptists in the hill country and in the southwestern states developed alternative theologies, schools, and publications. Their subregional religious culture valorized democratic localism and opposed urban affectations. Antimission Baptists, as they were called, rejected the notion that church people should advance the causes of the benevolent empire. They clung to a Calvinist orthodoxy that preached the uselessness of "means" to bring men to salvation. Their extreme localism was a religious expression of their isolation in a South increasingly divided by wealth, geography, and access to market-based, staple-crop economies. The antimission Baptists condemned political, economic, and denominational elites in the same breath. They compared denominational structures to power-seeking ecclesiastical or political hierarchies, while they viewed their own churches as defenders of the pure gospel of republican independence.[13]

The Landmark movement, a more theologically developed form of Protestant primitivism, offered the strongest intellectual alternative to the denominational establishment. The Landmarkists identified the local congregation as the source of all power and the Baptist minister as the locus of authority. The Landmarkers challenged the prerogative of centralizing denominational elites, substituting instead the "pure" local church as the authoritative voice of Baptists. Landmarkists arose as one part of the "democratization of American Christianity" in the antebellum era. They also voiced the Baptist version of a widespread movement known as "Primitivism," which called for a return to the pure church of apostolic days before the ravages of institutionalized Christianity. In short, the Landmarkers represented a folk faith with an ideological edge. In the early twentieth century the Landmarkist challenge to the SBC spent its force, and the Landmarkers split off into the Baptist Missionary Association, a small organization drawing most of its adherents from Arkansas, northeast Texas, and Missouri. The democratic and primitivist impulses expressed in Landmarkist doctrines permanently imprinted southern religious culture.[14]

The SBC constituency, lower on the economic scale than the other major southern denominations—Methodists, Presbyterians, and Episcopalians—but struggling for legitimacy and respectability, typified the average religious folk of the region. In fact, the struggles of the SBC parallel the relationship of the South to the nation as a whole. It was not quite in, and not quite of, the dominant world of the American middle class, uncertain within itself about whether it really wanted to be part of that world.

In the late eighteenth century, a moment of opportunity for a biracial religious order seemed fleetingly to present itself. Whites and blacks in backcountry congregations worshiped together. They called each other by the respectful evangelical titles "brother" and "sister" and wept to each other's exhortations. A few white Baptist ministers in Virginia declared slavery to be a sin, freed their own slaves, and advocated lifting restrictions on black men who wished to preach the Gospel in public.

But this apparent opening was illusory. It quickly became evident that whites valued the blossoming of their evangelical institutions and would make the necessary moral accommodations to maximize their growth.

Southern Baptists never accepted their African American coreligionists as equals. They lacked the will, the fortitude, the theology, and the intellectual tools to even contemplate doing so. As Virginians and Marylanders had established as early as the 1660s, freedom from the bondage of sin would never equal freedom from human bondage. Despite the presence of the occasional odd antislavery southern divine (such as David Barrow), white southern Christians erected a wall of separation between the realms of spiritual and temporal equality. By 1830, white Baptists who had questioned slavery in late-eighteenth-century Virginia were defending it as a divinely sanctioned social order. In South Carolina, where few whites ever challenged the peculiar institution, Baptists worked feverishly on a Christian proslavery apologetic. Richard Furman, a prominent cleric in the state, argued that God sanctioned American slavery in order to bring the Christian message to heathen Africans and teach "superior" peoples to care for the "inferiors" entrusted to them. God watched over humanity; husbands provided for and protected wives and children and received obedience and respect in return; masters provided for and protected slaves and demanded obedience. By the 1850s such a view reigned as a virtually unchallenged orthodoxy among white southern evangelicals, be they elite divines or uneducated exhorters.[15]

Enslaved Christians found in Afro-American evangelicalism a faith that provided many with the sustenance to fight off the worst psychological abuses perpetrated by whites. But black Christianity in the antebellum era empowered few slaves in any overt political way. It rarely intended to do so. When Nat Turner, the notorious slave rebel and Baptist messianist, was asked by his lawyer how he interpreted his impending execution for leading a bloody slave uprising, he answered simply, "Was not Christ crucified?" In Charleston, Denmark Vesey used his Methodist connections to organize an uprising of enslaved people in the region, narrowly averted when an informant divulged the plot. For most enslaved Christians, however, the evangelical faith provided not so much the fuel for violent revolt as spiritual protection from the heinous system of racial subjugation supported by their "white brethren" as God's plan to Christianize the heathen.[16]

Enslaved Baptists in the antebellum era could not establish an official institutional network. Whites carefully monitored black Baptist congregations and disbanded the early African Methodist Episcopal Church in the South after Denmark Vesey's aborted rebellion. But from the 1820s forward, black congregations sometimes were allowed a separate existence from their white parent churches. Over 150 separate black churches were formed. Despite the increasingly hostile attitudes of whites to black religious independence, institutions such as the First African Baptist Church of Savannah managed to maintain a separate if not autonomous existence. The presence of these congregations testified to the faith of enslaved people in the power of Afro-Christianity to overcome the most unpromising of conditions. The churches were not independent, but they nurtured independent spirits.[17]

Southern Baptist congregations in the antebellum era often claimed a substantial membership of enslaved African Americans. Presiding ministers solemnly recounted to them the biblical injunctions to obey their masters. This lesson on the cultural captivity of southern churches was not lost on the slaves. Frederick Douglass, the escaped slave and prominent black abolitionist, delighted northern audiences with his renditions of the hypocritical solemnities of white southern clerics. But blacks participated to a larger degree in southern white antebellum churches than historians once understood. White ministers tutored black protégés for missionary work, on occasion even setting them free. Black Baptists in white churches sometimes testified in church disciplinary actions against white defendants. Black members were considered part of churches, even if only their first names might be recorded on the roll book.[18]

Enslaved blacks embraced the Christian message of the ultimate equality of men before God. They also understood that the state and the master must be obeyed to the degree necessary for survival. But southern evangelical moralism failed to stamp out the expressive styles of enslaved African Americans. On the contrary, the evangelical enthusiasm of southern religion allowed for the adaptation and transformation of African customs of communal joy and sorrow. Whites interpreted the slaves' religious expression as evidence of an admirable, simplistic fervor and thus could hardly condemn it. But they feared it and sought to restrict its expression to services sanctioned and overseen by whites.[19]

Enslaved Christians in the antebellum South fashioned a religious culture that synthesized Euro-American Christian beliefs and African expressive styles into a sustaining Afro-Baptist faith. This faith took shape partly under the suspicious eyes of watchful but devout whites; but more important, it developed in the sacred spaces the slaves created for themselves in their own private worship. Sometimes noticed (and often ridiculed) by whites, slave religion found its fullest articulation in the brush arbors and secret places where enslaved Christians could express their faith freely. In these gatherings, the deepest desires for freedom found voice among people otherwise compelled to dissemble before old master. One black Texas minister, illiterate during slavery and told by the master to preach obedience, countered his restrictions in private: "I knew there was something better for them but I darsn't tell them so lest I done it on the sly. That I did lots. I told the Niggers, but not so Master could hear it, if they keep praying that the

Lord would hear their prayers and set them free." From these settings came some of the most beautiful creations of American culture—the spirituals, the ring shouts, and the African American chanted sermon.[20]

The Civil War revolutionized southern religious life for both blacks and whites. Before the war, the white southern ministry reaffirmed the view that "pure religion" involved defining and enforcing the proper behavior of individuals in their divinely prescribed social duties, not questioning the roles themselves. Ministers led in the "sanctification of slavery," realizing that the defense of chattel slavery in a liberal democracy necessitated the divine stamp of approval for "our way of life." The axiom that politics should be left out of the pulpit effectively muffled religious dissent. White southern evangelicalism served conservative ends from the early nineteenth century forward.[21] But this implicit prohibition against ministers engaging in "political-religion" loosened considerably during and after the war. Baptist ministers took an active part in secession discussions, some fervently supporting it, others fearing it as a rash and unwarranted move. The Alabaman Basil Manly Sr. exulted in his prominent role in secession discussions. The genteel Virginian John A. Broadus opposed secession but decided in 1861 that "it would be worse than idle to *speak* against it now" and that he should "resolve to do my duty as a citizen here." Southern political leaders understood the necessity of enlisting the spiritual authority held by Methodist and Baptist clerics for the war effort. A way thus opened for ministers to accept a greater sense of public responsibility. Chaplaincy in the Confederate army deeply informed the consciousness of a younger generation of evangelical ministers. Religious organizations such as the SBC flooded wartime camps with religious literature. After the war, elite ministers such as the Virginia Baptist John William Jones evangelized for the Lost Cause, the worship of Confederate heroes. They preserved the sense of the sacred in white southern history originally learned in the Confederate camps.

"Redemption" (meaning, in the religious sense, "washed in the blood") referred politically to the return of white Democrats to power in the 1870s. It also graphically symbolized the often bloody mixing of religion and politics in the postbellum South. During Reconstruction and into the 1880s, ministers preached a Lost Cause theology. The sacrifice of brave Confederate soldiers, they intoned, cleansed the South of its sin, while the cultural determination of whites after the war ensured the return of a righteous order. Once preached in this idiom—the language of the white evangelical South—this view hardened into an orthodoxy that pervaded southern historical interpretation for a century to come.[22]

The Civil War revolutionized black religious life as well. African Americans interpreted the war as a conflict about slavery long before white political leaders North or South conceded as much. After the war, organizers of African American religious institutions used this biblical interpretation of current history—the war and Reconstruction—to galvanize support for the Republican Party. And the separate religious life that enslaved blacks developed before the Civil War, even while worshiping in white churches, took an institutional form after 1865, as African American believers withdrew from white congregations.[23]

White and black Baptists profoundly influenced each other. Together, and separately, they created different but intertwined southern cultures that shaped Baptists in deep and lasting ways. Southerners of widely varying social groups, from plantation owners to yeoman farmers to enslaved blacks, accepted the evangelical Protestant mythology of mankind's unearned ability to achieve salvation. They rarely questioned the assuredness of salvation for the elect and damnation for the unconverted. They expected and demanded that believers exercise their faith by participating in a community of local Christians and by caring for those who were still "lost." By 1920 these beliefs had undergone challenges and some alteration, but the evangelical template still provided a pattern for the culture. The struggle against modernism marked southern religion as a distinctive element in the national culture. Fundamentalism originated as an intellectual movement in northern seminaries, but in the twentieth century it became identified with a group of southern evangelicals given to gloomy premillennial prophecies.[24]

The congregationalism of Baptist church governance also continued to shape the lives of southern believers and the larger culture. To be a southern Baptist meant to worship in a local congregation that exercised ultimate authority in church matters. It meant voting on who would pastor the church, how the church would expend its funds, and how the church's worship service would be conducted. Local congregational control—termed "Baptist democracy" by denominational apologists—also ensured that southern vernacular styles could be exercised freely in congregational gatherings. The localism and traditionalism so entrenched in southern culture found safe haven within the walls of self-governing congregations, where the people of a community could practice "watchcare" on each other and suspiciously guard against sinful influences from the outside world. Denominational leaders found some success in implanting in their constituency Victorian bourgeois norms of private spiritualities and public behavior, but their "progress" in achieving this was slow. The resistance put up by congregants to the visions of the reformers—whether continuing to sing in southern oral dialect, refusing to cooperate with centrally organized denominational programs, or resisting modernizing trends in theology—demonstrated the tenacity of rural culture in southern Baptist life. This resistance also meant estrangement from an increasingly heterogeneous and urbanized America. But Southern religious forms survived the programmatic piety of denominational reformers and gradually penetrated American popular expressions later in the twentieth century.

Southern religion in the white sense has usually produced a profoundly conservative stance, while southern religion for blacks, though rarely assuming any revolutionary bent in the postwar South, has supported prophetic voices of change. The religious cultures of blacks and whites in the South provided the moral and spiritual force both for the Civil Rights movement and for the dogged resistance to it. Blacks transformed the hymn "Woke up this morning with my mind / Set on Jesus" into the civil rights anthem "Woke up this morning with my mind / Stayed on Freedom." Conservative southern whites adopted southern evangelical strictures and added to them the technology of modernity.[25]

Into the 1940s, when white southern Baptists might be worshiping in a small church in Bakersfield, or black Baptists in scattered congregations in south Chicago, religious styles with rural roots endured and were adapted to new settings. Congregants lined out old hymns, listened to impassioned chanted sermons, set aside mourners' benches for the benefit of the unsaved under conviction, and condemned the traditional vices of drinking, dancing, and gambling. Even while many Americans moved to secular ways of perception and action, southern Baptists (many of whom no longer lived in the South) deliberately and proudly remained outside of the national mold set during the era of modernization. They remained instead firmly inside the evangelical consensus of the nineteenth century. By staying where they were, they found themselves in the twentieth century marginalized from the dominant culture. Today, while still seeing themselves as outsiders, their styles have become part of the dominant national culture, and they have claimed a political inheritance denied their forebears. Southern Baptists, white and black, were two peoples divided by religious cultures with different historical roots that ultimately nurtured a tree that sprouted diverse and unique branches.[26]

PART ONE

Religion, Race, and Reconstruction

CHAPTER ONE

Redeemed by the Blood

White Baptist Organizing in the South, 1865–1895

Brethren, is it a sin to love this
Southland more than other lands?
—Benajah Harvey Carroll, sermon
before a Texas congregation, 1891

We are a different people, a
different blood, a different climate,
a different character, different
customs, and we have largely a
different work to do in this world.
—*Biblical Recorder*, July 12, 1899

Early in 1865, while anxiously awaiting news of the fate of the Confederacy, a prominent educator articulated the fears that during Reconstruction compelled white southern evangelicals into action. "Under Yankee rule," he prophesied, "we may not expect to worship God but according to Yankee faith." Northerners, a North Carolinian angrily wrote during Reconstruction, read the biblical Great Commission to "preach the Gospel to every Creature" as a sectional diatribe: "go ye into the South and reconstruct the churches." Georgia Baptists defiantly declared that the region needed "no political-religious preachers, or higher law caste of eldership, sent to enlighten us or our people." White southern Christians would "labor, to preach the Gospel, *in its purity*, to our own people."[1]

From 1865 to World War I, southern resistance to "radical rule" in politics undergirded the rhetoric of white religious and cultural separatism. White southerners feared that northern religious leaders, like northern politicians, would foist a regime of social equality on the region. Once redemption was assured to all, fear of other forms of social disorder soon followed. Whether in manning the front lines in the battle for white supremacy, combating threats such as Populism, or fighting the demon rum, the Southern Baptist Convention (SBC) in the late nineteenth century defended the conservative, hierarchical social order of the South. In the twentieth century, with the SBC becoming the largest Protestant denomination in the United States, it became increasingly apparent that white southerners had lost the war but won their peace. White supremacy, bureaucratic centralization of authority, and paternalistic attitudes among elites all defined the "place" accorded to social groups in this order. The resistance such attitudes met—from the freed-people who rejected the place accorded them by whites, whites who distrusted centralized authority of any kind, and Populists who rejected conservative Redeemer rule—sparked confrontations in religion and politics that reshaped the cultures of the postbellum South.[2]

In public, southern Baptists rarely wavered in their certainty of God's partisanship for the Confederacy. Basil Manly Sr., a minister and educator in South Carolina and Alabama, played a key role in the formation of the Southern Baptist Convention in 1845 and later helped to author the secession resolutions. "I think we are right," he explained to his son after the secession convention, "and I do not shrink from the responsibility of all that I have done." Delegates to the Southern Baptist Convention meetings in the 1860s reaffirmed their belief that the war was "just and necessary" and acknowledged the "divine hand in the guidance and protection of our beloved country." They believed, as Virginia Baptists expressed it, that the course pursued by the North was "alike subversive of the teachings of Christianity and the genius of constitutional liberty and order." They felt secure in the "sweet assurance that our cause is a righteous one." In Edgefield County, South Carolina, churchgoers declared it the "sincere prayer of every true Southern heart" that the separation from the North "may be final, eternal." Even after Sherman's sacking of Atlanta, the pastor of the First Baptist Church of the city admonished his congregation that, "coming out of the fire purified and chastened, but still not destitute of hope, let us be a faithful, earnest, and devoted people." With the exception of churches in Unionist counties, which were often excommunicated from southern Baptist associations, congregations throughout the region sacralized the southern war effort.[3]

In private, however, there were doubts. In July of 1863, as he entertained thoughts of the eventual collapse of the Confederacy, Basil Manly Jr., a scion of the Baptist aristocracy, anguished that surely it could not "be God's will to expose us to the treacherous & fiendish malice & band of robbers & murderers." In South Carolina late in the war, looking after the recently opened Southern Baptist Theological Seminary in Greenville, Manly wondered what hope "in maintain[ing] our independence" would remain if Charleston fell, and felt "a gloom & great darkness" in envisioning the future.[4]

White southern Christians felt "gloom and great darkness" as northern troops leveled churches throughout the region in the course of fighting. Federal armies destroyed all the church buildings of Pine Bluff, Arkansas, Knoxville, and Fredericksburg. At least twenty-six Baptist worship houses lay in ruins in Virginia alone. Federal forces commandeered sanctuaries still standing for use as hospitals, barracks, and stables. Commanders turned over buildings to the appropriate northern missionary agencies. In February 1862, as a service began one Sunday in the Central Baptist Church in Nashville, news came of the surrender of Fort Donelson, "whereupon the congregation dispersed in the wildest confusion." The pastor fled South, and the care of the congregation fell to a northern missionary who never gained the support of the members. Andrew Johnson, the Unionist governor of the state, ordered the jailing of R. B. C. Howell, the most senior southern Baptist clergyman in Nashville, for Howell's refusals to take the required loyalty oath. Howell remained in jail for two months, while his congregation scattered. The black portion of the church, which met in an independent mission, doubled in size as freedpeople moved into Nashville. Years after the Civil War, the ex-slaves finished a new building and boasted of a membership of some 1,500, with meetings "full of life," while their white counterparts struggled through a period of financial difficulties. As white southern independence seemingly waned, black Baptist freedom beckoned.[5]

Churches faced puzzling questions of discipline and theological explanation when members deserted from the Confederate army or sought protection from the draft by fleeing to the Union side. They called up members before the congregation to explain questionable actions such as hiding sons from the draft or refusing to pray for the new nation. Churches excluded members for "unchristian conduct in leaving the bounds of the church in disorder and voluntarily going off with our enemies." In Burnt Corn, Alabama, a congregation disciplined a female member for pilfering bacon put in a storehouse "during the Yankee raid through this country last spring." The discussions about these cases often turned acrimonious. Even more troubling to churches was the number of black members who fled to Yankee army camps for protection. Congregants expelled pastors opposing secession and compelled them to leave the state. In the Upper South, where loyalties and sometimes families were split, the war decimated religious work. At one church in southeastern Tennessee, for example, no meetings were held in 1863 and 1864 because "there arose a Rebelion People in force and Arms Against the Cuntry and Drove the male members nearley all from ther homes and throwed the Cuntry in such a deranged Condition that we thought it best not to mete for a while." In Kentucky, Baptist minister and historian J. H. Spencer, accused of being a rebel by unruly congregants, found himself "threatened by a mob and a halter" during one service. The meeting ended, to his disappointment, with only "one accession to the church." Recalling the period, Spencer noted how the "presence of soldiers irritated the people, and party spirit rendered every attempt to exercise discipline in the church futile."[6]

After Gettysburg, as the war fortunes of the South declined, white Baptists pondered what lessons Confederate Christians should learn from their trials. Perhaps God was choosing this moment to chasten churchgoers in the region in preparation for greater glories to come. Whatever the theodicy used to interpret the Confederate decline, it appeared that the Divine had a different lesson to teach than the triumphalist one previously presumed. The final defeat of the southern forces proved difficult to accept, even for Christians who professed belief in God's foreordaining of events. In early 1865, a Virginia Baptist Association assured its constituents that "the sore trials through which we have passed and the darkness which now overshadows us are a part of the workings of Providence"; they were "chastisements" that would work for "a far more exceeding and eternal glory." By then, however, easy theological formulas no longer satisfied demoralized believers. The fall of the Confederacy "came as a revelation"; they learned that "their plans did not fit the divine purpose," a Baptist minister from Richmond later recalled. When William Wingate, a minister and educator in North Carolina, heard the news of the South's calamities in the spring of 1865, he "rose in rebellion against God," as a friend of his later remembered. Wingate "loved our beautiful Southern Country and could not bear to think that it had been conquered and lay at the mercy of our enemies."[7]

If the outcome of the war proved difficult to accept, Radical Reconstruction seemed an even greater cross to bear. Kentuckian and itinerant revivalist John H. Spencer questioned the institution of slavery and frowned on secession. He knew that war would disrupt his evangelizing. While maintaining a public stance of neutrality, his heart remained with white southerners as they fought what he deemed to be a war for their liberty. Recalling the condition of the South in 1866, he depicted the work of southern religious figures as "like that of God's ancient people on their return from Babylonian captivity. It was a time for rebuilding from ruins and repairing breaches. Not able debates nor sage counsel in conventions but earnest labor among the churches, was the need of the hour." D. P. Berton, a white minister in Alabama, tried to accept God's edict for the outcome but bemoaned the conquering of a government ordained by Providence. "I hope to submit like a Christian to the dealings of my creator," he wrote to a friend, "but I wish to have nothing to do with those who have ruined our country, stolen our property, burned our villages, and murdered our people."[8]

Clerics such as the gentlemanly South Carolinian Richard Furman, who had opposed secession while defending slavery, advised Christians to "reverently acknowledge the hand of God in the great events which have transpired and calmly to acquiesce in the orderings of his Providence." Few followed this advice, even in Furman's home district of Charleston. One religious Redeemer in South Carolina, speaking of the war's conclusion, granted that "God *has brought it about*," but disputed the necessity of loyalty to the reconstructed governments, a notion of "such daring and insulting blasphemy, that thousands here feel like abandoning a religion which gave birth to such atrocities." Charles Manly, younger brother of Basil Manly Jr. and pastor of the First Baptist Church of Tuscaloosa, swore in 1862 that he would have "lived too long" when he beheld "the horrors accompanying U.S. supremacy." The prospect of civil rights for black Americans especially disquieted him. He acknowledged that his region deserved "chastisement" but felt that "to undergo subjugation and extermination at the hand of the Yankees is too much." As late as 1904 he had not "learned to rejoice in our defeat" but had only "honestly and faithfully" submitted to an outcome "authorized by an almighty Providence, whose ways are often past finding out." A northern observer noted the reluctance with which their southern counterparts relinquished the Confederate dream of a slave republic: "They submit to the new order of things as a necessity, from which there is no escape, but claim that they have been conscientious in treason and beneficent in slaveholding."[9]

Lansing Burrows, a career Southern Baptist Convention official, witnessed the devastation of Richmond in 1865. He, too, struggled to accept defeat as "God's will" but still remained an "earnest rebel." A decade later, he came to understand the good purposes that the war served: "Many wrongs were perpetrated, but many rights have been established." Burrows's interpretation of the war as a divine instrument to unite Americans in a global mission crystallized into a resurgent nationalism in the late nineteenth century.[10]

After the war, prospects for the reconstruction of southern religious institutions appeared bleak. The centers of southern Baptist activity—Richmond, Charleston, Atlanta, Columbia, and much of North Carolina—were devastated. "The crops are destroyed, and the people have little religion," Charles Manly lamented to his brother Basil in 1866. "The churches are cold—almost frozen, and the impenitent recklessly pursuing wickedness," another southern Baptist educator wrote. A Texas pastor discovered his assigned province to be "almost an entire blank, so far as vital Godliness and spirituality are concerned." In Alabama, places "once enterprising and thriving, with prosperous churches," were by 1866 "without houses of worship, membership diminished, impoverished, dispirited and demoralized." Worse yet, "intemperance, Sabbath-breaking, licentiousness, infidelity, and irreligion in various forms—the legitimate fruits of war—are on the frightful increase." Where once the "voice of prayer and praise" was heard, Mississippi Baptists reported, "silence and desolation now reigns. Houses dedicated to the worship of God, have become the abode of bats and owls." In 1864, the First Baptist Church of Charleston, a congregation of considerable influence in the region, reported itself "in state of considerable dispersion—many members removed; no pastor; building struck by shells and broken into by robbers." Its fate in the immediate postwar years dramatized the devastation experienced by white southern Baptists.[11]

Before the war, churches affiliated with the SBC claimed about 650,000 members, many of them slaves. Church rolls registered severe declines in the years just after the war, as blacks withdrew from white congregations and as white members drifted away from religious affiliation. Contributions to denominational organizations plummeted, reaching a low in the mid-1870s. In the early 1880s, northern Baptists were spending almost three times as much as their white southern counterparts for missionary work in the region. Subscription lists for regional denominational newspapers dwindled. Baptist colleges were decimated, as entire student bodies fell on the battlefield and endowments vanished. At Mississippi College, only 8 of 104 students returned from the war. Richmond College, a flagship Baptist institution, lost nearly $100,000 of its endowment. Howard College (now Samford University), used as a Federal hospital at the end of the war, counted its loss at $58,000.[12]

The physical and emotional devastation of the white South led some moralists to question the sacralization of their own cause. The male self-assertion required by the code of southern honor always had clashed with evangelical notions of humility. Ministers now singled out honor as a cause for defeat. Intending to humble a "proud vain-glorious vaunting people," God allowed southerners to walk into their own destruction. It was, one minister intoned, "surely a most impressive lesson, if we had ears to hear, respecting the utter impotency of man, and our certain ruin without help from God."[13] Ultimately, however, white spiritual leaders preached that a sanctified, purified white South would rise from the ashes to serve as God's "last and only hope" in a modernizing and secularizing nation. The war, they believed, was the necessary chastening experience that the region needed. Evangelicals closed ranks around the defense of white supremacy and evangelical Protestantism as the bulwarks of a stable order. The term

"Redemption," used by historians to describe the end of Reconstruction in the mid-1870s, assumed an especially powerful connotation for southern believers. Redemption signified individual salvation as well as the deliverance of society from evil. Submission to the North in politics, they believed, would mandate Yankee faith—theological liberalism and racial egalitarianism.[14]

Whether viewed as divine punishment ("God's rod to scourge Israel") or simply as oppression, the opportunity during Reconstruction for African Americans to exercise civil rights appeared to white southern Baptists as an overturning of a divinely ordered hierarchy, as "Yankee faith" in its most frightening form. This specter of "Negro domination" (the term used to describe Reconstruction governments, which were in fact predominantly white), exhibited how the South would be "oppressed in every way in which a robbing, revengeful, blood-thirsty, unprincipled Party can oppress us." One South Carolina Baptist association thought it undeniable that Reconstruction legislation was *unconstitutional, corrupt,* and toward the South *unjust, oppressive, vindictive, and dishonoring,* all produced "by the most *unscrupulous, ungenerous and unchristian* use of the power of victory."[15]

White southern Baptists viewed political and religious reconstruction as the same process in different institutional settings. Just as carpetbaggers had "stolen" the reins of politics, so northern missionaries would seize control of the ecclesiastical government and religious customs of the South. Attending northern Baptist meetings after the war, John Broadus, the preeminent southern Baptist educator of the late nineteenth century, found himself "prayed at" and "cursed," experiences that left him skeptical of any postwar reunion of Baptist forces. "Unless we acknowledge ourselves to have been criminals," he wrote to his fellow southerners, "and ask forgiveness and absolution from these men, and admit their superiority, wisdom and integrity, they refuse to recognize us as equals and fellow-laborers in the Kingdom of Christ." Better to continue to labor apart, he argued, than work together with hearts that "would throb with suspicion and dislike and indignation."[16]

Despite the bitterness brought on by the sectional conflict, some practical and emotional sentiment for institutional reunion existed among both northern and southern Baptists. The issue causing the division, slavery, was dead. Southern Baptist officials maintained strong personal ties to Yankee Baptists, dating back to their days in northern seminaries in the 1830s and 1840s and their frequent meetings and pulpit exchanges since that time. A number of prominent clerics preached in both regions. But controversies over Reconstruction politics destroyed any chances of religious reunion. Since the "whole drift and spirit" of northern meetings suggested the Yankee obsession to "maintain the perfect religious and social equality of the races," a delegate to the SBC noted in the late 1860s, then white southern Baptists could not cooperate with northerners "without endorsing their reconstruction, both political and ecclesiastical." Meeting as "equals" with black Christians and their white allies would mean submission to the northern subversion of the social order. "As Seward found a higher law than the Federal Constitution, in politics," an Alabama Baptist reasoned, northern fanatics maintained "a higher law than the inspired Constitution [the Bible] in religion." He interpreted the events of Reconstruction as part of God's plan for allowing the "twin sisters" of "liberalism and fanaticism" to run their ruinous course and for southern piety to emerge cleansed and strengthened. "Who can tell," he exulted, "what the Almighty may have in reserve for his people in the Southern lands."[17]

White southern ministers were quick to complain of political preachers, but churches that served as organizing centers for resistance to Reconstruction rarely found themselves labeled as mere dabblers in politics. White southern Christians did not even recognize such activity as political in nature but as an extension of the cosmic struggle between order and disorder, civilization and barbarism, white and black. Federal authorities closed down the *Christian Index and Southwestern Baptist* for its advocacy of disloyalty as a moral and religious duty of the white South.[18] One South Carolinian condemned black ministers for delivering "political harangues" that "engender[ed] strife and bitter hatred" but advised his own ministerial troops to be "vigilant and active" in their state electoral contests. "I consider that minister recreant to his duty he owes to his country," he wrote in 1868, "who does not feel and *manifest* an interest in political affairs in the present crisis." He directed white Christians in April of 1868 to set aside "personal considerations . . . in the united efforts to save our state," and to elect those who represented "the white man's interest in the State and out of it." The issue, Jabez Lamar Monroe Curry (then a clergyman and later the head of the conservative Southern Education Board) made clear, was of "patriotism and religion—the feeling of life against death—of liberty against the worst form of enslavement."

In the 1870s, white southern Baptists joined in the battle to end Reconstruction and block the final civil rights proposals floating in Congress. The Civil Rights Bill of 1874 spurred the *Religious Herald* of Virginia, which claimed to eschew political questions, into laying out a set of alternatives remarkably like those of the white resistance to the Civil Rights movement of a century later. White southerners, they suggested, could counteract federal civil rights through state legislation. They could tax themselves to support public institutions for blacks while sending their children to private academies. Whites too poor to afford private schooling, the paper added, should allow their children to "grow up in ignorance" rather than be taught in mixed environments. Interracial schools would be a "greater calamity than barbarism, . . . pestilence, or our national destruction." Given these kind of stakes, white southern Baptists celebrated the return of white Democratic governments to power as "a Christian triumph."[19]

Yankee oppressors looked no more desirable even when outfitted in clerical garb. In Virginia, a well-known minister who accepted an appointment from the northern Baptist home missionary agency soon found that "his churches and the community had denounced and deserted him." He had become a pariah because he was a "political-religionist." In North Carolina, a Unionist association fell under vehement condemnation for endorsing the "very mild" measures of Reconstruction and suggesting that southern Baptists who "took the carnal sword in aid of the rebellion . . . violated the laws of God." Dissent in such matters was unacceptable. The much-vaunted Baptist democracy proved to be a Tocquevillean tyranny of the majority.[20]

White southern Baptists perceived their churches as religious forms of the republican ideal of localized, independent, self-governing institutions. This political language informed their interpretations of the centralization and extension of governmental powers during Reconstruction. A delegate to a state Baptist meeting in 1887 illuminated these ideological affinities between Redemption politics and white Protestantism in the post-Reconstruction South: "As a Democrat I love all Democrats. All Baptists are Democrats. . . . It is THE political faith of the great majority of the members of the church. . . . A Baptist is a Democrat because his church government is democratic and because it has about it none of the paraphernalia or trappings of monarchies and despotisms. . . . All power not DELEGATED remains in the individual churches. He believes in no strong centralized powers." Regional religious spokesmen assured their constituents that southern white Christians stood "distinctively and powerfully" on the side of "a sound and healthy conservatism in doctrine." By contrast the perpetrators of the new "isms," whether of racial equality or liberal theology, carried out their vision with "remorseless cruelty."[21]

The same sectional disputes that energized Baptist organizing also slowed the growth of southern Baptist women's groups. Just after the war, the *Religious Herald* advised evangelical women not to be "unsexed by fanaticism nor seduced by infedility [*sic*] under any of its Protean forms, but remember that *piety* is the chief glory of women, for which there is no substitute." The Civil War, in short, was not to undermine gender conceptions but reinforce them. The well-publicized leadership of abolitionist women in the early feminist movement heightened fears of the overturning of the racial and gendered social order. "Owing to the fact that the question of Woman's Rights in other fields has been pushed to such an offensive extent in more northern latitudes, our people have been bitterly opposed to our women being brought forward in any cause," a Mississippi Baptist association noted. Southern evangelical men urged women to glory in their domestic seclusion. The apostle Paul enjoined subjection to the husband "as unequivocally as he inculcates the passive obedience of the servant to master," a Georgia Baptist reminded readers of the *Christian Index*.[22]

But southern Baptist women were not content to sit that quietly. "The gospel is the magna charta of human liberty. It will eventually sweep away all despotism," a Texas woman proclaimed in 1881. In the late 1860s female members proved instrumental in the reconstruction of church life. Through Ladies Aid Societies, they raised money to rebuild churches, pay ministers, and support missionaries at home and abroad. A number of local congregations could thank women's activities for their reestablishment, including the First Baptist Church of Dallas, which later became the largest single Protestant congregation in the country.[23]

In the 1870s and 1880s, as women's missionary societies in local churches coalesced into state groupings, southern Baptist women talked of a national organization and solicited male allies in their cause. A central committee of women's missionary societies formed in nearly every state in the 1880s. They disseminated information supplied by and forwarded funds for SBC missionary agencies. In 1885, the SBC changed its constitution to ensure that no women would be seated as a delegate to the convention (rejecting two messengers who had come to represent their state conventions, including the wife of the Speaker of the House of Representatives in Arkansas). But denominational leaders recognized that women were becoming a financial backbone of the convention's work.

The women's missionary societies felt the need for a permanent committee to carry on the work during the interim between meetings. "If we do not accord to women places where their powers can be employed along with ours, they will do as our Northern sisters did, leave us and open up fields for themselves," a Mississippian pointed out. Women's missionary society leaders assured their male comrades that they had no interest in forming a separate and distinct board that pursued its own fields of work; that would be "out of harmony with the clinging tendril nature of the refined Southern woman." At the Woman's Missionary Union (WMU) organizational meeting at a Methodist church in Richmond in 1888, Annie Armstrong, who directed the coalescing of missionary societies into a national body, dismissed as "absurd" the accusation that her work contributed to "*women's rights*." She brushed aside opposition to her efforts, saying "religious work has not always been advanced by a majority." The WMU, "disclaiming all intention of independent action," was christened in 1888 to stimulate "the missionary spirit and the grace of giving, among the women and children of the churches" and to aid in fund-raising for "missionary purposes."[24]

The WMU became the single most effective means by which local churches were tied into larger, regionwide causes. In 1888, only 12 percent of southern Baptist churches housed denominational groups of any kind, and the majority of churches contributed nothing to the missionary agencies. By 1900 the number was substantially higher, and denominational agencies once floundering were on a firmer footing. The WMU proved to be the most effective fund-raising device in the history of the convention. In 1910, with only 7.6 percent of overall southern Baptist membership, the WMU raised approximately 30 percent of the total funds used for missions.[25]

The importance of women in revitalizing southern Baptist missions work also may be seen in the rebuilding of the Home Mission Board of the Southern Baptist Convention. The agency provided the means to spread the southern Baptist gospel throughout the South and, eventually, across the nation. After breaking from northern Baptists in 1845, the SBC carried on independent endeavors much like that of other agencies in the "benevolent empire." Convention workers distributed Bibles, preached to slaves and Native Americans, opened churches in newly settled areas, and evangelized fervently for their sect's doctrines. Funding disputes and theological questions raised by the defenders of the antimission tradition, however, limited the effectiveness of this work. During the Civil War the home missionary agency assisted in distributing religious literature to the soldiers, the most successful of its programs to that date. But after the war, the Home Mission Board struggled for survival. By 1882 it was nearly moribund. Paid sporadically and always uncertain of the receptiveness of local believers to outsiders, southern Baptist itinerants carried on difficult work in unpromising circumstances. The experience of an Alabama missionary in 1870 typifies the trials faced by these ministers. He found "ignorance" and "prejudice" against his efforts "and indeed, against everything among us that is systematic and organic." Antimission congregations raised obstacles "that seemed to be almost insurmountable."[26]

In 1882, the Home Mission Board moved from its previously obscure location (Marion, Alabama) to Atlanta, home to Henry Grady's *Atlanta Constitution* and the New South movement. Isaac Taylor Tichenor, a Civil War veteran and former college president, undertook the task of resurrecting the agency. He began with a meager yearly income for the board of about $28,000 and only about forty missionaries, few of whom worked west of the Mississippi. State conventions in the South often cooperated with northern societies, such as the American Baptist Home Mission Society, that sometimes refused to permit fund-raising for Southern Baptist Convention agencies. So Tichenor engaged district canvassers, who markedly increased the income of the agency. In 1892, he boasted that "there was not a missionary to the white people of the South who did not bear a commission from either the Home Mission Board of the Southern Baptist Convention, or one of our State Boards in alliance with it. Its territories had been reclaimed." In 1880, the Board claimed 35 missionaries, 435 converts, and about $20,000 in income. In 1902, 671 missionaries worked under the board's auspices or evangelized locally in cooperation with the agency. By that time home missionaries had established about one out of every eight churches in the SBC. By 1915, 1,409 laborers reaped an annual harvest of 44,000 new church members and 167 congregations.[27]

Tichenor activated the network of women's missionary societies as well. When they requested "mite boxes" to be placed in individual churches, a small investment by the Foreign Mission Board of the SBC netted some $75,000 in contributions over the next ten years. Home missions workers hoped to reap a similar windfall. By the early twentieth century, an annual regionwide offering for home missions accounted for hundreds of thousands of dollars annually. Their labor, a WMU advocate pointed out, simply encouraged women's work for women, not "speaking from the rostrums, Women's Rights, dynamite, Nihlism [sic]."[28]

The successes of the WMU and Home Mission Board in keeping alive the SBC soon produced a second major organizational success: the Sunday School Board of the SBC. For much of the nineteenth century, southern Baptists could not compete with the Philadelphia-based American Baptist Publication Society (ABPS), which boasted a large and highly literate northern constituency, carefully drafted materials suitable for all age groups and sections, and agents scattered throughout the South. One southern observer acknowledged the ABPS's service in supplying books and fostering religious literacy among white southerners but feared that it had already become a "huge monopoly, with its millions over-riding and crushing out any and all opposition or private and individual enterprise."[29]

Southern religious leaders since the 1840s had yearned for a major publishing endeavor of their own. They recognized the serious obstacles in their way, including the relatively low literacy rates in the region and the prevalence of antimission sentiment. As Basil Manly Sr. explained to his son, "our people have to be moved a long way forward, to get into a reading atmosphere." Manly argued that a regionwide publishing house would not snuff out private local efforts but instead would provide economies of scale in book and periodical production. He oversaw the distribution of a *Confed-*

erate Sunday School Hymn Book and involved southern Baptist writers in preparing religious tracts for Confederate soldiers. A children's monthly entitled *Kind Words* followed a few years later. Samuel Boykin, the Georgia minister who published the children's paper, included kind words such as urging young readers to pray that God would change the hearts of Yankees "blinded by fanaticism and infidelity." The centralization of this work carried on during the war presented a model for future publishing plans.[30]

The rhetoric of cultural sectionalism effectively promoted denominational publishing endeavors. In 1870, the SBC considered the establishment of a Sunday school paper that would "be alike free from offensive sectionalism and unsound theology." The creation of a new agency would save the white South from the materials laced with the "vitiated spirituality and rationalism of latitudinarianism of England, and the politic-religious mixture and doctrinal looseness of the North," a southern Sunday school publication advocate suggested. Southerners could not "look abroad" for literary efforts, argued Tennessee Baptists, any more than they should "expect our fields of manufactures and other industrial enterprises developed from the same quarter."[31]

By the mid-1880s the Home Mission Board brought the convention's publication efforts out of debt and began accruing capital for a denominational publishing agency. In 1891, the Sunday School Board of the SBC assumed direction of this work. Its success can be attributed largely to the work of James Marion Frost, who used the New South business ethic to develop the convention.

James Frost, who was born in Kentucky and was pastor of numerous churches throughout the South before 1891, felt called to a special task outside of normal pastoral duties. By 1890 the time had come, he believed, for the SBC to produce its own instructional materials. "God touched me and I thought it," he later declared. Using the widely read *Religious Herald* (the state denominational newspaper in Virginia) as a platform, he proposed the creation of a separate agency, owned and controlled by the denomination, to publish ephemeral religious literature for southern Baptist churches. Baptists from the older southeastern states, who retained close ties with the American Baptist Publication Society, worried that an underfunded new agency would embarrass the cause of southern denominationalism. Frost's proposal gained support when the American Baptist Publication Society considered the employment of black Baptist authors, a move viewed as an "incendiary" threat by many white southern Christians. Frost pressed the initiative, and in 1891 SBC delegates reached a compromise: churches affiliated with the convention would not be "required" to purchase material from the new Sunday School Board but were asked to give the agency a "fair consideration, and in no case to obstruct it." By 1892 Frost confidently, and correctly, predicted that through its periodicals the board would become "a great factor in our denominational machinery, second indeed to no other force."[32]

Frost's tenure at the board from 1896 to 1916 proved to be the turning point for the postbellum institutional history of the Southern Baptist Convention. In a few years the Sunday School Board quickly established a reputation as an efficient supplier of doctrinally correct and socially conservative materials, earning it support from those in the denomination who formerly had opposed it. By the early twentieth century the agency was producing Sunday school materials, periodicals, tracts, hymnals, and full-length books. In 1910, the American Baptist Publication Society withdrew from the South, clearing the field for SBC materials. Frost introduced denominational agencies to methods of corporate operation and significantly increased the capital wealth held by the convention's central bodies. The assets of the Sunday School Board, for example, grew from about $53,000 in 1900 to nearly $760,000 by 1920; the number of its employees increased from a handful in 1900 to 115 in 1920.[33]

In subsequent decades the board's large complex of buildings in downtown Nashville housed a corporate enterprise that churned out the largest volume of materials of religious instruction published in America. This religious literature inculcated a moderate, "systematic" spirituality, a "programmed piety," devoid of intellectual depth and full of religious pabulum. The Sunday School Board's material serviced its market quite well in providing simple evangelical catechisms and dispensing the kind of stories and homilies that *Reader's Digest* and other publications later so effectively employed. The publishing agency's growth in the 1890s served as a fitting climax to the reestablishment of "home rule" in southern politics and religion.[34]

The rebuilding of the Southern Baptist Convention also was evidenced in the rapid growth of churches affiliated with the denomination. After the creation of the Sunday School Board, for example, Baptist Sunday school enrollment in the region jumped from 377,000 in 1880 to 670,000 in 1900, and then to nearly two million by 1920. Membership in churches affiliated with the convention itself grew steadily from 1870 to 1910, moving from just over one million in the early 1870s to nearly two million by 1906. Following a period of rapid growth from 1906 to World War I, the SBC claimed three million members by 1920. The number of actual congregations rose from about 13,500 in 1880 to over 20,000 by the early twentieth century. In the 1890s, Southern Baptists overtook Methodists as the largest religious body in the region. Over the years the SBC solidified its claim as the denomination most broadly representative of the white South.[35]

The editor of the North Carolina *Biblical Recorder*, reflecting on the Baptist past and future, concluded that southerners had been given "the responsibility of preserving our national identity" and "the duty of maintaining the strength and the purity of our religion. This is the mission of the backwardness which has so often been flung upon us for a reproach, but which we are coming to be proud of." But even ideological antimodernists could use the latest in technologies and organizational planning to spread their gospel. The evangelical emphasis on individual voluntarism, personal choice in piety, the values of domesticity, and business-oriented agencies to conduct their affairs long had made evangelicalism consonant with modernization. The successful, profitable Sunday School Board of the Southern Baptist Convention was an outstanding example of this adaptation to the technologies, if not the theology, of modernity.[36]

White Southern Baptists and the Race Problem after the Civil War

We do not believe that "all men are created equal," as the Declaration of Independence declares them to be; nor that they will ever become equal in this world.—Henry Holcombe Tucker, *Christian Index*, March 22, 1883

That which God hath put asunder, let not man attempt to join.
—*Religious Herald*, November 7, 1901

The members of the Basil Manly family in Alabama and South Carolina, including three of the most prominent southern Baptist spokesmen, were among the wealthy white planters who faced the momentous question of the coming of African American freedom. The defeat of the South and the emancipation of the slaves shook them deeply. Charles Manly, the youngest son, released his black workers after the war but fretted for their future: "Poor creatures! Few, very few, will know how to profit by the change in their condition."[37] While Charles worried about whether the freedpeople would profit from emancipation, his brother Basil Manly Jr. contended with ex-slaves who seemed anything but "poor creatures." Shortly after the war Manly complained that his Negroes refused to work on Saturdays even though he extended the "generous" offer of feeding and clothing them "as before," with cash as a year-end bonus if they stayed on the plantation. He would provide for them until year's end and then, as he told his father, they would have to "scuffle for themselves, as I must for my family." Despite such irritations, Manly confidently assessed the prospects for the future of white supremacy. Dismissing any chimera of land redistribution, Manly scoffed at Thaddeus Stevens's "confiscation bilge" as a "sort of chained bulldog to frighten folks."[38]

Basil Manly Jr.'s professed imperturbability only thinly veiled anxieties for his personal safety. In July of 1866, blacks and whites in the area were fighting, and the situation was tense. After the immediate turmoil passed, he explained to his parents the precautions he had taken: "I loaded all my shooting irons—to be ready, if that was necessary: which I did not really anticipate any difficulty: but I had determined to shoot without delay, if there was any violence attempted about my place." Manly prepared to protect his worldly goods from confiscating freedmen: "I [could] deliver 16 shots— 2 from my double barrel gun, 6 from my revolver, and 8 from Spencer rifle I have (a Gettysburg trophy)." Manly never unleashed his arsenal of white resistance, but his formerly cherished assumptions about the God-given duties of whites to "protect" Negroes quickly fell away, leaving him with an attitude of fear and hostility. As he explained to his brother in 1868, "I should be satisfied—to live and raise my child in a 'white man's country'— and if I get a chance to do so, I may accept it."[39]

Unlike his sons, the elder Basil Manly maintained his paternalistic view of white-black relations. Manly Sr. pastored biracial churches in South Carolina in the 1830s, where he helped to formulate Christian proslavery arguments. In his pastorates he attempted to deal fairly with enslaved members of his church. He licensed black men to preach and allowed black members to pursue disciplinary actions against those of their own color. But Manly confronted dilemmas in his antebellum ministry that resisted satisfactory resolutions. In one instance, a black female congregant turned down communion one Sunday because of her forced submission to her master's sexual wishes. Manly urged the owner to desist. Failing in this effort, Manly purchased the woman in order to save her from living in sin with the master.[40]

Basil Manly Sr. later assumed the presidency of the University of Alabama and delivered the opening invocation at the formation of the Confederate States of America in Montgomery in 1861. He convinced the framers to invoke the "favor of Almighty God" in the preamble to the Confederate constitution. As he had in antebellum years, he worried that planters neglected their religious duties to slaves, sending them preachers who could not "make truth plain to those whose powers of apprehension is much better; who must therefore signally fail in regard to those whose powers of apprehension are much worse." He wondered if God was "chastizing [sic] our guilty people in this war" because of this failure. After the war he continued preaching to black congregations, thinking this would help maintain racial peace. Though confident that he could minister effectively to the freedpeople, in his early efforts he "failed to awaken the spirit of *work* and *self-improvement* among them." The congregants "seemed to enjoy and be affected by my preaching," he wrote, yet "the idea seems never to have entered them, that all which they see of power or attainment is the result of labor—labor such as they themselves can perform." The irony of a former slaveowner preaching to formerly enslaved workers about the "need to labor" was lost on him.[41]

The responses of the Manlys to the war and Reconstruction—father Basil's resolve to maintain the paternal bond, Charles's anxious forecast for the imminent degradation of the freedpeople, Basil Jr.'s brusque dismissal of his black workers and subsequent stockpiling of weapons—revealed a wide range of reactions to emancipation. White southern believers such as the Manlys groped to understand the social revolution unleashed by black freedom. They questioned why God allowed such a catastrophe among his "chosen people." Devout planters such as the Manlys also faced the troubling prospects of negotiating with a black labor force that they formerly presumed simply to command as masters. If, as the Bible clearly explained, God placed Negroes in the world to serve as slaves, then how was God's will to be fulfilled in a world without slavery?[42]

Most white Baptists were not of the class of the Manlys, but plain folk who owned few slaves. They confronted race questions most immediately within the bounds of their own congregations. Whites responded to the creation of independent black religious institutions in the same variety of ways they reacted to emancipation. Some expressed shock. Others puzzled over the inscrutability of divine will but gradually accepted these churches as part of the southern religious landscape. Once racial segregation became the norm both in practice and in law, white southerners could hardly remember a time when Christians of both races routinely worshiped together.

That Negroes were created as a separate and inferior race, that black worship consisted of heathenish revelries, that black preachers were unequipped to lead their flocks, and (during Reconstruction, at least) that black churches might become dangerous centers for political organizing— these were fundamental articles of faith held by nearly all white southern Christians after 1865. So was the belief that northerners would infuse dangerous ideas into gullible freedpeople and thus destroy the possibility for a stable and harmonious social order. As Andrew Broaddus of Virginia informed northern Baptists in 1868, "the freedmen are not understood at the North. They come from different races and tribes. . . . Many are mere savages."[43]

Blacks composed over half the membership of many southern Baptist churches before the Civil War. Prominent congregations such as the First Baptist Church of Richmond, Virginia, at one time claimed over 300 white communicants and over 1,100 black members. Enslaved Christians sat in segregated seating areas (often in balconies) but frequently participated in church affairs. They took communion, testified in church disciplinary actions (occasionally against white members), lined out hymns, and gave personal testimonies. That they saved their most deeply felt worship for their own services, often held at night and frequently in secret, does not lessen the importance of biracial worship in antebellum southern Baptist churches. White Christians thought of the black membership in their churches as emblematic of the paternalistic "community" created by beneficent slaveholders and grateful slaves. They also recognized the useful role of churches in instructing blacks on the biblical injunctions about the duties of slaves. On both counts, the black withdrawal from these churches involved, for many white southern Christians, rethinking the illusory construction of their social and religious community.[44]

The question of what to "do" with black members of white Baptist churches after the war resolved itself rather practically. As the freedpeople established their own places of worship, whites gradually accepted separation as divinely ordered. Just after the war, whites pondered religious segregation with trepidation. The "ignorance" of the freedpeople constituted "sufficient proof" that they were not "prepared for separate and independent churches," as a group of North Carolinians expressed it in 1865. Baptists in Edgefield County, South Carolina, in 1865 disapproved of separate organizations for blacks if this would result in "the guidance of ignorant, unqualified, and unauthorized persons." The freedpeople who remained in the white churches were usually afforded the same liberties as before—namely, the right to attend worship in segregated seating—but were now required to submit offerings to the support of the church. The Enon Baptist Church in Virginia resolved that "the regulation of the affairs of the church still belongs exclusively to the white male members . . . except in the election of the pastor, in which case the entire white membership of the church shall vote."[45]

By the late 1860s most southern whites accepted separation as necessary and inevitable. As Basil Manly Sr. expressed it, after black members of his church had petitioned to be set apart, "we think they are not yet prepared for the responsibility of an independent church state. We have told them so, but yet shall let go our hold of them, if after our advice, they desire it." In North Carolina, the Wake Forest Baptist Church secured a building for its former black members and authorized their pastor to organize Sunday schools for ex-slaves who wished to form a separate congregation. In 1866, Edgefield County Baptists reversed their position of a year before, suggesting that "where the colored members become restive . . . it will be wise, regularly to dismiss them, for the constitution of separate churches . . . and to persuade them to secure for themselves the benefits of an educated ministry." As one North Carolinian concluded in 1867, "disguise it as we may, our colored brethren are disposed to independent action—they want preachers and churches of their own." To those who feared that such a measure would give whites the rope with which to hang themselves, Jeremiah Jeter, pastor of a prominent congregation in Richmond, replied, "The Anglo-Saxons can have no cause to fear competition, in any department of enterprise, with any race of men; and certainly not with the African race." Separation thus grew more acceptable to formerly reluctant whites.[46]

Once separation appeared inevitable, local congregations dealt with the issue in myriad ways. In Charleston, white Baptists resolved to allow the freedpeople to remain in their churches "provided they studiously avoid occasions of irritation and offence." The church also encouraged whites to assist blacks in forming separate congregations and keeping watch over their ministers. "Should any of these become infected with a fanatical and disorganizing spirit," the Charlestonians warned, "it is easy to see how much they might mislead their class, of what widespread mischief they might become the authors." In Richmond, black members of the First African Baptist Church, who had met separately under white tutelage since 1841, moved out into a separate building, with the property being transferred to the trustees of the black congregation.[47]

In New Orleans, the situation was more complex. Southern and northern white Baptists in that city contested for control of the Coliseum Place Baptist Church. Originally constructed with money from the church edifice fund of the American Baptist Home Mission Society, southern Baptists had taken over the building lease, and its debt, in 1861. During the war the Union army assigned northern Baptists to use it as a public place of worship. In 1866, white southern Baptists demonstrated proof of ownership and intent to use the building for worship, thus regaining control over the property. This action angered northern abolitionists, but it accorded with Freedmen's Bureau directives to restore peace and normal civil relations as quickly as possible, even if that meant appeasing southern whites. The southern members then excommunicated members of the church who swore loyalty to the Union. In 1866, shortly before white southern members were going to expel the freed Christians, blacks left of their own accord and, with assistance from northern whites, established independent congregations.[48]

In other cases, whites themselves came into conflict over dealing with

Baptist freedpeople. In one Georgia town after the war, a white Baptist donor gave enslaved members of his church land for their own meeting house. After emancipation he tried to reclaim his property, saying he never intended the land to be used by freedpeople. But white members of a nearby church helped the black congregation regain the property through court action. For the longtime white Georgia minister who recounted this story, this action summed up the good feelings he imagined to exist between most white and black Baptists throughout his tenure. More accurately, his story exemplified the complexities of handling the black withdrawal from white churches.[49]

More common than direct conflict or close cooperation was simply parting with little notice or ceremony. Most local congregations quietly recorded the departure of black members, generally as part of enumerating gains and losses in membership totals. In 1866, the First Baptist Church in Jacksonville, Alabama, appointed black deacons to minister to their Christian freedpeople. In 1869, black members asked to form a separate congregation and sought white assistance in securing a meeting house. The Appomattox Baptist Association in Virginia advised its constituent churches to "quietly and promptly organize their colored members into separate and independent churches." Through the 1870s, final separations took place frequently, with whites often adding words of advice for the departing black brethren. In Tuscaloosa they "earnestly and affectionately" counseled colored members "to save their money weekly, to become economical in all their expenses, to use no more candles at meeting than necessary, to discourage expensive burials, [and to] avoid taking collection for things not connected with the church." Local white Baptists freely dispensed such admonitions, considering it part of their ongoing paternalistic duties. By 1880 a prominent white Alabaman concluded that "the races can be grouped into separate organizations, and they will be safer and happier so."[50]

Baptist associations (groupings of congregations in specific geographic areas) feared that any African American exodus would "be fraught with evil to the white members and destructive to the black membership." They initially resolved that the freedpeople should remain connected to white churches but worship in separate services, with black members voting only on matters pertaining to themselves (a practice common in antebellum southern churches). When their advice went unheeded, the associations advised black Baptists to form their own associations and accept white instruction. Members of the Goshen Baptist Association (white) in Georgia, which included prominent churches in the Savannah region, brushed their hands of their former brethren: "let the Yankees and negroes take care of themselves." But most other white Baptists declared themselves "ready at all times" to instruct the freedpeople in "the ways of Zion." White anxiety about their former subjects arose from immediately pressing practical concerns: "it is our interest because the more they are elevated in point of morality, the safer will be our persons and property."[51]

State conventions pursued a nearly identical pattern of response as Baptist associations. Initially they often advised against separation, insisting that "the Negroes cannot navigate alone." By the late 1860s they accepted separation as inevitable while imagining the dangerous perils that would accompany black religious independence. By the 1870s white associations and state conventions preached that separation was God's plan to ensure racial peace and to allow for the flowering of "Anglo-Saxon manhood.[52]

Texas Baptists provide a typical example of this evolution. During the war, they instructed their slaves that God sanctioned slavery and that Union promises to help the slaves were lies. Although accepting the separation of black and white Christians after the war, the white Texans still worried that the freedpeople were "moved rather by impulse and superstition than the pure precepts of Christ." In Waco, home of Baylor University and a center for Baptist efforts in Texas, white believers wondered how to confront the political questions arising from freedpeople "suddenly cut loose from that restraint and wholesome discipline which has heretofore been a safeguard and security against the exercise of the worst passions . . . as exhibited in the untutored and uncultivated mind." The freedpeople were, they imagined, "indolent, indisposed to voluntary labor, ignorant and vicious and with an extremely low standard of moral rectitude." Nevertheless, well-known clergymen in the state such as B. H. Carroll assisted in the organization of black congregations. Black Baptists in Texas later led national black religious organizations.[53]

From 1865 to 1870, white Baptists in Alabama moved from disapproval to acceptance of black congregations and Baptist associations. They recognized as early as 1865 the right of the freedpeople to establish separate churches but determined that their "highest good" would be preserved by remaining tied to white congregations. In 1866, the Alabamans asked how whites could help ex-slaves find this highest good:

> Shall we abandon them to the inevitable fate of the masses, if uncared for by the white man—indolence, superstition, and the rapid return to barbarism—or shall we leave them to the teachings of others who are strangers to their character, and who, however pure in their motives and purposes, must, from the very nature of things, labor under many and serious hindrances to success. Or shall we demonstrate to mankind by a frank recognition of our responsibilities, and assiduous care to meet them, the

truthfulness of what we have heretofore claimed—that the master is the negro's best friend.[54]

A white North Carolinian in 1867 summarized many of the perplexities troubling white southern Baptists: "Shall we press ourselves upon them when they seem to suspect us? Shall we encourage them to form separate churches? Are we willing to receive their delegates in this convention, and in our Association? How can we decline to receive the representatives of a regularly constituted church on account of color? Are we not too timid in this matter?"[55]

At the 1869 Southern Baptist Convention meeting, a definitive consensus emerged. The messengers rejected merging with northern Baptists or meeting in interracial southern Baptist associations or conventions. The Bible never intended to "abolish social distinctions," they said. Jesse Campbell, a white Georgian and longtime minister to the slaves, was not "disposed, and never expected to be disposed to be on terms of social equality" with the freedpeople. He impatiently asked when white Baptists were "ever to be done with discussions about the colored man?" Any discussion of reunion with northern Baptists was effectively squelched.[56]

Most white southern churchgoers believed devoutly in the divine sanction for racial slavery but feared for the inadequacy of their efforts to Christianize those they enslaved. Since the early nineteenth century southern Baptists had urged evangelism among the slaves, even to the point of questioning laws prohibiting the teaching of literacy to black people. They foretold divine retribution if the white South failed in this task. A Georgia minister chastised slaveowners who failed to make a "distinction between the immortal minds that they control and the brute animals that they protect and use for the sake of gain." After the war, clergymen pointed to Appomattox as the divine chastening they had once prophesied. Baptists in Mississippi concluded that the "present condition" of the white South arose from "a failure on our part to discharge the duties and obligations to a race naturally gentle and docile, that God has placed under our protection for their good and our welfare." White southerners, these Baptists suggested, had thus sealed their own doom: to live with freedpeople unable to care for themselves outside of the tutelage of slavery. The "varnish of civilization" acquired by blacks during slavery, a prominent South Carolina Baptist wrote, could "not conceal the barbarism of the race."[57]

The same freedpeople who had acquired only a "varnish of civilization" appeared eager to seize the reigns of government—abetted, of course, by scheming northern politicians and turncoat white southerners, the agents of divine retribution. It seemed clear to white southerners why the controversy over the racial politics of Reconstruction overwhelmed all other questions. "We would infinitely prefer any form of government, military, aristocratic, royal, or imperial," explained a Virginia Baptist, "to that of the ignorant, lawless and rapacious negroes, led by a few white men who affiliate with them to gain office and fill their empty pockets." E. T. Winkler, a prominent Alabaman, connected his fears of a landless peasantry with broader concerns for the safety of the ruling classes: "Emancipation has given us a proletariat and communism is the first article of its political creed," he warned in a commencement address in 1871. To discount the profound racial gulf between white and black, added a North Carolina Baptist, was a "hideous and revolting lie" that had "deluged this continent with blood and . . . probably turned over to barbarism and ruin some of the best and most useful laborers upon the face of the earth." Instruction in religious duties was not only a moral imperative but also a practical way to ameliorate noxious northern influences. As Mississippi Baptists pointed out, it was a "matter of self-interest for us to elevate them into a better life. They will be better servants and better citizens."[58]

Northern missionaries who might "come among us to preach politics rather than religion" personified this concern for the loss of control over "our Negroes." Isaac Taylor Tichenor, savior of the denomination's Home Mission Board and president of what later became Auburn University, explained why Yankee activists represented a particularly insidious threat to the southern social order: "with their ideas of negro suffrage, of social equality, of miscegenation, of agrarianism, and every mischievous outgrowth of the fanaticism of that clime, prolific in such baneful fruits, they will infuse these things into the minds of the negroes." If northern missionaries, for instance, insisted "on equal suffrage rather than repentance, and . . . excite the colored people to consider their former masters and real friends as their enemies, then their influence will be mischievous." White southern Christians repeatedly asserted to northerners that "we know them better than you do, and we love them better than you do." Ministering to the freedpeople without "amalgamating" with them involved great tact and patience, qualities that white southern Baptists found lacking in the northern religious carpetbaggers. "The elevation of a gross people rather by a higher social style than by a descent to their level is the Protestant style of civilizing them," one southern minister reminded his northern colleagues. Amalgamation in religious matters, he added, would lead inexorably to mongrelization "such as now disgraces the earth in Central America." Educators such as Jabez L. Monroe Curry warned that the freedpeople had been "cut off from instruction of an intelligent ministry"; they were "degenerating into superstition and barbarism and idolatry." This analysis of independent black religious life echoed the attacks of the Redeemers on black political activists: black leaders were taking their followers back into their "natural state of savagery." W. J. Northen, a Baptist leader and future governor of Georgia, warned of what might happen if the rhetoric of racial equality ran unchecked: "anarchy in government, wretchedness in society, and wild desolation in the church."[59]

Early segregationists among white Christians, a vocal minority in the 1870s, questioned whether whites still retained any "duty" to the freedpeople. "Some of our people *can't* accept the idea that *we* should take part in the *intellectual* as well as moral culture of this *now* most unfortunate race," a South Carolina minister wrote privately in 1866. Some suggested that the same northerners who had freed Negroes before they were "ready" for citizenship now should assume responsibility for them. Others insisted on the "spirit of independence and self-help" as the key to postbellum religious endeavors.[60]

Even supporters of evangelizing freedpeople remained cautious and skeptical about what results might ensue. "We know," wrote a white Alabama pastor, "that the great majority of their religious teachers are corrupt in their lives, and totally unfit to instruct them in Christian duty. We know, too, that their forms of worship in many instances partake more largely of the nature of Buddhism than of Christian assemblies." John Broadus, the southern Baptist best known by northern colleagues for his lectures on preaching, found the prospects for Negro evangelization equally gloomy. At first, he said, northern missionaries "imagined that the faults of the Freedmen were chiefly the results of slavery, and would disappear after a few years of freedom, partial education, and their own earnest and loving influence." But, he continued, the northerners now understood that the culture of the freedpeople, being "inherited from untold generations," would not easily change. "It is a vast and difficult task to lift up the lower races of mankind into Christian enlightenment," Broadus concluded philosophically.[61]

These disparate views on racial self-development crystallized into an orthodoxy expressed in Redemption politics and later in Jim Crow social legislation. Denominational officials often hailed from modest slaveowning families, and something of the paternalist ethic sunk in. "Nothing is plainer to any one who knows this race than its perfect willingness to accept a subordinate place," the Home Mission Board of the SBC declared. In 1867, E. T. Winkler, pastor of the Citadel Square Baptist Church in Charleston, preached that unequal races should "neither be inflamed with mutual hostility and summoned to arms . . . nor be persuaded into an unnatural social equality." With a rhetoric typical of white southern conservatives, he suggested that "a respectful subordination on the one side, a condescending kindness on the other, and virtue and religion on the part of both, will enable them, each in his own sphere, to contribute to the happiness of all." The Georgia minister H. H. Tucker wrote to members of the First African Baptist Church of Savannah, who were celebrating the centennial anniversary of their congregation, that while "the creation of God made us one, . . . it is also true that the providence of God has made us two. . . . If God himself has drawn the color line, it is vain as well as wicked for us to try to efface it."[62]

In the 1890s, with a growing national sentiment of imperial mission, northern elites learned to emulate and appreciate the language of southern evangelical conservatism. By that time, the romantic liaisons between northern officers and southern belles in the works of popular novelists and the nationalist fervor surrounding the Spanish-American War exemplified the growing racial consensus of North and South. Both professional and amateur historians acknowledged Reconstruction to be the "tragic era," the term popularized by Claude Bowers's bitterly partisan history of the period. Challenges to the egregious misrepresentations rife in these works were ignored. White Americans, North and South, agreed on the superiority of "Anglo-Saxon manhood" and collectively worried for an America then being flooded by swarthy and Catholic immigrants. Despite the commitment and heroism of some northern missionaries and the exposés of journalists, who wrote of peonage camps and lynching posses, the larger issue of the "race problem" was considered settled.[63]

Southern Baptists were instrumental in the mythologizing of the "horrors" of Reconstruction, boilerplate that quickly insinuated itself into the folklore, and soon the accepted history, of the era. Before Republicans took control of the House of Representatives in the 1866 elections, for example, two prominent Virginia Baptists rebuked Yankee faith in the conventional language of white southerners as victims of northern marauders. Northern Christians, they asserted, had

waged against us a lawless war, which, instead of being regulated by the rules of warfare, . . . has been conducted in a spirit of savage, or rather, draconian cruelty and devastation. Not satisfied with the unbridled spoilations, robberies and thefts, which we have suffered; or with the midnight screams of naked females escaping from their burning houses; or with our incarcerated ministers, separated from the people of their charge, and doomed to lose their health and strength in filthy prisons; not satisfied that we have accepted the issues of the war, and declared our allegiance to the existing government, or with the impoverished and ruined condition to which we have been reduced; . . . not satisfied with all this their unsatiated and insatiable malice (what else can we call it) is still ever pouring upon us its bitter and dirty streams of vituperation and abuse.[64]

During Reconstruction, white southern Baptists prepared for a cultural and political war to defend white supremacy. If violence was necessary to this end, they were prepared to use it. In North Carolina the Sandy Creek Baptist Church, one of the original Baptist churches dating from the eighteenth century, questioned the action of a "vigilant committee" in the county that had executed a black man suspected of political activity. "But under the excitement of the times," it added, ". . . we forgive all who were concerned." Other churchmen felt no need even to make this kind of back-handed apology. E. T. Winkler explained to northern Baptists in 1872 why groups such as the Ku Klux Klan were justifiable: "In a state of society where there is no law, and where men must form temporary organizations for the redress of intolerable grievances and the maintenance of social order, justice itself is perverted by attacks on these organizations." The Force Act of 1871, which authorized action against groups that blocked the exercise of civil rights, seemed to Winkler an example of the "oppression" to which the white South had been subjected. Winkler offered no such justifications for "temporary organizations" (such as Union Leagues) which defended the precarious rights of the freedpeople.[65]

Southern Baptist Convention messengers in 1891 endorsed the standard canards of the "tragic era" school of Reconstruction mythology. Biracial government in religion would have led, they decided, to the same "corruption" and "degradation" as when "Negro domination" supposedly fastened its hold on the South. Resistance to northern religious radicalism appeared as heroic as the fight against northern political radicalism. This account of history, already standard in academia and popular perceptions by 1890, failed to mention the corruption of the white Redeemer governments, the murderous guerrilla groups that terrorized freedpeople attempting to exercise their civil rights, and the tightening stranglehold placed on southern lives by the policies of the Redeemers. It reinforced the misremembering of Reconstruction, with tragic political consequences for African Americans.[66]

In 1886 and 1887, J. L. Johnson, a professor at Mississippi College and a minister in the state, grew disgusted at his enforced contact with Negroes in train cars. He prayed to God, " 'Is there no way out of this but blood? . . . Shall the Anglo-Saxon sit still and see these poor, ignorant, deluded creatures used as a mop to blot out the finest civilization the world has ever known?' " The idea of state-mandated separate cars came to him. He later boasted of his role in creating the "Mississippi Plan," the template for the segregation and disfranchisement laws of the 1890s and 1900s. The Ku Klux Klan, he later explained, was the salvation of whites, and segregation the greatest blessing for the Negro.⁶⁷

White southern Christians immortalized those who engaged in the struggle to defend white supremacy, whether in politics or religion. They remembered when "designing political demagoguery laid its polluted, scourging hand" on the region and led it "away from the truth, happiness and prosperity." A Baptist editor praised Thomas Dixon's novelistic evocation of *The Clansman* for retelling the inspiring story of an "Invisible Empire of defeated soldiers who in poverty and weakness by the might of right and courage of consecration to all that is holy, terrorized the aliens that had assumed to rule them, disarmed the black cohorts, struck down their white satraps, and drove out from the Temple of our Liberties the horde that [had] been put into possession of the holy of holies itself." Baptists thanked God for having been redeemed "by the blood of the Lamb," and added another hymn of praise for "redemption" from "political-religionism"—that of the blood of the Ku Klux Klan.⁶⁸

CHAPTER TWO

A Wall of the Lord 'Round Me

Black Baptist Organizing in the South, 1865–1895

I am sho' glad slavery is over. I glory in it.—Ex-slave from 1930s quoted in *Oklahoma Narratives*

I sho' did my part buildin' de church atter freedom. . . . I dug a heap o dirt for de Lawd. I was smart way back dere.—Black churchgoer quoted in Orville Vernon Burton, *In My Father's House Are Many Mansions*

For missionaries of Christianity and bourgeois American civilization, the rapid growth of independent black churches after the Civil War augured well for a brighter era in African American history. At last, they exulted, the oratorical powers of African American preachers could be harnessed in the service of pulling forward newfound institutions of black freedom. As a black Baptist woman explained in 1868, the momentous events of the war "quickened" the freedpeople's "sense of inviolability of the divine law," and their faith in the "justice of retribution for national guilt." Two years after Appomattox, Charles Satchell, a black missionary in New Orleans, evoked the significance of independence in black religious life. "These churches," he wrote in a northern Baptist publication, "stand amid their people as springs of water in a desert land," wielding "a controlling influence" over the minds of the freedpeople. The debilitating legacies of slavery, he warned, meant that most ministers were "generally uninformed brethren" more adept at inducing spiritual ecstasies than teaching the lessons of a mature Christian faith. They instilled in their congregations "too little idea of business, and of church discipline." Satchell suggested that "enlightened Christianity and intelligent worship" would take root slowly among the formerly enslaved people. With faith and education, the missionaries believed, such barriers could be overcome, and the freedpeople could claim their full citizenship rights. This deep faith emboldened postbellum black Baptists and their few white allies and carried them through decades of tribulation.[1]

45

The growth of independent African American congregations was remarkable. To whites, it was a disturbing reminder of the disappearance of the antebellum community. When possible, black congregations, even in the antebellum era, carved out a separate niche, meeting in services that whites supervised (as by law they had to) but did not control. In many cases, such meetings were required simply by the racial demographics of local church membership. Of the 442 members of the First Baptist Church of Natchez, Mississippi, 380 were African American; in Columbus, Mississippi, 80 percent of the Baptist church membership before the war was black. In antebellum Georgia, about 35 to 40 percent of Baptist church members were black. After freedom, white southern intransigence and northern paternalism compelled black Baptists to form independent state and national organizations. By 1890, 54 percent of African American Christians were Baptists, numbering slightly over one million. The 1906 religious census listed about 2,250,000 black Baptists, comprising about 60 percent of black churchgoers. In 1883, black Baptists in Georgia outnumbered whites in the state 131,216 to 123,851. In the early twentieth century Georgia could claim the largest number of black Baptists, 334,000. The racial segregation of religious institutions was complete. As a prominent minister explained in the 1890s, "the emancipation of the colored people made the colored churches and ministry a necessity, both by virtue of the prejudice existing against us and of our essential manhood before the laws of the land."[2]

W. P. Price, a longtime white Baptist minister in Georgia, remembered the exodus of blacks as a confusing period of unparalleled upheaval in the churches. Customarily, those withdrawing from one Baptist church to join another carried letters from their previous congregation testifying to their conversion experiences and upright moral character. Many black Baptists after the war received such dismission letters from white ministers. But some "bad spirits" among the freedmen, as Price called them, tried to convince congregants that "they owed no allegiance" to the white members and should organize churches when and where they wanted. Price extended dismissal letters only to those he deemed worthy, a practice followed by many of his white colleagues.[3]

Like Price, white Baptists often expressed satisfaction at their amicable relations with many formerly enslaved congregants while puzzling over freedpeople who ignored their advice. Jeremiah Jeter, a longtime Richmond minister and editor of the flagship denominational paper the *Religious Herald*, encountered freedpeople who looked suspiciously on offers of assistance from white southern Christians. This hesitancy originated, Jeter supposed, in the "persuasion that those who were opposed to the emancipation cannot be their friends" and the "apprehension that all protestations of friendship from such persons are designed to allure them back to slavery." Andrew Broaddus, an eminent divine in Virginia who had been jailed briefly during the Civil War, found the ex-slaves impatient "of even the *appearance* of control—and counsel has that appearance *to them*—by their former masters." Broaddus grew disturbed at the thought of ex-slaves receiving instruction from "false preachers," men whose claim on the freedmen derived "from their ability to incite excitement."[4]

As many freedpeople saw it, these so-called false preachers bore the gospel tidings of freedom, while the same whites who claimed to be the black man's "best friend" had been the staunchest defenders of slavery. During the war, enslaved Baptists who joined with the Union forces were often summarily written out of their congregations by the remaining white members. The Rappahannock Baptist Association of Virginia excommunicated a group of enslaved church members for "joining our enemies." After the war black members continued to ignore the advice of whites. Imbued with his duty to instruct freedpeople in the "ways of Zion," Charles Manly urged black members of his Tuscaloosa, Alabama, church to organize a separate congregation. They were "rather 'dull,'" he reported, more concerned with daily survival than with spiritual matters. Whites in the church expressed their disapproval of the actions of a black congregant named Prince Murrell, who traveled to Mobile for a freedmen's convention and received an ordination from northern Baptists. Manly "pointed out the uncandid and unfair proceeding as well as unscriptural and disorderly way of pronouncing a sort of *quasi ordination*" for Murrell. Black members responded by organizing their own congregation with Prince Murrell as pastor. Writing in 1868 from Tuscaloosa, where he worked for the American Baptist Free Mission Society (a group of northern Baptists aligned with the Radical Republicans), Murrell explained that his congregants held no "hard feelings against our former owners," but that the southern churches would not "have anything to do with any northern churches. They say that religion is the same as it was before the war. They will have nothing to do with any colored churches that think they ought to have the same rights to serve God in their own way." Murrell wanted to cooperate with whites in religious work but found that they "drive us further and further from them." White Alabama Baptists viewed Murrell's missionary employer as a purveyor of "fanaticism" that would "sow among the freedmen the seeds of political religionism—seeds apt to bear only a more luxuriant and more noxious harvest in the soil of ignorance."[5]

Congregations that had conducted their own affairs in the antebellum era moved rapidly into the new era, assuming legal title to property formerly held by white trustees and generally benefiting from the cooperation of their original churches. The First African Baptist Church in Richmond, for example, assumed property rights to a building in which, just a few years earlier, delegates to the state secession convention made their fateful decision. When the longtime white pastor of the church, Robert Ryland, was ordered out of the pulpit during the war, the congregation voted to retain him. He voluntarily stepped down, believing that his parishioners would rather hear a preacher of their own color. His black protegé James Holmes, formerly a slave in Richmond's tobacco factories, purchased his freedom during the war and began a long pastorate in 1867. During his tenure, First African of Richmond grew into the largest black congregation in America, later meeting in a massive edifice constructed at a cost of $35,000. Walter H. Brooks, who as a boy received instruction from Ryland in Sunday school, later was educated at Lincoln University in Pennsylvania, and served as a missionary appointed by northern Baptists to Louisiana. After returning to Virginia, he spoke to the white Baptist state convention in 1879, assuring his audience that separate black churches were safe teachers of orthodoxy, not centers of radical organizing. Brooks's efforts pronounced a kind of benediction on the racial separation of religious institutions.[6]

Congregations such as the Gillfield Baptist Church in Petersburg, Virginia, established in the early nineteenth century, continued a longstanding tradition of independent worship. In 1818, a permanent site had been purchased for the church, and the congregation erected a new building in 1874. With a membership roll of some 1,700, Gillfield emerged as one of the leading black churches in the region, supervising fledgling congregations in its area as well. The Reverend Henry Williams, a native of Spottsylvania, served in the church's pulpit from 1865 to 1899, using his post to campaign for more black teachers in Petersburg schools. The tradition of lengthy pulpit tenures continued in the twentieth century, with the Reverend A. S. Brown serving as pastor from 1913 to 1951.[7]

In antebellum Nashville, black members of the First Baptist Church of Nashville met, worshiped, and conducted business separately, with only nominal white supervision. Pastor R. B. C. Howell encouraged separate black religious development and assisted in the pastoral education of Nelson Merry, an ex-slave who assumed the pulpit of the black mission in 1853. After the city succumbed to Federal forces in 1862, the black congregation, numbering about five hundred communicants, thanked the whites "for the kindness done us in times past" and asked for a deed to the lot of their church building. In later years, they erected a "splendid house of worship beautifully painted and elegantly frescoed," with an auditorium accommodating 1,500 worshipers.[8]

Long-established black congregations, particularly the First African

Baptist Church of Savannah, played key roles in organizing new churches. First African sent missionaries, often apprenticed preachers, to evangelize among the freedpeople in the Georgia low country. These emissaries supplied about a dozen "praise houses" (or "pray's houses") with ministerial leadership who reported back to the mother church in Savannah. Low-country black believers saw in W. J. Campbell, minister of the congregation during Reconstruction, visual representation of the same traditions of independence that low-country workers had carved out toiling in the rice and cotton fields. "The people around the coast would hail his coming among them as a priest," a minister recalled of Campbell's work.[9]

Freedmen's Bureau agents and northern missionaries secured buildings in Andersonville, Georgia, and numerous other locales for use both as schools and church houses. Charles Corey, a Canadian-born white missionary with the American Baptist Home Mission Society (ABHMS), organized clandestine congregations in Charleston during the war and operated more openly afterward. The KKK issued him "warnings" about his efforts to establish a black theological institution. "Bad passions" were "still rampant" after the war, he recalled; it was a time "when hate prevailed, and not love." Few white Christians, he continued, would dare to sell or lease a building "in the face of their pro-slavery neighbors to be used as a school for Negroes." Whites would "almost turn pale with fear when I asked them to sell me a piece of land" for a mission school. But Corey also received assistance from local white pastors, and succeeded in maintaining Richmond Theological Seminary (later merged into Virginia Union University), which trained many of the best-known ministers in the region.

In Atlanta, Frank Quarles, supported by the American Missionary Association, worked out an arrangement to use a building as a school during the week and as a church on Sunday. Local whites complained of the plan and sold the property. Quarles then purchased a lot for Friendship Baptist Church, whose original handful of members had been meeting in a railroad boxcar, on the west side of the city. By the 1890s, E. R. Carter, a well-known minister and temperance activist, presided over the church's 2,500 members and $60,000 worth of property. The basement of the church later became the first home of Spelman College, a center for the higher education of black women.[10]

Instances of relatively amicable relationships with whites provided hope for a new kind of religious community in the South, one separate but equal. In Twiggs County, Georgia, the full black conference waited until 1874 until requesting to withdraw from the parent congregation "not from ill will but for the better government of ourselves." Many white churches donated land and other kinds of assistance for new congregations. One of the largest black gatherings in Virginia, Shiloh Baptist Church in Northumberland County, was formed in 1867. "We should be wanting in fidelity if we did not seek to place ourselves in that position in which we could best promote our mutual good, both in reference to ourselves and our posterity. In this new relation the subject of a separate church organization presses itself upon us as the best possible way in which we can best promote those indispensable interests, such as an ordained ministry, a separate congregation with all the privileges of a church organization," they explained. The deacons of the white church provided a plot of land for the black congregation. The Baptist church of Darien, Georgia, lost its building to Sherman's raid and later gave over this land to the freed Baptists. In Montgomery, the First Colored Baptist Church organized itself in 1867 when seven hundred black members withdrew from their antebellum congregation. Nathan Ashby, who had preached to slaves in the basement of the First Baptist Church of Montgomery, pastored the black church after the war. The three hundred white congregants of the First Baptist Church assisted in raising a church house for blacks. "The colored church moved into it with its organization all perfected, their pastor, board of deacons, committees of all sorts," a white minister later recalled. Local instances of cooperation provided a significant helping hand to fledgling black congregations. As a Florida black Baptist leader who enlisted the aid of whites in moving his Tallahassee congregation to the heart of the city advised white Baptists, "aid them to build their churches and schools and you will thus build the surest protection around your dwellings and your henroosts."[11]

Elite white ministers imbued with a paternalist ethic assisted in the organization of black congregations and frequently preached in the new churches. In 1877, Dexter Avenue Baptist Church in Montgomery (later the home of Martin Luther King Jr.) split from the city's First Colored Baptist Church and met in a former slave trader's pen purchased for $270. In the 1880s, congregants raised money for a permanent structure with the assistance of J. B. Hawthorne, a well-known white Baptist minister. J. O. B. Dargan, a white South Carolinian, spent considerable energy, by his own estimation, preaching among the freedpeople, ordaining ministers, and organizing churches. The ex-slaves were "accessible to any minister" who would approach them "with a true desire to promote and advance their spiritual interests," he believed. Ex-slaves later remembered whites who donated land and helped to build churches "out o' pine logs and chinked de cracks up wid clay an' straw, and dis wuz de school too, de white teacher wuz first, den de Marster got us a niger teacher nex'." In Texas, the well-known minister Benajah Harvey Carroll preached to black churches around the state. An ex-slave in Texas remembered how Carroll directed the rebuilding of a church house after the war and gave it "to us old slaves for our color, an' to dis day hit stands as a monument to de work of dese good folks of de Brazos bottom." A black candidate for the ministry in Mississippi, in a situation repeated often in the postbellum South, asked his former white congregation to examine "his call and qualifications to the ministry and if said examination result satisfactorily to them to set him apart by ordination to the Gospel ministry." John A. Whitted, a black Baptist historian in North Carolina, remembered the "kindliest and most friendly relations" between the brethren, with whites "often going to considerable sacrifice to serve" black Baptists "with advice, with instruction and with money."[12]

Such interracial cooperation, however, was carefully bounded. Ultimately, it was less important than the initiative of the freedpeople who established an independent religious life in the face of poverty, illiteracy, and oppression. Black Baptists frequently rented or purchased buildings in which they formerly met as quasi-independent missions. They felt title in sweat equity in land cleared or structures erected by their own labor. Blacks with some accumulated wealth earned by hiring their own time purchased land or older buildings for use by new black churches. In Edgefield County, South Carolina, David Graham, a carpenter and mechanic, donated property for the Rock Hill Baptist Church, where he served as deacon. He remained popular among local whites until his entrance in politics in the 1870s, he testified, "and they have hated me ever since." Newly formed congregations not fortunate enough to receive donated plots or buildings paid market prices or higher for pieces of land. The resources scrabbled together by household production—the sale of eggs from a chicken, milk from a cow, meat from a hog, or the independent lines of credit opened by black farmers with their stock animals as collateral—provided the meager surplus that allowed for the building of schools and churches and the bare-bones salaries afforded to preachers and teachers. In Granville County, North Carolina, members of the New Corinth Baptist Church purchased a one-acre lot from one of its own members for $10, about the going price for a good acre of farmland in the area. In Beaufort, South Carolina, ex-slaves used a building that was the property of a white church. When whites returned to the island after the war, they offered to sell it to the black congregants for $350. Blacks in the area raised nearly half of it. "The times are very hard down here," a correspondent wrote to northern Baptists, "but thank God our people have this year, men and women, gone to work."[13]

As frequently as not, black Baptists congregated with little or no assistance from whites, often under difficult conditions. In Memphis, Rev. Morris Henderson, born a slave in Virginia and for years the property of a white woman in Shelby County, Tennessee, persuaded parishioners out of the First Baptist Church of Memphis and into a shelter of tree limbs and branches. The Woman's Sewing Society of the fledgling congregation raised $500 in nine months and later deposited $1,000 in a Freedmen's Bank, money that made possible the construction of a building. By 1870 Henderson's congregation, the Beale Street Baptist Church, was the largest in the city, with a membership of more than 2,500. In Edgefield County, South Carolina, Paris Simkins and Lawrence Cain, two black ministers and political leaders, founded the Macedonia Baptist Church. Simkins served as a local school commissioner in the 1870s and was a rival to the most prominent black Baptist minister in the region, Alexander Bettis, a man known for his accommodationist attitude toward whites. And in Georgia, a black Baptist organizer cited the case of a group of freedmen who, growing weary of their treatment and "feeling that they were now men," declared themselves an independent congregation and selected one of their own as pastor.[14]

The dialectic of paternalism and violence in southern race relations deeply imprinted the region's religious life. While white Baptists frequently spoke of their "moral obligation" to guide the freedpeople, they just as often ignored their own advice, or pointedly reminded blacks that they would be "servants in fact to the end of time," as E. B. Teague, a white minister in Selma, told one black congregation. An ex-slave in Texas remembered one minister and former slaveowner who was "a Baptist Preachah an' preached to de cullud fo'ks, an' m'ybe de Klux don't lak fo' him to does dat." White Baptist congregants often would have "nothing to do" with ministers who preached to freed men and women, a white Texas pastor complained. One Baptist minister and slaveholder announced freedom to his slaves with "tears in his eyes w'en he tells weuns dat he laked weuns, dat weuns had all been good fo'ks to him, an' he hates to part wid weuns, but 'twas law." But the ex-slave once owned by this minister remembered how little the ex-master's ministerial status counted to Reconstruction era vigilantes: "Father don't lak to leave Marster's place but him gits so 'fraid something am gwine to happen to his fam'ly. 'Specially after two niggers gits shot by de Klux. He 'cides to leave de country."[15]

Black missionaries discovered that the same whites who claimed to have the "best interests" of "their Negroes" at heart abetted those who most actively oppressed the freedpeople. Black Baptists in North Carolina thanked God for allowing the freedpeople the opportunity to "worship according to the dictates of our minds and consciences" and expressed their opposition to "any white person's having the whole control of the colored churches." One of the earliest organized black associations in the state resolved to "use every exertion . . . to harmonize the white and colored races, so that they may live in peace in the same country, and that both may prosper spiritually and temporally." Two years later the association acknowledged the "spirit of coolness" between the races but regarded the whites "as brethren and sisters, Pilgrims to a better land," praying that God would soften their "obdurate hearts." In 1872, the association determined to work "to civilize our people both white and colored, temporally as well as spiritually." In the South Carolina low country, Arthur Waddell, a black missionary and pastor in Beaufort, discovered that the freedpeople would be obligated to accept "the same portion allowed us in the days of slavery" in their old congregations. In other words, whites still demanded that racial habits in the church retain the old "slavish custom," that is, for blacks "to stand up out of doors with hat in hand" or else sit in the balcony. But Baptist freedpeople asserted their independence from these everyday gestures of submission: "We act toward them as brethren," concluded Waddell, "but never shall we again let them rule us as masters."[16]

Throughout the South, black Baptists found themselves harassed by lawmen, unprotected by federal authorities, and at times hunted by white terrorist groups. An ex-slave in Texas recalled "the turrible things" perpetrated by the Klan in her younger days. "But I just built a wall of the Lord 'round me so they couldn't get at me," she told her interviewer. Black Christians throughout the South replicated her personal fortitude. Charles Satchell's church in New Orleans, organized in June 1866, soon grew extremely large and spawned other congregations. Black Baptists in the city created a local association to oversee their work and settle internecine disputes. The churches in Satchell's association frequently were turned out of their meeting houses by local vigilantes. Many of his congregants feared attending evening services "owing to the insecurity from being assaulted in going to and from church." City policemen absented themselves when parishioners were assaulted. And one of Satchell's colleagues found himself pursued by armed men while he was looking for land for a new church house. As Satchell realized, whites feared the idea of black ministers "imparting information to the people that would result in their [whites] losing control over them."[17]

Satchell assumed that the obvious moral character of his parishioners would spare them from attacks. That this moral character might appear, in the eyes of whites, as "impudence" or "insolence" would have undermined the whole project of the missionaries. It was unthinkable that uplift of the race would not eventuate in respect for black people. But evidence to the contrary mounted in the years to come. "If you got so you made good money an' had a good farm de Klu Klux'd come an' murder you," a minister later remembered. "De gov'ment built de colored people school houses an' de Klu Klux went to work an' burn em' down." In Edgefield County, South

Carolina, white vigilantes attacked black prayer meetings that were assumed "to terminate politically and not spiritually." In Richmond, whites harassed members of the Second African Baptist Church because it housed a school for freedmen and was a site of an emancipation celebration in April of 1866. An ex-slave in Arkansas remembered the numerous stories she heard of how white gunmen "used to come 'round and bother the church services looking for this one and that one." As one ex-slave admonished his interviewer, "I guess you be scared. They run the colored folks away from church a lot of times." An elderly woman in Arkansas recalled that when the freedpeople held church with a black minister, "here come the Ku Klux and run em clear out. If they hear least thing nigger preacher say they whoop him. They whooped several." The lesson she drew from this experience would be one that a later generation of black ministers would take to heart: "They sure had to be might particular what they said in the preachin." The ex-slaves were clear about the cause of these troubles: "That was about equalization after freedom. That was the cause of that."[18]

Black Baptist ministers were in fact imparting subversive information to the ex-slaves—that they were free and equal people under the laws and under God, and that they should act and vote as such. For an America baptized in the blood of racism and slavery from its birth, this message constituted a radical break with the past. For example, Steve Robertson described the minister at his church in Texas after the war as a "pow'ful preachah. Him cause de fo'ks to 'membahs de things dat him talks 'bout: how de Lawd answers prayahs, how many niggers prays fo' dis freedom weuns have now en' now dey's persecuted for de 'prayin'." And as another ex-slave summarized his beliefs, "prayer is bes' t'ing in the worl'. Everybody oughta pray, 'cause prayer got us outta slavery."[19]

During Reconstruction, messages not only of moral equality, the stock-in-trade of slave preachers, but also of political rights sounded forth from black pulpits throughout the South. An ex-slave in Florida recalled his father telling him how he "often heard the preacher point out Negroes who attended the meetings and attained prominence in politics as an example for members of his flock to follow." At a church service in Virginia shortly before one election, a student of southern political life described prayers being "offered up as fervently for the Republican candidate as if the very existence of the blacks depended upon his election." In this congregation, if word leaked out that a member voted for the Democrats, he faced the possibility of removal—"and a sentence of excommunication means as much to him as it meant to a European in the middle ages." During elections, Sir George Campbell observed that the preachers' advice carried a good deal of weight as did that of "the negro women, who are very strong republicans."

In South Carolina during a gubernatorial election, an ex-slave recalled, "de preachers sure got up de excitement 'mongst de colored women folks. They 'vised them to have nothin' to do wid deir husbands if they didn't go to do 'lection box" and vote for Franklin Moses, Republican candidate for governor. Philip Bruce, a condescending analyst of plantation life in Virginia, described how "the affairs of the Hereafter and a contemporary political canvass" were "mixed in inextricable confusion" in a black service he witnessed. The church, he concluded, was "thus converted into a political organization that is consolidated by the religious fervor that pervades it."[20]

In black churches, associations, and convention meetings, stump speeches for Republican candidates rang out as fervently as evangelical themes. In 1868, a Mississippi Baptist association recognized that blacks were still "a down-trodden and oppressed race." They prayed for the success of "that great party," the Republican Party, and resolved to defeat candidates who were "opposed to us having equal rights before the law." Delegates to black Baptist meetings thanked God and "the great Republican party for our present political status." During the Liberal Republican revolt in 1872, they warned that the demise of the Radical Republicans would mean a "fast retreating step back again to the land of whips for our own backs, to labor unrequited, to all the laws forbidding the peaceful and happy enjoyment of our rights as American citizens."[21]

Prominent ministers inspired church organization and prompted electoral excitement as well. The historian Eric Foner has counted 237 black ministers who held local, state, or national office during Reconstruction, including 55 who were Baptists. In Georgia, home to the largest contingent of black Baptists in the South, clerics in Savannah, Augusta, and Atlanta took the lead in black political organizing during Reconstruction. For example, William Jefferson White, who conducted clandestine literacy classes for Savannah blacks in the 1850s and was ordained in 1866, pastored churches in Augusta, edited the *Georgia Baptist*, and attended conventions of Georgia freedmen during Reconstruction. He also authored the constitution of the Missionary Baptist and Educational Convention of Georgia (organized in 1870), acquired lots on which the Freedmen's Bureau built schools, and organized educational societies. He was, according to one account, the first to make known to the freedpeople in southwest Georgia that Congress had extended them the right to vote. "These were dangerous times," a contemporary of his commented, "and frequently it looked as though Mr. White would be murdered by the whites, who could not bear at that time even the thought that colored people were to be equal citizens." During his editorship of the *Georgia Baptist*, he publicly supported the Populists and lambasted conservatives such as Booker T. Washington. Inspired by the Niagara Movement of 1905, a predecessor to the NAACP, he organized the Georgia Equal Rights Convention in 1906, despite repeated threats to his life and property. William Heard, an African Methodist Episcopal bishop in the late nineteenth century, remembered William J. White as one of his inspirations. After hearing him, "I determined from that night to be a MAN." ‖ White was "always outspoken for Orthodox Religion and the Republican Party," Heard recalled.[22]

In January of 1865, African American ministers from the Georgia low country advised Union leaders on dealing with the slaves set free by Sherman's march. Garrison Frazier, an elderly ex-slave who purchased his freedom before the war and pastored Baptist congregations for thirty-five years, informed General William Tecumseh Sherman and Secretary of War Edwin Stanton that "the way we can best take care of ourselves is to have land, and turn it and till it by our own labor . . . and we can soon maintain ourselves and have something to spare." He assured Union officials that "if the prayers that have gone up for the Union army could be read out, you would not get through them these two weeks." And his alliance with top Union personnel did not stop him from vigorously protesting the unequal treatment of African Americans in the Union army.[23]

Ulysses L. Houston was particularly influential among blacks in the Georgia low country. Born in South Carolina and brought to Savannah as a house servant, he learned to read from white sailors while he worked in the city's hospital and earned money by hiring out his time. Licensed to preach in 1855, from 1861 to 1880 he pastored the Third African Baptist Church (later renamed the First Bryan Baptist Church), a congregation of about four hundred. In the early days of Reconstruction, Houston helped to lay out a village on Skidaway Island, taking advantage of Sherman's plans to set aside conquered lands for black settlers. In later years, Houston served twice as president of the black Baptist convention in Georgia. During his tenure in the Georgia legislature, however, Democrats in Savannah worked behind the scenes with local ministers, including members of Houston's own congregation, to displace him from the Third African pulpit. Houston also incurred the ire of a local rival, William J. Campbell, who pastored the imposing First African Baptist congregation.[24]

James Simms also pursued an active career as a "minister-missionary" and politician. Born a slave in Savannah, he purchased his freedom in 1857, using the resources he accumulated from working as a master-builder. Avoiding work in Confederate war industries, he traveled to Boston and returned as a northern-appointed missionary. His ordination was rejected by William J. Campbell, who feuded with Simms as he did with Simms's pastor, Ulysses L. Houston. Working for the Freedmen's Bureau, the American Baptist Home Mission Society, and as a Union League organizer, he later won election to the Georgia House of Representatives and became the only black district judge in Georgia Reconstruction. Shortly after his election to the House, however, Klan activity chased him out of the county and into Atlanta. Simms later wrote that during this period ministers "had to leave their flock and legitimate field of labor to enter the arena of politics to secure right and justice for their people . . . notwithstanding the white citizens among whom they lived and served, and the late owners, [who] constantly spoke disparagingly of the ministers who served in these positions." At a meeting concerning black suffrage, the efforts of white ministers to "manage every thing their own way" were subverted by Simms, who "said it was the first time he ever had such an opportunity of speaking to white men, and should improve it to tell them *some plain truths*. . . . For once, at least, they heard the unvarnished truth." Simms "traveled about the State extensively since the war and mingled with the colored people." He testified before Congress and addressed the freedpeople "upon political questions and upon their general interests." His editorship of the Savannah-based *Freedmen's Standard* provided him another forum for his leadership in religious and political work. Meanwhile, Simms's colleague Thomas Allen, who was an active politician in Jasper County during Reconstruction, reminded his congregants that the Yankees had freed them and that "they ought to vote with them; to go with the party always. They voted just as I voted." Simms, Allen, and Houston were "almost the only ones capable of looking out after our people," as Simms later explained.[25]

In Mississippi, Henry Jacobs and Jesse Boulden assumed roles of spiritual and political importance. Their personal rivalry carried over into church work, as each formed rival state Baptist conventions partially as personal vehicles for their political ambitions. Born a slave in Alabama in 1825, Henry Jacobs escaped to the North in 1856, was ordained to the ministry in 1858, and moved to Natchez after the war to organize for the Baptist cause and the Union League. He served in the state constitutional convention of 1868. Jacobs was unpopular with some in the state, especially among ministers in Boulden's convention and congregants who resented his tendency to high-handedness. Later he left the state to take medical training in Louisville. Jesse Boulden, a free black educated before the war in Quaker schools, served as a minister of the Mt. Olivet Baptist Church in Chicago, a congregation that in the twentieth century would become the largest black church in the country. He moved to Lowndes County, Mississippi, in 1865, where he worked under the American Baptist Home Mission Society. While in Columbus, Mississippi, he "found more to do than preach to the people. He considered it his duty to give all the instruction he could to them." Both

Boulden and Jacobs served successfully in dual roles as ministers and political organizers, especially for the freedpeople in the plantation districts.[26]

In Montgomery, Alabama, Holland Thompson, a former slave, served on the city council and in the state House of Representatives. Though a layman, he was instrumental in the formation of the Alabama Baptist Missionary Convention and the creation of the Dexter Avenue Baptist Church. He fought for decent black cemeteries, an African American presence on the police force, and equal public school systems. Toward the end of Reconstruction, however, his religious and political activism came into conflict. At one point his colleagues removed him from the very black Baptist convention that he organized, allegedly for neglecting his financial duties. Future Alabama Baptist leaders carried on his legacy. Jesse Duke, for example, editor of the Alabama black Baptist newspaper, the *Baptist Leader*, and an activist in the Republican Party, was a trustee of Selma University, a black theological institution, and the first president of the Alabama Colored Press Association. After publishing inflammatory editorials in 1887, he was forced to flee the state, eventually settling in Arkansas. The costs of religio-political work could be great. Richard Burke, a minister, teacher, and Union League organizer, served in the state House of Representatives in Alabama from 1868 to 1870. Rumors circulated that he advocated the arming of blacks, and he was murdered. Testifying at the Ku Klux Klan hearings, his former owner remembered that while Burke was a "quiet man" he nevertheless "had made himself obnoxious to a certain class of young men" through his work in the Loyal League "and by having acquired a great influence over people of his color."[27]

As "Redeemed" governments wrested back control of southern politics in the 1870s, black Baptists lost faith in the federal government as a transforming agent in the South. Religious organizers blasted the Republican Party for betraying "the confidence *we* put in it." A North Carolina minister and professor lambasted southern politicians, including the Republicans, for preferring that the freedpeople remain "blind to the shameful fact that our *postbellum* masters have existence, as our *antebellum* masters once had, and that we are, therefore, not yet free." William J. Simmons, a powerful minister and educator in Kentucky, advised an audience of black Baptists in 1886 that rather than counting on government action as "a panacea for all our ills," race leaders should "court the favors of the people of the state. We must be for progress wherever found." The Republican Party, he argued, could not help black people even if it willed to do so: "They are debarred by statutes and by sentiments stronger than statutes." Black southerners, another Baptist organization lamented, were "so trammeled in some places that they dare not express an opinion on any subject if it differs from a white man." They could not exercise their voting rights, he complained, and "in other places they feel the sting so badly that they arise and depart, considering that they have no rest in the present cultivated districts." By the late 1870s, blacks moving to Kansas, dubbed the "Exodusters," personified the despair at the broken promises of Reconstruction life. While expressing disapproval of the "sudden emigration," black Baptists in Virginia nevertheless hailed these blacks' showing "to the world that they have the spirit of men." The Exodusters served as an example before "the civilized world [of a] condition of barbarity unknown in the annals of history among a people who profess the Christian religion."[28]

Historians of Reconstruction have detailed both the importance and the limitations of black churches as avenues of political organizing. Just as significantly, churches were moral and spiritual guides during dangerous and difficult times for the freedpeople. "Visit them in their churches, and observe them in praying, and singing, and preaching, and the reason why they themselves do not ask or desire to be admitted to the communion of the white churches will be readily understood," one British observer commented. Religious gatherings reunited families scattered under slavery, provided avenues for courtship, and sustained a social life for impoverished freedpeople dispersed through the countryside. The freedpeople "made their churches their rallying places, and poured out their souls in praise and thanksgiving," a black Baptist historian wrote. The pastors of large congregations spent much pulpit time "advertising and reading letters from all parts of the South making inquiries for members of scattered families . . . who were sold like cattle in the market," a visitor to Richmond observed. In Virginia's black churches, another visitor noted, "there was not an evening or afternoon that had not its meetings, its literary or social gathering, its picnic or fair for the benefit of the church, its Dorcas society, or some occasion of religious sociability." A minister's wife who traveled with her husband for twenty years on the camp meeting circuit remembered how "people would come in ox wagons to de big camp meetin's, we sure had fine times. . . . On dem camp meetin' groun's de folks brought dere pots and pans and baked and cooked de food right on the groun'. . . . Folks sure believed in one another at dat time." Black Christians congregated "to worship, to hear the choir sing, to listen to the preacher, and to hear and see the people shout," Benjamin Mays remembered of his boyhood in South Carolina. "The young people went to Mount Zion to socialize, or simply to stand around and talk. It was a place of worship and a social center as well. There was no other place to go." Mays was "motivated by people in the church who made me believe that I could become something worthwhile in the world." Mays recalled that when his father's buggy accidentally threw dust on some whites passing by, his father apologized profusely to the offended party. "Did this mean that my father mentally accepted or emotionally approved this cringing behavior?" Mays later asked himself. "I doubt it. It was a technique of survival. But I have always wondered how long one can do a thing without eventually accepting it." For a boy who grew up with memories of whites on horseback firing at black voters and recollections of his proud father cringing before common whites, the encouragement of his elders in the pews every Sunday was of lifelong significance.[29]

Whether it concerned differences in worship customs, disputes over church politics, or quarrels over the necessity of education for the pulpit, conflicts between black Baptist organizers (many of whom were free before the war) and the local ministers (most of whom were ex-slaves) were widespread. To northern missionaries of both races, the worship of the freedpeople was reminiscent of barbarism. In asking the American Baptist Free Mission Society to fund a general missionary for Mississippi, Rufus Perry lamented that "our people" were "not rational enough here to act from principle"; they were "impulsive, and go as their feelings not reason moves them." Their naïveté left them "often at the mercy of the designing." Charles Satchell depicted the provincialism of the spiritual leaders of the freedpeople in New Orleans this way:

> The greatest trouble we have, arose from an imperfect ministry, and from this source we shall have trouble for some time to come; men wedded to the old customs of the country, ignorant, selfish and domineering, and who can only live by keeping the people in a state of ignorance to uphold their pretensions. They ignore everything like system, have no respect for moral obligation, and poison the minds of the people against every thing of northern origin, as Yankee measures to cheat the slaves out of their money.

The result of such ministerial leadership was painfully obvious. "Visit the South and see," one missionary concluded, then "weep and pray, and give to the cause of education."[30]

The missionaries who came to the South sought the cooperation of formerly enslaved preachers. But the entrance of these outsiders with higher formal qualifications in ministerial training threatened the traditional place of uneducated ex-slave preachers who "contended for old customs." A Virginia missionary, for example, wrote of the bitter "persecution" black Baptist reformers in that area faced, originating in the "jealousness of those known here before the war as plantation preachers, and who are used as tools of the old rebels in opposition to the 'carpet-baggers.' " In Mississippi, according to another missionary, church deacons spread fears that educated men aimed "to subvert the true principles of religion, and to make merchandise of them." He condemned the power politics practiced in ministerial satrapies: "These things are kept alive by a class of men who control them as leaders. So long as they can keep the people in this ignorance they will hold their influence and control and filch from their small earnings." Some preachers came to be known for pleasing both the missionaries and the local congregations. A black missionary in Savannah told northern Baptists of exhorters who professed support for "intelligent" and "progressive" practices yet preached in an unrestrained style to their congregants. Such men "hold with the hare and run with the hounds. . . . They want to be thought well of on all sides." The different masks they wore according to the situation would undermine the work of progressive-minded church leaders, he warned: "Believe me when I tell you that I have found much of this amongst our people."[31]

With such an array of problems facing them—racist terrorism, illiteracy and ignorance, and apparently backward religious customs—black religious leaders knew that immediate organization was imperative. With optimism, faith in God's plan for the freedpeople, and courageous leadership drawn from both formerly enslaved and free people of color, black Baptists during Reconstruction organized associations and state conventions throughout the South. In forming one of the first state conventions in 1868, black Baptists in Virginia evoked the trials they faced, with many freedpeople spiritually demoralized by the physical struggle for existence in this promising but economically difficult period: "The great struggle between contending political parties in this country has scattered, and virtually exiled, many of the children of God, and caused them to be as sheep without a shepherd and a flock, and are hungering and thirsting after righteousness, as presented in the gospel and its melodious sound, and panting, not only for spiritual food, but also for spiritual protection." When whites refused to meet in the same associations with churches that would send black delegates, black Virginians responded, "the Convention will not mourn at the non-interchange, nor slacken her progress but will move on trusting in that God who has . . . proven . . . to be void of prejudice, of colorphobia, of caste, or lines of demarkation." The Virginians prayed that God would "help us to show ourselves men—God's freedmen, endowed with certain inalienable rights" and that the freedpeople would rise above "mere hewers of wood and drawers of water, above back seats and figure heads." They hoped to "carry on the work of evangelization and education as well as any other race of men that God ever breathed into the breath of life."[32]

When black churches in Georgia who applied to white associations for membership were told that they would not be allowed to send black delegates and were encouraged to forward funds to the white-run association instead, they countered by forming separate associations. By 1877 twenty-six such groups in the state accounted for a combined church membership of some 91,000 communicants. By the 1890s, freed Christians throughout the region had formed an impressive number of state and local Baptist groups that figured centrally in aiding educational institutions (academies, high schools, and colleges). Churches were members of these associations by voluntary consent. The associations held no formal powers but exerted considerable informal local influence. "There is as much scheming to get churches to join some associations," Texas Baptists acknowledged, "as there is practiced in political circles."[33]

After the war, state conventions also sprang up throughout the South, replicating at a state level what associations accomplished at regional and local levels. North Carolina Baptists led the way, organizing a state convention as early as 1866. By 1888, there were 132,000 black Baptists in North Carolina, mostly in the eastern part of the state. In Virginia, the Shiloh Baptist Association, comprised of churches in and around the Richmond area, counted seventy-five churches and over fourteen thousand members. In 1868, ministers of the Shiloh Association and the Norfolk Union Association founded the Baptist State Convention of Virginia. In the same year, twenty-seven churches in Alabama met in Montgomery and formed the Colored Baptist State Convention. Mississippi followed in 1869 with a state convention organized primarily by Henry Jacobs, who served in Natchez pulpits and various political posts in the state. Jacobs's nemesis Jesse Boulden formed a rival convention, but the two bodies merged in 1890, bringing together nine hundred churches and seventy-nine thousand Baptists. Texas Baptists convened their state meeting in 1874 and soon boasted of twenty-three associations with nearly fifty thousand communicants. In 1896 their roll had increased to over one hundred thousand believers. In South Carolina, the prominent minister E. M. Brawley brought together Baptists into a state convention listing nearly 124,000 members in 1895.[34]

Black Baptists understood that a strong national organization was necessary for the protection and development of their people. But the localism of Baptist polity, the ability of any group of believers to form a congregation, meant that churches were often small, weak, and schismatic, and larger organizations were difficult to support. Soon after the war, for example, representatives from a number of smaller black Baptist groups formed the Consolidated American Baptist Missionary Convention (CABMC). During its existence, from 1866 to 1879, it represented a significant attempt to centralize the various regional associations that free black Baptists had formed before the war along with new associations created by the churches of the freedpeople. Most of the CABMC men hailed from the North or the West. A few were born as slaves but had either purchased their freedom or else escaped from slavery. Several of its leading members came directly from the ranks of the American Baptist Free Mission Society, which during its short life worked on the principle that "the sooner freedmen cease to be treated as children, the sooner will they cease to be children" and especially emphasized education, because "what slaveholders found it most necessary to withhold, we consider most necessary to give." By 1869, the CABMC listed thirteen affiliated associations and seventy-two member churches and was involved with a school for ministerial training in Richmond. The convention's spokesmen stressed the symbolism of a black–controlled central organization carrying on business competently: "Brethren, we are watched. We are not accepted as a body or denomination qualified to manage our own missionary and educational work, and many of those who most discredit our capacity . . . have set themselves up as our benefactors, and call upon our friends to aid us through them. But our very organization is our proclamation to the world that we are able to do this work, and that we *ought* to do it."[35]

Delegates to the CABMC stressed their readiness to manage missionary work among the freedpeople, with money coming from their own fund-raising efforts and from white northern assistance. Rufus Perry, a CABMC spokesman, argued that the aid extended by the American Baptist Home Mission Society, the major northern Baptist missionary society in the post-war era, had set back the cause of true freedom: "The principle of helping us to help ourselves, regarded by the intelligent of every denomination as the best, has hitherto been totally ignored." But white northern Baptists in the Home Mission Society responded negatively to Perry's request for black control over the expenditure of missionary funds. If they funded Perry's group they would soon be swamped with other requests, they explained. To CABMC members, this episode exemplified how whites deliberately steered the development of free black institutions away from self-reliance. White northern money "presented ostensibly for our improvement," asserted Perry, tended "by a peculiar Yankee involution" to bear "its first and last fruits unto the opulence and glory of the nominal benefactor." The dispute over who should oversee mission money illustrated some of the difficulties that bedeviled relations between black Baptist men and their northern white benefactors. Black leaders resented their lack of meaningful black participation on the committees of the Home Mission Society. The society's "mode of operation," H. H. White declared, "makes the colored people entirely passive and completely unmans us." White's critique of the paternalism of white benefactors toward blacks resembled the views expressed by black abolitionists, such as Frederick Douglass, before the war, who felt the avuncular hand of the Garrisonians become a restraining grip.[36]

Internal controversies and funding shortages also afflicted the CABMC. The black missionary force in various states suffered heavily from the failure of the Freedmen's Banks. Politically active CABMC members were accused of neglecting religious work for the political arena. Such men, a black Baptist organizer warned, could "become more or less contaminated with political corruption, and defective, inefficient and depreciated as ministers of the gospel." The CABMC also never recovered from the closing of the Freedmen's Bureau, which ended support to the convention's schools. The CABMC apparently disbanded in 1879, after limping along for its last years.[37]

During the war, the American Baptist Home Mission Society had initiated work among the freedpeople, directing its money especially at the creation of academies and colleges. At its height sixty-eight missionaries worked the southern field. By 1879, however, as the society sought to stretch its resources to projects scattered across the country, only twenty-one missionaries of the ABHMS were stationed among freedpeople. The prominent Virginians Jeremiah B. Jeter and John Broadus, though fond of sectionalist polemicizing, recognized that laborers from the North were bound to be present and would need suitable advice from southern whites. "By thus co-operating with good men in this work," Jeter suggested, "we neutralize the effect of ultraists who may come from the North to preach to the colored people." This endorsement of safe and conservative northern whites provided yet another motivation to contend for black Baptist independence.[38]

If the paternalism of northern aid sat uncomfortably with Perry and other black Baptist separatists, the offers of southern whites to assist the freedpeople seemed egregiously self-serving. It would be better to fail in an "honest, manly effort to lead, govern, and elevate ourselves," Rufus Perry announced, "than to suffer the shame of committing this important trust either to our late masters that made merchandise of us, or to those who proscribe us and deny us the social and ecclesiastical rights and privileges . . . necessary to constitute a recognition of our manhood." Churches in black communities, he insisted, must teach not only "the way of salvation" but also the means of "social progress." John Gregory, a white northern Baptist, recounted his experiences at a conference where "nearly every speaker announced himself as a 'race man' and avowed his determination to 'stand by his race.'" He grew alarmed over the implications of this rhetoric: "Even the more sensible colored men themselves confess to its unwisdom and danger." Black Baptist officials responded that requests for greater participation in religious and educational labor among their own people were not equivalent to an unthinking separatism. After all, as one black minister reminded Gregory, "it is the whites who want to keep separate."[39]

Table 1 lists the twenty-eight institutions supported by the American Baptist Home Mission Society. The local academies and institutes were significant primarily in providing literacy training and other forms of basic education to African Americans. North Carolina black Baptists, for example, boasted the strongest series of institutes and academies. The Waters Institute, located in Winton, North Carolina, stood as probably the premier private academy of black Baptists in the South. Established as Winton Academy in 1886, in 1891 it took the name of Waters Normal Institute to honor a New York Baptist who donated $1,500 to support its founding. A board of trustees from the Chowan Baptist Educational Association, made up of over sixty Baptist churches in the eastern part of the state, presided over the school. Waters provided both primary and normal instruction and trained teachers. The first principal of the school, Calvin Scott Brown, was educated at Shaw University, one of the premier institutions of higher education supported by the Home Mission Society. Asked by the president of Shaw to head the institute, Brown moved to Winton in the 1880s. By the time of his death, in 1936, he presided over a campus with twenty-one teachers and seven buildings valued at nearly $80,000. Most of the other academies were not as fortunate. During the Depression, many of them folded. Also, because of the philanthropy provided by the Rosenwald, Phelps-Stokes, and other funds, states built schools superior to those run by the religious associations. State school boards eventually took over the property of numerous black private schools.[40]

The higher educational institutions supported by the American Baptist Home Mission Society served as the linchpin of northern Baptist missionary efforts. Training a generation of black Baptist ministers at these institutions, their northern benefactors assumed, would accomplish more than any other form of work to "uplift" the ex-slaves into productive citizens. In the first twenty-five years of this effort, the ABHMS devoted about $2 million dollars to establish or support fifteen institutions. By 1890 the society could boast of some thirteen thousand students who had been through their schools, and about $763,000 worth of school property. In the next twenty years the expenditures would double, and many of the younger institutions (such as Spelman College in Atlanta) would flourish, while others would

Table 1. Educational Institutions for Black Baptists, Founded 1865–1902

Institution	Location	Founded
Selma University	Selma, Alabama	1878
Arkansas Baptist College	Little Rock, Arkansas	1884
Florida Baptist Academy	Jacksonville, Florida	1892
Florida Institute	Live Oak, Florida	1876
Americus Institute	Americus, Georgia	1897
Jeruel Academy	Athens, Georgia	1886
Atlanta Baptist College	Atlanta, Georgia	1867
Spelman Seminary	Atlanta, Georgia	1881
Walker Baptist Institute	Augusta, Georgia	1892
State University	Louisville, Kentucky	1879
Coleman Academy	Gibsland, Louisiana	1887
Leland College (originally established by American Baptist Free Mission Society)	New Orleans, Louisiana	1870
Jackson College	Jackson, Mississippi	1877
Western College and Industrial Institute	Macon, Missouri	1890
Thompson Institute	Lumberton, North Carolina	1900
Newbern Collegiate Institute	Newbern, North Carolina	1902
Shaw University	Raleigh, North Carolina	1865
Waters Normal Institute	Winton, North Carolina	1886
Mather Industrial School	Beaufort, South Carolina	1867
Benedict College	Columbia, South Carolina	1871
Howe Bible and Normal Institute	Memphis, Tennessee	1888
Roger Williams University	Nashville, Tennessee	1866
Houston College	Houston, Texas	1885
Bishop College	Marshall, Texas	1881
Tidewater Collegiate Institute	Chesapeake, Virginia	1891
Hartshorn Memorial College	Richmond, Virginia	1883
Virginia Union University	Richmond, Virginia	1865
Storer College (originally established by Free Will Baptists)	Harpers Ferry, West Virginia	1867

struggle. Meanwhile, controversies over the direction of the institutions often stirred conflict between black Baptist leaders and the northern benefactors. The experiences of Shaw University and Roger Williams University in Nashville reflect the varied history of these schools.[41]

Shaw University, one of the success stories of black Baptist higher education, was established originally in Raleigh, North Carolina, just after the war ended. In 1870, despite Klan hostility to his work, founder Henry M. Tupper secured a site for Shaw in the suburbs of Raleigh. By the late nineteenth century, with a medical college attached to it and relatively secure funding sources, it stood as one of the most successful of the Baptist missionary colleges. Shaw's close relationship with its white northern bene-factors ensured that black Baptists in North Carolina would remain loyal to notions of cooperation, refusing to join the separatist-oriented National Baptist Convention. Shaw rarely experienced the kinds of racial conflicts between administrators, students, and black Baptist conventions that often plagued other schools. In 1894 Shaw claimed 353 students, with thirteen teachers. By 1910, 565 students attended the school, including 51 at the college level and 43 at the high school level. Shaw's medical program pro-duced missionaries to Africa. In the school's periodical the *African Exposi-tor*, E. H. Lipscombe, a Shaw University professor, explained the philoso-phy of teaching dominant at the institution: "Our minds must cast off the old shell in which slavery incased [*sic*] them, and overtake and control our bodies for our own good and for the good of the great country of which we are citizens."[42]

Roger Williams University in Nashville provides a second and less happy example. A flagship institution for black Baptists, Roger Williams was founded in 1864 as the Nashville Institute. D. W. Phillips, the school's longtime president, met with his first students in the basement of the First Colored Baptist Church of Nashville. Phillips developed a following among black ministers in Nashville, who later reminisced, "We went with him over the city, and he ate at our tables, as poor as we were. He identified himself with us to lift us up, to bring life to us and open a way by which we might be educated." Phillips raised the money to buy a government surplus building, with a two-story structure as the original classroom. In the 1870s, with a gift of $30,000 from Phillips's former classmate Nathan Bishop (a northern Baptist who also endowed Bishop College in Marshall, Texas), Roger Wil-liams acquired thirty valuable acres and a large brick dwelling in a prime location. The school began to offer the A.B. degree in 1877. From early in its history, the school had black members on its board, including Nelson G. Merry, pastor of the black First Baptist Church of Nashville. Incorporated in 1883, the school changed its name from the Nashville Institute to Roger Williams University. By 1890 it boasted of several hundred students, about $100,000 in property, and a place in the community second only to that of Fisk University. A number of future black Baptist leaders passed through its doors, including Joseph Booker and E. C. Morris, future presidents of the National Baptist Convention, and Lewis G. Jordan, a longtime foreign missions advocate. In 1881 Roger Williams became the first Home Mission Society school to offer college-level work, and until 1905 it led all schools of the ABHMS in the number of students in higher grades. John Hope, later president of Morehouse College, taught at Roger Williams for four years, and the school acquired the backing of some local white Baptists, including William Palmer Jones, who, as a state senator in the 1870s, favored free public schools.[43]

Roger Williams began to come apart in the 1880s, however, when black students charged T. E. Balch, treasurer of the school, with assaults on female students. "You *dirty grand rascal* yo think that Negroes are blind fools but we will show you how to come here acting a dog and calling us rogues. . . . This is our home and you dirty pup we will kick your ass out if you do not act better," an anonymous group of students wrote to him. The Educational Board of the ABHMS, headed by Henry Morehouse, came to Nashville to adjudicate the dispute. They insisted that the two student ringleaders, who brought up the charges, be denied degrees and stated that the board would "expect in the future as in the past to have a voice in the management and discipline of all schools whose property it owns, and whose support it assumes." The statement further alienated faculty, who objected to the "arbitrary dictation" of the board. The majority of students enrolled at the school, meanwhile, asked to be discharged. Student enrollment dropped to about two hundred. The board offered to sell the property to black Baptists in the state, but they could not raise sufficient money. In 1905 a fire destroyed the main building of the campus, and the property was sold, to be used later as the site for Peabody College. In 1907 Tennessee black Baptists voted to assume responsibility for the school, with a black faculty and predominantly black board. The ABHMS provided financial assistance and approved of the transfer of the corporation to new trustees. The college reopened on January 1, 1908. Twenty years later it moved to Memphis, where it merged with Howe Junior College, but it did not survive the depression years.[44]

The language of separatism that informed the organization of black Baptists proved less useful in formulating specific policies about whether and how much to cooperate with whites. State conventions of black Baptists struggled to balance a desire for black independence along with the necessity for white financial and administrative assistance. Black religious leaders faced the same questions that sparked controversies in many black organizations of the era. Did accepting white money inevitably mean bowing to white dominance of efforts toward education and independence? If whites donated money to black institutions on the condition of white leadership, was this a sacrifice of the principle of black autonomy? If a black teacher was added to a school, or a black member to a board of trustees of a missionary college, was this tokenism or real participation? In the state conventions, which served as intermediaries between local congregations and large national organizations, no clear victor emerged from the battle of separationists and cooperationists, just as no clear intellectual victor came out of the "debate" between integrationism and separatism. Ultimately, these racial strategies pointed to the same end. Both drew from an ideology of uplift that would ultimately prove disappointing.[45]

Delegates to Texas Baptist conventions were among the first to skirmish over ground that would soon witness numerous intraracial battles. Within their own institutional context, the black Texans of the 1880s debated the issues of integrationism and separatism. In 1884, Black Baptists in south and east Texas founded Guadalupe College in Seguin, which was supported primarily by the Guadalupe Baptist Association. In 1888, the black convention in Texas voted to divide its money between two preparatory schools and two colleges, Bishop College (established by the American Baptist Home Mission Society in 1881 in Marshall, Texas) and Guadalupe. The plan of the ABHMS, however, called for making Guadalupe a lower-grade feeder school, with higher educational resources concentrated on Bishop College. The result was a split between those who supported the plan and those who argued that Guadalupe should serve as an example of independent educational projects. Complicating the situation, Bishop's white president, S. W. Culver, was accused of assaulting a female student, leading to a boycott of the school. Allen R. Griggs, leader of the cooperationist Baptist Missionary State Education Convention of Texas was accused of "working for the white people." But he angrily denounced the charge as being "superstitiousness" that forced "some of our people to believe that every dollar a white man turns loose on a colored man he sees where he can make two out of it."[46]

Texas Baptist separatists, including Sutton Griggs (a graduate of Bishop), Richard H. Boyd, and Richard Abner, son of a Reconstruction legislator and a former faculty member at Bishop, founded the General Missionary Baptist Convention of Texas. They justified their move with language that even the cooperationists could appreciate: "The Holy Spirit come to us and forbid the Negro taking a second place." Griggs emphasized how white money and power, channeled for Baptists through the Home Mission Society, hindered the development of "black manhood": "We believe in letting all our Baptist schools live. . . . [Whites] simply say let your field grow up in weeds and work my land for fifty years. Let your wife and children do without the home for fifty years, and work for me; but they forget when the fifty years are out the Negro is just where he was when he started. Not one whit higher, cornered and unprotected." Black Baptist separatists in Texas criticized the cooperationists for accepting white money, but the separatists themselves accepted donations from white Baptists, with the stipulation that the funds would not be contingent on specific policies.[47]

In other states, especially Georgia and Virginia, disputes between separatists and cooperationists ended in similar schisms. In Virginia, the cooperationists agreed to consolidate educational efforts into one major location, Virginia Union University in Richmond, rather than scattering institutions across the state. Under this plan, the seminary operated by the black state convention, Virginia Seminary in Lynchburg, would be made into a secondary school that would feed theological students into Virginia Union. But Gregory O. Hayes, president of the black-run seminary, objected to the agreement. An Oberlin College graduate and charismatic leader, Hayes headed the creation of Virginia Seminary in 1888. He soon thereafter was compelled to accept money from the ABHMS, which was a blow to his plans for black independence. The Virginia Union agreement embittered him further. At the state black Baptist meeting in 1899, dubbed the "Battle of Lexington" by students, Hayes led a majority of delegates to oppose the Home Mission Society's plans to concentrate resources on Virginia Union in Richmond. After being outvoted in the black Virginia Baptist State Convention, the cooperationists met and formed a separate convention, the General Association of Virginia, in 1899. "Those of us who have any idea of country life in the South and in our own State can see at a glance the absurdity of those who claim that the Negro has the ability to take an independent attitude in this country," the cooperationists explained. "These so-called independents are slaves to their own personal ambition and seeking to satisfy it by sacrificing their brethren and sisters."[48]

The gathering currents of black separatism came to a head in the 1890s, resulting in the formation of the National Baptist Convention in 1895 and, soon thereafter, the National Baptist Publishing Board. A dispute over a series of articles to be published in 1890 in the *Baptist Teacher*, a northern Baptist quarterly publication used in Sunday schools throughout the nation, galvanized sentiment for a separate publishing board. In the wake of the controversy, southern white and black Baptists each formed publishing agencies that soon made significant inroads into a market formerly dominated by the northern American Baptist Publication Society.[49]

The incident grew out of an offer made by Benjamin Griffith, director of the American Baptist Publication Society, to three notable black Baptist ministers—William J. Simmons, Emmanuel K. Love, and William H. Brooks—to publish their doctrinal articles in the quarterly publication *Baptist Teacher*. Black Baptists in Virginia and North Carolina had convinced Griffith that publication of black authors would expand the market for the materials of the publication society. They trumpeted Griffith's proposal as evidence of their intellectual progress. But white southern Baptists who favored the creation of a publishing agency within the Southern Baptist Convention (SBC) blustered that Griffith's plan encouraged "the wickedly ambitious, unprincipled elements" among African Americans and encouraged a "contempt for law and order and to deeds of violence and death." The SBC was assured that the society would not employ "objectionable Negroes" or any that advocated "assassination and arson." But the southern separatists carried the day, and Griffith withdrew the offer, asking instead that the same authors write a series of tracts, marketed to black churches, that would cover the similar doctrinal matters. Griffith insisted to blacks that he meant no "indignity upon any of your race." But black Baptists countered that the northern publication society could not possibly expect black Baptists to patronize the society "unless it believes us void of manhood." As a concession, Griffith hired more black agents for the society in the South and supported the publication of articles written by prominent black Baptists.[50]

In the early 1890s, black Baptists came together for the creation of a separate publishing endeavor and national denomination. But much opposition to their effort remained. The American Baptist Publication Society had begun to place inexpensively produced materials in the hands of black churches and had hired black agents to sell its publications. The death of Benjamin Griffith, director of the publication society, was a blow to the efforts of those who wished to continue cooperating with the white northern society (who were known as "cooperationists"). They insisted, to no avail, that God would "raise up just as wise and conscientious a leader . . . who will respect the rights of the colored Baptists." If the proposed new black Baptist publishing agency collapsed, the cooperationists added, this would prove to whites the inability of blacks to conduct their own affairs. These opponents of the new board defeated a proposal in 1895 to establish a publishing agency within the constitution of the new National Baptist Convention. "It was hoped by the more learned," a black Baptist historian explained of the opposition, "that the idea of printing was stamped out." The most strident opponents of the establishment of a separate society, mostly employees of northern publication societies, "felt that such steps would be construed as enmity against our white brethren and friends who had given so much, and endured so much for us." E. M. Brawley, a well-educated South Carolinian who worked closely with the northern publication society, warned his colleagues not to "rush poverty-stricken, comparatively, into the face of wisdom, experience, and might." African Americans should "want no organizations on the color line," he argued, but should strive to "merge race feeling in the broader spirit of an American Christianity."[51]

Backers of the publishing house pointed out that such an agency would serve as a vehicle for resisting the growing tide of white supremacist rhetoric. "All races have a literature," one advocate pointed out. A black Baptist publishing effort could help African Americans avoid "absorption" into the white mainstream, he asserted. Black Baptists would "never attain to the broad influence and elevated dignity worthy of so vast a body of Baptists so long as our literary productions remain unpublished," a black denominational leader explained in 1893. Supporters of the publishing endeavor also pointed to practical reasons for backing the prospective firm, including "race employment." Black Baptists should assume the responsibility "to provide better things for our children, than our fathers were allowed to prepare for us," argued another proponent. Only when race leaders in the church created solidly grounded institutions, he concluded, would American Christianity be able to "sign the death warrant" of racist prejudice.[52]

By the mid-1890s, influential black ministers such as Emmanuel K. Love, pastor of a large congregation in Savannah and president of the Missionary and Educational Baptist Convention of Georgia, supported a separate publishing agency. Until the 1880s, Love's close contacts with officials of the American Baptist Publication Society, especially with Benjamin Griffith, kept Love in the cooperationist camp. But Love gradually concluded that because of their dependence on white northerners, black Baptists had "grown too largely to be parasites," too prone to assume a "begging attitude." As he told one congregation in 1897, "he is both blind and foolish who does not recognize the fact that the color line is already drawn. I do not believe that any white man is color blind." The publishing house was also, he argued, a "question of race pride and of race gain in dollars and cents and it gives employment to Negroes which they cannot hope for in a white publishing house." He concluded that, "there is not so bright or glorious a future before a Negro in a white institution as there is for him in his own. . . . A people who man no enterprises show that they can have no spirit of progress . . . and a people without this cannot command the recognition of nations and the respect of the world." He lambasted the "deceitful, disloyal Negroes and Hirelings" of the American Baptist Publication Society, "who are ingloriously opposing this laudable Negro enterprise to curry the favor of white people and to be called a good sensible Negro."[53] Eventually, the arguments of the supporters proved successful. In 1896, the National Baptist Publishing Board, headed by black religious entrepreneur Richard H. Boyd, was chartered. In the early twentieth century it became the largest black-owned publishing enterprise in the country, a story told in fuller detail in chapter eight of this book.

In addition to establishing the publishing house in the 1890s, black Baptists were working toward uniting into a single national denomination. Up to this point, the Baptist Foreign Mission Convention, formed in 1880, oversaw missionary work abroad,the American National Baptist Convention, chartered in 1886, organized home mission and educational endeavors, and the National Baptist Educational Convention, created in 1893, centralized fund-raising for educational institutions. Despite internal dissent, each of the groups eventually supported separate and independent black religious enterprises.[54]

Representatives from each of the organizations met in Atlanta in 1895 and created the National Baptist Convention. The convention appointed boards to oversee the various programs formerly carried out by separate and distinct organizations—home missions, foreign missions, publishing, educational work, and church building funds. Unlike the white Southern Baptist Convention, the National Baptist Convention was not specifically a southern organization. But the convention numerically would be dominated by southern churches until the migration of African Americans out of the South after 1915. And in spite of its stormy early history of periodic schisms and infighting, the National Baptist Convention grew to be the largest black organization in the country.

In response to the forming of the convention, black Baptists from Virginia and the Carolinas who opposed separatist rhetoric in religious work founded the Lott Carey Baptist Foreign Mission Convention in 1897. The Lott Carey group maintained their cooperative ties with the northern Baptist societies. North Carolina Baptists stood "firm and unchangeable in their high esteem and loyal support of the Home Mission Society," a Lott Carey organizer explained. He found it a "sad spectacle . . . to see a few men educated in the schools" of the mission society "turn away with the basest ingratitude, and with their greatest efforts, though feeble at best, strike back at the Society." Most importantly, in their mind, black Baptists working alone would not be able to support successfully a costly and difficult foreign missions program.[55]

In the early twentieth century, however, the rift healed. The Lott Carey group and the National Baptist Convention established cooperative relations, and in most states the separate state conventions reunited. The separatists lacked the financial resources to carry on independently; the cooperationists were compelled to admit that white racism necessitated efforts by African Americans to establish a "world within a world." With the victory of white supremacist forces in the South, and to a large degree in the nation, the black separatist organization—the National Baptist Convention—emerged as the most important and influential of the groups. The fact that it cooperated with southern whites whenever possible in home mission work and in the construction (three decades later) of a black seminary in Nashville pointed out the ambiguities that softened the rhetoric of racial "separatism" and "cooperation."[56]

In the 1890s, black religious organizers knew that their battle only had begun. While the "intelligent and progressive element in our churches have composed the vanguard of God's great army among the Negro Christians of the world," National Baptist Convention president E. C. Morris suggested, most of the nearly two million black Baptists remained "crude and under-developed." During the Progressive Era, both white and black Baptists found in "intelligent worship" a strategy for bringing their denominations into a new age of separate racial development and, they hoped, "all things working together for mutual progress."[57]

PART TWO

Religious Cultures and the Social Order in the New South

CHAPTER THREE

These Untutored Masses

Spirituality and Respectability among White Southern Baptists

Our membership is composed largely of the masses of the people, and what the common people are that must our churches be. . . . To take these untutored masses and culture them and organize them for the world's great battle is the grandest duty of this convention.
—Southern Baptist Convention *Proceedings*, 1885

"The churches throughout the rural districts were dilapidated in the extreme, and frequently . . . inhabited by hogs, sheep and other animals," wrote Solomon Conser, a cleric in Virginia during Reconstruction. Even those buildings not disturbed by wandering livestock often housed congregants who worshiped in primitive ways, he continued, describing the "extravagant devotions" of the freedpeople, how they fell "into trances and cataleptic fits and professed to see visions of angels and demons." Such "spasmodic excesses," he added, characterized worship styles among churchgoers of both races: "In various forms and divers places they had made their appearance." This religious "fanaticism," he concluded, was "encouraged by a class of zealots and divines of limited physical learning."[1]

Mary Allan-Olney, an unsympathetic observer of southern life, expressed her disgust that both black and white women would not believe they had experienced conversion "unless the process had been ushered in by a good, strong, unmistakable fit of hysterics." In the 1880s, Stephen Powers observed the "quaint and simple antiquity of certain usages, such as that of standing in prayer, [and] of lining out the hymn" in southern worship. Southern preaching, "even in the largest metropolitan cities," Powers claimed, was more comedic than spiritual: "You can almost hear the solemn 'whangdoodle whine' the moment you enter." In the 1930s, an ex-slave saw "both white and colored people responding to preaching in much the same way as in his early life," with preachers appealing "to the emotions of their flock."[2]

Denominational modernizers perceived that southern vernacular spirituality would be inadequate for progressive churches in the developing region. A Mississippi minister in the 1880s acknowledged that much of the southern countryside was "comparatively undeveloped in benevolence, and resting in a rather low state of religious activity." Few churches supported Sunday schools, while much "drinking, ungodly reveling and lawlessness even among the church members" embarrassed the community. "This is true of a great many of the Baptists, who live on as their fathers lived, feeling little responsibility for the world's salvation," he concluded.[3]

White and black Baptist denominationalists shared similar ideas of proper spiritual expression. This concern for the regulation of spirituality arose most immediately from the impulses of progressivism, especially in the desire for "efficiency" and "rationality" in worship ritual and denominational structure. In the late nineteenth century bourgeois conceptions of appropriate public behavior in urban social settings spread to a growing middle class. Urban elites cordoned off high culture from unruly spectators, pronounced the formation of a canon of great literature, and depicted the South as a hopelessly backward, albeit appealingly romantic, region of ignorant whites and primitive blacks. While the advocates of bourgeois respectability were winning the battle to change public behavior in the nation as a whole, evangelical believers in the South still worshiped in ways that were suggestive of camp meeting excesses.[4]

The conflict between bourgeois codes of behavior and vernacular expressions of spirituality provides a case study of the way southern Baptist churches absorbed outside influences while remaining a repository of regional cultures. Many urban congregations accepted the "programmed piety" offered to them by denominational modernizers. But the religious culture of rural southern Baptists proved far more resilient than church leaders recognized. This was the reality of Baptist democracy and of the free market of American Protestantism.

J. B. Cranfill, a longtime Texas Baptist official, grew up as a Primitive Baptist. Derisively termed the "Hardshells" for their "hard" views on predestination, the Primitives opposed the use of means (Sunday schools and missionary work) to induce salvation and were generally skeptical of Whiggish notions of social improvement. The services in Cranfill's boyhood church were lengthy affairs, including three sermons and communion before a footwashing ceremony concluded the service. Modeled after Christ's bathing the Disciples' feet during the Last Supper, footwashing was taken by the Primitive Baptists (unlike their mainstream denominational counterparts) to be one of the prescribed ordinances. Its effect was powerful: "They would grasp each other's hand, shed tears of Christian joy, give voice to expressions of tenderest Christian love. . . . Many were the misunderstandings and embryo feuds that would be settled on these footwashing occasions. No man could ever allow an enemy to kneel and wash his feet, and no man could ever remain an enemy of the man whose feet he had washed."[5]

Home missionaries building up congregations in "unchurched" regions romanticized the older spirituality. The nephew and grandson of two Baptist preachers, Adoniram Judson Holt, spent much of his adult life as an itinerating missionary in the frontier Southwest. In his youth he learned to fear "the jerks," the physical seizures accompanying spiritual fervor. While serving as a medical orderly in the Confederate army, he struggled against falling in with his comrades' drinking excesses. Although feeling no "electric shock" at his conversion in 1868, he recognized that his efforts at "seeking religion" finally had succeeded. Soon afterward he announced his call to preach and asked the local believers to "liberate him to exercise his gifts." He collapsed from fright during his first preaching engagement but recovered to become a success. "That was the way they did in those days," he explained. Churches "taught a young preacher to preach by making him preach. It was like breaking a colt; they just put the harness on and made me pull."

Holt enjoyed success in his exhortations, starting churches in numerous small towns in Texas and Arkansas. He decided to further his career by attending Southern Baptist Theological Seminary in Louisville, despite the objections of church members who insisted that seminary training ruined exhortatory powers. Holt felt out of place among his more cosmopolitan fellow students. "I used such provincialisms as were in vogue among the people where I lived," he recalled, and dressed so differently from his comrades that he frequently felt "humiliated." Contrary to the fears of his friends in Texas, Holt believed that theological training enhanced his preaching abilities. Holt's own life demonstrated how the fervor of rural religious customs could be directed to strengthen Baptist organizational life.[6]

Denominational modernizers found much fault with the backwardness of rural churches. But rural churches still remained "nurseries of pure religion," a Texas Baptist wrote, because they stood far removed from the "vanity, liquor, gambling, Socialism, Sabbath desecration, infidelity and cesspools of shame of the cities." Urban northern churches, he continued, were "increased in goods, respectable, influential and yet passionless," and the northern minister all too often played the part of a dandy, "cultured, elegant in manners, with a perennial smile petting and fondling a great church, and in turn petted and feasted and fondled by the church, and all perfectly satisfied." Country life advocates in the twentieth century reinforced this rhetoric. Although the "rural atmosphere" might be "somewhat uncongenial to progress and activity," one Texan asserted, it also discouraged "loose thinking and living." Self-educated preachers in the countryside still preferred the "social simplicity of rural life" to the "artificial conventionalisms which hedge and harass the pastor of a fashionable city church." Congregational democracy possessed a "peculiar appeal to people who live out in the open," argued an exponent of Frederick Jackson Turner's frontier thesis.[7]

White southern Baptists most often met in small rural churches that convened once a month. They voted once a year on calling a pastor, exercised discipline over members for transgressions of behavioral codes, and focused attention on saving souls and reclaiming straying members of their flocks. Services in most Baptist churches were infrequent and lengthy. In Mississippi, for example, only 23 of the 948 churches affiliated with the state Baptist convention in 1892 held a weekly service. Thirty-eight met every other week. The remaining 887 churches convened once a month. Part-time bivocational ministers supplied most pulpits. Monthly meetings often entailed two days of preaching and two sermons on Sunday, with dinner between the services. Widely scattered parishioners used meetings to catch up on news, speculate on cotton or tobacco prices, spread local gossip, and find appropriate mates.[8]

Older churches followed a patriarchal model of family organization. As the historian Ted Ownby succinctly put it, "the church followed the model of the home in that, while men were primarily in power, women were most revered and respected." Urban churches gave up the practice of gendered seating in the mid-nineteenth century; country churches retained the custom longer. But as the bourgeois family model spread, women participated more frequently in matters of church government. Gradually churches adopted resolutions similar to those of the Antioch Baptist Church in rural Virginia, stating that "the female members shall have an equal right with the male members to vote on all questions coming before the Conference." Jesse Mercer, a longtime Baptist leader in Georgia, opposed females voting in any church matter, but rightly suspected that a majority of churches practiced otherwise. While white males usually ran disciplinary committees, female members sometimes sat in when the defendant was a woman. "Females constitute the larger portion of our church members, and they ought to be consulted as to who shall preach to them, and as to who shall have their fellowship," an Alabama Baptist man acknowledged.[9]

While steadily gaining more rights to participate in church decisions, women's real religious influence, churchmen suggested, lay in their status as moral exemplar. Woman's work, a prominent cleric pronounced, remained that of "shining the steady flame of a genuine piety which will warm a cold world." As one minister intoned, "Let no Christian woman chafe beneath this subordination. Let her remember the pit from whence she was digged. Her Savior has taken her from among the bondslaves of Satan, and placed her in charge of a flowering garden, not amid the dust and blood of battle. There has he bid her stay—away from the crushing responsibilities of the mighty conflict of Truth with Evil."[10]

If women were assigned the role of pious defenders of a domesticated evangelicalism, then men could never exist as comfortably in this world. While women participated avidly in the services, men hung outdoors, often sauntering in late with a decided air of ambivalence. Pastors were often "afflicted for years with men who will get to church late, and walk like oxen to the very front seat, interrupting the preacher and the whole congregation," a North Carolinian reported. In a backwoods county in North Carolina, according to one missionary, patent medicine books outnumbered Bibles, and churchgoers lacked even the most rudimentary notion of worship etiquette. His patience was sorely tried: "Drunken men would interrupt church conferences by taking part in the discussions. While services were being held in the church, fisticuff fights and pistol shots were common in the church yard." Congregants and pranksters would "stick pins" in one of the ministers "as he knelt to pray" and "twist forked switches in his hair." Congregations in cities such as Richmond posted guards outside the door during services to discourage irreligious elements of the city from causing a commotion, particularly during revival services. Younger men delighted in parodying the proceedings, so much so that it became a convention for religious leaders to be converted at services that they originally attended for sport. Men "professed an easy toleration for profanity, drunkenness, gambling, and gross immorality," another minister recalled of his early years of work. A Primitive Baptist preacher who began his work in the 1910s remembered "some very ugly sights in the meeting house on the 'men's side,'" which no one thought anything about, or at least said nothing about," coming from the same church members that would not " 'have any fellowship for the organ.' " He probably encountered many men such as the horse trader in North Carolina in the 1930s who felt that "religion is a fine thing for women and children" and who found little time for spiritual matters as he was "busy as hell tryin' to make money." Rural men improved houses, land, and machinery, but still conceived of religion as a "nickle-and-dime" business "to be fostered chiefly by women," a Baptist home missions worker lamented.[11]

Faced with quarrelsome congregants and disorderly behavior in church conferences, congregations struggled to regulate themselves. A church in northern Mississippi amended its rules in the 1890s so that "no personal remarks shall be indulged in or personal reflections made during the discussion of any subject before the conference." Shiloh Baptist Church in Virginia required every member to "address each other by the title of brother, or sister" and proclaimed that "no whispering, talking, nor useless moving about shall be allowed, nor any member to absent himself, without permission." Outside the church grounds, members were forbidden "the indiscreet use of intoxicating beverages, the playing at any game for the purpose of gain, and the indulgence of any such or similar practices," all of which had "the tendency to injure the cause of Christianity."[12]

Church members in the nineteenth century exercised a constant and intrusive watch over each other. Jeremiah Jeter, a longtime minister in Virginia, recalled that Baptists in an earlier day were still "quite ascetic" in their practice: "On becoming a Baptist, one was expected to renounce the pleasures of the world—not only dancing, but all games, sports, and amusements—and to be grave, avoiding mirth and frivolity. This rule was not rigidly enforced, but its observance was deemed essential to high Christian character, and peculiarly necessary to ministers of the gospel." In Georgia, according to a precisely detailed study of church discipline, congregations excluded (excommunicated) about 2 percent of their members a year from congregations. An even higher percentage of congregants were issued reprimands and compelled to repent publicly. Disciplinary patterns varied according to gender, race, and social status. Young men most often came under scrutiny for drinking, fighting, and social misconduct. Older men were forced to repent for misuses of power. Church conferences indicted women most frequently for adultery and other forms of more private misconduct. Church discipline, then, both shaped and reinforced societal norms of behavior. Baptists intended not so much to cleanse society as to exercise the biblical command to "keep up a Godly Dicipline [sic] and to Deal faithfully and tenderly with those if any, who shall Depart from the faith which was once Delivered to the Saints, Either in principle or practice." Their foremost concern was with ecclesiastical, not social, control. Baptists considered the family and government responsible for the civil punishment of individuals engaged in explicitly antisocial acts. Baptist church discipline arose from an exclusivist vision of religious purity. This is why so many church members were excluded for violations of standards of belief in addition to disorderly conduct. If churches ignored false doctrine, a North Carolinian argued, it would be "as fatal to the cause of Christ . . . as if they become loose about morality and fail to exclude wicked men and wicked practices."[13]

While the problem of behavior and theological discipline occupied church conferences, doctrinal disputes over predestination, missionary work, and orthodox creeds also tore apart congregations. Baptists were "not the same people so far as doctrinal points are concerned," an Alabama Baptist association acknowledged in 1868. Members of churches affiliated with the Southern Baptist Convention (SBC) ousted members who professed opposition to missionary endeavors, while Primitive Baptist churches excluded those "joining another order calles themselvs misionary babtist," as did one church in Tennessee. The Second Baptist Church in Atlanta revoked the license of a preacher who claimed that "the impenitent dead were annihilated." Entire churches attempted to withdraw fellowship from other congregations that strayed from proper practices. One congregation in Murfreesboro, Tennessee, in 1888 engaged in a long discussion of whether to exclude from its fellowship another local church that was allegedly not "sound in doctrine," since it did not practice footwashing and "had a hired preacher." Eventually the church dismissed the charges and instead removed from its fellowship the accuser, rescinding his license to preach. A Virginia Primitive Baptist congregation urged sister churches that endorsed Sunday schools and missionary societies to recognize that these agencies subverted "the great purpose for which the Gospel was given, namely to bear glad tidings of salvation to such as are made above by the spirit." They beseeched brethren "entangled in this Arminian net, to prayerfully ponder and boldly retreat from such heresies." In July of 1890, a church in Tennessee voted that "as we believe the doctrine of the absolute Predestination of all things whatsoever comes to pass, causes confusion and divisions in the Baptist family," that members who espoused this "doctrine of fatality" should be expelled. Seventeen years later, a motion to rescind this resolution as being "to strong against Predestination" again aroused controversy. During the proceedings, the moderator (the pastor) made an "illegal objection" to the new motion by "getting up out of order and leaving the church without a moderator and Broke up servises in Disorder." This church never recovered from the spat over the exact workings of one of Christianity's most mysterious doctrines.[14]

Later in the century, as the disputes over predestination and similar controversies receded, new challenges to orthodoxy provoked disciplinary action. Congregations faced decisions, for example, over whether to retain or exclude members in good standing who professed belief in Christian Science or Holiness doctrines. Even more significantly, the spread of popular amusements, especially dancing, concerned guardians of morality. Opposition to dancing was, as one Texas minister put it, "a Baptist *land-mark*." The Penfield Baptist Church in Georgia in 1866, thinking it incumbent on churches to "define clearly their views on questions of disorder at all times, and especially after periods of great political convulsions (like the great war), which naturally tend to efface the lines of distinction between the church and the world," condemned "practices and amusements not sanctioned by the word of God." The newer styles of dancing, the Mississippi *Baptist Record* proclaimed, placed a "wrong emphasis upon the physical and animal nature, making woman a thing to be adorned and to be made physically alluring instead of exalting the mental, moral and spiritual virtues." Converts were assumed to reject sinful recreations, but church members were increasingly recalcitrant about being disciplined for behavior outside the church walls. Church trials for dancing rose significantly after the Civil War, but members were generally more reluctant to engage in serious disciplinary sanctions. A Baptist church member in Georgia in 1878 admitted that he had "attended dancing parties, and had dances," and "that he did not think it a Sin and was not sorry for dancing."[15]

The democratization of popular amusements in the twentieth century spelled trouble for traditional southern evangelical moralism. In one Mississippi community, a hotel that provided opportunities for recreational dancing attracted local Christians, who found nothing wrong with such diversions. When some members of a Baptist congregation tried to exclude the dancers, the church found itself split. The "errant" members simply professed their lack of concern for what they saw as anachronistic mores. When upper-class recreations were made readily available to the common people, it became clear that discipline would not function effectively in controlling mass culture. By the early twentieth century, Baptist theologians suggested to inquiring pastors that "those who might afterwards become useful Christians are cut off by a discipline that is too peremptory." They advised instead "a patient but persevering effort to reclaim the dancer[s] and lead them to a higher ideal of Christian life."[16]

Regarding the use of tobacco, leading ministers hoped that even the most uncultivated of church members judge when it was appropriate to chew tobacco and when not to indulge. Yet God's house was often "badly defiled with tobacco expectorations to the grief of people of refined habits," sighed one pastor. Preachers often chewed tobacco while preaching, aiming for a spittoon on the floor at convenient intervals. A number of churches responded to such indignities by disciplining people who persisted in tobacco use, while other churches provided spitting cups on the backs of pew benches.[17]

Churches also employed discipline as the primary enforcer of temperance in the nineteenth century. Southern evangelicals created "islands of holiness" in their congregations while distrusting state-enforced measures of prohibition. Many (though certainly not all) churches disciplined individuals for the public use of alcohol. Members of the Carrollton Baptist Church in Mississippi were "admonished against" drink and "kindly requested to withdraw their support from such a cause and give their influence to the maintenance of the cause of temperance and a pure Christianity." It was "inconsistent with the Christian profession" and "injurious to the harmony and usefulness of a church" for members to drink or rent houses "to those who traffic in whiskey." But the rules of temperance were observed as often in the breach. A Virginia Baptist remembered when "moderate social whiskey-drinking, and friendly, fraternal and pious *mellowing* of the heart . . . was esteemed an essential prerequisite to a proper exhibition of an appreciation of the 'good creatures of God,' and a needful preparation for the duties of the sanctuary." A longtime Baptist minister recalled how a preacher of the earlier era might take a "julep to prepare himself for the duties of the pulpit, or his toddy to brace up his wearied powers after the services were over."[18]

Despite repeated sermons denouncing the demon rum, church members persisted in imbibing—"even deacons, and good men, too—walk into the 'bar,' take their drink, come out and wipe their mouths, and stand and talk at the door as if there were not harm in such a course," exclaimed a North Carolina minister. It was "no strange thing," another Tar Heel cleric concluded, "to hear of drunkenness, profanity, brawls, uncleanness of life, dishonesty, and almost any other sin, in members of churches." Despite their repeated attempts at enforcing teetotalism, churches balked at disciplining prominent members who were otherwise upright but sold liquor at their stores or drank it quietly at home. A survey by a North Carolina association in 1875 discovered that about 70 percent of male Baptist church members drank occasionally, most at "tippling shops." An Alabama Baptist association in 1861 found that church members indulged in the "erroneous and dangerous habit of dram drinking, and others of vending spirituous liquors to be thus used." Even the pulpit, "God's divinely constituted agency for the suppression of vice," was not free "from its foul infection." Church members opposed restrictive measures on alcohol, "thereby encouraging the traffic of this vile stuff." In earlier days "almost the entire male population would indulge in the drink, preachers in some instances included," a South Carolina Baptist later recalled. Churches in North Carolina, an associational speaker acknowledged in 1877, differed on whether abstinence should be required of Christians, let alone on whether the state should enforce it. The Wake Forest Baptist Church postponed for years a resolution in favor of Prohibition, as the church could not come to consensus. The *Christian Index* of Georgia advised against excluding people who voted "wet" in local option elections, acknowledging the divisions among evangelicals on such matters. At one church in Georgia, an early-twentieth-century minister watched a prominent member who was also a liquor dealer storm out of a service and cut a hickory switch to beat the pastor. Another deacon in the church toted a gun along with communion bread and wine to services. Drunken men, the pastor remembered, sometimes lurched to the mourner's bench to be saved. He stumbled over the brandy bottles strewn about church members' homes. At a church in Louisiana, the pastor, a "poor but Godly man," was nicknamed the "old club" for his "fearless denunciation of sin, especially the matchless evil of drinking whiskey." He influenced the congregation to declare itself open only to teetotalers; "this caused the church to be divided, and many good brethren withdrew." Historically, southern Baptists generally aligned themselves with Democratic notions of limited government, resisting notions of social improvement (such as Prohibition) accomplished through the mechanism of the state. Thus, state-centered reform movements in the South struggled.[19]

The rhetoric of modernization and the drive to enforce bourgeois codes on evangelicals was remarkable given the nature of the southern Baptist constituency. In the early 1920s, a survey of over nineteen thousand SBC congregations revealed the extent to which rural people and churches dominated the region's largest religious group. About 80 percent of Baptist church members were farmers; 35 percent of these were tenants. The nomadic life and endemic poverty of southern rural life made rocky ground for planting a stable community and church life. Southern Baptist leaders, who understood only vaguely the larger forces leading to increased tenancy, condemned the profligacy of renters for their precarious economic status.[20]

As late as the 1920s, about 86 percent of churches connected to the SBC stood in areas defined as rural, that is, in or near places of less than one thousand people. If the varieties of Primitive and Free Will Baptist organizations were included in the tally, the percentage of rural congregations would be even higher, as they were concentrated in isolated up-country counties and in Appalachia. In Deep South states such as Mississippi and Alabama, over 90 percent of white Baptist churches stood in rural areas. Despite the efforts at church-building sponsored by the Home Mission Board of the SBC, rural churches were often either nonexistent or in need of repair. As one denominational official noted in 1912, although Baptists believed "most emphatically in the local church," they had "a greater number of homeless churches than any other denomination in America." One out of four rural congregations lacked any official worship house, while about one in five met in school houses or rented halls. Eighty-five percent of congregations with church houses met in one-room structures, often "in little cabin-like meeting houses with no carpets on the floor, no organ, no song books and not even a Bible on the desk." The slovenliness of the buildings—or, in many cases, the lack of any regular meeting house at all— was a painfully visible symbol of backwardness in church life. "We cannot with ramshackle sanctuaries command the respect of either ourselves, our children, or our neighbors," the *Biblical Recorder* pointed out in 1912. Three-quarters of currently existing rural white Baptist churches had been organized since the end of the Civil War, the survey concluded. Despite their recent vintage, they were hopelessly out of date in their "equipment, the leadership, and the methods of work." About one in three pastors lived in or near the same communities they served. Over one-quarter of the ministers lived from twenty to seventy-five miles away from their churches; 40 percent lived six to nineteen miles away, a considerable distance in a region with relatively few good roads.[21]

The Sunday school programs of these churches were either nonexistent or deficient. Some 23 percent of rural white Baptist churches in the early 1920s were without Sunday schools altogether, and another 22 percent held them only part of the year. Of those rural churches with Sunday schools, only about 40 percent of the membership enrolled, and only one-fourth of these enrollees "regularly attended." Three-quarters of rural congregations held no denominational rallies or institutes and received no state or regional denominational visitors during the year. "We face mountains of ignorance and prejudice, prejudice largely due to ignorance of the facts about our denominational machinery," a Baptist leader concluded. As late as 1916, fully half of constituent churches provided no support to SBC programs. "Many of our most substantial members live in the country and most need developing. What shall I do?" a North Carolina Baptist asked.[22]

The distance between the ideal of "efficient" churches and the reality of undertrained rural ministers leading lethargic flocks impressed the dozens of academic and denominational surveyors of rural religion in the early twentieth century. According to Charles Hamilton and William Garnett in their study *The Role of the Church in Rural Community Life in Virginia*, most ministers and rural churchgoers believed that the "church as an institution should not be concerned with rural social and economic problems; but rather the church member as an individual citizen should so live as to help solve such problems." The social service programs of Virginia's rural churches, they found, generally consisted of sending flowers to the sick and giving food to the poor on holidays, actions that reinforced rather than ameliorated social stratification. Rural pastors encouraged these sentiments by preaching that monetary success lay in the hands of an omnipotent God. The fragmentation of rural church life into "small, inefficient church groups" had "all but bankrupted the rural church," these surveyors concluded.[23]

Baptist officials shared Garnett and Hamilton's views about the backwardness of rural churches. Deeply influenced by models of the good citizen drawn from contemporary progressivism, denominationalists depicted poor southern whites as descended from virtuous and sturdy stock but degraded and indolent. The South's population was "twelve million strong but eighteen million weak," wrote John E. White, a prominent Atlanta minister and progressive southern Baptist. Twelve million soldiers for the army of the New South, he continued, were trailed by eighteen million "undrilled, undeveloped, uninstructed, raw recruits of civilization, who do not know the rules of the march and who easily riot among themselves." With poor whites, mountaineers, and a "thick and sluggish mass" of blacks, progressive southern citizens faced a huge trial, White suggested.[24]

Though churchmen boasted of Baptist democracy, the centralizing efforts of denominational leaders, accelerated greatly through corporate organizational methods, clashed with the pervasive localist ethic of rural congregations. These differing visions set the stage for the drama of folk South battling New South. In this struggle, defenders of traditionalism would not be without theological arms. The theology of antimissionism and Landmarkism served as the rallying cry for Baptist localism.

In the pluralistic environment of nineteenth-century denominationalism, Protestant sectarian leaders sought to distinguish their own organizations and theological tenets as uniquely valuable. Southern Baptist Landmarkism was one such movement. It was based on a few rigidly held tenets, all of which emphasized and exaggerated certain characteristic Baptist principles. Landmarkists insisted that the local church was absolutely sovereign, its collective will greater than any individual or any organization above it. Only those converted and baptized by ordained Baptist ministers could partake of the ordinances administered in Baptist churches, namely baptism and communion. Baptisms performed by ministers not ordained in a proper church were "alien immersions." Landmarkists also resisted cooperative endeavors with churches of other denominations. The true Christian church, they believed, had existed since apostolic days; current-day Baptist churches were its pure successors.

In Landmarkist thought, Methodism was the chief mischief-maker in American Protestantism. *The Great Iron-Wheel*, Landmarkism's best-known polemical work, castigated Methodism as a bankrupt old-world ecclesiology of centralism. The image of the "great iron wheel" was itself a parody of the Methodists' own description of their polity. James Robert Graves, its author, asserted that only Baptist churches maintained true Christian liberty, because only they upheld the sovereignty of the local church. Critics labeled Landmarkist ideas "ecclesiastical squatter sovereignty," but Landmarkers fired back at critics with weekly fusillades launched from their polemical base of operations, the *Tennessee Baptist and Reflector*, a paper ✳︎ Graves edited. By 1860, during his heyday, Graves's publication reached about thirteen thousand subscribers, making it the most widely circulated periodical in the Southwest. Many Baptists grew up in homes where, as a later seminary professor recalled, the Bible and the *Tennessee Baptist and Reflector* constituted the complete canon of works necessary for an understanding of Christianity. Landmarkism drew its strength from the support of local congregations concentrated in the Southwest—Texas, Arkansas, Tennessee, and Missouri. They were acutely aware of how the sides split—urban versus rural, Southeast versus Southwest, settled places versus frontier. Graves used a language full of the same images employed by nativists, nineteenth-century republicans, and Populists. "Little by little," warned one Landmarker, convention officials had made "their incroachments upon us from Eastern hotbeds of indifferentism, not to say liberalism."[25]

Those opposed to Landmarkism accused its leaders of being "designing ecclesiastical politicians" who arrayed the "country brethren against the town brethren." Virginia Baptist officials, leading opponents of the Landmarkists, castigated these supposed preservers of Baptist liberty as in fact the "most tyrannous in their attempts to fasten the yoke of doctrinal subjection upon the necks of their brethren." Despite these attacks from well-heeled Virginians, by the 1870s Graves could boast of the victory of his principles: "I do not believe," he wrote triumphantly, "that there is one association *in the whole South* that would today indorse an alien immersion as scriptural or valid, and it is a rare thing to see a Pedobaptist or Campbellite in our pulpits." Graves carried on unceasing warfare against the Baptist orthodoxy of the Southeast—the "VIRGINIA *principles* and *sympathies*" of denominational toleration. Attacks from Virginia against him, Graves argued, were in fact aimed "against the rising influence of the West in directing the counsels of the Convention; therefore men, and papers, and Boards, and Secretaries favorable to the West must be depreciated and put down and away." In North Carolina, correspondents to the state Baptist newspaper railed against the activities of Virginians who edited the *Religious Herald*, the state denominational newspaper and the leading voice opposing Landmarkism. Graves's influence spread even into the state where his ideas were most rejected by denominationalists. In 1866, the Leigh Street Baptist Church in Richmond, a prominent and respected congregation, adopted a resolution that "strictly required . . . all persons joining this church except from churches of the same faith and order to receive baptism at the hands of a regularly ordained Baptist minister."[26]

The Landmarkist opposition to "conventionism," their term for the growth and centralization of the SBC, was rooted in the antebellum frontier tradition of antimissionism and the theological heritage of primitivism, a broad nineteenth-century evangelical movement to recapture the "purity" of the apostolic church. In Alabama, a minister discovered, many Baptists saw denominational agencies as a " 'money machine,' for the support of a few favorites from which no good can result. They think it is composed of aristocrats, who would scarcely speak to a 'poor country Baptist.' " Descendants of Graves and of antimissionism in the late nineteenth and early twentieth centuries adapted the heritage of localism for a new era. J. A. Scarboro, an Arkansan and twentieth-century Landmarkist, wrote that conventionism had "fooled us a good while," as "it looked like a Baptist, but it talks and works like a Papist." The SBC, he charged, was "but Romanism in a Baptist cloak." The "Protestant bishops" of the major American denominations had involved "the whole Christian world in confusion, strife, division, and failure." These latter-day Landmarkists excoriated the missionary boards as centers of power through which elites presumed to command their subjects. A colleague of Scarboro's accused the boards of the SBC of making preachers "but the bill-stickers and collecting agents of a set of ecclesiastical masters who lord it over God's heritage." Edgar Young Mullins, president of the Southern Baptist Theological Seminary, bemoaned the long-lived effects of Landmarkism in a letter to a ministerial colleague in the early twentieth century:

> It is really difficult for other people to understand the exact nature of the problems which confront Southern Baptists. You may be familiar with the word "Landmarkism," but perhaps you do not know all that is implied in it. The center of gravity of the Southern Baptist Convention has in recent years shifted towards the Southwest, and the type of opinion described by the above word is very much in evidence in the present constituency of the Convention, especially when it meets within range of that territory.[27]

In the early twentieth century, the Landmarkers retreated from the SBC to their own southwestern fortresses. They formed regional organizations in Arkansas, Tennessee, Texas, and Missouri, and united in the General Association of Landmark Baptists in 1905. "Ours is an old-fashioned truth-loving people," a Landmarker proclaimed in 1917, "in the main clinging with death-like tenacity to the old-fashioned religion of the Fathers." Modern churches and conventions, in their view, were "hasty to adopt worldly plans, copied after war methods and commercial affairs." The "gospel mission" movement, which urged that missionaries be supported by local congregations rather than by centralized denominational boards, drew from the Landmarkist doctrine of the absolute sovereignty of the local church. Legal tussles in state denominations between modernizers and their critics (many of whom were associated with the Populist movement and, later, with Fundamentalism) also exemplified the tenacious hold of Graves's ideas.[28]

Landmarkism arose as one form of the resistance to the organizational ethic of denominational officials. Populism was another. Populism carried on the kind of crusade against the ethic of corporate centralization that paralleled the one carried on within religious denominations. Populism combined evangelical forms of communal bonding—camp meetings, singing, fervent oratory—with a socio-political program that challenged the rule of Democratic redeemers. The Bourbons of the Democratic Party discovered in Populism a dangerous political contender. Likewise, the Baptist Bourbons found such political radicalism to threaten their control of southern religion.[29]

Populists in the 1890s skillfully meshed the language of southern evangelical pietism and agrarian protest to capture God-fearing farmers living in difficult times. Religious Populists preached a form of rural social gospelism, tying their reform programs to the realization of the Kingdom of God on earth. "Very many preachers in this and other states are Alliance men, but not cranks," suggested one Baptist supporter of the farmer's movement. Acknowledging the criticism of preachers' involvement in politics, he countered that "instead of the Alliance leading a preacher away from his high calling of God it will lead him to it; he becomes more intimate with his flock, knows more of their needs, learns more of their cases, their joys and their sorrows." Sam Adams, a Populist activist in Alabama, advised Baptists that "those Christians who believe in freedom of the mind, soul, and body, will have to take hold of the politics of this country, or we will be enslaved by the rule of a class of men in this life who have no regard for the souls of men."[30]

Denominational leaders initially appeared sanguine about Populism, viewing it as a mild reform movement. The "infusion into politics of fresh blood from the most moral class of our people would be an unspeakable blessing," one leading minister suggested. Influential clerics such as the pastor of Atlanta's First Baptist Church joined Populists in condemning "class legislation, despotic monopolies, political rings, bribery and ballot box stuffing."[31] By the early 1890s, however, denominationalists grew alarmed over the way that the movement had co-opted the rhetoric of radical pietism. When Populist Baptists spent more time, in church and elsewhere, glorifying the Omaha Platform than evangelizing to the lost, ministers grew concerned over their "priorities." Southern Baptist laymen, predominantly farmers themselves, lambasted the overly conservative stance of church leadership. In response to an editorial that suggested that high interest rates were acceptable when business conditions warranted them, a North Carolina Baptist farmer retorted that the Bible condemned usury and that those who practiced it would lose their souls, even if they were doctors of divinity. He saw no way people could better themselves "unless those who lord it over them see their error and cease from their oppressions." In October of 1892, with strife running high over the fall elections, the *Biblical Recorder* in North Carolina reported talk of boycotts of professional men "and even of preachers, for their political views and preferences. . . . There is division in the pew." A conservative Alabama minister despaired that "politics and money-making [are] getting to be absorbing topics among the preachers—it is so common, indeed, that one seldom hears them discuss anything else." As a result, he thought, "the people have lost faith in us and the gospel we preach." Disputes over the stock law (involving requirements to fence in open range), a minister later remembered, dominated church meetings and split congregations. Populists attacked Baptist leaders who were prominent politicians and landholders. In Georgia, Tom Watson wrote acidly of Joseph Brown, a wealthy Baptist, former scalawag, and sometime governor of the state: "Joe Brown is a millionaire. Of course. He is a convict lessee. Of course. He is a rigidly correct member of the church. Of course."[32]

Denominational leaders felt the sting of the infighting. Divisions over Populism, an SBC official wrote in 1890, had "caused more division and strife among neighbors, and more injury to churches and the cause of Christ, than was ever before known." Preachers should tend to spreading the message of Christ rather than the gospel of the Farmer's Alliance, he insisted. They lambasted preachers who were "being drawn into the political whirlpool" and "taking decidedly more interest in politics, and have been, for a number of years, than they manifest in the cause of Christ. . . . By long continued practice [they] have become champions on the hustings of considerable notoriety." A Georgian described how Baptists in his town had "turned statesman and must attend all the barbecues and public speakings to applaud or disapprove, or fortify, or advise the candidate. . . . Men labor six or seven months in the year instead of twelve, and blame God and the government that they are behind." He advised those unsettled over political contests to "settle down somewhere; maintain a school, build up a church, be still long enough for the preacher to teach you something, to mould and be moulded." Ministers condemned the mixing of religion and politics and reminded their constituents that no matter what threat Populism might pose, "the white people of the South mean to rule, and they will rule."[33]

Southern evangelical individualism eventually won out over the Populist critique of corporate evil. Populists themselves often failed to overcome their distrust of collective solutions, not to mention their racism. Yet the extent to which Populist politics affected religious meetings in the 1890s showed how rural evangelical piety, transplanted into Populist camp meeting fervor, could threaten the conservative social order of the region. Here was a political reason for Baptist officials to wage the battle for a regulated spirituality. Enthusiastic religious expressions could carry with them implications of social disorder.

Holiness doctrines in the 1890s represented in the spiritual realm the same challenge that Populism raised in the world of politics—the use of southern evangelical forms for culturally or politically radical ends. Holiness was an apolitical response to many of the same social symptoms that Populists addressed at the political level. Holiness doctrines, drawn both from a Methodist heritage and from the more conservative Reformed tradition, taught that one could achieve the higher life through a "second baptism" of the Holy Spirit (the "first baptism" being that of conversion). The more moderate advocates of the doctrine interpreted "sanctification" as a gradual process of nurturing more pure Christian believers, while those who split from mainstream denominations to form Holiness churches argued that sanctification was an immediate life-changing event in which God's spirit permanently indwelt the believer. Twentieth-century Pentecostals, heirs to the more radical Holiness sects, insisted that this second baptism would be evidenced through the gift of speaking in tongues. Some Pentecostals even discovered a "third blessing" following conversion and baptism in the spirit, one in which tongues speech signified the believer's ascension to the highest rung of Christian perfectionism. Holiness doctrines soon sprouted offshoots into a variety of Pentecostal sects, especially after the famous Azusa Street revivals in Los Angeles in 1906. Holiness and Pentecostal congregations virtually recreated the ambience of the camp meetings of the early nineteenth century, complete with shouting, speaking in tongues, and physical convulsions.[34]

Holiness and Pentecostal churches were apolitical. They focused on the internal experience of the believer and the communal expression of spiritual emotion. They could be culturally radical, especially where they encouraged interracial worship and female preaching. But they also inured poor and marginalized people to the idea that the otherworld would right the injustices of this world. Abolitionism grew out of the Second Great Awakening, with its visions of postmillennial optimism, while political quietism accompanied a Holiness movement that increasingly took on pessimistic premillennial visions of the endtimes.

Holiness doctrines found their way into Baptist churches despite the vigorous efforts of leading ministers to anathematize the teachings. Ethel Hilliard, a mill worker in North Carolina, understood little of the specific Holiness doctrines but knew that "they was good people. I always thought they was. I enjoyed helping them out. And when they washed feet, I washed with them." With respectable Baptists taught to celebrate their complete "sanctification" with emotional release, the battle for respectable worship was far from won, denominational leaders realized. Theologically, the perfectionism of the Holiness sect ran against the grain of conservative evangelicalism. A potent sense of personal sin and the relatively narrowly drawn boundaries encompassing the elect still defined orthodox southern Baptist thought. One North Carolina Baptist was "a little puzzled," he reported in 1896, when he witnessed how the "holiness craze" had "taken such root" in his home state. "It is a fearful disease among Christians," he warned. A North Carolina Baptist reporter scornfully noted the widespread presence in state associations of the " 'wholly sanctified' brother with his Bible, well-marked, carrying it around under his arm, ready for a discussion with anybody who is thoughtless enough to go into it with him." Such straying sheep should be taken out "from under the influence of a set of ecclesiastical tramps who get their living by imposing on the credulity of simple-minded, but, on the whole, good people." Local controversies over Holiness beliefs plagued churches. In Thomaston, Georgia, for example, a young pastor invited in a revivalist who preached Holiness doctrines. The congregation nearly split over whether to declare itself a "Holiness, Oilpouring and man healing church." The pastor himself publicly expressed a belief in faith healing. The deacons finally forced him out in a stormy meeting in which he accused them of being possessed.[35]

Holiness churches claimed numerous adherents among working-class southerners, both white and black, who increasingly found the established Baptist and Methodist churches theologically and socially inhospitable. A few prominent ministers, including one who was trained at the University of Chicago and was pastor of a large Baptist church in Ft. Worth, left their southern denominations and became leaders in the Church of the Nazarene, the Assemblies of God, the Church of God, and other Holiness-Pentecostal groups. This development made it all the more imperative for church leaders to denounce the Higher Life doctrines, the intellectual base of Holiness practices. One denominational official condemned the "half-fledged minister" who evangelized for Holiness doctrines. "That is precisely what the exhorter—the men of old time unable to preach the Gospel did," he explained. The Holiness minister failed to understand that "Christianity is a deeper thing than sentimental mysticism; that it requires of its ministers somewhat more than readiness in exhortation to lead their flocks into a higher life." Sanctification, wrote one guardian of orthodoxy, was not an experience or state of sinless perfection but rather a matter of "Christian culture," of the "development of Christian character." Baptist and Methodist leaders wrote off Holiness enthusiastic practices as "eccentric religious phenomena."[36]

The religious passions invoked by Holiness doctrines and Pentecostal practices were also uncomfortably close to those traditionally experienced at revivals. Since the camp meeting days of the early nineteenth century, evangelical leaders across the denominational spectrum sought to regularize revivals. Methodists set up camp meeting grounds with strict rules and regulations, seeking to bring order to the tumultuous scenes that accompanied Cane Ridge and other holy festivals in the early Republic. Many of the denominational reformers led countless "protracted meetings" themselves and later recounted with self-satisfaction their heroic soul-winning exploits on the revival circuit. But church leaders grew increasingly uncomfortable with such meetings as the nineteenth century progressed. Revivalists, they argued, substituted evanescent passion for the serious commitment required of the true Christian. One meeting in South Carolina in 1867 was notable for how it was not like most revivals, as it had no "shouting, nor clapping of hands, nor any of the theatrical exhibitions sometimes indulged in by shallow-brained enthusiasts,. . . nothing but the plain, Scriptural means of awakening." Those drawn into churches from revivals, critics noted, were "rarely objects of further concern and were strangers to all training in church duty or benevolence." During services shouting women interrupted the preacher just when he was "in the most solemn and impressive part of his sermon." The presence of overly enthusiastic congregants pointed to the larger problem. "Together with a worthy desire for the salvation of souls," scolded a Virginia Baptist spokesman in 1870, churchgoers who craved revivals "mingled a hungering and thirsting not so much after righteousness as after religious excitement." The "great want in the churches" was "training"; the "vast amount of moral power latent" in the churches needed to be "liberated, brought out, set to work." Revivals were not the means to this end because they awoke "animal excitements" that disgraced the churches in the public eye.[37] Despite such objections, however, revivals retained their central role in southern evangelical culture. Increasingly routinized and professionalized, they produced an annual harvest of souls and replenished church membership rolls. "Say what we will,"

EVAN GEL ISTS

an SBC committee acknowledged in 1905, "our people believe in and they will continue to demand these protracted meetings, special efforts, revival services, or whatever we may be pleased to call them, and wise are we if we study the sanest and safest methods of conducting these services."[38]

The spectacular rise of professional evangelism in the late nineteenth century discomfited the same evangelicals who distrusted the passion of revival seasons. The converts won at meetings such as those Dwight Moody led in northern cities left the impression that it was the special province of the professional evangelist to harvest souls, while the normal preacher's task was to attend to the more quotidian affairs. "We have rarely known a professional evangelist who has not fallen into reproach from a real or supposed thirst for gain," the *Religious Herald* commented in 1875. While the office of the evangelist was a biblical one, a Virginia Baptist argued, evangelists aroused widespread distrust because "any sapless and half-cracked preacher who chooses may label himself an evangelist and go bumming up and down the walks of Zion."[39]

But even if some evangelists were "more noisy than efficient," some swept "through a church or Sunday school like a bosom of destruction, leaving enough problems on a pastor's hands to last him for years," and some became "vain and belligerent and bumptious," the practice of evangelism was still essential. Just as the ministry was partly professionalized, so was the office of the evangelist. Many churches accepted only those officially commissioned by some associational or convention body to be traveling evangelists. The success of Dwight Moody and Ira Sankey's revivals, where the message was wholly amenable to conservative southern evangelical views, contributed to the acceptance of traveling evangelists. Even the somewhat haughty editors of the *Religious Herald* in Virginia admitted that Moody must have the sanction of God, for what else could explain his success? His "style betrays a want of high education; his vocabulary is meagre; he never rises to vehemence, [and] knows little of logic." But he claimed tens of thousands of converts. If God had not meant professional evangelists to exist, He would not have invented Moody, the editor concluded.[40]

Despite the reigning doctrine of moderate Calvinism, many southern Baptist churches were becoming increasingly Methodist in practical, popular theology by the late nineteenth century. The ken of people to whom God had extended the promise of salvation grew wider, the means of claiming that salvation easier. The personal manner one was supposed to exhibit in public professions of faith was not the ecstatic shouting of the stereotypical convert but rather a low-key friendliness and earnestness, much like the relatively businesslike displays at Moody's larger urban services. Despite warnings about "dead formalism," most southern evangelicals endorsed the standardized salvation experience to be a proper safeguard against excessive passions.[41]

In addition to the close scrutiny of revivals, another central part of the campaign to regulate spirituality lay in the reform of singing. Baptist associations recognized that church members were "greatly deficient in musical training" and advised their pastors to "organize classes in music and make it a part of their educational efforts in training the disciples of the Lord in church work." Denominational reformers emphasized the importance of "good" hymns. Seminaries started music training programs and encouraged the use of professional music ministers in churches wealthy enough to afford them. Pastors promoted revivals with music leaders who could bring crowds to a proper sense of the sacrality of these occasions. Denominationalists ridiculed the slow, seemingly discordant style of singing characteristic of country congregations as well as the more upbeat modern gospel hymns. As a Mississippi minister wrote of the music he heard during his rounds of churches in the 1880s, "the singing is often unworthy of an assembly engaged in the worship of God, and tends to diminish rather than to increase the devotional spirit." Few children learned and most adults could not read music. Southern Christians fortunate enough to attend singing conventions learned a shape-note form, in which individual notes were "shaped" distinctively to indicate their place on the "fa, so, la" scale (hence the use of the term "fasola singing" as a synonym for the shape-note format.) Schools that taught shape-note singing brought an accessible form of musical education to southern believers. But in urban churches, standard hymnbooks with just words, or with lyrics and standard four-part notations, gradually replaced the older shape-note books and primitive psalmodies. Rural song styles came to be thought of as backward. Those who raised the tunes in most congregations, a South Carolina Baptist wrote of older a capella musical styles, often had "no idea either of harmony or of time." The result, in his view, was "an inharmonious jingling of nasal sounds—all is discord from beginning to end . . . and a positive feeling of relief is experienced when the singing is ended." His description was "no caricature," he assured his readers, but "a truth familiar to many."[42]

Proper hymn selection, good singing, and a limited but effective use of choirs would ensure doctrinal orthodoxy and congregational comity, denominationalists believed. "The Church that sings error, or caters to 'rag time' music is as far from right as the one that deals in mere sensational reading and preaching," the Mississippi Baptist State Convention advised its churches in 1905. Churches should select hymnals "in line with the soundest interpretation of the Scriptures" and use choirs to add to the sacred tone of meetings. A seminary professor taught his students that

SANKEY

hymns and choirs should remain "*subsidiary*" in worship, with the hymn selection controlled "by the more spiritual and at the same time the more intelligent of the church, with careful consideration of what is good for all classes."[43]

The enthusiasm with which congregants adopted the Moody–Sankey genre of gospel hymns showed how urban practices could penetrate country churches. The spread of "these pious jigs" dismayed denominational modernizers, who held to the eighteenth-century classics as the standard. "When I go to some city churches and hear music that has the jim jams," wrote a Texas Baptist denominationalist, "there is nothing to do but to crawl into my shell and wait till the rain of discordant notes ceases to fall."[44] Caretakers of southern evangelicalism issued quasi-official statements warning of the theological traps hidden in the gospel tunes. For southern Baptist critics of revivals, the easy emotion aroused by the music associated with Moody's meetings symbolized the shallowness of the services. "It requires no expert in hymnology and Bible doctrine to notice that the doctrine of many hymns that are now quite popular is not at all sound, from a Baptist standpoint," warned one North Carolinian. An Alabama minister recognized and cautioned against the lure of the new music: "The glow of sentiment in these hymns is inspiring. The lively or pathetic music with which they are associated, has given them popularity. . . . Yet, in many instances, there is no substance in the productions, and in many they encourage a diversion of thought and feeling from the practical duties of Christian life."[45]

In response to their dissatisfaction with both old-time singing practices and the newer gospel songs, southern Baptists produced hymn books for their own churches. Their work drew inspiration from the life of the father of southern hymnals, William Walker, known as "Singing Billy." As compiler of the widely known *Southern Harmony*, first published in 1835, Walker changed the singing culture of the South. In 1859, Walker introduced musical instruments at his home Baptist church in Spartanburg, South Carolina, and paved the way for the spread of modernized instruments in churches throughout the region. *Southern Harmony* was probably the most popular hymn book in the South before the Civil War, surpassing even *The Sacred Harp*, a shape-note publication that taught the fundamentals of singing to many southern church people. By sponsoring singing schools and introducing musical instruments into churches, Walker and his followers helped a generation of southern believers learn the rudiments of four-part singing. Walker's hymnal mixed tunes from diverse traditions and notated them in a way comprehensible to those with little musical training.[46]

Extending from Walker's work, SBC officials produced a variety of hymn anthologies. Basil Manly Jr. and his father made their first effort in 1851 with a collection entitled *Baptist Psalmody*, which was distributed through the Southern Baptist Publication Society in Charleston. Later, Basil Jr. edited *The Choice*, an anthology designed to bring SBC congregations back to emphasizing older standards. The "rage for novelties in singing," he wrote, was "driving out of use the old precious, standard hymns." Manly directed *The Choice* against the growing influence of gospel hymns, including southern compilations such as *Sacred Bell*, by the noted hymnist W. E. Penn from Tennessee. Manly much preferred the stately cadences of "How Firm a Foundation," an Isaac Watts classic, to newer gospel tunes with a bouncy beat such as "Love Lifted Me." The lyrics also indicated a shift in conceptions of God and salvation in hymnody, from the "firm foundation" of eighteenth-century theologizing to the domesticated imagery of the good, rescuing father of nineteenth-century gospel songs:

("How Firm a Foundation")
How firm a foundation, ye saints of the Lord
Is Laid for your faith in His excellent Word.
What more can he say, than to you He hath said?
To you who for refuge to Jesus hath fled?
("Love Lifted Me")
I was sinking deep in sin, far from the peaceful shore
Sinking, sinking deep within, sinking to rise no more
Then the master of the sea, heard my despairing cry.
From the waters lifted me, now safe am I!
Love lifted me, love lifted me,
When nothing else could help, love lifted me!

Baptist officials in the twentieth century assumed Manly's role as the promoter of orthodox hymnology. Lansing Burrows, for decades a prominent figure in SBC work, introduced in 1904 a compilation designed as a "book of praise to Almighty God" rather than one simply "to gather in convenient form a number of pleasing songs."[47]

Despite the standards of taste set by denominationalists, southern Baptist congregations and pastors demanded gospel hymn books, and hymnologists gradually responded to this market opportunity. Robert Coleman, business manager for a Texas Baptist denominational newspaper, greatly influenced regional hymnology in the 1910s and 1920s, especially by his appointment of B. B. McKinney as a musical editor. While head of the music department at Southwestern Baptist Theological Seminary, McKinney distributed gospel hymns to churches throughout the South with the imprimatur of the denomination behind them. Hymns intended for use in Sunday schools and revivals came to dominance in regular church services. Older standards were relegated to formal services needing more stately music. McKinney made a number of his own contributions to the gospel hymn repertoire, including "Wherever He Leads I'll Go," which became popular for its soothing music and heart-tugging lyrics:

> Take up thy cross and follow Me
> I heard my Master say.
> He gave his life to ransom me.
> Surrender your all today.
> (Refrain) Wherever He leads, I'll go.
> Wherever He leads, I'll go.
> I'll follow my Christ, who loves me so.
> Wherever He leads I'll go.

Southern Baptist congregants made clear their attraction to the hymnody of sentimental Victorianism, a compelling force in popular religious culture that inevitably overpowered the efforts of the guardians of orthodoxy. By 1913, a prominent seminary professor advised ministers to adapt to the kind of hymns congregants wanted: "One of the severest tests of the devotion and adaptability of the cultured minister is his ability and willingness to lay aside the fringes and adornments of culture and so come at the heart of realities as to hold and help the plain man in his worship. . . . Popular gospel hymns, sung with verve and vigour, may not satisfy the artistic taste of the cultured, but they serve the purpose of worship for the common man far better than more elevated efforts."[48]

Ministers who insisted on rooting out the musical practices customary among plain-folk congregants found the task difficult. Many churches could ill afford hymn books and were slow to give up the practice of lining out hymns—the custom common in American Protestant circles since the days of the Puritans of using song leaders to call out the lines of hymns, one at a time, to teach the words and tunes to churchgoers. In many backwoods churches, controversies over musical instruments, particularly over the installation of organs, were common, with many southern Christians opposed to any form of musical accompaniment to congregational singing. "I verily believe God will not suffer this *Beast* to rule in Baptist churches," a South Carolinian exclaimed of the organ. Yet he found it "little use to speak and argue against it" as churches which had purchased the instrument wanted to keep it.[49]

But as early as the mid-nineteenth century, Baptist congregations were moving away from hymns lined out by individuals without musical accompaniment to unanimous congregational singing with a piano or organ for background. Soloists and other special performances made their way into the musical lineup of urban worship services. Questions on the theology of performance troubled believers who were musically gifted but who considered "mere display" sinful. "Harmony is voluptuous," a Virginia Baptist wrote in his diary. "It requires no pious emotions for a man to love harmony. In fact, by singing base and suffering my mind to be distracted from the words, by the 'lascivious pleasing' of chords, I am often unfitted for the other exercises of the Sanctuary." Yet he knew parishioners were pleased with his voice. Southern Baptists such as this Virginian gradually accepted stylistically refined music as spiritual.[50]

Choirs were becoming a more frequent (and costly) part of urban churches in the late nineteenth century. A number of congregations followed the practice of the Leigh Street Baptist Church in Richmond, which hired a professional choir and periodically, if grudgingly, resolved to raise its pay. The First Baptist Church of Nashville spent one-sixth of its church budget in the 1890s to support its elaborate music program. The previous effort of the church to give up paid singers had ended in failure, as the short-lived all-volunteer choir could not sustain a suitable musical program. Other major congregations, such as Citadel Square Baptist Church in Charleston, struggled to maintain organs and choirs. Of the $300 budgeted for its music program, organ upkeep alone consumed $100 a year, leaving the rest to employ an organist and pay a choir. After unsuccessfully attempting to form a volunteer choir in 1897, the church raised a choral group by subscription of funds outside of normal church contributions. Such examples showed a growing professionalism in southern church musical practices.[51]

Some denominationalists worried that the development of formal choir singing was part of a "modern tendency" to make "a mere display of musical talent, or a bid for the encomiums of those who study taste and aesthetics, more than they do religion." They suggested that watching choirs perform rather than joining in heartily in congregational singing could diminish sacred emotion. Choirs should "discard the more artistic and operatic music, and select the simple and devotional, ever keeping it in mind, that they are not to sing to secure pewholders, nor to develop artistic excellence," advised B. H. Carroll, a Texas Baptist stalwart. North Carolina Baptists approved of choirs for educational value but worried that "our almost rigid informality threatens to become austere formality. . . . We pursue the same order of service week after week as faithfully as those who have a prayer-book to go by." They contrasted this formalism with a "full-voiced congregation rolling some old-time hymn forth to earth and heaven," one that could produce a "contagion of emotion which takes one all and all and moves his heart to swell." This combination of simple but proper musical technique and communal emotion represented the ideal for Baptist music.[52]

Even with the gradual decline of shape-note singing, the influence of professional music ministers, the trend toward paid choirs, and the spread of hymn books with standard notation and classic hymns, southern oral dialect still offended trained ears. Styles remained diverse, as much influenced by time-honored customs as by standard forms. A new generation of twentieth-century gospel tunes, epitomized in the 1930s classic "I'll Fly Away," ensured that southern evangelical singing retained a special quality treasured by its participants but that it would be ridiculed by denominational officials and national cultural elites. Furthermore, the use of radio in spreading white gospel music again placed the control of music outside the purview of denominationalists.

The program of denominational modernizers ultimately depended on raising money. Baptists searched for effective but spiritually acceptable methods of fund-raising. Since numerous congregations distrusted organized fund-raising and preferred instead the silent and unsolicited contribution, pastors often wrangled with congregations over the nonpayment of clerical salaries. Providing a steady flow of funds for the collective endeavors of the SBC proved even more difficult.

Methods of individual church financing were as diverse as were the size, location, and incomes of the congregations. Denominational modernizers despaired of cultivating a truly effective regionwide system. "General and systematic giving" among churches in the denomination was "unknown and unattempted," Alabama Baptists acknowledged in 1893. Despite the constant pleas for "systematic beneficence," collections for Baptist endeavors remained anything but systematic for decades. "The financial methods of the churches belong to ages past, and no one seems to be making any serious effort to improve conditions," a convention spokesman complained in 1912.[53]

Unlike churches in other denominations, relatively few Baptist churches collected pew rents. Many congregations owned no pews on which to collect rent: 20 percent of Baptist churches in 1923 lacked a permanent meeting house of any kind, while a large number of others rented spaces. The farmers who filled most southern Baptist pews often made in-kind contributions to the church—feeding the pastor on a Sunday, contributing labor to building the church house, or providing hay for a minister's horse. But basing financing purely on voluntarism nearly bankrupted many congregations. Urban churches with full-time ministers sometimes collected pew rents, the best way to keep up with expenses. But pew rents raised the specter of class distinctions. Many churches that had used "pew-holders societies" abol-

MONEY

ished them after the Civil War. In Columbia, South Carolina, a major Baptist congregation appointed a treasurer to assign pew rents, with the admonition to be "careful not to assess to pew-holders more than they can bear." This church was relatively successful—its pastor's salary rose from $700 a year to $1,500 a year (paid quarterly) between 1870 and 1874. Few other congregations managed to do as well.[54]

Many churches stimulated fund-raising through an envelope system. Treasurers assigned quotas to each church member, and contributors would fill and sign their names to the envelopes placed in pews. Congregants who failed to meet their financial obligation were subject to church discipline and even expulsion. The Wake Forest Baptist Church in North Carolina adopted this method as early as 1875. Every member "who shares in the inestimable advantages of the church" was under as much obligation "as to pay for any other comforts or blessings of life," the congregation resolved. Members assessed their financial situations themselves, contributed weekly in envelopes provided by the church, and were subject to the inquiring visits of deacons. By 1885 this plan allowed for a budget of nearly $1,400. Nearly 60 percent went to the pastor's salary and contributions to ministerial education, with the remainder split between church expenses (about 5 percent), state and foreign missions (nearly 20 percent), and contributions to various Baptist orphanages (10 percent). By the mid-1880s the congregation allowed for specially designated offerings for denominational causes at a time when few churches allowed special fund-raising for objects outside specific congregational needs. Most other Baptist churches were reluctant to allow preassigned offerings. In most places the pastoral salary remained an obligation that churches struggled to meet each month, quarter, or year.[55]

Until well into the twentieth century, itinerant agents took up collections for endeavors outside of the local church: educational enterprises, foreign missions programs, orphanages, special denominational programs, and the like. SBC institutions relied on peripatetic fund-raisers to collect money and teach congregations to contribute without requiring the presence of a designated pleader. The agent's success was ultimately measured by the extent to which he could achieve these difficult tasks.[56] For example, if the agent's visit coincided with a national depression or local crop failure, even the most emotionally moving of presentations would come to naught. Despite his heartfelt efforts, an itinerant fund-raiser in Greensboro, North Carolina, in 1884 collected only $3 "owing to the great scarcity of money at the time." Agents desperate to raise cash could fall into embarrassing displays. "The public beggar, knowing what is expected of him," wrote one church member in 1893, "often apes the very airs of the clown in the circus," extending yet another "opportunity to harp on the old string that told of the *ignorance* of Baptists." In addition, the seemingly endless procession of agents wearied congregants of the special pleas for individual programs. And because agents were commissioned, they were tempted to skim more off the top than was their due. Yet few ideas for an alternative to the agent system proved effective until the 1920s. Congregations again resisted the visions of standardization that obsessed denominational modernizers. As one church member wrote in 1914, ideas for systematizing church finance came from men who did not understand "the spirit and genius of Southern Baptist churches. The New England policy is to have a line of cleavage as clear and cold as ice between the spiritual functions and the administrative and finance."[57]

Women organized in missionary societies encouraged systematic rather than spasmodic giving. The Woman's Missionary Union (WMU) in 1889 produced its first "Lesson in Stewardship," and in 1890 advised that "no unchristian or questionable methods be employed" for fund-raising. A steady cash flow, they asserted, could be achieved through women's self-denial and the cultivation of "so many rows of potatoes, etc., such a proportion of eggs, butter, land," and town women could save their pennies by denying themselves entertainments. "We earnestly deprecate the employment of any method that would put the cause of Christ before the world as a beggar, . . . or by catering to the lower elements of human nature," wrote one WMU leader.[58] Many of the most effective ideas of the SBC for systematic fund-raising, such as the tithing envelope, originated in local women's missionary societies. By 1910 women had contributed nearly a quarter of a million dollars for missions and tens of thousands of dollars more through in-kind donations. The head of the WMU, Annie Armstrong, sent literature to 5,625 churches describing the "New Century" fund-raising campaign and instructing local members on how to form missionary societies. The result was 616 new societies and a growth in WMU contributions of nearly 30 percent. Armstrong also devised the idea of a Church Building Loan ⏐) Fund. SBC agencies worked in a kind of symbiosis with the female missionary societies.[59]

Denominations as institutions required constant efforts at propaganda, exhortation, and fund-raising for their continued expansion. The language of business enterprise increasingly shaped denominational organizing. Beginning after World War I and extending through the 1920s, denominational modernizers pushed their ideas of the systematization of southern Baptist church life. In the wake of the Great War, southern Baptists engaged in major organizational drives patterned after the voluntarism of the American war effort itself.[60]

In 1919 the SBC centralized its fund-raising efforts under a new initiative dubbed the "Seventy-Five Million Campaign." It paralleled the Interchurch World Movement, a massive campaign from 1919 to 1922 that enlisted mainstream Protestants in raising hundreds of millions of dollars for home and foreign missions. As first drawn up in spring of 1919, architects of the Seventy-Five Million Campaign set an overall goal of $75 million worth of pledges, to be paid out over a period of five years. Agencies and crusades once competing for the same Baptist dollars would now peaceably draw from the same well of funds. The crusade was not only to raise money but to nurture "many of our churches, through adequate preaching services and pastoral work, whose members are second to none in their sound Americanism and evangelical faith, but who have not been adequately taught in the life of faith."[61]

In only one year SBC churches pledged $92 million and contributed $12 million. As the postwar economic recession took hold in 1921–22, however, actual receipts for the campaign plummeted. The Woman's Missionary Union contributed all of its quota, but total receipts equaled less than $60 million. The postwar Protestant crusades, a Baptist seminary professor wrote, came during a "high plane of idealism," when "the spirit of sacrifice was everywhere." But these moral enthusiasms quickly evaporated. "Our moral life has declined, as seen in our crime record and our salacious literature," he concluded. The collapse of the Interchurch World Movement was small comfort to SBC officials who had already spent dollars pledged but never received, leading to a major financial embarrassment in the mid-1920s. Denominational leaders constantly praised Baptist democracy, but their dreams of the international expansion of evangelicalism were frustrated in yet another way by the localist ethic of southern congregationalism.[62]

Brooks Hays, a congressman who supported civil rights measures in the 1950s, recalled what Baptist democracy meant to him in his younger years:

> In Western Arkansas at the turn of the century, the typical congregation covered the whole spectrum of community life. . . . My first Sunday School teacher was a blacksmith. Later I was instructed by a coal miner, whose gnarled hands symbolized for me the hardships of the period's life. There sat on the same pew with my parents the woman who did my mother's washing. . . . Her vote in church conference had the same weight as my mother's and father's, and her presence on that third pew with them remains for me an authentic symbol of Baptist democracy.[63]

Hays found it unnecessary to mention that the participants in this democracy were all white.

No doubt many Baptist ministers of refined habits dreamed of donning the robes of an Episcopal cleric and directing a service in which none of the congregants shouted at inappropriate moments, used the floor as a spittoon, belted out undignified hymns, or closed their pocketbooks to pleas for denominational programs. Yet this was the price of Baptist democracy. For the black Baptist folk, the defense of distinctive spiritual expressions took on an even greater importance.

CHAPTER FOUR

God Stepped in My Soul

Spirituality and Respectability among Black Southern Baptists

I stays independent of what white *
folks thinks when I shouts.
—Cordelia Anderson Jackson
quoted in *South Carolina
Narratives*

"With freedom, the negro, *en masse*, relapsed promptly into the voodooism of Africa," wrote Myrta Avary, an unsympathetic commentator on life in Virginia during Reconstruction; "emotional extravaganzas . . . were indulged without restraint." Intent on ridiculing the religious life of the freedpeople, Avary, in fact, observed the reason for its strength: "It was as if a force long repressed burst forth."[1]

In 1886, attending a meeting in New Orleans, missionaries of the American Baptist Home Mission Society delighted in the "progress" they perceived in African American churches. When some women were overcome with shouting at the service, the presiding elder threatened them with expulsion. But the missionaries found the sermon exasperating. The black minister preached on Baptist doctrine but added heterodox interpretations of biblical events that met with the vocal approval of his audience. At the Pentecost, he thundered, the Disciples were not drunk but were shouting. "Some folks preaches style and says 'keep still, stop that shoutin,' but I doesn't preach style. Who dares to say to a soul filled with the spirit, 'stop shoutin!'"[2]

Urban Baptist reformers were modestly successful in spreading norms of bourgeois spirituality. But black folk used the democracy of Baptist congregationalism as a means to preserve and reinvigorate folk worship rituals. Elias Camp Morris, president of the National Baptist Convention from 1895 to 1920, insisted that respectable worship practices would better reflect on the rising race. "We make no effort to eliminate the worship

107

from our worship or our service," he said, "but we think the right to regulate it, so that it may be more profitable than injurious, should be reserved by the leaders and disseminators of thought who are laboring faithfully to advance the Christian system."[3] Yet the missionaries of bourgeois spirituality worked in a region where Afro-Baptist spirituality lived on strongly, and where the polity of congregationalism was reinforced by the reality of small church units with bivocational ministers who preached from an oral tradition. Black worshipers incorporated certain of the reformers' ideas— new hymns, more regularity in service times and manner, standard sermonizing. But pastors and church members alike, wrote a northern Baptist missionary in the 1880s, were "as tenacious of their rights and prerogatives as the most intelligent churches in the land." The freedpeople eloquently evoked the significance of Afro-Baptist expressive culture. Said a former slave, "I feel good in the church. Ain't feared of nothin' to tell nobody." Even more pointedly, the former slave Cordelia Jackson told her interviewer, "I stays independent of what white folks tells me when I shouts. De Spirit moves me every day, dat's how I stays in. White folks don't feel sech as I does; so day stays out. . . . Dey tries me and den I suddenly draps back to serving de Holy God."[4]

The evolution of southern black worship practices suggests one of the central themes of this work. Southern white and black worshipers borrowed freely (if sometimes unwittingly) from each other. They withstood the same attempts at rooting out their expressive spirituality while adopting certain forms suggested by the advocates of respectable religion, leading to services that smacked both of their rural southern past and of the modernizing present. Whites taught blacks the Christian story. African Americans showed Euro-Americans compelling physical expressions of experiencing the sacred. But what they learned from each other was expressed in separate congregations. And their mutual cultural influence hardly mitigated the racial violence and hostility of the so-called southern way of life.

Baptists in eighteenth-century Virginia seemed to elites of the Old Commonwealth to encourage a dangerous mingling of racial bodies in ecstatic worship. Critics of the great camp meetings of the early nineteenth century highlighted the jerking, howling, and barking of new converts. Church leaders, the beneficiaries of the raft of new souls wading to their shores by way of camp meetings, were uneasy about the communal passion unleashed by these epochal events. But in the covert religious rituals of the slave community, where African traditions mingled so deeply with camp meeting styles that the "roots" of black worship remain too entangled to be definitely sorted out,

Afro-Baptist expressions girded generations of believers through the tortures of enslavement. This faith mixed the spiritual and the secular in ways more akin to African spirituality and premodern European folk culture, than to the Victorian religious sensibility of Anglo-Protestant America.[5]

White southerners alternated between viewing "their Negroes" as reassuringly childlike and frighteningly savage. During Reconstruction, fears that blacks would "revert to barbarism" slowed white acceptance of independent black religious life. Later, whites retreated to the view of the "faithful Negro," repeated endlessly in nostalgicized reminiscences of servants protective of their masters' goods during the Civil War. White southerners had learned that even "faithful Negroes" could fight for freedom, ally with Republican politicians, and develop religious institutions. This explains why white Baptists would fall back to the reassuring image of simpleminded but orthodox Negroes.[6]

White Americans of the nineteenth century disparaged black culture, mocked it in minstrel shows, and enacted their revulsion through rituals of physical humiliation and violence. But they were also fascinated with it. John Jasper, famous black pastor of the Sixth Mt. Zion Baptist Church in Richmond, attracted crowds of tourists with his best-known sermon, "De Sun Do Move." Many came strictly for amusement but professed to be emotionally moved almost in spite of themselves. Jasper was the reassuringly orthodox Baptist par excellence. "He clung far more to the traditions and sentiments of his bondage days than to the new things which freedom brought," his Virginia ministerial colleague William Hatcher wrote of him. Jasper claimed numerous converts, and many ministers adopted oral styles influenced by him.[7]

Missionaries and northern reporters in the late nineteenth century detected a growing gap in southern vernacular spirituality and the practices of respectable churches. Walter Hines Page remembered religious meetings in 1866 in which "mourners" (those seeking salvation) would fall into trances and be carried off by ushers. To find similar customs decades later, he added, "one must now go to remote regions where the religious habits of the whites are of a similar kind." The "many very orderly congregations," a *Harper's* correspondent remarked, annoyed the "old Negroes," who found the new rules of conduct to be a "great trial" to them. Another missionary recounted a service where, when a few ex-slaves raised a shout, "they were sternly and promptly suppressed by a stout black matron, a leader in their church." The observer recognized that "such emotional demonstrations doubtless still occur in the remote rural regions among what the Africans call 'old issue black folks.'" Upon hearing a "powerful good sermon" one Sunday, an elderly congregant said that "it most killed me to hold in them shouts." Her exertions demonstrated the influence of notions of respectability. Observers discovered that black worshipers would not "give way to their wildest gesticulations or engage in their sacred dances before white people, for fear of being laughed at." Respectable ministers discouraged shouting "since it did not conform to the conventional pattern of the white man's service," reported Lydia Parrish, a folklorist of black song styles. She recognized that such religious exercises remained part of black religious life, even if hidden from the "more fashionable Negro preachers" and from musicologists.[8]

Larger urban congregations increasingly employed full-time ministers with substantial educations, leading to the spread of Victorian propriety. In the 1870s, Edward King observed a congregation in Richmond listening "with tearful and rapt attention to the emotional discourse of their preacher, or singing wild hymns as they are read out, line by line, by the deacon." But later correspondents at this same church remarked on the sedate nature of the services, as did reports from other urban settings such as Atlanta's Third Baptist Church. Lord Bryce, the renowned English student of American politics and culture, contrasted the "enormous difference" between black churches in the urban areas of the upper South, where, as he believed, the "ideas of decorum [were] modeled on their white neighbors," and black meetings in the deep South that retained the "old superstitions" and had relapsed "into the Obeah rites and serpent worship of African heathendom." In the churches of coastal South Carolina, a prominent black minister explained, there was as much "dignity, decorum and quietness . . . as one will find in the average white assembly." The solemn demeanor in these congregations was preserved precisely because worshipers found other outlets for emotional expression, especially in the praise houses on the nearby Sea Islands. "In the churches they act like 'white folks,'" he concluded, "but in 'praise houses' they are 'cake walkers.'"[9]

Frequently the resistance to lectures on proper spirituality was more open. E. C. Becker, a northern white missionary among the freedpeople, concluded that he was "thrusting myself upon the colored people where I am not wanted." During his final sermon, a white southern colleague of Becker's found himself interrupted by a woman who jumped up before he finished preaching, led an exuberant prayer, to the delight of the congregants, and finally collapsed on the floor. The preacher denounced her action. The woman suddenly revived her spirits and led the congregants in deserting the hapless minister. With this ignominious end to his preaching career among the freedpeople, he resumed "fighting along the white line, which is much more pleasant."[10]

Black Baptist missionaries encountered a similar resistance to lessons in proper spirituality. G. B. Mitchell, a missionary in Georgia in the 1880s, condemned the "erroneous, impious, and irreligious doctrine, which has been heeded as one should the truth." Ministers in his area preached messages "too painful to mention," including a pronounced emphasis on dreams as the key to salvation. A cleric in Savannah angered worshipers because, "instead of teaching dreams and visions," he emphasized the necessity of an "intelligent Christian experience." Because of his refusal to countenance such customs, he had been "cast out as an evil" among those who clung to a belief in "dreams, visions, and root-work superstition." In 1913, a missionary in Mississippi recorded his unsuccessful attempt at preaching to a local congregation about involvement in denominational work. Upon arriving at the church, he discovered that "the pastor had gotten it into his head that I was coming to reign king over him and had instructed his officers to shut the door on me."[11]

The reformation of southern religious ritual was a central aim of the white northern Baptists who educated black ministers in denominational schools and colleges. Henry Morehouse, coordinator of northern Baptist educational work among the freedpeople, reported that congregations on Alabama plantations held "low conceptions of religion, most crude ideas of Biblical truths, grotesque notions about conversion, and exceedingly narrow horizons concerning their responsibility and duty in the age of the world." But even some of the educated were still attracted to traditional worship styles. In Villa Rica, Georgia, Thomas Madison Dorsey held a ministerial position while toiling the other six days of the week as a tenant farmer. Even after getting a degree from Atlanta Baptist College in 1894, the preacher/farmer did not become a "race leader" but returned to itinerant preaching while he raised his son, Thomas Andrew Dorsey, the so-called father of gospel music. For the elder Dorsey, this "abrupt change of course reflected a deep ambivalence toward assuming his duties in the acculturative church over which the Society had trained him to preside." In this family, one senses the same ambivalence that many congregants felt toward notions of respectability. Thomas Andrew Dorsey, a product of this upbringing, experienced years of shuffling between classical, bawdy secular, and religious styles before settling on a form that came to be known as the gospel blues.[12]

Black denominationalists felt the contradiction between a congregationalist polity and their notions of proper spirituality. William Wells Brown, a well-known ex-slave and prominent African American writer, witnessed a minister at "one of the most refined congregations" in Nashville raise a shout. The hope for an educated ministry was distant when the "uneducated superstitious masses" refused to "receive and support an intelligent Christian clergyman," he lamented. "We cannot place in our pulpits educated pastors until the masses are lifted up to a point where they will *demand* it," a black missionary in Louisiana explained in 1881. "Let us hope that the truly progressive brethren in our colored churches, who believe in church order, and who would have their church affairs rightly administered, may be able to gain a more abundant hearing among their brethren," a northern missionary wrote in 1882. He found steady gains being made but noted the continued widespread use of "plantation methods of revivalism."[13]

As the decades progressed, the reformers grew more hopeful. Despite the "wide-working leaven of old-time shouters," one minister suggested, younger clerics were delivering quiet sermons "without any long agonizing or shouting" in churches filled with African Americans of all classes. "This may not mean much to New England," he concluded, "but it means everything in the New South." The *Savannah Tribune*, a well-known black newspaper, highlighted the "modernization and progressiveness of a large percent of the management of some of our churches." Educated ministers now commanded "the attention of the community." The editor of a biographical dictionary on the lives of black Baptist clerics issued this hopeful assessment: "Intelligent worship is steadily gaining ground among the churches all over the country. Many unnecessary (I was about to say unchristian) customs have been relegated to the background. . . . In every community the churches are beginning to appreciate a pure and simple Gospel sermon. Mere sound no longer satisfies the thirsting souls."[14]

Bishops of the African Methodist Episcopal Church, most famously Daniel Payne, traveled their circuits in the late nineteenth century, intending to stamp out "heathen" practices. Black Baptist denominationalists, lacking the authority provide by the episcopal church structure enjoyed by Daniel Payne and other African Methodist Episcopal bishops, could rely only on scolding, advising, or encouraging individual congregations to learn the ways of respectability. A black Baptist missionary in the 1880s told Texas denominational leaders that in his work he met "with some strange customs and teaching not warranted by the Word of God. These I deal with gently, but earnestly and pointedly." Baptist literature was scare, and congregants had not learned "to bring the movements of the world and the doings of the day" into their meetings.[15]

The visions of modernization and standardization in the late nineteenth and early twentieth century made inroads on all aspects of rural southern culture. A kind of regional enclosure movement rationalized southern agriculture and reduced older customs of free-range grazing and food foraging. Cotton mills, lumber companies, and turpentine camps brought national industries southward. The railroads penetrated isolated parts of the countryside. Mail order catalogs brought urban consumer goods within reach of rural households. In addition, denominational publications advocating respectability in religion reached thousands of homes, and schools of ministerial education gradually placed their graduates in rural pulpits. Two generations of worship reform seems to have been at least modestly effective, as evidenced by ex-slaves who bemoaned what they perceived as the decline of spirit in worship. "Colored folks nowadays is jes' ruinin' singing' 'cause all dey is think 'bout is style, and dey don't sing no more with de old time spirit in it," lamented one ex-slave interviewed by the WPA. "You has to 'bide by Jesus to get de spirit, and not iffen you has better clothes den other folks." Jane Cotton, a longtime churchgoer in Texas, remembered the old-time camp meetings: "people them days had religion, cause they was neighborly." In later years, she reported sadly, worshipers "get in one of these here cars and go to the church, the preacher he talks about thirty minutes then they goes home. Thats [*sic*] not religion, cause the devil had done got the whole bunch."[16]

Peter Goldsmith, a scholar of African American church life, provides a contemporary description of the effects of worship reform in his study of the Emmanuel Baptist Church in current-day Savannah. Pastors at Emmanuel frown on talk of the influence of the Holy Spirit, discourage religious dancing, and limit physical manifestations that suggest something uncomfortably close to spirit possession. When older members extemporize prayers, the pastor apologizes for allowing the service to continue past the designated closing time. The minister receives a regular and stable salary and in return reports to the deacon board, which controls the hiring for church positions. Women serve as choir directors and in other limited capacities, but their informal roles as "gospel mothers" have long since disappeared. The congregants, who represent working people of the community, pride themselves on their distance from the disreputable practices of the local Holiness assembly, where unpaid ministers chant sermons and induce spirit possession. In the case of Emmanuel Baptist Church in Savannah, black Baptist reformers were relatively successful.[17]

Walter Pitts's close study of contemporary black congregations in Texas balances Goldsmith's account. Pitts details a pattern of worship that moves through the whole range of the black religious experience in America. Services begin with a devotional period, usually led by elderly congregants, where the raising of slow eighteenth-century hymns and the use of archaic English in the preliminary oratory enhances the subdued mood. In the second phase of the service, the use of black vernacular overtakes the stilted English of the first part, livelier gospel tunes replace the slower hymns, younger people become much more actively involved in the service, and physical passion accompanies the high points. Pitts's study of how the solemnly devotional transforms into the exuberantly spiritual in the context of a single service demonstrates the effect of respectability of worship and the staying power of black spiritual traditions—of "the Frenzy," in W. E. B. Du Bois's terms.[18]

The best place to start in understanding "the Frenzy" lies in the conversion experience. Black converts from 1865 to 1920 gave vivid accounts of their soul's sojourn in the other world, with supernatural spirits wresting over the fate of individuals, and of emotionally compelling encounters with God's spirit. Those feeling stricken by the spirit often removed themselves from daily life and fasted during the time of their journeys (usually two or three days). In some close-knit communities, especially among the Gullahs in the Sea Islands, candidates for conversion donned special clothes signifying their transitional status, and excused themselves from normal chores while struggling to achieve redemption. As they sought to become church members, the "seekers" would tie cloths around their heads, "drop all work and look very woe-begone." Seekers later recited their accounts of being "carried in spirit to heaven and hell." "Raw souls" gained admission to the praise houses of the Gullahs after proving the sincerity of their "striving," depicted by a local missionary as a "long process of self-examination and solitary prayer 'in the bush.' . . . So unremitting must be the devotion during this stage that even attendance at school is thought to interfere with the action of the Spirit." Successful candidates passed through a probation time followed by baptism and church membership. The visionary travels were considered a necessary rite for a full entrance into the community. By such means "the church is there a real power in society," a missionary concluded.[19]

These experiences normally occurred late in teenage years or in young adulthood, indicating their status as rites of passage in rural black communities. "I was an awful wicked boy when I was growin' up. I thought it was best for me to change. I couldn't raise a family like I was," an ex-slave said of his decision to convert. A young Mississippian in 1872, working in a field near Holly Springs, told of having "an awful time with the devil," who "kept trying to throw me off the track." He retreated repeatedly to his special prayer location but "the devil he allus went to. 'Peared like he'd say, 'Come on Preely, go with me.' I could't get away from him, but kept fighting and praying and I finally whipped him." Since his conversion he had been "steadfast an' immovable so far" but worried that the devil was "watching me all the time trying to get in his dirty work."[20]

African Americans conceived of the devil as a "powerful trickster who often competes successfully with God," a figure akin in his wiles and ambiguously admirable intelligence to Legba, the trickster god of West Africa. Legba was "far from the fallen angel of European dogma, the avenger who presides over the terrors of hell and holds the souls of the damned to their penalties," the anthropologist Melville Herskovits explained in his classic study of Africanisms. As a trickster god, the devil was a constant presence, alternately amusing, admirable, and malevolent. God, the individual, and the devil engaged in daily skirmishes, and as the most adaptable and even creative force of the three, the devil might win as often as not.[21]

The bluesmen also started their careers at young adulthood, suggesting the importance of where one chose to align one's sympathies—with the church, or with the bluesmen and -women, the church's most severe and telling critics. The Georgia-born gospel musician Thomas Dorsey paid the bills by writing tunes of sexual bravado such as "It's Tight Like That" even while yearning to put his soul in the hands of the Lord. A series of personal tragedies, including the death of his beloved wife, threw him back to the Lord, by his own account, for consolation and sustenance. He soon thereafter wrote the gospel classic "Precious Lord, Take My Hand." The spectacular success of his subsequent career justified his renewed faith. By contrast, bluesmen such as Son House struggled through their lives with the call of Christianity and the temptations of the bluesmen. His efforts to remain faithful to God, he sang, met grief at the hands of "the womens and the whiskey." Son House's struggles duplicated those of a generation of talented men who saw in the church one avenue for redemption but could not reconcile themselves to the self-denial required of southern evangelical lives.

The visionary tales of converts and bluesmen both drew from a long tradition of African American spirituality that emphasized the role of spirits in guiding individual lives. Robert Johnson, the great Mississippi Delta bluesman of the 1930s, for example, sung of how "me and the devil was walking side by side," saw the blues as "walkin' like a man," and expected his spirit to be laid by the roadside to wait on the Greyhound bus. Johnson related his Faustian bargain at the crossroads, where he purportedly received special power to play the guitar, with a narrative structure similar to that of a typical conversion narrative.[22]

In their conversion stories, as in blues lyrics, narrators borrowed, shaped, and adapted prototypical experiences and story patterns. Just as blues lyrics passed from one singer to another, with local references and peculiar incidents constantly added to the store of available lore, salvation narratives varied by individual but eventually settled into the familiar formulas that assured hearers of their authenticity. There was the same reticence and fear, awe at the sight of a supernatural power, and feeling of release and "calling" in life following the event. This theology of the active supernatural eventually found its way into the practices of both white and black Pentecostal churches in the twentieth century, where tongues speech evidenced the movement of the Spirit. In such ways white and black worshipers influenced each other to an extent that they rarely acknowledged, most especially in the sects that, as one writer discovered, "grew up like mushrooms" in the South.[23]

For blues musicians, spirits were usually some identifiable demonic entities, whereas for most black Christians, the spirit remained without a specific personage. "It's not anything you can touch, of course, but you know it's there," Charley White, a longtime Baptist and Holiness preacher in Texas, said. A vision was something like a dream, but, he added, "it's not exactly like that neither. When God gives you a vision your whole body kind of soaks up the message, like a biscuit soaks up red-eye gravy. And sometimes you can hear the message as well as feel it. And sometimes you can see it."[24] In the belief systems brought to this country by the forced African migration, spirits "rode" the possessed and used them as the carrier for specific messages. African Americans believed that individuals were not mounted and controlled by independently acting spirits. Believers inspired by visions of divine origin recited the imagery of their own salvation, rather than serving as a channel for the direct unmediated voice of a possessor. They conceived of the spirit in specifically Christian terms, as the presence of Jesus or the "holy spirit."[25]

For both whites and blacks, public conversion tales formed a central part of the extemporized liturgy of Baptist worship. They reflected the deep need of worshipers in low church settings to have a comforting sameness to rituals while leaving room for the spontaneous action of the spirit. The narratives related by ex-slaves to Fisk University interviewers, compiled by Charles Johnson in *God Struck Me Dead*, stand as eloquent tributes to the influence these stories had on individual lives. Amy Perry, interviewed in South Carolina in the 1930s, for example, professed her disbelief in dreams or conjuration. But her conversion occurred while she was asleep, when she was twelve years old. Walking in a "large green field," she spotted a girl "I didn't had no use for" carrying a large bundle on her back. "I honey de girl up and love um and de bundle fall on de ground," she said. "Dey put me in de church den." Many others "had the hardest time to get religion," as did Mary Ellen Johnson. In Johnson's younger years, "sin had a hold on me that was hard to break and it got so that I were a different one in my own house and my folks wouldnt have anything to do with me because I was ageable and did'nt have the religion." Taken sick when she was fifteen, she lay in bed alone one morning when suddenly "sin formed a heavy white veil just like a blanket over my bed and it just eased down slowly over me until it was mashing the breaf' out'n me." She cried out to be saved until the veil lifted off her and "went away in the air. I jumped out'n the bed and I were'nt sick no more and I ran to the field where my mammy and pappy and the others were and I went a runnin' and shoutin' and the joy they had when I told them I was saved from sin."[26]

These conversion tales carried a marked similarity well into the twentieth century. Rossa Cooley, who succeeded the pioneer northern missionary Laura Towne in the Sea Islands, observed the continuity of religious customs among black Christians in an area where African traditions directly influenced belief and behavior. The young candidates in her area, still called "seekers," had to " 'see visions and dream dreams,' which are interpreted to [them] by a 'spiritual father' or a 'spiritual mother,' who is closer after having been seen in a dream." The seekers ceased all other activities and stayed all night in the woods. Later they related these stories to the church elders, who judged their authenticity.[27]

Church boards and elders routinely challenged the validity of the conversions, often requiring greater proof of the experiences from the candidates for membership. As a northern Baptist discovered, supposed converts who went before the church "with an intelligent Christian experience" were not rewarded but rather " 'sent back to seek further,' until they [came] with the usual stranger visions and physical demonstrations." The Gillfield Baptist Church in Petersburg, Virginia, found one supposed convert "not to understand her self or the Principles of Christ's dealings with his people." It voted to send her back "to a Throne of God's Grace which is able to make her wise unto devotion." Black Christians interviewed in the twentieth century related how examination committees initially rejected candidates for church membership, saying " 'The devil is trying to convert you. Fooling you boy! Go back!' "[28]

One of the most moving of the conversion stories comes from Ned Cobb, a sharecropper in Alabama known through his luminous and eloquent oral history. Converted while in prison, Cobb vividly remembered in the 1970s the spiritual experience that overpowered him in the 1930s. Cobb's activities with the Southern Tenant Farmer's Union had been discovered by local white planters. Determined to punish all those involved in this brief and radical challenge to the rural southern social order, they jailed Cobb for taking up arms to defend his neighbor's property. Normally a man of immense nerve and heroic self-control, Cobb "was a raw piece of plunder that mornin in jail," he remembered. His subsequent salvation steeled him for his upcoming twelve-year stint in prison. One morning, after days of praying in his cell, he found himself "leapin everywhere, in a trance," while the other prisoners stared at him uncomprehendingly. "All of a sudden, God stepped in my soul. Talk about hollerin and rejoicin, I just caught fire. . . . Good God almighty, I just felt like I could have flown out the top of that jail." Two years later, on a temporary leave from prison, he admonished his rural Alabama congregation "let us act like a nation of people should act." No one sent him back to seek further.[29]

Nineteenth-century whites were uncomprehending of the liturgical role of black conversion stories. Missionaries reported that "a bare rehearsal of a dream or some startling vision is all that is necessary to secure fellowship in their churches." Dreams and visions were "considered necessary to a good Christian experience," and the "physical excitement" produced by loud preaching "is thought to be the result of the influence of the Holy Spirit operating upon the heart," a northern reporter observed.[30]

Anthropological observers of African American life in the early twentieth century, who normally commented with a more sympathetic eye than the earlier travelers and missionaries, provide some of the most sensitive accounts of the conversion saga as community ritual. For example, Zora Neale Hurston, daughter of a Baptist minister in an all-black town in Florida, was a lifelong religious skeptic who knew intimately of the shortcomings of the believers. Churchgoers in her home town "plowed, chopped wood, went possum-hunting, washed clothes, raked up back yards and cooked collard greens like anybody else." Even with her doubts and questions, she enjoyed the oral artistry of the salvation narratives. She felt moved in churches "not by the spirit, but by action, more or less dramatic." Candidates for membership, she recalled, were pursued by "hellhounds" as they "ran for salvation" (perhaps the same "hellhounds" that trailed bluesman Robert Johnson as he ran from the "blues falling down like hail"). They would dangle precariously over the fires of hell, call on Jesus, see a "little white man" on the other side calling them, and finally traverse to heaven. In publicly describing their spiritual journeys, Hurston remembered, they sometimes extemporaneously created variations on the scripted narrative: "These visions are traditional. I knew them by heart as did the rest of the congregation. Some of them made up new details. Some of them would forget a part and improvise clumsily or fill up the gap with shouting. The audience knew, but everybody acted as if every word of it was new." Converts added their own flourishes to tales of redemption already sanctioned by the community: "The individual may hang as many new ornaments upon the traditional form as he likes," Hurston explained, "but the audience would be disagreeably surprised if the form were abandoned."[31]

In certain parishes, particularly in Louisiana and in the Sea Islands, candidates sought guidance from a "mother of the church." The church mothers of the Sea Islands "settled quarrels and difficulties among members, visited the sick, encouraged the dying, washed and coffined the dead, mourned over those believed to be lost, [and] draped the church in black for the dead." As the unofficially sanctioned oracles of dreams and visions, these church mothers powerfully affected the quality of individual religious experience. "By virtue of her supposed sanctity and religious activity," the church mother was "gifted with power to make spiritual excursions into the other world," one missionary explained. Few of these women achieved the status of renowned female exhorters such as Jarena Lee and Zilpha Elaw, but in local congregations, they exerted a daily influence that made them as important as their better-known and publicly controversial Methodist sisters. Church mothers displayed a strict virtue and kept tabs on the quality of congregants' lives. Their duties presaged the gender-specific roles of women in Holiness churches early in the twentieth century.[32]

Church mothers also have been seen as variants of the older female guides common in African secret societies, women responsible for shepherding young people through rites of passage. "Ostensibly this respect is given to her for her constant prayers," one postbellum missionary in the Sea Islands noted of a church mother, "but undoubtedly there is some occult element in the reverence for this old African whose source is not revealed to any white person." They were also women who creatively adapted to the restrictions imposed on women in southern Protestantism. In urban congregations such as the Gillfield Baptist Church of Petersburg, members considered the question of whether it was "right to suffer Females to be Holding Public meetings in the Houses." A committee of three men concluded that women should not "Teach or Exercise the Position of a Minister of the gospel at any time or at any place." But pious women throughout the region found ways around such rulings. Pastors complained that they were not allowed enough authority in church, with women exercising too much informal control.[33]

For the reformers, the power of these "gospel mothers" and "old shepherds" provided a painfully persistent example of the lack of "system" and "intelligent worship" in their churches. In New Orleans (a city with a tradition of older black women renowned for their esoteric spiritual powers), Charles Satchell opposed the authority of these spiritual guides. In his parish, the women with the most status were the church mothers, with younger women dubbed "gospel mothers" who served as their assistants. They exercised control over members, Satchell wrote, "on the ground [that they had been] sent to them by the Spirit." The consequences of crossing their will could be severe. "If a member can keep [on] the right side of these officials he need have no fear of church displeasure; they can gain access to the church. But woe to that disciple who is so unfortunate as to be out of their favor," he explained. He saw "no way these things can be overcome but by a more enlightened ministry." Congregants were eager to break free of enshackling superstition, he told northern Baptist supporters, and "unite with the friends of reform and progress."[34]

But change came slowly. Black Baptist association and convention minutes from the late nineteenth century indicate that progressive ministers remained "troubled by the Deacons and so-called Shepherds assuming authority over and controlling the pastor in the discharge of his duties, all of which we disapprove of." Laypeople with specially designated authority provided one means for individual congregations to shape their own destinies. Pastors came and went, but the mothers, the deacons, and other laypeople preserved distinctive Afro-Baptist practices.[35]

Those who were converted, whether in visionary excursions through the otherworld or in less dramatic encounters, celebrated their passage to a new life in the rite of baptism, the central ordinance for southern Baptists of both races. Ned Cobb's oral history evokes the rite's meaning for black Christians. Unlike most others, his baptism was not a communal affair. The pastor present for his conversion narrative refused to baptize him immediately, insisting that he wait until the customary annual ceremony in December. Affronted by the pastor's decision, the congregation, as Cobb recalled, "wouldn't 'amen' him, wouldn't say, 'that's right' or nothin. . . . And when they wouldn't agree with him, he took it in his own hands and refused me. Well that brought on a commotion but it didn't move him." Cobb finally received the ordinance the next Christmas, after his congregation "had done got shed of" the original preacher. Wearing a blue robe over his best Sunday dress, he was brought by the church deacons to a creek and handed over to the new pastor waiting in the water. After the immersion, he celebrated the rite in the traditionally exuberant way: "I felt, when I hit the air—and it was early winter when I stepped up out of that water—I felt just like somebody done poured a kettle of warm water over me. I weren't cold a bit. And I commenced a shakin hands all around and laughin and goin mad for joy."[36]

While not considered necessary to conversion, baptisms were still symbolically powerful. Being lowered into the water and completely immersed depicted the cleansing of sin. The emergence out of the water symbolized one's rebirth into the Christian community. "The Baptist is my deah belief, 'cause I was baptized by the Spirit an' then by the water, nothin' but the Baptist," an ex-slave told his interviewer. Elderly black Christians remembered the riverside gatherings common in the nineteenth century. "I don't believe in these pools like they have in churches now," commented one. He remembered the baptizing "down by the side of the creek" and said of later practices, "religion ain't what it was when I was a boy . . , there's too much style now." Philip Bruce, a condescending critic of plantation life, described the significance of the rite for black converts: "Its ceremony of immersion particularly is full of meaning to their minds; the vast crowd, swaying, shouting, and gesticulating, the strange and picturesque local details of the vicinity, the canopy of the sky and cloud over head, the late hour, the emotional rites, all tending to impress the occasion upon which they are received into the bosom of that church most deeply on their minds."[37]

During Reconstruction, whites distrusted black baptisms as potentially subversive gatherings, assuming (not without justification) that political organizing occurred at such ostensibly religious ceremonies. For most believers, however, baptisms were essentially spiritual events that girded them for a life of struggle and turmoil. Still a slave when she received her baptism, Easter Lockhart was accompanied by white folks who "went to see their negroes go under." Just before immersion, she recalled, "I seemed to walk real light. While we were getting in our baptizing clothes we shouted praises as the people on the banks sang." The whites returned home after the ceremony but the slaves processed back to church, where they "shouted till we could not shout no more." Her baptism was a central event in her life: "I ain't had nothing to come against me since I was baptized. My head loses lots of things, but not my religion." Bill Thomas's baptism was a "big time" in which other congregants shared in his happiness by shouting. "A man can get so happy, he cain't hold it," Thomas explained. When Cindy Kinsey was baptized, the preacher ducked her under the water until she almost drowned. "De debbil he got such a holt on me an jes wont let go, but de Preacher-mans he kep a duckin me and he finaly shuck de debbil loose an he aint bother me much since," she remembered. Forty people entered the water with Ellen Payne. The accompanying congregants sang "Let's go down to Jordan," with "plenty of shouting" all around. "I still shouts at meetings," she said. "It hits me jest like a streak of lighting and there ain't no holding it." Though she tried to "behave," she found that "when I gets in the Spirit, I jest can't hold that shouting back." Her retort to the younger people who ridiculed her emotionalism was simply that "style is crowded all the grace out of religion today."[38]

Communal baptisms frequently served as preludes to lengthy services held at a high emotional pitch. Typically, the pastor led a procession followed by converts "all in emblematic white robes and white cotton gloves." Providing musical accompaniment, worshipers wound their way to the river: "There after prayer, exhortation and more singing they are dipped in the muddy water; and struggle out through the yellow slimy mud, shouting in religious frenzy 'Glory to God.'" In the afternoon, the crowd returned to

SHOUTS

the church, "the converts dressed in 'ball costume' and bridal array, to hear more preaching, and join in congratulations and singing. This is kept up until evening, with gradually increasing fervor until the climax of the holy dance." Formal acceptance into the church, Rossa Cooley noted, was "only a final ceremony that crowns all the days and nights of praying, prayer interpretations, and the great act of baptism."[39]

Worship reformers lamented that the crowds at black baptisms produced "such confusions and excitement, and sometimes such a display on the part of those baptized, that the whole scene becomes a farce, and intelligent and sober-minded people go away disgusted." In Louisiana in the 1880s, Walter H. Brooks, a black Baptist missionary among the freedpeople, witnessed a "disorderly and disgraceful ceremony" in which the converts, after leaving the baptismal waters, bound to shore while still in a trance. In the service that followed, two young ministers served communion while preaching "in a wild and disconnected manner." Brooks delivered a carefully worded and orderly sermon, according to his account. After his talk, a female member, feeling the Spirit, marched in the aisles and sang "in a rapid, wild, exciting style." The congregants joined in her song "and sang and intensified the excitement until the young woman fell, exhausted and almost breathless, into the arms of one of the 'mothers of the church.' " The presence of Brooks, a well-educated minister, would not block exuberant Afro-Baptist expression.[40]

Just as important as the visionary conversions and communal baptisms was the continued practice of "pagan" and "heathenistic" rituals such as the ring shouts. Even the most obtuse of white observers during the antebellum era recognized their African origins. With freedom, many assumed, would come a more "advanced" form of worship. But adaptations of the shouts remained central to black worship expression, particularly in areas retaining more "Africanisms" than elsewhere. Few nineteenth-century missionaries found much to admire in them. George Stetson, a northern writer, described ring shouts as "vehement, impassioned, ecstatic prayer and exhortation; profuse psalmsinging (often absurdly improvised), the whole culminating in the 'holy dance' or 'walk in Egypt.' " Laura Towne recorded what she perceived as the "remains of some old idol worship" in the Sea Islands. A few of the participants would stand apart to lead the shout, while others shuffled around them in a circle, "following one another with not much regularity, turning around occasionally and bending the knees, and stamping so that the whole floor swings." Francis Leigh, daughter of the actress Fanny Kemble, witnessed a shout on Butler Island in 1866 in which the freedpeople "lit two huge fires of blazing pine logs, around which they began to move with a slow shuffling step, singing a hymn beginning 'I want to clim up Jacob's ladder.' Getting warmed up by degrees, they went faster and faster, shouting louder and louder, until they looked like a parcel of mad fiends." At another service, congregants who suffered through a quiet sermon had three of the better singers among them stand to the side to lead the music. The remaining worshipers danced in a circle. Dozens of people followed in the ring, the white observer reported, "each one seemingly in a state of exaltations, and wholly unconscious of all earthly things." The appearance of shouts in areas outside the Sea Islands and coastal low country dismayed those observers who expected the freedpeople to be more acculturated. An observer at a Primitive Baptist Church in Florida witnessed a "Rocking Daniel" ceremony at the close of communion, in which participants circled in front of the pulpit and moved around a leader in a single file, singing hymns and clapping. A white Baptist minister discovered that a similar style of shouting and sacred dancing had spread to Texas churches by the 1870s. Preachers led the congregations in marching around and bowing to a red flag, while singing their "peculiar" songs. Only a proper religious education would check this "manifest tendency to heathenish superstition," the missionaries surmised.[41]

In the twentieth century, missionaries, folklorists, and scholars presented a more positive assessment of the shouts. W. E. B. Du Bois argued that there was "no true American music but the wild sweet melodies of the Negro slave" and described the tenacious hold of "the Frenzy" on black worshipers, "when the Spirit of the Lord passed by, and, seizing the devotee, made him mad with supernatural joy." The movement of the Spirit could vary, Du Bois wrote, from the "silent rapt countenance or the low murmur and moan to the mad abandon of physical fervor—the stamping, shrieking, and shouting, the rushing to and fro and wild waving of arms, the weeping and laughing, the vision and the trance. . . . Many generations firmly believed that without this visible manifestation of the God there could be no true communion with the Invisible." Written under the influence of Hegelian notions of the dialectic operating through the world's races, Du Bois's work suggested how black spiritual expression could serve as an antidote to the "dollars and smartness" of Anglo-Protestant America. Rossa Cooley found in the praise houses of the Sea Islands "the simplest, and the most real form of the Christian religion I have ever seen." She thought religion to be the "gift of the Negro to our American life. There is its strong dramatic expression found in the praise houses on the plantations. It wells up through the songs of the race."[42]

"If freedom has lessened their fondness for their peculiar amusements," wrote an observer of the lives of freedpeople, "it seems to have increased their love of funerals and revivals and religious gatherings of every descrip-

Revival

tion." For both whites and blacks in the rural South, revivals, footwashings, and funerals were cherished times of ingathering, particular occasions for celebration and sorrow, and release from the constraints of everyday life. Black Christians regarded the revival as the "spiritual festival of the year," as a "homecoming day" for people of the community who had moved elsewhere, and as a "general holiday season" for average working people. Preachers gifted at chanting sermons and leading singing and shouting drew the largest crowds. Congregants sang revival songs, a genre reserved for such occasions (as opposed to "classical songs" that were "considered appropriate only for the Sunday school or more formal religious services").[43]

Revival services followed set routines. At a service in Mississippi in the late nineteenth century, to cite one typical example, singing began the meeting while a collection was taken up for specifically announced objects. Afterward two ministers preached "with machine-gun rapidity" while a woman danced down the aisle "shrieking and wailing in a most uncanny voice" before falling into a trance. "All these give an impression of the tremendous energy and earnestness of these plantation people," a white missionary in attendance commented. At a service in the Sea Islands, laymen conducted a prayer meeting while women walked to church singing softly. Prayers beginning the service turned into song, and the exhorters entered. The preacher mostly chanted his sermon except for the occasional spoken reproofs directed to the congregation in a "sharp, ironic, conversational tone." As was customary, accessions to the church were celebrated with tears. Even at colleges where the leading ministers were trained, the periodic revival was encouraged as an outlet for the religious emotions presumably the students had pent up the remainder of the year. The advocates of respectable worship would allow emotions at revivals to "break the bounds of a decorous spiritual propriety."[44]

Missionaries, academicians, and journalists depicted the "glowing, tumultuous, uncontrolled fervor of the revival, where hundreds writhing in inward agony literally cast themselves in the dust"; or the "highly emotional, sometimes hysterical, almost madly corybantic [services], combining with a half-Christian service a half-pagan frenzy"; or of communal rites full "of awful mystery, of intoxicating passion, of excruciating pain, of supernatural joy, of dire and occult communion with the Invisible." Such commentary mixed patronizing sentiments with a fear of the latent sexual power of the services. Similar reactions would greet early jazz music and serve as well as haunt the Harlem Renaissance writers. Langston Hughes, for example, realized that whites weaned on images of sexual savagery in representations of African American culture expected black writers to personify the primitive.[45]

Footwashings served similar communal functions to baptisms and revivals. They allowed congregants to resolve differences with each other and celebrated the bonds of Christian love. In mainstream white churches (except in Appalachia, where the custom lives on to the present day), the practice of footwashing gradually died out, but it remained common among small black congregations in the rural South. Sometimes the footwashing accompanied a regular service but more often it constituted a separate ceremony, often held on the midnight before Christmas. At one footwashing in Alabama in the 1890s, the ceremony began in the evening with supper. One part of the congregation ate bread while the other half sang. To begin the ritual, the minister washed the right foot of the head deacon, and the deacon returned the favor. The minister then tied a towel around his waist, washed the foot of a man in the congregation, and handed over the towel, the process passing similarly from one male congregant to another. A similar ceremony took place on the female side. After the washing, worshipers moved church benches to leave room for a ring shout led by a layman. During the shout the participants danced around in "a perfect circle, with little twitches and jerks of the body, the feet only gliding on the floor." At a ceremony in Virginia, female footwashers robed themselves in white with caps while one older man, the "shepherd of the flock," dressed in a long gown with a handkerchief on his head. Following a supper served separately to men and women, the "old shepherd" removed his garment, and with a towel washed the feet of the man to his right. The churchgoers followed him in succession. A correspondent in Florida described a similar ritual that took place at a bread and forgiveness festival. Members put bread in the mouth of those from whom they were begging forgiveness and emotionally proclaimed their resolutions to reconcile. Such ritualized events in the low church liturgical calendar of white and black southerners yielded moving accounts of long-remembered times of togetherness. As a Hampton Institute scholar wrote, black worshipers found the "big-meeting day" a time of "great rejoicing" in which "those who cherished grudges against their neighbors forget them, and those who were on unfriendly terms became reconciled."[46]

Just as revivals and footwashings provided sanctioned gatherings of communal bonding, burials and funerals allowed communities to come together to mark the passage of souls. Friends and neighbors remained with the deceased during the three days between death and burial, with the whole neighborhood gathering for the " 'setting up,' " or preparation, for burial. Burials preceded funerals, sometimes by a short time and other times by months. Relatives of the deceased took no part in preparing the body. Pallbearers bore the white-sheeted coffin to church and placed it in front of the pulpit, after which preaching began. From the church to the grave ritual wailing filled the air. Music at the funerals, especially the popular hymn "Hark from the Tomb a Doleful Sound," illustrated the older style of slow a cappella singing with the verse couplets read out by the preacher. As a New Englander put it, "I have sometimes thought that such singing must be designed to tone down the emotional zeal of the Negro's religion, for its effect cannot but be depressing. Some of the people swayed softly backward and forward to the music, seeming to find a certain solace in its mournful rhythm." The congregants sang over twenty verses and choruses of the songs "without apparent fatigue, while I was ready to drop." John Jasper in Virginia cemented a regional reputation for his ability to induce emotion through his funeral sermons: "Before the torrent of his florid and spectacular eloquence the people were swept down to the ground, and sometimes for hours many seemed to be in trances, not a few lying as if they were dead." At some funerals, communal celebration took the place of somberness. Charles Corey, head of a black theological institution in Virginia, remarked disapprovingly that through the serving of wine and cake at funerals "the solemn services attending the burial of the dead are often converted into scenes of merriment and frivolity."[47]

Whether professed Christians or not, African Americans commonly believed that spirits inhabited the house for three days or more after death, watching the preparation of the body. Spirits not admitted to heaven could return to haunt the living. If the living neglected their duties to the dead they could also be troubled by the "hants," for the dead could return and demand a funeral "for the repose of their souls."[48] Belief in the powers of conjure, defined by one historian as "an extensive area of magic, practices and lore that includes healing, spells, and supernatural objects," was widespread, and vitally influenced local beliefs in spirit travel during conversion and after death. Christianity and conjure could be two sides of the same coin, one representing eternal salvation and security, the second protecting one's life from the evil forces in this world (or enacting revenge on an enemy). Black Christian leaders fought to root out this "superstition" and could claim some success. Works Progress Administration interviews conducted in the 1930s include numerous instances of ex-slaves insisting that "anybody that believes in conjuring is just a liar" and that "God is the only one who can do any conjuring."[49]

But ministers and otherwise pious laypeople often confirmed the presence of the otherworld. Sometimes it was a simple acknowledgment of unseen presences. Riding down the road one evening, Jacob Aldrich saw something without a physical presence go through a fence. "I tell de preacher 'bout it and he say it was a ghos'. Dat what I thought it were too." Conjurers such as Allen Vaughan from North Carolina (from a clan widely known for its efficacious powers) and "Uncle" John Spencer in Virginia were devout Baptists, but they used magic for purposes of revenge, finding in that no contradiction to their Christian faith. Observing such beliefs in the 1870s, D. F. Leach reported that plantation people lived "in constant dread of evil from these various imagined sources. Even those who profess to be Christians have a stronger faith in those things than in the Bible." White southerners also provided a clientele, albeit often a surreptitious one, for conjurers and other practitioners of hoodoo.[50]

Conjure could induce physical manifestations of divine powers and could be healing or malign. Sometimes ministers were asked to "break spells" placed on parishioners by conjure men. William Adams, a Christian and respected conjure specialist in Texas, disputed the characterization of conjure as "superstition" and explained how "special persons" were chosen to "show de powah" of God:

> 'Membah dat de Lawd, in some of His ways, am mysterious. De Bible says so. Thar am some things de Lawd wants all folks to know, some thing jus' de chosen few to know, an' some things no one should know. Now, jus' 'cause yous don' know 'bout some of de Lawd's laws, 'taint superstition if some udder person undahstan's an' believes in sich. . . . Thar are some bo'n to sing, some bo'n to preach, an' also some bo'n to know de signs. Thar are some bo'n undah de powah of de devil an' have de powah to put injury an' misery on people, an' some bo'n undah de powah of de Lawd fo' to do good an' overcome de evil powah. Now, dat p'oduces two fo'ces, lak fiah an' wautah.

Even those pastors who preached against the powers of conjure maintained their own pragmatic respect for conjure men.[51]

Nothing more fascinated observers of black worship than the rich tradition of black sacred music. Baptists of both races used and reshaped a variety of musical materials, including the shape-note hymns and spirituals of the antebellum era, or the Moody-Sankey gospel hymns filtering south from northern revival services. Songs of all sorts were interspersed through the lengthy services characteristic of southern meetings, with both spontaneously raised hymns and prearranged programs guiding musical choices. Southern oral traditions influenced cadences and melodies, slowing down the songs and encouraging active congregational participation in spontaneously altering lyrics, flattening notes, or emphasizing the two and four beats. Some Baptists of both races opposed modern means of music making, but most southern believers gradually incorporated musical accompaniment to hymn singing. Enslaved blacks demonstrated remarkable resourcefulness in creating musical instruments from the simplest materials. The freedpeople developed their own strongly held but flexible traditions about what constituted proper instruments for religious music, a standard that excluded the fiddle and banjo but included pianos, organs, and virtually any sort of rhythmic instrument.[52]

Historians have explored the interaction of white and black believers in the creation of southern sacred music. The ex-slave Wayman Williams in Texas remembered how this dynamic worked in antebellum days: "De white folks taught de 'Exhorters' to read de Bible and de songs, he would sing de songs 'bout two verses to de niggers and den dey would all sing togedder an dat is how dey learn de songs." He recognized the significance of singing for influencing the sacrality of the services: "We all helps wid de songs for dey is de gateway to enter into de spirit of services. De exhorter caint do much wif out de help of de congregashiun." Another Texan, Leo Mouton, remembered that "dey uster sing d' song d' w'ite folks sing 'n' den had some dey mek deyse'f." One of the most vivid recollections came from Vinnie Brunson. In her church building, which doubled as a schoolhouse, the congregants removed the benches at night after preaching was over and gathered to sing. During the music "if de spirit moves dem dey jus up an dances to de tune of de song and sings and de crowd keeps de time pattin de feet and de hands." Brunson concluded with a philosophical reflection on the meaning of singing for African Americans in the South:

Yes'm de nigger used to sing to nearly everything he did, Hit wuz des de way he 'spressed his feelin's an hit made him relieved, if he wuz happy, hit made him happy, if he wuz sad hit made him feel better. . . . [They] sang things different ways for different occasions, fast for joy and slow for funerals. Hit is de niggers mos' joy, an his mos' comfort w'en he needs all dese things. Dey sing 'bout de joys in de nex' world and de trouble in dis. Dey first jes sung de 'ligious songs, den dey commenced to sing 'bout de life here and w'en dey sang of bof' dey called dem de "Spirituals.[53]

Northern missionaries in the postbellum South, and later southern black denominationalists, attempted to acculturate black singing styles to standard Protestant practices. Charles Satchell of the American Baptist Free Mission Society moved to New Orleans just after the war and organized several black churches and associations in the area. With northern financial assistance, Satchell's flagship congregation in New Orleans bought an organ and recruited a "reasonably fair choir of singers." Satchell forecast a finer style of worship for his church: "I think when we get fairly on the way, with the improvements in singing, order in worship &c., the people who may attend will see the advantages of an enlightened state of things, and it will be the leaven that will work until old fogyism and the tyranny of the old churches, with the popish idea of old shepherds and gospel mothers, lords over God's heritage, will be unknown."[54]

New gospel hymns made inroads and choirs were formed even in smaller rural churches, but the spirituals, the "old-time songs," still expressed the deepest religious yearnings of many African American believers. Although younger black Christians were said to disparage these hymns, "they could all sing them," a northern observer reported, and were "quite as easily enthused by them as were the generation from whose toil and travail they spring. No music moves them as this does." Joseph Earnest, a student of religious life in Virginia, wrote in 1914 that the newer hymns interested the black worshipers but did not "delight them." At Thomas Dorsey's home church in Georgia, congregants learned the rudiments of Protestant hymnody through shape-note singing, a nineteenth-century tradition that brought musical education to illiterate folk. But the moaning of congregants extemporized from the hymn tunes brought the most shouts.[55]

The way in which black worshipers responded to their own song styles comes across clearly in accounts of musical selections sung during offering times. Preachers lined hymns while congregants filed forward to a table where deacons collected the money. When worship leaders struck up spirituals, Rossa Cooley reported, "the money comes fast as a rule." Visiting a church in Kentucky, William Barton described a scene in which two deacons sat in the front awaiting the collection. The preacher interrupted a "new-fashioned" hymn midway, "saying 'Breddern, da hain't no money in dat tune. Sing one of de good ole tunes.'" A spiritual followed, and "there was every indication that this song brought a good collection." Lillie Chace Wyman also witnessed the practice of waiting until the end of offertory time to raise "some sweet wild melody," which inspired a final surge of almsgiving: "The musical faculty of the Africans fails them when they attempt the congregational rendering of church music. . . . [But] when the audience becomes excited and ceases to struggle with these alien harmonies, it will . . . burst into a wild song whose musical and emotional qualities are fascinating." With such a demonstrated success, the sorrow songs, as W. E. B. Du Bois called them, survived every attempt at elimination from the repertoire of black sacred music. "It will no doubt be a long time," conceded a white southern Baptist in 1911, "before the negroes are developed to a point where they shall in their worship prefer a type of song that does not consist so much in repeating the same doggerel line over and over."[56]

Black religious music in the late nineteenth century grew more diverse as congregations absorbed musical influences from missionaries, popular secular tunes, and black and white gospel hymnists. Observers of services commented on the range of styles and how black traditions of expressive culture influenced the sound regardless of the genre. At services on Alabama sharecropper plantations in 1894, Henry Morehouse heard plantation songs, standard hymns, and gospel tunes, all of which were lined out. Morehouse approved of musical modernization in black services but realized that "nothing so alters their souls like the plaintive, weird, old plantation songs born of their bitter experiences, old slave songs of supplication to God for deliverance from their woes." The only antidote to primitive singing, he argued, was to "teach good music in our schools." Another northern Baptist felt certain that "no one thing can be a greater blessing than to get those songs and relics of the past barbarism out of the way, and displace them even by the ordinary Sabbath school songs."[57]

Whites were not alone in their efforts to replace the spirituals with standard hymns. A reporter in 1882 found that the "strange, wild songs" were "coming to be regarded as relics and badges of the old conditions of slavery and heathenism, and the young men and women are ashamed to sing them." Music leaders in revivals attracted crowds who traveled twenty or thirty miles in a day to hear the latest Moody and Sankey songs. They returned with "music enough in their heads and hearts to stock the plantations, and a new era in their church music has been inaugurated." Those dismayed by this musical evolution made similar observations. Younger people in the 1890s willingly learned the "cheery and attractive songs taught in their 'free schools'" while allowing "those marvelous melodies of their people drift into oblivion." Orra Langhorne provided a condescending account of changing black song styles: "Many of the colored congregations that are now beginning to have trained choirs and musical instruments, formerly sang the lines given out by the preacher, or improvised as they went along. The ignorant class are growing diffident in the presence of choir leaders, who sing from printed notes and are scornful of old fashioned people."[58] Worship reformers also could take heart from the frequent expressions of frustration about the gradual decline of the "old-time" songs. Fannie Yarbrough in Texas told her interviewer of lying in bed, remembering the singing of spirituals, when she "heard all those foolish songs and jubilee [gospel] songs that came over the radio—then some of those good ole time spirituals came and it jest made me feel like I was in ole times." The Reverend Squire Dowd in North Carolina condemned "the way they have messed up our songs with classical music."[59]

Black worshipers altered tunes from varied sources into music that fit the cadences and needs of their own rituals and allowed for improvisation even within the formulaic structures of Sunday school songs. The four or five lines of gospel hymns sung out by the leader would simply be repeated, each time getting louder, and soon the "ordinary Sabbath school songs" would be transformed into Afro–Baptist call-and-response style. The same hymns with different tunes might be sung several times over, with interruptions as congregants rose up spontaneously to relate conversion experiences, "always talking in a scream, as if crying." The congregations would supply rhythm with clapping and bodily movement, "gradually increasing to a stamp as the exercises proceeded, until the noise was deafening." Melville Herskovits documented the way ordinary gospel hymns of the late nineteenth century, sung conventionally for a verse or two, gradually would be transformed "into a song typically African in its accompaniment of clapping hands and foot-patting, and in its singing style. All that is left of the original hymn is the basic melody which, as a constant undercurrent to the variations that play about it, constitutes the unifying element in this amazingly illuminating music." Such descriptions explain the inability of reformers to eliminate Afro–Baptist song.[60]

Through their efforts in the publication and distribution of standard hymnals, black denominationalists spread the "classical singing" disparaged by many of the WPA interviewees. Richard Boyd, owner and manager of the National Baptist Publishing Board, published the *National Baptist Hymnal* in 1903, modeled on the American Baptist Publication Society's own compilation of 1883 (except that this latter hymnal contained nothing authored by blacks). "The books containing old-established hymns are the best," he explained. "Adopt those, and hold to them. Do not be carried away by 'catchy' tunes adapted to words that may be either destitute of all sentiment or full of that which would be positively injurious. Many an error is sugar-coated by music popularizers." Boyd's hymnal featured 146 selections of Isaac Watts, the great hymnist of the eighteenth century, and 37 tunes of Charles Wesley, the founder of Methodism and a prolific eighteenth-century hymnist. Several black-authored tunes made the cut, most of them written by Charles Rosoborough, Boyd's collaborator in the hymnal project.[61]

Boyd's publishing house produced a variety of song books adapted for multiple uses. "Doctrine can be more easily taught in poetry set to music than it can be by dry prose," Boyd wrote. Church members and ministers called for pocket editions, which were popular in the nineteenth century, so that each member could "select and sing the old metered songs of his or her choice." Pocket hymnals were cheap, portable, and flexible enough for congregational use. An anthem book published by Boyd in 1906 met this need. Boyd produced hymnals for use in Sunday schools and compiled formal anthems for church choirs. In 1916, the National Baptist Publishing Board released the *National Jubilee Melodies*, a collection of spirituals that, Boyd said, expressed "the emotion of the soul of the Negro race as no other collection of music—classically or grammatically constructed could possibly do." The hymnal, he continued, would "build a monument to the memory of our Negro ancestry and show the rising generation who may yet become a great and educated people that they sprang from a deep and prayerful religious race.[62]

In the 1920s, black denominationalists sponsored contests to encourage the writing of new hymns, reintroduced congregations to the spirituals, and fostered the growth of a new sensibility about African American sacred music. The printing of spirituals was a key turning point in this process, because it allowed to be passed down to future generations a tradition that once had been wholly oral. In 1921, the Nashville physician and hymnologist Arthur Melvin Townsend directed the production of the classic compilation *Gospel Pearls*. The collection turned the mainstream black Baptist hymnody away from an almost exclusive reliance on the white hymns of the eighteenth century and gospel songs of the nineteenth and incorporated more of the music of the black tradition. In 1924, Townsend put together the *Baptist Standard Hymnal*, which served for decades as the standard reference for thousands of congregations. Comprised mostly of traditional Protestant songs, it also showed the imprint of the Moody–Sankey era of gospel tunes and included works by prominent black hymnists such as W. M. Nix. At his performances at National Baptist Convention meetings, Nix's incorporation of microtonally flattened notes and other trademarks of the bluesmen into his music vitally influenced a generation of black gospel musicians. Thomas Dorsey's performance of his tunes at meetings of the National Baptist Convention in the 1930s were so affecting that gospel music soon came to be synonymous with urban black religious culture. Gospel grew into a widely appreciated (and, very early on, highly commercialized) form of music that profoundly influenced the later course of twentieth-century American popular song. Doo-wop, soul, funk, and rock-and-roll artists incorporated the melismatic, "sliding" phrasings considered primitive by earlier generations and turned them into pop music clichés.[63]

The efforts of church leaders to model a more acculturated form of spirituality was partially successful, but for a price: the black churches lost some of their most creative impulses to newly forming Holiness and Pentecostal groups. The rise of the Holiness movement in the late nineteenth century perturbed the "friends of reform and progress" and those who made careers rooting out the very "heresies of emotionalism" that Holiness practices deliberately induced. In the 1890s, former Baptist minister Charles Harrison Mason, feeling a need for entire sanctification, preached Holiness doctrines to his congregation, which resulted in his being kicked out of the black Baptist convention of Mississippi. When he received the gift of tongues at the Azusa Street Revivals in 1906, Mason returned to the South, moved to Memphis, and formed a new black Pentecostal denomination, the Church of God in Christ. By the time of his death in the 1960s, services at Mason's Tabernacle Church in Memphis were renowned for vibrant music and impassioned preaching and shouting.[64]

The success of a man such as Mason befuddled the advocates of respectability, who understood that Holiness and Pentecostal worship revived the very sacred dances and shouting that the respectable leadership sought to stamp out. For example, A. W. Pegues, a black minister and professor in North Carolina, worried about the "tendency of our people to erroneous views on the question of sanctification, Holiness, [and] the 'New Tongue.' " Pegues traveled as a sort of theological caretaker in the Tar Heel state, which, along with Georgia, was one of the hotbeds of early Holiness-Pentecostalism. He attended numerous Baptist meetings, explaining the incompatibility of Holiness belief (such as the "second blessing" of the Holy Spirit leading to the "sanctification" of the believer) with Baptist doctrine. Ministers such as James Henry Eason fought the new spiritual sects. In *Sanctification Versus Fanaticism*, published in 1899, Eason argued that "the sanctification that takes away from the church these choices and privileges, and leads members of the church to leave the church, combine themselves in bands to denounce local churches and sectarianism, while they rebaptize and establish as sect themselves—the sanctification that does that is not the sanctification of the Bible." Influential clerics such as J. A. Whitted, pastor of a large congregation in Winston-Salem, pronounced these doctrinal defenses a success, but the continued appearance of spirit possessions in black Baptist churches and the impact of ministers converted to Holiness-Pentecostalism must have given pause to the orthodox.[65]

If the specific theology of the enthusiastic sects failed to overturn Baptist doctrine, the vivid style of expression in Holiness congregations—one of exuberant emotionalism and unabashed spiritual joy expressed through dynamic music—proved far more powerful than bourgeois church liturgy. Charley White, a popular Holiness preacher in southeastern Texas, remembered when he and his fellow Baptist ministers "got all stirred up" from rumors that incoming Holiness evangelists "could put some kind of spell on folks." White and his colleagues challenged them to a Bible duel, believing that "we knowed the Bible and we didn't think they did." But the Holiness men carried the day, much to White's consternation. Having lost the duel, he considered transferring his allegiances, but the thought of humiliating himself in public was a chastening one. "I'd been telling other folks about their sins, and how they ought to live," he ruminated. "What would they think when they saw me on the altar?" Of even greater concern, White's wife already had converted and brought a Holiness woman into the house, challenging his spiritual authority. When he found himself "all the way down flat," he received the gift of the Holy Ghost. "Wasn't nothing to it after I got myself straightened out," he said. "It sure felt good. I'd never been anyways near this close to God before." He preached for the Church of God in Christ, a rapidly growing Pentecostal denomination of the early twentieth century, and members of his Baptist congregation followed him. The church, he concluded, "didn't belong to the Baptists. It belonged to the people there and me—we built it." White turned Baptist congregationalism to his own favor.[66]

Black southern Baptists sustained a religious culture that later fed into the freedom movements of the Civil Rights era. From 1865 to 1925 their customs endured attacks from within and outside the black religious community. But the personal liberation black Baptists experienced in conversion and the communal joy at their baptisms and revivals were rarely translated into the broader themes of social freedom. As a former slave put it, "Does I believe in 'ligion? What else good for colored folks? I ask you if dere ain't a heaven what's colored folks got to look forward to? They can't git anywhere down here. De only joy they can have here, is servin' and lovin'; us can git dat in 'ligion but dere is a limit to de nigger in everything else."[67]

Just as slave religion provided both a critique of an unjust order while it allowed an accommodation to the reality of enslavement, the postbellum Afro-Baptist faith sustained those enduring the daily humiliations of white supremacist rule without staging many obvious frontal assaults against that pernicious social order. But the apparent satisfaction of whites with the "orthodoxy" of "their" Negroes could leave a bitter taste. "It just worked in a way," Ned Cobb remembered bitterly, "that the nigger wasn't allowed to have nothin but church services and, O, they liked to see you goin to church too."[68]

Academic observers of rural religion in the early twentieth century decried the isolation of rural southern churches from modern life. As Charles Hamilton and John Ellison wrote in 1930, "the Negro church, being always conservative and often primitive, has not kept pace with progress in the social and intellectual life of the Negro." But to condemn the black church for not staging a revolution in the Jim Crow South is to overlook its role in holding people together during a period when sheer survival was an achievement. A Depression era historian of black life in Virginia captured this idea of sustaining spirituality: "Leading the song, dressed in Sunday best, or testifying at great length of wallowing in darkness and then seeing the light, or walking up the aisle to place coins on the collection table, or lifting quavering voices in a well-known spiritual, or exhibiting knowledge of parliamentary procedure at board meetings, or watching a loved one 'come through,' many Negroes find on the seventh day an importance, which six days of hardship, worry, and insult do much to diminish."[69]

Martin Luther King Jr. envisioned a land where all people could live together peaceably. His was a "dream deeply rooted in the American dream," he said in his epochal speech in 1963. His vision grew out of the deepest roots of conservative yet creative black vernacular practices sustained weekly in thousands of worship services throughout the South, a spirituality that eventually cleared one way out of the American racial wilderness.[70]

CHAPTER FIVE

The Character of Ministerial Manliness

White Southern Baptist Ministers, 1870–1925

In 1917, a Baptist minister in Henderson, North Carolina, privately wrote of the obstacles pastors encountered in teaching their congregations a "progressive" religious ethic: "Nearly all of us are driven by the force of circumstances to be a bit more conservative than it is in our hearts of hearts to be. I am frank to say to you that I have found it out of the question to move people in the mass at all, unless you go with a slowness that sometimes seems painful; and I have settled down to the conviction that it is better to lead people slowly than not at all." Such frustration was common. As a young and well-educated minister from Tennessee entered in his diary after one Sunday's work in a small church near Louisville, Kentucky, "this is a hard audience to preach to. They have small ideas and low ideals, as a rule."[1]

Both of these accomplished southern clerics might have taken comfort from the experience of an aspiring minister in a North Carolina mill town in the 1920s, who, although of a laboring background, set himself apart from his congregants, including his former comrades at the cotton mill. "Travelin' helps him a whole lot," his wife observed. "He'll go to the Association and hear big preachers talk and recollect might nigh everything they say." He understood the critical importance of proper salary, a respectable family life, and carefully tailored dress. A preacher, he explained, was burdened with "more expense than a laborin' man. He's got to be dressed up. Who wants his pastor goin' around lookin' like a hobo? I've said lots of times I'd like to sit around at home in my overalls, but it wouldn't do."[2]

From the 1890s to the 1920s, when a new generation of ministers reached adulthood, denominational modernizers spread the gospel of pastoring as a vocation rather than a calling. To a larger degree than historians have understood, plain-folk farmer-preachers in rural pulpits accepted this ethic, even when they could not put it into practice. Congregations throughout the region both encouraged and resisted the professionalization of the pulpit.

The postbellum South was impoverished, and its believers deeply entrenched in the customs of rural evangelicalism. Yet ministerial spokesmen learned to seek specialized training and demand regular salaries adequate to maintaining a middle-class standard of living. They cultivated restraint and decorum in personal behavior, as seen in the norms governing personal conversions and calls to the ministry. They sought professional training either in colleges and seminaries; barring that, they pursued programs of self-study with the help of denominational literature and informal institutes. They formed ministerial associations and exerted their influence in political debates.

Ambitious southern Baptist clergymen sought their niche in the emerging corporate capitalist models of American religious enterprises. They saw themselves as God's public relations experts, instructed to inspire congregants to support centrally organized programs. This professional ideal informed the lives of well-educated urban clerics and also reached the farmer-preachers who dominated rural pulpits. When professional pastors encountered resistance in exercising their roles as moral professionals, they experienced the kinds of frustration that made them "more conservative" than it was in their "heart of hearts to be."

Elite ministers in the antebellum era practiced a careful personal decorum to distinguish themselves from the untrained exhorters abounding in those days. Broadly educated clerics with wealth, elegance of style, a paternalistic view of slave-masters' duties, and socially conservative views represented the summit of ministerial status in the antebellum South, a region that paid primary allegiance to a rural landed class. Cultivated clerics, in the ideal at least, would not have to work at mean occupations. These "gentleman-theologians" provided moral guidance to southerners troubled about the existence of slavery in a free society and frightened by periodic slave revolts. In the antebellum years, as well, a generation of energetic preachers spread the gospel of a primitivist and democratic evangelicalism to plain folk in the countryside. A widening gulf opened between the parishioners of elite churches, who took their guidance from the gentleman theologians, and plain-folk congregants, who communed in simple wooden structures for evangelical exhortation.[3]

In the late nineteenth century, educated divines still delivered erudite sermons, and enthusiastic exhorters held forth throughout the region. But conceptions of pastoring as a middle-class professional occupation gradually took hold. Visionaries of the New South enshrined bourgeois values, diversified agriculture, and industry as the salvation of the region from its economic backwardness. Ministers took up this call. In their weekly or monthly homilies, the ministers stressed to congregants the need for restrained personal behavior, the imperative of respecting those with professional aspirations and education, and the critical importance of a progressive vision of "manhood."

The autobiography served as a primary means of communicating these values to a wide religious audience. A large number of Southern Baptist clerical narratives suggest the degree to which bourgeois models of private piety and public spirituality took hold in a region better known, and caricatured, for seasonal outbreaks of religious hysteria. No matter what the tradition of "the call to preach" may have been, these ministers decided on their occupation more through a gradual realization of their professional talents and a conviction of duty than through any epiphany. The Calvinist call metamorphosed into the Weberian call.

Jeremiah Jeter, a powerful influence among nineteenth-century Virginia Baptists, narrated in his autobiography what later became a prototypical conversion to Christianity and summons to the ministry. Jeter's subsequent retelling of his life illustrated the evolution of southern spirituality from communal religious emotions in late-eighteenth-century Virginia to the more private, controlled, and dutiful experiences normative a century later. After attending revival meetings in the 1820s, Jeter was burdened by his unbelief. Following a period of struggle, he felt at last that he could with confidence pronounce himself a believer. Immediately after his conversion the "burden of guilt and anxiety" that he had long felt "instantly departed." He sensed an inner peace that was "inexplicable" and that he was "not careful to analyze." Jeter expected a rush of overwhelming emotion, but the process climaxed instead with an inner calm. It was common practice for revival exhorters to set aside mourner's benches as sacred places where grown men and women could experience the sacred with the full approval of the community, but Jeter frowned on those who embarrassed respectable Christians by collapsing into public hysterics. His efforts at teaching restrained public behavior in the most personal of spiritual moments and the similar conversion accounts of others suggest that the stereotypical pairing of southern evangelicalism with public emotionalism has been overdrawn.[4]

Jeter's contemporaries in denominational work encountered the sacred in equally unspectacular ways. Son of an elite planter, minister, and university president, Basil Manly Jr.'s early religious impressions were but "very temporary, superficial, and evanescent." In the 1840s, studying the life of Jonathan Edwards (the eighteenth-century theologian whose thoughts revolutionized American religious and intellectual life), he learned to "loathe" himself and decided to "try" to become a Christian. "I have kept on trying every since—sometimes in doubt, mostly in hope," he later wrote. Conversion came less from an overwhelming spiritual infusion than a long, conscious effort to achieve intellectual contentment. Jeter and Manly both consulted with Christians older than themselves, looking for affirmation that their intellects had not fooled them. Manly was a gentleman-theologian who received a sterling education in both southern and northern institutions. As a prominent minister in Richmond and a seminary professor, Manly taught men of modest backgrounds, many of whom had been raised in rural churches that scorned "money-grubbing" or "hireling" preachers, to use the ministry as a means of achieving a professional status.[5]

By 1900, few Southern Baptist Convention (SBC) spokesmen apologized for using the ministry to achieve not just spiritual satisfaction but also social fulfillment. James Marion Frost, future head of the Sunday School Board of the SBC, rose from a less patrician background than Basil Manly Jr. Shortly after the war, he sensed an inward "growth of grace." The feeling that he "ought to preach" came over him, and after years of struggling, he reached "the point of feeling it [to] be duty." Thinking himself inadequately prepared for the ministry, he suddenly envisioned God speaking through the burning bush to Moses. The image symbolized the sacred answer to Frost's own personal doubts. Yet this experience induced not ecstasy but inner calm and purposeful duty. Frost and others used the term "surrender," a favorite image employed by camp meeting converts. But the word now lacked its former implication of a cataclysmic struggle between the sinner and God. Instead, "surrender" came to mean "decide."[6]

Men of poor rural backgrounds, who perhaps were better candidates for conversions in the camp meeting style, struggled to comprehend their own surprisingly staid spiritual awakenings. The spiritual metamorphosis of George Blount, an obscure pastor in Georgia in the late nineteenth century, failed to produce the expected holy fervor. Though feeling a "calmness of mind" on the evening of his salvation, he remained dissatisfied: "I worked myself to feel fearfull [sic] lest I should quench the Holy Spirit from my Breast and thus the whole of my experience at first was one of trying to feel." Blount admitted to falling into "many errors while my mind was worked to such a point." Finally, he accepted his transformation as undramatic but genuine. I. H. Goss was plowing the fields when he felt the influence of the Holy Spirit. "When this sudden change took place with me," he reported, "I heard no voice of words with my literal ear, and [saw] not God or Jesus with literal eyes, but felt delivered from the burden, guilt, and condemnation of sin." Otis Webster Yates encountered God at a revival in rural North Carolina, where a deacon told him of the great light he should see at salvation. "I looked for that wonderful light," Yates later wrote, "but have never seen it to this day." Even ministers raised in the Primitive Baptist tradition, which emphasized the necessity of focused moments for salvation, experienced undramatic conversions and calls. James Carroll, a Texas Baptist official in the late nineteenth century, grew up with family members who prepared themselves for the day with a shot of whiskey and retired at night after a Bible reading. Carroll avoided the dissipations of youth but still was burdened by his precarious spiritual status. He "resisted" God's call to him but finally, at a revival service, yielded when he felt a purposeful determination about his life. J. B. Cranfill, a fellow Texan and Carroll's future partner in Baptist work, noted a "sudden conviction" in his soul during conversion, but his call to preach was "not audible" but instead simply a "distinct impression."[7]

Men who would become ministers in the late nineteenth century learned also that conversion alone could not provide a clear life path, another move away from traditional conceptions of the sacred moment. While fighting in the Confederate army, Edwin Hansford Rennolds, a native of Tennessee who resisted conversion as a teenager, "began to consider how uncertain were all things earthly, and there came a longing for something sure and certain." After the war, talks with his wife finally persuaded him that he was a Christian. He never thereafter doubted his regeneration but struggled to discern his role in life. While he maintained his "faith in God's accomplishing his plan of evangelizing the world," at the beginning of his ministerial career he lacked "a clear view of the part I was to perform." William Owen Carver, a Tennessean who later became an authority on the theory of missions, wanted to be a missionary but eventually settled on pastoring at home. "It has been hard for me to thus let go a fixed purpose and hope," he wrote in his diary, "and I have often felt that I might be lacking in the proper determination. Yet I have felt that it was not due to a vascillating [sic] . . . mind." His exertions to achieve self-control may have been too successful. After a quarrel with his fiancée in 1896, he wrote privately, "I am conscious that I have not been a nice and considerate lover as I might have been. I do not—and I fear cannot—love with the wild passion of some. God forgive me and help me to be a true and tender man."[8]

Denominational newspapers imparted to their readers the emerging norms of professional competence, while acknowledging the retention of old-fashioned conceptions of the ministerial calls. Congregations still expected their young ministerial candidates to encounter "some sort of special revelation, some articulate voice, some overwhelming and phenomenal experience, which he is unable to relate to ordinary causes," a Virginia Baptist spokesman unhappily acknowledged in 1910. A North Carolina minister urged Baptists to give up expectations of the "personal and miraculous interposition of God" with "attendant theatricals of seasons, visions and visitation of angels" in decisions to enter the ministry. The further Baptists moved away from such anachronistic folkways, he believed, the nearer they would "accord with truth, Scripture, and common sense."[9]

Self-control in the personal experience and public display of spirituality constituted one central part of the emerging norms for southern ministerial conduct. Proper pastoral training was a second. In the early nineteenth century, southern Baptists hailed their ranks of untrained exhorters as one of the glories of American religious democracy. Baptists never considered it a "disqualification for a minister to be destitute of this or that particular kind of mental training," according to a pioneer Baptist educator. The major prerequisite remained that the prospective minister "had some power to preach, and people were willing to hear him." Young men with no training except for their call typically went before churches asking to be ordained. In 1897, at the age of twenty-two, A. W. Duncan knelt before his church elders. Because he had been a member of the church for years already, there had been "ample opportunity to become acquainted with his piety, and ministerial gifts," so one of the elders scrawled out a license saying, "trusting that God has called him to preach the Gospel, we hereby license him to engage in the great work." Duncan thus became a minister. Even well-off churches such as the Leigh Street Baptist Church in Richmond simply asked for a "statement of Christian Experience, Call to the Ministry, and Views concerning doctrine and denominational polity" from those they ordained. Elite clergymen of that era worried about the social stigma attached to their sects because of this corps of minimally educated pastors. They erected academies, schools, and Baptist colleges to train properly a respectable portion of ministers. And even "uneducated" ministers were expected to learn their trade much as would any artisanal apprentice.[10]

Many aspiring clerics who felt the call lacked the knowledge and resources to prepare themselves adequately. Starting out in his ministerial career in the 1870s, George Blount recognized that the "one great qualification" necessary for his work was a sound education. Lacking money and knowledge, he wondered where to turn. "I have no books that I can study safely," he worried, "and some of them are not standard now." By Blount's definition, a lack of "education" meant a paucity of specifically theological training, a considerable advance from the days when an "educated ministry" simply meant a literate one. Feeling a call to the ministry often meant starting a long and difficult road to education, whether through formal schooling or self-study. Sometimes family members encouraged prospective clerics in their educational pursuits. In other cases, kinfolk proved hesitant in supporting them, particularly if it drew them off the farm. For instance, Joseph Martin Dawson, who was reared by a Populist father, attended a church in rural Texas where "not infrequently a few women shouted, whirled in unrestrained emotion or sank into a trance which I fancied was death." Upon telling his congregation of his determination to preach, church members cried and embraced him, but at home "neither father nor mother shared the church's joy, but asked how I expected to live, much else pay for schooling." His success at a trial sermon the next Sunday convinced his parents of his oratorical abilities, but Dawson struggled for years before later graduating from Baylor College.[11]

Following a course of theological training proved difficult for illiterate and impoverished young ministerial prospectives. Access to education, especially to advanced theological study, remained severely limited. In the 1880s in Tennessee, only about forty of the six hundred Baptist ministers in the state received anything beyond a few years of schooling. There were few secondary schools and the Baptist college in Union, Tennessee, was a small, struggling institution. Few congregations, moreover, insisted on any ministerial training from the men they chose for the pulpit. "Beyond the very narrow circle in which they move they know nothing and care as little," a northern Baptist in the state observed of Tennessee ministers. John T. Oakley of Tennessee already had received his first pulpit posting in the 1870s, but at the urging of his mother, he struggled to achieve literacy and teach himself the basics of theology and church history. He later presented his own life as evidence of the transition in the Baptist ministry from the nineteenth-century exhorter to the professional cleric. The "unlettered fathers" of southern Baptists, he wrote in the 1920s, had "wrought well in their day," but the consecrated modern minister should at least "avail himself of a good English education" and study basic theological subjects. The days of the untrained exhorter were over.[12]

The intellectual challenges presented by newer forms of theology and the rising authority of scientific explanations of the world also furthered an insistence on ministerial education. John Broadus, the preeminent southern Baptist theological educator of the late nineteenth century, immersed himself in theology and church history during his years at the University of Virginia. In the past, he argued, the low social status of Baptists made it necessary to accept a "comparatively uneducated" ministry. Broadus devoted his life to making sure that this situation would not be duplicated in the future. "Errors are constantly being developed in new shapes and more fascinating forms," and only well-read Christians could combat them, a Mississippi Baptist association argued. "A world that is beginning to ponder the mighty revelations of science," a denominational official added in 1875, would no longer be "satisfied with the impassioned exhortation of the uncultured minister." The older struggle against religious heretics, won by evangelical passion alone, had shifted to a battle between "Revealed Truth [and] a partially revealed science."[13]

By the 1880s, the comparatively uneducated preachers often smarted from their sense of low status in emerging ministerial and denominational hierarchies. Defenses of untrained exhorters took on an apologetic tone. Churches increasingly chose seminary graduates over plain-folk preachers for pulpit openings, a move "well calculated to create in the minds of these older brethren a prejudice against theological schools in general. . . . Age and experience ought to tell for what they are worth in the ministry more than in any other calling," the *Biblical Recorder* advised. Older exhorters were "not devoid of the sense of human feeling" nor "wanting in the exercise of a well-regulated gentlemanly pride," an Alabama minister reminded his denominational colleagues. Baptists should remember that "whomsoever God calls, has a right to preach the Gospel; although his education may be limited," a Mississippi association instructed its churches. In the earlier nineteenth century, this idea would have been a point of pride. By the 1880s, it was a matter for some embarrassment.[14]

Denominational officials urged ministers to forsake worldly occupations and devote themselves to their particular calling. A Texas Baptist expressed this view of the professionalized ministry in an 1890 associational gathering: "There is a brother in my church who believes that I ought to plow six days in the week and preach on Sunday, but I assert, with Scripture warrant, that a man who can, with any peace of mind or conscience, follow any other profession or business, should never enter the ministry nor be ordained by a Baptist Church. . . . A preacher is called for the ministry but he is educated in it." B. J. W. Graham, who later would become the owner of a denominational newspaper in Georgia, was a successful cotton ginner and knew what sacrifices entering the ministry would entail. But the conviction that a formal theological education would be necessary if he was to live out his call grew in him. He entered Mercer University, a Baptist college in Georgia, at the age of twenty-seven, with a wife and five children in tow. He graduated in five years while pastoring four churches on the weekends. Later he served as a trustee of a Baptist high school and tirelessly supported Mercer in fund-raising activities. His life modeled how the call to preach should coincide with more secular interests.[15]

Southern Baptist officials saw their seminaries as a primary agency for spreading the professionalized norms of the ministerial call and work. In 1859, four well-educated and moderately wealthy men founded the Southern Baptist Theological Seminary in Greenville, South Carolina. James P. Boyce, the wealthiest and most accomplished of this group, hailed from a prominent family in Charleston. He studied at Brown University with Francis Wayland, one of the foremost theologians of the antebellum era, and later furthered his education at Princeton University, a center for intellectual formulations of Calvinist doctrine. After pastoring for a short time in Charleston and serving on the faculty of Furman College, he grew increasingly interested in theological education. Boyce realized that the democratic explosion of American religious life in the nineteenth century required that Baptists recruit their spiritual leaders from "classes as varied as the membership" of the churches. To those who deemed it inadvisable to open the seminary to Greek scholars as well as frontier exhorters, Boyce answered, "We cannot prevent this diversity, if we desire to do so."[16]

In 1856, Boyce enunciated the principles that served as the fundamental institutional philosophy of the seminary. He argued that theological education should include for all students both the higher subjects of scriptural exegesis as well as basic courses in English Bible. He insisted on an adequately endowed library with books carefully screened for orthodoxy. Finally, he required faculty members to sign a statement of principles ensuring that students under their tutelage would learn to "distinguish truth from error and to embrace the former, and that the same precious truths . . . will be propagated in our churches." The seminary creed reiterated basic Baptist doctrines but avoided taking specific positions on issues (such as Landmarkism) that divided churches in the SBC.[17]

The seminary had its critics. Primitive Baptists opposed professional theological education, and Landmarkers interpreted the opening of the Southern Baptist Theological Seminary as another move by Virginians and Carolinians to solidify their control of the denomination. Both suspected the institution to be an entering wedge of heresies and a tool of denominational centralizers. "The money power of our great schools have become golden calves and all sorts of infidelity is now singing and dancing around them. They, our schools, have become bigger than our churches and to tell what will be the final outcome would be a sad prophesy," one critic of Baptist theological education wrote in 1896. Leaders of the school recognized the social base of their opponents. As one of the founders explained, referring to Landmarkism's stronghold in Tennessee, "Nashville will try to crush it [the seminary] like everything else *Atlantic*." The institution's founders, however, vowed that Landmarkist opposition was "but a reason why we should stand up to it."[18]

The effects of the Civil War and Reconstruction proved far more difficult to overcome than Landmarkist opposition in keeping the school alive. The founders had invested the seminary's initial endowment in Confederate bonds, losing it all in the war. Greenville, South Carolina, the institution's initial home, lay physically wrecked in 1865. James Boyce, whose personal credit had been instrumental in establishing this "school of the prophets," had sunk large sums of his money down the Confederate sinkhole and witnessed his estate burned. In the late 1860s, with just a few students and little financial backing, the prognosis appeared bleak. "The only hope I can see for the preservation of our country and your Institution is in God," a supporter wrote to James Boyce. With the imminent "humiliation and danger of being placed under the control and government of the negro" and "the Tyrant Sickles your only lawmaker," there seemed little reason for hope.[19]

Despite these real and imagined obstacles, the founders determined to press on. "Suppose we quietly agree that the Seminary may die, but we'll die first," one of the original professors reportedly vowed to the others in 1865. In 1877, they moved the school to Louisville, Kentucky, gambling that this would alleviate fears that the seminary was a special haven for southeastern Baptists and hostile to southwestern Landmarkers. Boyce took up fund-raising work in earnest, traveling to numerous churches and hiring financial agents. By the 1880s, with a gift of $50,000 from former Governor Joseph Brown of Georgia (an ex-scalawag who ensured political support in the post-Reconstruction South through well-placed philanthropy) as well as substantial contributions from northerners, the institution entered a period of steady growth. The student body grew from a dozen students in the early 1870s to about three hundred in the mid-1890s and nearly four hundred by World War I, making the school by then one of the largest theological institutions in the world. By the 1920s, it had become a revered center of southern religious education, one known to stand "against the looseness and isms of Chicago and the North."[20]

The seminary recruited students from North and South and attracted many aspiring clerics with relatively little formal education. Faculty members assured interested applicants, many of them marginally literate men, that the curriculum included basic courses designed for those of limited attainments. The school also enrolled college graduates, though most of the better-trained students from the South still traveled North for advanced training (generally to schools with a reputation for theological conservatism). The seminary curriculum rewarded talent in preaching ability. "Our Southern people think much of this, you know," president E. Y. Mullins wrote of the key position of the professor of homiletics in the seminary.[21]

The democratic model of education also characterized the seminary's social world. Bernard Spilman, an alumnus and later an untiring organizer of Sunday schools in North Carolina, recalled his days there as a time of close quarters with a diverse group of men. Doctoral candidates and scholars from German universities sat next to men "caught wild on the plains of Texas without knowing what kind of thing a high school was," he wrote. "Men from the South and from the North, a great mixture." Living together in dormitories, traveling in tandem to churches on the weekend, and sitting in daily chapel services and basic courses with one another enforced a degree of mingling that prepared students to deal with diverse congregations. The faculty discouraged social segregation while encouraging men of lesser backgrounds to pursue elementary theological studies. The seminary placed its trainees in the most important pulpits throughout the South, ensuring the spread of the professionalized ideas of clerical work. By 1920, congregations of two hundred or more members rarely considered untrained men for pulpit postings.[22]

As the seminary's curriculum expanded and evolved, Baptist traditionalists feared that the fundamentals of the faith might be eroded among its students. In fact, conservative forces ousted Crawford H. Toy, a professor at the institution in the 1870s, for his apparent questioning of the divine inspiration of the Bible. Despite his reassurances that the Bible was no less divine even if it was "set in the framework of a primitive and incorrect geology," Toy's academic articles expressing sympathy with newly developing methods of textual criticism enraged denominational conservatives. If God sent a message "by the stammering tongue of a man," Toy offered in response, "I will not reject the message because of the stammering." But southern Baptists rejected Toy, hounding him from Louisville. He eventually accepted a post at Harvard, where he flourished as a prolific scholar in religious studies.[23]

The Toy imbroglio was one of a number of controversies over higher criticism that tormented theological institutions of the late nineteenth century, and the first of many such fights at Southern. Critics of the school repeatedly charged the faculty with attacking basic dogmas such as the divine inspiration of the Bible as well as discrediting the Landmarkist emphasis on the ancient origins of immersion. Thomas T. Eaton of Louisville's Walnut Street Baptist Church quizzed students who left the seminary or renounced their faith, attempting to discover evidence of infidelity. One former student, who had worked in the library and later renounced Christianity, received a letter from Eaton that concluded, "you being in the library made me think that you had read a great many books there." If students studied Hegel and Fichte rather than works of faith, they would "take a bath of filth from which they may never recover themselves," the *Biblical Recorder* feared. The "new theology," a North Carolina minister felt certain, would "overturn the Christian faith and plunge the world into doubt and uncertainty." He was "anxious to know where we stand" on the questions raised by higher criticism of the Bible. "It is enough to make the heart sick to see what things are advocated in the name of 'liberty in teaching,' and then excused in the name of 'academic freedom,'" James Frost exclaimed. He wished for "a vigorous conflict concerning the great doctrines" that would purge liberalism from the region's religious system. Responding to these criticisms, seminary professors assured their frightened constituency that modern methods of understanding the Bible only strengthened evangelical doctrines. As one New Testament scholar explained, "not all the criticism in the world can put Jesus back in the grave." Such reassurances rang hollow to those who felt the double assault of textual criticism and contemporary science on long-cherished tenets of the faith.[24]

Advocates of Landmarkism devoted themselves to enforcing Baptist sectarianism in the school. They won their greatest victory in 1899 when they forced out William H. Whitsitt, president of the institution from 1895 to 1898. Whitsitt's critics lambasted him for research published under a pseudonym in a northern theological review proving that Baptists had practiced immersion only since the early 1640s rather than since apostolic times, as Landmarkist doctrine held. Whitsitt's work fueled charges that heresy had slipped into Southern.[25] The forces opposed to Whitsitt, led by Thomas T. Eaton, a conservative minister and trustee of the seminary, broadcast the news of his disloyalty and bombarded faculty members with letters demanding his resignation. If Whitsitt failed to leave Louisville, wrote one Texas physician, then the "principles that Babtists [*sic*] have contended for during the past centuries will perish from the Earth." Pastors told the faculty that the "the Baptist backbone of the State . . . feel that Dr. Whitsitt has not acted in good faith." The question, several correspondents assured Eaton, "narrowed down to a difference between our city churches on the one hand and our town and country churches on the other." Whitsitt's critics praised Eaton for opposing the "aggressive liberalism" he represented. One correspondent asked a new professor at the seminary in 1897 if he taught his students the Whitsitt view of the recent origins of immersion. "If so," he continued, "you ought to be carried off in the fields somewhere and shot. That would save the trouble of draging [*sic*] you off."[26]

A respected member of the faculty, Whitsitt commanded strong support in the Southeast, especially in his home state of Virginia. Whitsitt himself confessed considerable sympathy with Landmarkist views earlier in his life but later broadened his theology as he came into contact with those of different persuasions. His backers argued that compromising with his opponents would only make them more aggressive in their attacks. But Whitsitt gradually lost their support as well. As a correspondent to the Virginia *Religious Herald* (a paper sympathetic to Whitsitt) explained, while free investigation of historical questions should be encouraged, Whitsitt had been indiscreet in his publications. B. H. Carroll, an influential denominational spokesman in Texas, decided that Whitsitt's removal would reassure "a vast host of good men now alienated" who were "as loyal to the Southern Baptist Convention unity as any who draw the breath of life." After a long series of maneuverings, Whitsitt resigned in 1899 and took a position at Richmond College.[27]

The Landmarkist victory was short-lived. Edgar Young Mullins, a native of Mississippi who studied in Louisville in the 1880s, assumed the presidency of the institution in 1899. With his appointment, there was "now not a smell of narrow and intolerant Landmarkism about the Seminary," a Virginia Baptist editor exclaimed. "We have won the fight. You will be able to utilize the victory in a nice way," exulted a nearby minister. In his tenure of three decades, Mullins raised a permanent endowment, oversaw the institution's move from downtown Louisville to a larger lot on the outskirts of the city, expanded the curriculum to include the study of missions and sociological topics, and initiated a program that trained women interested in religious social work. As he proclaimed in his inaugural address, the faculty adapted the seminary's program to the "needs of its entire constituency all over the South." The faculty reassured those concerned with heresy that they avoided propagating liberalism, "which seeks to . . . renounce the Biblical authority for a purely subjective conception of religious authority," while they also eschewed "ultra-conservatism," defined as the tendency to "ignore missions and the development of the spiritual life of our people." As a result, Mullins suggested, the SBC constituency maintained faith in the seminary, even while northern Christians lost confidence in their own theological institutions. Mullins explained what he believed to be two erroneous ideas of the ministry: "one that the minister should spend his force in trying to correct public evils; the other that the preacher of the gospel has nothing to do with public life whatever."[28]

Possessed of a greater sense of diplomacy than Whitsitt and thoroughly convinced of the righteousness of his "middle course" between extreme Baptist sectarianism and liberal theology, Mullins successfully deflected attacks against the seminary and its faculty. "You seem to me to be in position to soothe and quiet the excitable and intolerant men, to whom theological difference is occasion for unstopping the vials of wrath," the pastor of the Second Baptist Church in Richmond wrote to him. Mullins bridged the theological and social gaps between the ethic of professionalization taught at the school and the conservative rural constituency of the denomination. "We are progressive as well as conservative," he blithely announced. By 1907, Mullins could write to a candidate for a new post in religious sociology that there was now "greater freedom than there used to be" in the seminary's program, with "less attention . . . paid to the would-be mischief-makers." At the same time, he warned a colleague that the institution's critics, particularly the powerful faction of Fundamentalists in Kentucky, would "behave only so long as they feel they must. They would attack any of us at any time if they felt free to do it." He wearily noted, "We are subject to a persecution which has gone on through all the years." To the dismay of conservatives, Mullins permitted students to read "infidel" works under the guidance of professors, a practice, one correspondent charged, comparable to allowing "a child to have poison while near some wise and learned physician, who could give it an antidote." But the seminary's supporters remained confident that they would prevail in the "warfare for freedom among Southern Baptists."[29]

The notebooks and diaries of students indicate how professors drilled students in the southern evangelical faith. C. M. Thompson, a student in the mid-1890s, jotted down these notes from lectures he heard about the faults of contemporary northern divines: "Uncertain theology. Lack of deep and genuine experience of religion. Influence on preaching great and not altogether wholesome." Thompson's professor suggested an eclectic reading list for ministers, including everything from St. Augustine's *Confessions* to Mark Twain's *Innocents Abroad*. Yet his teacher added that, for the harried preacher unable to tackle the entire list, philosophical and scientific books could be omitted safely. Unceasing Bible study remained the only requirement. Baptist traditionalists worried far more than necessary about theological liberalism at the seminary.[30]

The seminary fostered the development of a professional ethos among its students. Its alumni contributed to the seminary magazine, raised money even from congregants suspicious of heresy at the school, and proudly talked of the camaraderie of the men with whom they communed while in Louisville. Mullins publicized examples of students who praised the rigid loyalty to biblical truth and denominational principles they absorbed at the school. One former student from the North wrote that in the theological institutions of his area he heard the Bible ridiculed, while in Louisville professors taught students to subject their "proud rationalism" to God's word. The seminary was not "cursed by any of this so-called New Theology," another alumnus announced. The faculty periodically fanned out to lead revival services, raising money for the school while also consciously exhibiting some old-time evangelical fire. Many of the professors supplemented their income by preaching at churches in the Louisville vicinity. The faculty also compiled a respectable list of publications, ranging from a textbook for the study of ancient Greek to numerous (if unoriginal) essays on the relationship of Christianity to modern problems.[31]

Conservatives, however, rightfully worried about the influence of nascent social gospelism in Louisville. Social gospel teachings at the seminary received a major boost from the appointment of Charles Spurgeon Gardner, who published significant works in the field of religious sociology. Professors in the early twentieth century, usually themselves graduates of the seminary, successfully encouraged modern conceptions of ministerial roles. W. J. McGlothlin, successor to the influential nineteenth-century scholar John Broadus as professor of homiletics, taught his students that while the minister's distinctive work was spiritual, it was also the obligation of clerics to encourage "better homes, adequate wages, reasonable hours; sanitary, safe, healthful working conditions; moral and healthful amusements, good schools, the prevention of contagious and infectious diseases, protection from the dangers of vice and other moral contaminants." Professors gradually added courses on the immediate issues of the pastor's life, denominational programs, and sociological concerns. "We are in no degree sacrificing scholarship," Mullins advised one correspondent, "but we are seeking at every point to vitalize our teaching, by living contact with the world as it is and conditions as they are." The seminary's newspaper, the *Baptist World*, spread social gospel notions institutionalized in the curriculum.[32]

Conservative critics of Southern were somewhat appeased with the opening of Southwestern Baptist Theological Seminary in 1908 in Ft. Worth, Texas. From its inception, Southwestern remained decidedly more conservative and sectarian than its brother seminary in Louisville. Its curriculum deemphasized the traditional subjects of nineteenth-century education—ancient languages, exegesis, and moral philosophy—and replaced them with practical courses in church management. Students learned of the practical techniques for church growth while also imbibing the "best Baptist orthodoxy, but that means a militant orthodoxy." Southeastern Baptists complained of a "Texas theology" in Ft. Worth that was "not of the most tolerant kind," but this was precisely what the founders of Southwestern had intended.[33]

Southwestern derived its financial support and attracted students mostly from areas outside the prime fund-raising and recruitment grounds for

Southern. Despite the fears of those who decried the liberalism of their seminaries, both schools steadfastly adhered to orthodoxy in doctrine. The happy medium that E. Y. Mullins sought for Southern—being "progressive as well as conservative"—defined itself within the provincial limits enforced by the southern evangelical constituency. When compared to other major theological institutions, southern Baptist seminaries appeared remarkably more conservative than progressive.

Faced with the overwhelming reality of racial slavery, antebellum southern evangelicals expressed far less optimism than their northern counterparts about the future of a Christian America. Southern doctrine and practice remained more oriented toward the private, to reforming individual behavior rather than overhauling the social order. Later in the nineteenth century, while liberal theological elites in the North moved away from evangelicalism into modernist theology and social gospel concerns, and while northern conservatives refined their Calvinist cosmologies and invented intellectual fundamentalism, the evangelical emphasis became the primary domain of popular revivalists. Dwight Moody, the Chicago-based interdenominational preacher who perfected the techniques of late-nineteenth-century urban revivalism, combined religious fervor with political quiescence, thus making the world safe for mass evangelism. His success demonstrated that evangelical Americans were receptive to the narratives of sentimental Victorianism, which discouraged stern admonition and encouraged the use of family metaphors to communicate the Gospel. The decline of terrifying visions of "hell" in revival preaching and elaborations of "heaven" as a place remarkably like an ideal middle-class home furthered this connection.[34]

Responding to these trends in the intellectual history of evangelicalism, southern Baptist ministers of the era moved away from the austere Calvinism widely accepted in the mid-nineteenth century to more optimistically evangelical attitudes. This popular evangelicalism better suited visions of a New South than the fulminations of the older exhorters. Southern Baptists in the early twentieth century increasingly assured congregants of a place in the bourgeois world. By implication, ministers proclaimed that they too should enjoy the security of a professional niche in the emerging social order.

The decline of classical Calvinism may be traced from 1870 to 1920 in the three most important theological works of southern Baptists. The first, James P. Boyce's *Abstract of Systematic Theology*, represented "old, straight, up-right, outright" southern Calvinism at its pinnacle of theoretical expression. This tome presented in stark form the rigidly outlined doctrines of

Soul compet ✗

election, predestination, and eternal damnation. In the early years of the Southern Seminary, students "inclined to Arminianism" were "brought up to the standard of Baptist orthodoxy" by Boyce's demanding schema.[35]

In the early twentieth century, E. Y. Mullins's *Axioms of Religion* and *The Christian Religion in Its Doctrinal Expression* signified the waning of Calvinism as a major force among SBC theologians. Influenced by William James's ✗ *The Varieties of Religious Experience*, Mullins insisted on thinking of religion as a "fact of experience" which merited close scrutiny. "We must rigidly insist that the data of the Spirit are really data," he explained. His theory of biblical inspiration allowed room for the "human powers of the divine messenger," since "man is not converted by the inspiration of the Almighty into anything akin to a mere mouthpiece or machine." Overemphasis on doctrinal teachings hindered true spiritual transformation. "We must not become ⁑ spiritual vivisectionists," he warned, "and kill the vital experience in the ⁂ process of unfolding the truth about it."[36]

Mullins's pamphlet-length contribution to *The Fundamentals*, the moderately phrased manifesto of the original Fundamentalist movement, showed his concern for defending the central tenets of evangelicalism and biblicism. He dismissed those who suggested that Christianity was an advanced form of a mystery cult, arguing that it was instead a "spiritual force which is as uniform and steady and reliable in the personal realm as is the power of gravitation in nature." Mullins warned off those "swept from the supernatural interpretation of Christianity by the modern spirit" from seeking pulpits in southern evangelical churches. "You would not find yourself in a hospitable atmosphere in the South," he informed one such northern-born ministerial prospective. By cultivating an image that was theologically solid but socially moderate and levelheaded, Mullins attracted national recognition to the seminary while warding off heresy hunters. Mullins's theology demonstrated that, even in an era of modernism, theological professionalism could be compatible with conservative evangelicalism. "Baptist belief and life dynamically stated appears much more biblical" than the previous orthodoxy of Christianity "as formulated and fixed and set down from Heaven for all time," an Alabama Baptist argued in defense of Mullins.[37]

SBC clergymen such as Mullins reshaped (and sometimes simply jettisoned) Calvinist doctrines from election to predestination to fit the pragmatic evangelicalism that characterized much popular theology in the nation. W. R. L. Smith, a denominational official in North Carolina, happily pronounced the death of the "stiff, cold, unworkable scheme" of Calvinism) and rejoiced in the "larger warmer conception of our Father which has come to us." Baptist spokesmen contrasted Calvinist rigidity with the Baptist emphasis on freedom of the spirit and "soul competency." The doctrine of predestination, once the object of endless theological skirmishing, no longer dominated pulpit polemics. As early as 1880, an Alabama minister scoffed at the idea that "God saves or damns men in the very act of creating them." In 1912, a longtime denominational worker suggested to his congregation that predestination simply meant that "somehow these little lives of ours are interwoven with God's eternal purposes," thus robbing the term of any specific power to define narrowly the elect. Ministers steered around the doctrine of election, another fundamental of Calvinism. God's selection of a few elect for reprieve from eternal damnation could not be squared with the equally fundamental tenet of the spiritual accountability of all men, they admitted, but such conflicts could be dismissed as beyond man's limited understanding.[38]

Urban southern clerics developed sermon styles and emphases that attracted the emerging middle class of southern cities who were sympathetic to moderate theologies and professionalized conceptions of ministerial practice. Denominational statisticians quantified growth in church attendance and financial contributions and used the information in determining appointments to SBC agencies. If pastors aided church growth by junking Calvinism in favor of a "warmer conception of our Father," then that justified practicing in individual congregations what seminarians had already systematized in theological discussions.[39]

Twentieth-century Fundamentalists excited their followers with dire predictions of the time of tribulation that would precede Christ's Second Coming, a doctrine known as premillennialism. Prominent southern Baptists, however, distrusted precise prophecies on the unfolding of the millennium. In part they feared opening up theological issues to a disputatious constituency only recently cooled from the fires of the Landmarkist debates. Southern believers "must not make imagination the interpreter" of scripture, the *Christian Index* warned. John Broadus argued that controversies over millennialism rested on "very doubtful interpretations of very obscure expressions." E. Y. Mullins held to this same view through his career, telling one correspondent in 1908 that the Scriptures did not "warrant assertions on this point." An Alabama Baptist minister questioned why men should "foolishly demand an explanation of things before the time? What if God conceals his purposes for a time to make them better known?" Baptist postmillennialists such as B. H. Carroll pictured God as a supreme arbiter of conflict, with churches in the future acting as heavenly courts on earth, adjudicating international strife. His views, if not typical of southern Baptist thinking, were a natural extension of the progressive idealism shared by many Protestant figures in the early twentieth century.[40]

Those who disapproved of the idea of popular evangelicalism argued that contemporary preachers inordinately stressed "human agency" and free will over the sovereignty of God. Exhorters in the Primitive Baptist congregations proclaimed the uselessness of "means" (including Sunday schools and missions work) to bring one to salvation and the awesome glories of the doctrine of predestination. Even well-established urban divines worried that contemporary sermonizing, as exemplified by Henry Ward Beecher in the North, threatened to become mere "lecturings on evolution and politics." Christianity was being assailed by science but more importantly was "being betrayed and stabbed from within," lamented one cleric. "Many of its professed followers are busy trying to undermine its foundations." Contemporary theology was "as old, at least, as the garden of Eden—the same old hissings of the serpent." Such jeremiads kept alive an older tradition of worldly pessimism and theological disputation.[41]

Most southern Baptist ministers, however, relegated primitivist Calvinism to the dustbin and delivered messages that appealed to the widest audience possible. They feared modernism but they modernized southern evangelicalism. In the early nineteenth century, when a belief in the Bible as God's literally inspired word was firmly entrenched among most Protestants, issues separating the denominations dominated religious polemicizing. This was the heyday of exclusivist theologies such as Landmarkism. In the early twentieth century, conservative Protestants felt most threatened, not by those with slightly differing readings of a few scriptural passages, but by secular scientific explanations of the natural world and literary forms of biblical analysis. Tolerance for religious modernism in southern pulpits, an Alabaman exclaimed, would "sow the seeds of moral poison in churches and communities." Liberal theology was a "freedom which means spiritual slavery to those who imbibe the evil teachings." Southern Baptist conservatism, by contrast, had "kept out dangerous doctrinal error which has crept into other sections, honey-combing the faith, weakening man's reverence for the Bible." Southern Baptists possessed "the kind of religion which, we believe, God wants given to the world," he concluded.[42]

Even northern evangelicals trained in the South appeared suspect simply because of their northern origins. Some of these prospective theological carpetbaggers wearied at the thought of the constant scrutiny they would endure in towns full of southern evangelical zealotry. "I love the Southern people, their hospitality, their religious enthusiasm, and their social ideals," one northern man wrote to a seminary professor. He made his preaching "constructive and positive" but still feared that "in the close contact of a small town" his few doctrinal differences would "inevitably come out; for I must be honest when pressed on my views." As a result, he declined an offer of the pulpit of a congregation in Georgetown, Kentucky. A young cleric from Illinois, after studying in Louisville, failed to secure a pulpit in the South despite his heartfelt desire to serve in the region. On some visits to southern churches he was "examined doctrinally half a dozen times," an experience that had "nearly destroyed" his "confidence in securing pastoral work among any southern people—much as I like them—for here a northern man is distrusted doctrinally simply because he is from the North." By contrast, a southern-born minister who preached in the North for five years wrote requesting information on southern pulpits. "You are so familiar with the religious atmosphere of New England, that my desire will seem natural enough no doubt. The missionary from the foreign field needs to tone up at home now and then," he wrote to Mullins.[43]

Rank-and-file ministers concerned themselves less with the evolution controversy or the difficult issues raised by textual criticism of the Bible than with the far more immediate issues affecting their daily lives. They filled their personal letters and diaries with concerns over pay, relations to their congregants, and the constant obligation to add new church members to their ministerial scorecard. But most importantly, they engaged in constant self-examination of pulpit performances and adjusted sermon technique and content to appeal to demanding congregants.

Jeremiah Jeter, a genteel Virginian, remembered the preaching styles of an earlier day with an attitude of mingled affection and embarrassment. Old-time sermons came from "an exuberant imagination" rather than from the "oracles of God," he recalled, but the messages often contained something of value: "Amid much that was puerile and disgusting, there was frequently mingled momentous truth." Preachers intoned their sermons and tried less to woo the unconverted than to "wound, overwhelm and bring into contempt their opponents." The sermons followed predictable, monotonous patterns:

> Most sermons contained an account of the conversions, conflicts, sorrows, and perplexities of a soul in its passage from death to life, somewhat after the manner of Christian in the Pilgrim's Progress. . . . Many sermons began with the fall of man, touched on the principal doctrines of revelation, gave a Christian experience, conducted him safely to heaven, and wound up with the resurrection of the dead, the general judgment, the retribution of eternity, and an application of the subject according as "light and liberty" were granted.

A longtime Texas minister recalled that the ministers in his early days of preaching were not broad-minded, "but their very narrowness made them mighty. Their concentrated convictions forged a terrible bolt which they launched against sin with deadly effect."[44]

Even elite clerics felt the call of traditional pulpit styles in their preparation. Before leading a public prayer for the Alabama secession convention, Basil Manly Sr. explained to his son that he could not "study the form and words of a prayer I am to offer; it seems like impiety and hypocrisy, as well as mere formalism." Jabez L. M. Curry, who would later become a conservative director of southern educational philanthropy, confessed that "at times I love to preach" and worried that "sacerdotal ideas connected with the ministry, or preaching have been productive of untold evil." Like Manly, he too cultivated a compelling pulpit performance that complemented his preparation as a gentleman-theologian. Even if the old Gospel was unpopular, one Virginia minister commented, it remained preferable to the "sugar-coated, dancing, theatre-going, card-playing, wine-drinking, society-worshipping religion of our day," which would "fill the world with infidelity" if left unchecked. F. M. Jordan, a self-taught minister in North Carolina, summed up his long career in the rhetoric of the antebellum exhorters: "For fifty years I have done nothing but preach salvation by grace through faith." Ministers of his day should do likewise, he suggested.[45]

Southern Baptist ministerial spokesmen at the turn of the century made occasional bows to such sentiments for an earlier style of evangelical oratory but moved firmly in the direction of respectable preaching. The modern sermon, as denominational leaders conceived it, would express an evangelistic spirit but be thoughtfully composed and calmly elocuted. "Fifty years ago the common sing song delivery of the preacher was all right with the masses of our people," wrote one prominent cleric in 1894, but these older styles were a "ludicrous failure" in his day: "As the people advance in intelligence there must be a corresponding advance in the preachers." W. J. McGlothlin urged his ministerial students to speak "of the vital, of the experimental, of life." Pastors should "not to try to preach great sermons" but instead use personal experiences to "become the vehicle of God's saving power," he advised.[46]

The ideal of pulpit manner not only appeared among the ranks of urban clerics but also reached rural churches. Denominational newspapers, widely read by countryside preachers, provided instructional tips on sermon organization and delivery. Southern and northern Baptists cooperated in creating informal institutes and workshops conducted by trained ministers that transmitted the ideals of professional demeanor to both white and black rank-and-file preachers in the late nineteenth century. For example, pastors flocked to institutes held at Mercer University for lectures on sermon preparation and delivery given by B. J. W. Graham, owner/editor of the Georgia denominational newspaper. Graham stressed the importance of preparing sermons that would "conform to the science of discourse." The gatherings, he believed, cemented relations between pastors of varied backgrounds and provided them with common standards for pulpit manner and sermon forms: "For thirty five years I have had fellowship with the brethren who studied with me in Bible institutes. In those meetings, we learned to believe in each other, to believe the same truths and to believe them in the same way." Preachers accustomed to improvised exhortation thus learned a uniform system for sermon preparation and delivery.[47]

Southern Baptist ministers in the late nineteenth century exerted much energy to control emotionalism in the pulpit. They worried less about "dead formalism" than about losing control of their physical self while preaching. A young Georgian in 1883 critiqued his pulpit performance one Sunday: "I preached too loud and was really boisterous. I do wish to be calm in my preaching and self possessed. I shall try from this [time] on to preach in a more conversational style." Preaching in 1895, William Owen Carver, who later became a respected seminary professor, expressed his disappointment that he "made a poor out of it. I was nervous, uneasy and unable to put myself in the Holy Spirit. . . . I am sometimes afraid I shall never be able to preach." The following year, before a funeral sermon he was to give for a man who was "moral and well respected" but also a liquor distiller, Carver prayed that God would enable him "to do and say what and only what is right and proper." John H. Spencer, a longtime minister in Kentucky, could never be satisfied with being a "mere revivalist." Rather, he "tried to indoctrinate every church I held a meeting with both in the theory of the plan of salvation and the practical duties of Christians." Lansing Burrows, who spent more than fifty years in the ministry, told the congregants at his final sermon that he taught "the plain orthodox obvious doctrines of our honored Baptist Fathers." But his neatly outlined sermons often lacked overt evangelical phraseology, stressing instead personal respectability, American patriotism, the proper uses of money, and other shibboleths of Gilded Age oratory. Clerics such as Burrows developed and disseminated the models for pulpit oratory that defined the norms (if not always the practice) for twentieth-century southern Baptist ministers.[48]

Proper pay and respect in their communities were two other key cornerstones to the professional model. The southern Baptist minister of the early nineteenth century, even if an untrained exhorter, was not necessarily lacking in pretensions of a conspicuously respectable life. When John Spencer, who lacked any theological education, entered the ministry in the 1850s, he knew that poverty would be part of his lot, but he was not reconciled to it: "A young man, constantly in society, as my calling forced me to be, wants to dress well, indulge in social luxuries and be liberal with money." This was impossible at a time when it was rare to "live off the gospel." He quickly learned to be frugal. Later he resigned his pastorate and resumed what he felt to be his true mission, itinerant evangelism. Spencer fought the temptation of choosing sites to preach according to his financial needs. He sought to avoid making "merchandise of the gospel or to impair my influence by seeming to do so." To finance his labors, he simply let worshipers know that he was dependent on them. Sometimes his wants were "amply supplied," most other times not.[49]

Preachers in the countryside measured professional status as much by regular pay, in cash or in kind, as by knowledge of ancient Hebrew. But even those who were successful by this standard experienced frustration. The destitution of common folk in the postwar South largely explains the strapped finances of clergymen in the 1870s and 1880s. In the immediate postwar years, even larger churches were reduced to promising their pastors payment such as twelve barrels of corn for the year, as was the case for the Wake Forest Baptist Church in North Carolina. A Georgia minister in 1867 wrote in despair that he knew of only two preachers in the state "whose wants are amply supplied by their flock." Pastors with families to support generally pursued other work to supplement their income. A Texas association in those years reported that two of every three churches in the Austin area were without preachers. "While we believe it to be the duty of ministers, with other citizens, to make sacrifices while we are struggling for our independence, yet they must make a living," this Texas association acknowledged during the Civil War. Missionaries didn't establish new churches because they could see no possibility of providing them with preachers. "It is greatly to be regretted that so many of the ministry have been compelled to resort to secular pursuits in order to secure their daily bread and save their families from suffering and starvation," a missionary observed in 1868. In Alabama, one cleric reported, pastors were "suffering for necessary wholesome food for themselves and family. Their churches cannot feed them and keep them in health." Ministers throughout the region left their congregations because their salaries were not paid.[50]

Thousands of congregations, especially those in frontier areas, simply felt that they should not have to "pay for preaching." Ebenezer L. Compere, a home missionary in Arkansas, recounted the number of ministers who wrote to him looking for promising pulpits in the growing state. Compere warned away such applicants: "Brethren wish to know if there are churches here that will support them. We say to you positively *there are none*. This is a frontier people, unused to 'paying for preaching,' and our little churches are composed largely of little babes and children in Christ. They have not yet been trained to giving. Their preachers have been too fearful lest they should 'hinder the gospel.'" Preachers who asked for a "stipulated salary were often ridiculed even in public assemblies," a self-educated minister in Missouri recalled of his work in the Reconstruction era. Those opposed to paying clerics "swayed the popular mind, and the ordinary country pastor had to suffer the evil consequences of it." This cleric routinely made between $35 and $70 a year for his pastoral work after the Civil War.[51]

Even in more established areas than Arkansas or Missouri, ministerial pay remained a touchy issue. George Blount provides a good example of the difficulties with which clerics of the era contended. As a pastor and home missionary in Georgia in the 1870s, Blount often selected locales for his preaching where he thought he might receive some pay. His monetary expectations were hardly extravagant: "The Lord has provided for me most graciously, in the things of this life, I have not been without something to eat in the house, since I commenced to preach [though] the food has sometimes been of the humblest kind," he wrote in his diary in 1875. Still, Blount expected that a dedicated clergyman such as himself should receive more than a mere miserly subsistence. Lacking the means appropriate to his station, he felt he could not fulfill the role of a professional pastor. His wife, for example, avoided the streets of their Georgia town because of her shabby dresses, and Blount's own personal appearance was an embarrassment: "My hair has grown so long that I look wild, the food we eat is not paid for, and what we have is the very plainest." His church promised $25 a month, but that March he collected only $.75. Blount also received nothing from the Home Mission Board of the SBC, technically his employer, because it was nearly defunct. Blount's poverty was such that he feared the "better clan of people" in his church would no longer associate with him. He avoided social interaction with the "poor and vicious folk" in his pews, thinking that they "might be the cause of ruining my character." Yet they were part of his flock and he felt obligated to tend to their spiritual needs. Blount's desire to make ministering a professional career was also frustrated by his congregants' penuriousness, but his pretensions to a better status remained strong.[52]

 The difficulties pastors experienced in persuading congregants to provide them with adequate recompense in later decades suggests even more strongly the resistance of congregations to the professionalization of the pulpit. Southern Baptist laypeople usually eked out modest livings at best. In the late nineteenth century, white farmers who tilled small acreages of soil scrambled to retain their holdings, an effort that often proved fruitless in the face of declining cotton prices and exorbitant interest rates. The attraction of work in cotton mills drew many away from farms and toward growing mill villages. In this economic context, conflict between ministers

Pay

who expected regular pay and social respect and laypeople who held deep economic resentments was inevitable. One pastor in North Carolina, who preached in a growing mill village, had attended seminary in Louisville for one year in the 1890s and left because of typhoid. He wanted to return and complete his studies but found it "a hard matter to save any money ahead with which to go." Salaries for ministers were meager, and he sensed a widespread "feeling among the churches that pastors are overpaid." Church records document the difficulties congregations faced in collecting the salaries promised to their spiritual leaders. Many churches decided on the preacher's salary early in the year, failed to meet the obligation, and scrambled later in the year to meet the deficiency. Churches canvassed the members to raise their promised amounts, but this exacerbated economic antagonism.[53]

Despite these obstacles, men of the pulpit increasingly insisted on, and sometimes received, prompt and adequate pay from their congregants. When they could not get it, they changed churches, accepted other positions (especially schoolteaching), or deliberately reduced their work. Recognizing these eventualities, congregations increased their efforts to come up with adequate salaries. The First Baptist Church of Huntsville, Alabama, for example, appointed a Ladies Aid Society in 1879 to help raise the $1,100 it promised to pay its full-time pastor. For years afterward the women raised over half of the pastor's pay, a remarkable achievement for a congregation whose church building was destroyed during the war. A Kentucky church offered William Owen Carver, a recent seminary graduate, use of a parsonage and a substantial salary of $1,200 for the year. But Carver declined the offer, citing the fact that the church rolls included "four members engaged in the whisky business who cannot be moved or removed." In earlier years, Carver probably would not have had such an option.[54]

By the turn of the century, white ministers in the countryside made it clear that economic security would be a component of their professional status, particularly if they had some training. The Clear Creek Baptist Church in northern Mississippi called for a pastor in May 1891. One agreed to preach once each month only if the congregants paid him $126 until Christmas, covered his traveling expenses each trip, and collected extra offerings during revival season. In response, church members indicated secretly how much they would "agree to pay the pastor who might be elected." Candidates for the pulpit learned to negotiate the terms of their yearly preaching stints from congregants who previously condemned "hireling preachers." Public disparagement of money-grubbing ministers eventually diminished as carefully planned church budgets incorporated salary obligations. A pastor in one small congregation in North Carolina boasted in 1906 that he never "had a word to say to the church concerning salary; the

deacons attend to that. In other words, it is the best small church I know of."
Hight C. Moore, who was "licensed" to preach at seventeen (which simply
involved a paper testimony from his church of his good character and desire
to exhort), recalled that his devout grandmother "never wanted to hear of
me preaching for money." But after he earned his degree from Wake Forest
College and taught school, this rural North Carolinian accepted an offer
from a congregation that promised him $500 a year. He pastored in a series
of successively larger churches, eventually taking in $1,500 a year while also
producing a corpus of denominational literature. Moore was one of the
thousands of youths who found in the ministry an avenue into the respectable middle class.[55]

Ministerial salaries were one of a number of contentious issues that
distanced pastors with professional orientations from congregations with
deeply imbedded customs. The practice of the annual call created another
barrier. Church members voted each year on whether to retain their pastors
or call another. The annual call served as a kind of electoral check. Most
pastors served two to three years in their monthly preaching posts. Urban
pastors' tenures were somewhat more stable, but even those were remarkably short on average. Many ministers voluntarily left churches because of
disputes over salaries, and congregations often exercised opportunities to
remove men who angered local members. Ministers complained of repeatedly leading congregations where they lacked the intimate knowledge of individuals and communities necessary to their job. Denominational officials
likened the annual call to tenantry—an unequal contractual relation that
allowed for no plans of steady improvement to a larger goal. Urban churches
gradually granted a more flexible tenure, but about three-quarters of rural
congregations retained the yearly plebiscite. It served as the ultimate guar-
antor of congregational authority, the foundation of Baptist democracy.[56]

Denominational officials insisted that annual calls blocked the development of professional pastoral authority and the cultivation of proper pulpit
manner. The constant traveling of ministers necessitated by their part-time
status "frequently wore the preachers out," critics argued. Congregational
control over pulpit posts too often punished those who pursued the "sober
work" of the pastorate while rewarding those who practiced "spasmodic
popular preaching." Rather than thinking of their pastor as a "spiritual
guide and overseer," religious folk instead demanded an itinerant showman,
"a man hired to entertain the congregation with rhetorical flourishes, and
bursts of declamation," wrote one minister.[57] When the wishes of the congregation collided with clerical directives, moreover, local divines grew
frustrated at the tenuousness of their status. When churches were split over
controversial matters, preachers were "too much afraid of hurting some

one's feeling to preach the Gospel with force and feeling," a Texas minister charged. "The old guard in nearly all of our churches must be constantly coddled," explained another Texan, "and the pastor is the official coddler. His life is harassed out of him by meetings innumerable, conferences, committee gatherings, church suppers, bazaars, dinners, pink teas, and old ladies embroidery clubs." He thought of congregational authority as tantamount to "ecclesiastical anarchy." Doctrinal differences also highlighted the relative powerlessness of pastors. "I myself believe in church sovereignty," one Arkansas cleric fumed, "but I do not believe that a majority vote of a church or anything else takes precedence over God's precious word."[58]

While the professional ideal of the ministry advanced to an impressive degree throughout the region, it often met determined resistance in the democratic workings of local congregations. Many ministers learned the same lesson as did J. L. Johnson, who pastored churches and helped to author Jim Crow laws in Mississippi. Johnson's last tussle with his congregants generated such ill feelings that he left permanent pastoring altogether and took to the road as a traveling evangelist. To retain his "independence of thought," he discovered, he had to escape the confines of the local pulpit, where the necessity of pleasing congregants stifled "freedom of utterance." When ministers spoke out on social issues, they risked alienating vested interests in the community. In Kentucky in the early twentieth century, night riders and lawlessness disrupted life in urban areas. During this period, one minister who preached at the funeral of a black man beaten to death by a mob put the "lessons of the hour calmly enforced and plainly applied." As a result, the "politicians and Elks went wild and pressed fairly against me by all sorts of lies," with the leaders being "democratic politicians and Elks in our church." He soon thereafter resigned his pastorate.[59]

The evolving daily interactions of pastors and congregants suggested the spread of the clergy's demands for professional respect not only in terms of salary requirements but also through expectations for social deference. Remembering her girlhood in the rural South, one woman recalled the stuffy preachers who ate at her house, men who knew themselves to be superior to mere exhorters. They "expected to be fed. They thought they needed better." She reminded her interviewer that ministers were "just servants of God, that's all. But they did eat at our house a lot." The ubiquitous regional folklore of the chicken-eating preacher suggests that the plain folk in the pews could interpret behavior demanding professional respect as little more than personal pretension. A professor in Louisville in the 1890s warned ministerial candidates of the perils awaiting them: "In the first charitable glow of the young preacher's heart he is apt to drive suspicion away and to put his faith in all men. He is deceived alas! too often and this experience tends toward misanthropy. . . . Among some people, whether justly or unjustly, the stupidity of the preacher has grown into a proverb." The zeal characteristic of young clerics, he suggested, was often "not born of holy desire—it is carnal and worldly, and its ultimate result cannot be other than degrading and disastrous."[60]

Ministers with substantial educations sought to bridge the gap between themselves and their communities. If they failed to do so, their tenures could be short and unpleasant, but if successful they could become widely respected figures. After completing seminary work, Edgar Young Mullins searched for his proper role among his ill-educated congregants. The "alienation of pastor from people," he wrote to a friend, inevitably resulted from their "dwelling apart in the matter of intellectual tastes." These distinctions would inevitably remain visible, for any "self-contraction" on the part of the minister represented a form of "self-abnegation." He felt the necessity of "popularizing my conception and treatment of the text" in his sermons but strived to be a "man of books and a man of the people both." Yet his own experience exemplified the difficulty many educated clerics had in achieving this ideal. His "exceedingly hospitable" Kentucky congregants loved "to entertain and *feed* above all things. If I would permit myself to do it I could spend my whole time in social intercourse with the members of my church." However, this would have required forsaking his books, a calling he deemed more important than socializing.[61]

Even congregants separated in intellectual tastes from the minister still considered it his pastoral duty to engage in frequent and hearty visitation. Families were proud, as one minister remembered of his boyhood, that they had a "familiar" connection with their pastor at home and were easily offended by aloof clerics. Pastors likewise took pride in their familiar connection with local residents. "How can it be expected, if the minister is a man of God, that he should be satisfied with doing nothing more than preaching the Gospel," asked the *South Carolina Baptist*. It advised pastors to follow a course chosen by W. T. Tardy, a longtime cleric in Texas, who felt compelled not only to preach to his particular congregants but also to "project" himself into the lives "of everyone within the bounds of my diocese."[62]

Specialized training, regular pay sufficient to support middle-class needs, and carefully regulated personal and social decorum all helped to define the norms of moral professionalism. All of these elements drew from conceptions of bourgeois occupations but took on special meanings in a region still dominated by racial obsessions, staple-crop economies, and a culture of localism. The ideal of manliness emerging among middle-class southerners from the 1890s to the 1920s, particularly the emphasis on competence and self-possession in public, provided a gendered language that also shaped the emergence of moral professionalism in the ministry.

Evangelicals defined manliness as self-control. Benjamin Riley, a Baptist minister and educator in Alabama, described the proper public behavior of the ministerial professional: "Humility and self-assertion, courage blended with gentleness, having strong convictions, and yet regardful of the opinions of others, this gives in symmetrical shape the character of ministerial manliness. . . . His bearing is that of a respectful gentleman always, coupled with a consciousness of his true manhood." Riley contrasted these characteristics with those of the "ecclesiastical brawlers" of the early nineteenth century, the demagogues who excited frontier people with wild sectarian polemics. The religious hysteria of camp-meeting exhorters, once the very essence of evangelical fervor, now symbolized a loss of self-control.[63]

In the Progressive Era, a time of redefining conceptions of masculinity and femininity, evangelicals across the nation decried the "feminization" of religion and linked evangelical virtues with middle-class manly honor. As one minister explained, "preaching is a man's game and he who successfully preaches must be a man." Liberal northern ministers were "disgustingly effeminate"; they turned "serious people away from the church." By contrast, "a church should be like a well disciplined army," explained a southern Baptist in Mississippi. "Every member should have his place in the ranks, know what to do, and be ready to do it, whenever called upon." Any pastor who refused to lead congregants "ought to stand in the army of Christ as a disobedient officer stands in a well regulated army." Denominational modernizers carefully defined how rural pastors would meet this emerging definition of manhood. The rural minister provided the key to unlock the door to the newly awakened church: "It is he who must not only preach the doctrines of self-development and neighborliness, but must also, in his daily intercourse with his members and with others, unveil before them the possibilities of community development, link them onto governmental information and agencies, and, by his example, inspire and unite them in cooperation for better things." Pious yet practical, full of spiritual homilies and agrarian wisdom, equally at ease with biblical injunctions and the latest in agricultural techniques, the figure of the manly minister seemed the ideal synthesis of nineteenth-century evangelicalism and twentieth-century social Christianity.[64]

The professionalization of the southern Baptist ministry advanced further than scholars have realized but less so than denominational leaders envisioned. The process was limited by both the lack of a secure white-collar niche in southern society and the hesitancy of many congregations in accepting the demise of rural evangelicalism. But it is significant that preachers expressed dismay at their lack of training and acquitted themselves as professional men despite their inability to meet the educational and salary requirements for such a claim. Just as significant, many congregations throughout the region remained unconvinced that clerical professionalism represented a higher spirituality than the practice of impassioned exhortation.

CHAPTER SIX

Intriguers and Idealists

Black Southern Baptist Ministers, 1870–1925

Then, brethren, let us preach
Christianity and not Anglo-Saxon
civilization.—W. B. Johnson,
National Baptist Magazine,
July 1894

From the Civil War to the 1920s, southern Baptist ministers, white and black, were mostly bivocational men of limited educations who occupied quarter- or half-time pulpits for low pay. Rank-and-file preachers traveled to different churches on successive weekends, generally exiting pulpits every two to three years. Ministers sought to find paying pulpits, develop reputations as orators, and establish themselves in local communities. They tread carefully in relations with their congregations and acquired as many of the accoutrements of a middle-class pastoral life as possible.

Like their white counterparts, African American Baptists sought to replace untrained exhorters in part-time preaching stints with professionally self-conscious clergymen in stable pulpit positions who would practice an acculturated worship and teach the values of the "better classes." Black ministers were charged with the task of providing moral uplift and race leadership for the congregants. They maneuvered uncomfortably between white society and the common black folk and faced the impossible task of pleasing both.[1]

In the twentieth century, the cultural authority vested in the ministry came under severe challenge. Itinerant exhorters were increasingly marginalized by a new class of relatively educated clerics. The growth of secular institutions such as the National Association for the Advancement of Colored People partially displaced the central role of ministerial leadership, as did new ideologies of protest that scorned faith in improvement as a panacea. Just as important, innovative cultural forms (such as the blues and Holiness spirituality) competed for the attention of men and women dissatisfied with the pieties offered by the mainstream denominational preachers.

Because of their relatively cautious position, black Baptist ministers and their organizations came under attack for being complicit with the Jim Crow establishment. The accusation stung. Impoverished as many of them were, ministers still enjoyed a place of relative prestige in black life. Clerical leaders condemned the injustices perpetrated by white America, but they trusted in self-help and uplift for race advancement. When the faith in improvement failed to deliver, its major proponents, the preachers, were vulnerable to the attacks of the disillusioned. Ministers were easy targets: the authority granted them in African American culture was diminished in light of the powerlessness of black people in Jim Crow America. But the spiritual hope offered up by the preachers sustained millions of men and women whose spirit might have been broken by the relentless racism of American life.

In a survey conducted in 1903, Henry L. Morehouse, executive secretary of the American Baptist Home Mission Society (ABHMS), counted some ten thousand ordained black ministers for twelve thousand churches of just under two million members. Thousands of other licentiates and informal exhorters as well as ordained but unemployed ministers filled the ranks of those who felt the call. Only about one thousand clergymen preached every Sunday. Fifteen of these ten thousand received $1,500 or more annually for their preaching, one hundred of them netted about $1,000 each, while approximately fifteen hundred received $500 to $700. Most preachers received $200 to $400 a year. Most of the exhorting, Morehouse reported, was "emotional, hortatory, imaginative, visionary, . . . the close of the sermon being delivered with powerful intonations and gesticulations to arouse the audience to a high pitch of excitement." Educated clerics shied away from the countryside, where they enjoyed few "congenial intellectual associations" and where, "in accommodation to the tastes of the people," they were required to "descend, more or less, to the old style of preaching."[2]

Studies conducted by twentieth-century academic researchers demonstrate how stable this picture of the ministry remained through the century. According to their findings, most pastors were older men embarrassed by their lack of education, defensive in personal manner, careful not to reveal their income, and ambivalent about what benefits would derive from training. They were in a nether land between being informal exhorters and professional divines. Since frays with congregants or local whites could endanger their positions, most preachers shunned controversy and stuck to time honored and racially neutral themes of evangelicalism. Laypeople (especially boards of church deacons) much more than pastors controlled church decisions. The dearth of opportunities for ambitious men in other fields created an oversupply of applicants for pulpit openings, hampering efforts to raise meager wages. The one southern theological institution for training the black Baptist ministry, the American Baptist Theological Seminary in Nashville, was small, underfunded, and conflicted by its place in a region that had never come to terms with black higher education. Preachers who sought professional status were caught between anachronistic customs and professionalized standards that were usually impossible to realize.[3]

The demands placed on black ministers were extraordinary given their limited training, low pay, and lack of real authority beyond the power of exhortation. And given these limitations, the achievement of the clergy was also extraordinary. Their human frailties, satirized in folklore and song, were apparent precisely because they were under intense public scrutiny. W. E. B. Du Bois depicted the black preacher as "a leader, a politician, an orator, a 'boss,' an intriguer, an idealist." In his book *The Souls of Black Folk*, Du Bois generously assessed the minister's success in filling these varied roles: "The combination of a certain adroitness with deep-seated earnestness, of tact with consummate ability, gave him his preeminence, and helps him maintain it." They were of the people but set apart from congregants by their special social role. "Us preachers has to be careful 'bout where we goes and what we does. We's held up as shinin' lights for sinners to go by," a Georgia minister concluded. Men of the cloth were expected to "stand for the people in nearly every avenue of life," denominational leaders acknowledged. The black cleric, wrote another observer, was required to know "the best remedy for teething infants" and serve as a "horse doctor, ever the prophet, must attend the living, bury the dead, tell the farmers when to plant, [and] act as bondsman for his people."[4]

Ministers expected to receive their divine summons to preach in dramatic fashion, and congregants reinforced the custom of emotive calls. For example in South Carolina Thomas Dixon entered the ministry in 1886, when an earthquake in Charleston "drove many sinners to their knees." He recollected: "I resolved to be a soldier of the cross and ever since I have carried the shield of faith in my left hand and the sword of the Word in my right hand." George Briggs, a longtime preacher in South Carolina, never achieved literacy but still felt a yearning for the pulpit. "It's de Spirit of de One in Three dat gits into you, and dat's de Holy Ghose or de Holy Spirit dat gives me my enlightenment," he explained. A former doctor in Arkansas who attended Meharry Medical College and entered the ministry in 1900 told of the "deep call" that compelled him to acknowledge that he "was a real preacher and not a real doctor."[5]

Young men conscious of their social and oratorical skills considered themselves naturals for pastoral work. As Isaiah Norwood, a retired Texas minister, told his interviewer, "early in life I got to doin' Baptist missionary work, and I [liked] dat. Dis allowed me to git around and visit de folks." He had given up preaching because of his age but knew that "dat's all right 'cause I still got de spirit in me." James Smith was a farmer in Texas from the end of the Civil War until 1895. After learning to read and studying the Bible he realized that "I's a natural talker, an' gifted fo' de Lawd's wo'k, so I's started preachin'." After many years of vigorous exhortation, he retired: "W'en I's preach, I's preach hahd, an' de doctah says dat am dangah fo' me to do so."[6]

Congregations and associations tested prospective ministers for proof of their divine call. Gillfield Baptist Church in Petersburg, one of the first independent black Baptist congregations in America, brought young ex-horters before an examining council, usually testing erstwhile preachers several times before ordaining them. Licensing boards expected the candidates to demonstrate their command of the oral biblical tradition while a dozen or more older men tried to fluster them. Independent exhorters in the countryside were summoned to the church and required either to provide their credentials or cease their work. One such member used his spiritual freedom to exhort "in years gon by" but told a disapproving church council in 1868 that he "had not bin Preaching" but just calling meetings together. The council rebuked him for trespassing on pastoral authority. Urban congregations such as Gillfield increasingly relied on ministers drawn from the ranks of those educated in mission colleges.[7]

Informal congregational councils remained the most common method of licensing and ordination, allowing for freelancing exhorters to shop around for credentialing. Churches and associations condemned "the actions of such so-called ministers, who go through the country ordaining men to preach the gospel without knowing anything of their character, fitness, etc." These organizations were responding to embarrassments such as the credentialing of one self-styled preacher who, despite being excluded from his Savannah congregation, repeatedly presented himself before an associational board for ordination, finally getting his certificate from a sister church. Instances of this kind of informal licensing were legion. When Charley White, an unlettered Texas farmer, wanted to preach, he built his own church on a farm, conducted Sunday schools there, and asked local Baptist ministers for a license. Impressed with his command of the oratorical tradition, the council ordained him on the spot. "I guess I just like to preach. I always felt better when I was on good terms with God, and when I was preaching seemed like him and me hit off awful well," he later commented. The prevalence of men like White ensured that skill in exhortation as much as educational background would determine ordination decisions.[8]

Pastors of large congregations were understood to be community spokesmen. Thus, the larger the church, the more momentous the selection of the minister—and the more difficult. The selection of the pastor at Springfield Baptist Church in Augusta, Georgia, in 1885 provides a case in point. The congregation first raised one man's name and then rejected him. A second candidate lost out by one vote. A third candidate was elected, but the congregation rescinded the call because of reports of his intoxication. He appealed to the church for forgiveness and reconsideration, but after considerable debate, the congregation removed his name permanently from contention. The church trustees took over the electoral responsibilities but also could not agree on a candidate. Finally, the congregation settled on Charles T. Walker, a minister soon dubbed the "Black Spurgeon" for his fervid oratory. Disagreement remained on whether to extend to him an indefinite call or hire him for one-year terms. The whole tortuous process revealed the unstructured roles of pastors, deacons, and trustees in running church affairs. They agreed in 1886 to "meet in Council and define their duties."[9]

Lengthy and delicate searches continued to characterize pulpit selection procedures in the twentieth century. The *National Baptist Union-Review*, a denominational publication, fielded numerous inquiries for preachers to fill empty pulpits. Churches specified in exacting detail the necessary personal and professional qualifications for their posts. One congregation in 1919 advertised for "an educated man, married, without children, light complexion, tall in stature, neat in appearance, one who will be satisfied with $50 a month." Emmanuel K. Love, the powerful pastor of First African Baptist Church in Savannah, explained why a call to a pulpit should be unanimous. Churches expected ministers to "gather the congregation, do the preaching, do the praying, do the singing, lead the prayer meetings, teach Sunday School, make the people do right, and keep the spirit in the church," he wrote. Demonstrating his conception of the patriarchal role of the urban cleric, Love demanded that the congregants officially pledge to honor and obey him before he would take up his post.[10]

Black ministers and their parishioners constantly negotiated the rules governing their relations. They interacted in ways akin to the complex, two-sided norms that define and limit the roles of democratically elected politicians. In larger urban churches, clerics developed powerful bases of support and ruled their congregations firmly. W. J. Campbell was one such example.

In the 1870s, he firmly directed his Savannah congregation of approximately four thousand members. "His people would do just what he told them to do. When he spoke it was law," his successor in that pulpit recollected. Skilled at raising hymns, organizing missionary work among blacks in the low country, and bringing recalcitrant members to heel, Campbell enjoyed a wide popularity and was paid handsomely. Though eventually ousted from the pulpit in an ugly controversy, Campbell left his mark through an authoritarian style.

Successful clerics assumed key roles as community spokesmen and expected salaries commensurate with their status. For example, the Reverend James Marshall of South Carolina, a powerful rural clergyman, received $800 per year from his four churches in the late nineteenth century. He was probably the best-paid rural minister in his state. Benjamin Mays, once a parishioner of Marshall's, remembered the "rare privilege" of having the pastor "spend the night in one's home. The house was spic and span when the preacher came, and the best food was served. He was the only hero we had around Zion to worship."[11] Most preachers, however, received small recompense from churchgoers. Those who pursued a full-time ministerial and teaching career without other means of remuneration guaranteed themselves poverty. A missionary for the National Baptist Convention indicted rural Alabamans for their view that after they gave their contributions to the church "the preacher must go and cut boxes or work at the mills as they do." One Virginia minister and teacher reported back to his alma mater that since leaving Hampton in 1874 he had worked for "the upbuilding of my people." In fact, he preached at three churches, taught school, and worked as a carpenter. His experience typified the struggles of bivocational ministers of this generation:

> All of these points had to be promptly met and are in a very mountainous country. It is traveled on foot. After the close of my school on the 11th, I preached on Sunday, after walking about fifteen miles on Saturday, and then walked six miles and preached on Sunday night, and on Monday morning I went to Rocky Mount at Franklin Court House, and back Tuesday, the distance of sixteen miles. And after all, I got no money. The treasurer told me he had no money, and had not finished paying for the year '77.

A rural Floridian informed Harriet Beecher Stowe in the late 1870s that "for a long time yet, in the country, the *preacher* must be only an educated farmer."[12]

The tradition of the bivocational ministry continued into the twentieth century. In established associations in North Carolina, for example, salaries before World War I—even for fairly substantial congregations of two hundred to five hundred predominantly female members—ranged from $180 to $420 a year. In Brunswick County, Virginia, according to a study conducted in the 1920s, the average minister received $193 yearly per church, and his income averaged less than $400 annually. In this county of nineteen Baptist churches, twelve congregations reported nonresident ministers who manned the pulpit once or twice a month. In the entire state, just sixty-nine rural churches owned or rented parsonages, an important in-kind contribution to pastoral support. A longtime minister and former mail carrier in Georgia found that his church members wanted him "just to preach for 'em and visit 'round 'mongst the disabled members." But he had to "work out 'cause I had a family to look out for and my chillen was in school. . . . I just had to keep on the job every day and preach on Sunday."[13]

Clergymen who retained strong bases of support or developed reputations as effective orators or educated men demanded more pay and social respect. Educated ministers could attach themselves to northern (and, occasionally, southern) missionary societies, increasing their opportunities for steady salaries. Missionaries employed jointly by white and black Baptist conventions in the late nineteenth century, for example, supplemented their regular ministerial pay with between $200 and $400 annually for the denominational services. In individual congregations, ministers sponsored raffles, organized excursions to local towns for entertainment, and raised two or three collections during services while announcing the names and exact amounts of generous contributors. Pastors of larger churches divided their congregations into clubs who vied with each other in fund-raising events. The competitions organized by the Reverend Emmanuel K. Love in Savannah raised sufficient funds to refurbish the historic sanctuary and sponsor a celebration for the one hundredth anniversary of the First African Baptist Church. Love "did not mean to beg out of Savannah, nor to beg a single church in the city" for centennial celebration funds, and he fulfilled his promise.[14]

Preachers with talent and charisma could also wield immense authority in local communities, leading to the charge that the black Baptist polity tolerated and encouraged "one-man rule." As a black denominational writer noted disapprovingly, "every Baptist minister is a law unto himself. His actions are not reviewable by a higher authority." Except for the workings of public opinion, this critic concluded, there was no way to "disrobe him if his conduct is unbecoming." Many preachers were not shy about using their power. Alexander Bettis, a longtime pastor in postbellum South Carolina, ordered those who disrupted services to be seized, and "with his buggy whip he would then and there inflict a whipping wholly commensurate with *responsibilities — Power*

the offense." James Marshall, a colleague of Bettis's, forcibly stopped the "fighting and heaving drinking on church property" common elsewhere in his county. Ministers freely quizzed employers for personal information on the congregants and disciplined those reported to have engaged in disreputable activity. Embattled pulpiteers seeking to preserve their posts sometimes refused to issue letters of recommendation to congregants who wanted to join another Baptist congregation. Other untenured clerics used disciplinary proceedings to oust those likely to lead campaigns in favor of dismissing them. The influence of the nineteenth-century folk preacher was "almost boundless," an *Atlantic Monthly* correspondent wrote in 1883. "Excommunication is his most trenchant weapon." The minister's powers of "censorship of the morals and deportment of his flock" were great, an influence generally "exerted to make [congregants] honest and faithful men and women."[15]

But to term the authority of the folk preacher "boundless" is to ignore the restrictions imposed by the congregationalist polity of the Baptist tradition. Church disciplinary proceedings, for example, evidenced clerical control but just as often demonstrated the autonomy of deacons or congregants from pastoral dictates. Ministers faced the task of disciplining wayward congregants while not alienating important members as a result. The pastor of the Gillfield Baptist Church in Petersburg, Virginia, for example, condemned congregants in his church in 1868 for attending a local fairgrounds on a Sunday evening. The admonishment soon became a "much talked of matter." Dissatisfied members who complained to the pastor and deacons about the restrictions against Sunday excursions were asked to repent. Some did but others refused. One of the accused announced that he had not done "anything Rong, in what he had said or don in the wole matter that he Had Said the Pastor and Deacons had no Right to make Laws for the Church." Another recalcitrant member brought to task for allegedly castigating the deacons as "masters of the church" denied the accusation but pointedly added that "it looked so much like mastering when he had to go to them for the privilege of his daughters marriage in the church." Disturbed by the constant disagreements over disciplinary action, the Virginia congregation entertained ideas "for the more becoming manor of dealing with certain delecate cases that may claim the church's attention." But the church rejected as "foreign to Baptist usages" a proposal calling for a council of deacons to hear cases. As a result, the congregation as a whole, acting under the authority of the minister, retained disciplinary powers, apparently willing to countenance the messy situations that arose from the encounters.[16]

At the Springfield Baptist Church in Augusta, questions over dances and circuses sparked similar controversies. In 1887, the church resolved that those attending "balls or any place of dancing shall be excluded from the church even if they ask the forgiveness of the church. Said members to be dealt with the same as <u>drunkenness and adultery</u>." But one member ordered to answer to the church for <u>circus attendance</u> told the deacons "that the church had no claims whatever upon him, and that he did not intend to obey the summons." In the early twentieth century, the church relaxed this restriction, reprimanding rather than expelling those who attended circuses or danced, but its disciplinary hand remained firm.[17]

Tension between pastors, deacons, and parishioners <u>split many churches.</u> Congregations in larger urban areas usually appointed a trustee board to oversee property matters and entrusted deacons with supervising disciplinary proceedings and pastoral selection committees. In the First Bryan Baptist Church in Savannah, a <u>deacon named Alexander Harris</u>, whose "highly intelligent mind and indomitable will gave him the leading place in the affairs of the church," took control of the congregation as if he were pastor. The other deacons licensed him to preach, hoping to encourage him to exercise his ambitions elsewhere. Failing in this attempt, they rescinded his license and restored him to his deaconship. Because the pastor, James Simms, was often away attending to political matters during Reconstruction, Harris succeeded in installing himself as the minister, compelling Simms to organize another congregation from blacks who withdrew from a white congregation in <u>Liberty County, Georgia</u>. Eventually the congregation removed Harris, but he retaliated by calling on the police one Sunday to arrest Simms. A disorderly scene ensued, but Simms was later restored to his pastorship. Simms recounted this cautionary tale as a warning against ceding too much power to important congregants or deacons. Continued problems with <u>ministerial selection</u> procedures were exemplified in the troubles of Savannah's Shiloh Baptist Church in 1914. When congregants called a conference to dismiss a relatively new minister for contracting unnecessary debts, the pastor posted police officers around the church building, reportedly saying that "God gave him the church and he was not going to let it get away." This church resorted to legal action to oust the recalcitrant cleric.[18]

Maintaining <u>good relations with churchgoers</u> was particularly important for ministers because of the practice of the <u>annual call,</u> the custom common in southern Baptist churches of voting each year on whether to retain the pastor's services. Reports from associations and convention meetings from the 1870s to the 1920s point to the complex nature of the relationship between clerics and congregants. Ministers employed fear tactics, subtly (or not so subtly) hinting at divine punishment should the church not renew a call. Sometimes preachers convinced those in the pew that churchgoers were connected to some higher episcopacy that could exercise authority over local church branches. Mississippi Baptists in 1870 admonished any minister who made his congregants believe that "because they organized a Church it has no power to act for itself, unless he gives them power, and at the same time makes them believe that they are a branch of some other church." Clerics often used spectacular instances of prophecy to bolster their divinely ordained authority and to ensure that their call would be renewed. Benjamin Mays, for example, recounted how James Marshall, his boyhood pastor in South Carolina, foretold a severe punishment for a man and his female companion engaged in sexual misconduct. When whites with their own designs on the woman murdered the man, the minister's accurate prophecy of doom "skyrocketed his prestige in the community. Thereafter nobody wanted Preacher Marshall to 'put bad mouth' on them." Pastor Marshall guarded his reputation carefully. He was circumspect with women and shunned liquor, Mays remembered, although "the same could not be said of all the ministers who pastored in Greenwood County."[19]

Despite the power of such men, the cliché of "one-man rule" in Baptist churches ignores the large number of local congregations that never relinquished democratic control of their own affairs. Ultimately, if a minister proved unsatisfactory, congregants could unite to oust him, no matter what action he took to lengthen his incumbency. "Takin' it all and all, you're only at a church as long as you'n the members agree on everything," an elderly minister in Georgia concluded of his career. "Just let something come up in the church where the pastor don't see things just the way all his members wants him to, and right then they'll throw him out for sho, before he knows what's happenin." Pastors worked to keep congregants happy, hesitating before denouncing publicly church members' wayward doings. The pastor who would fill his pews "must be a 'jolly good fellow,' giving himself no airs, but meeting his people without the semblance of affectation or reserve," a commentator observed in 1897. A black Baptist association reported in 1917 that with an annual election imminent, the minister's "knees get weak, and he winks at many sins that he should strike square from the shoulder." As a Mississippi Baptist leader lamented, "it is to be regretted that we have so many preachers who claim that they have been ordained of God to lead the people, and yet the people are leading them."[20]

The annual call proved to be a serious obstacle to denominational modernizers. "Churches have divided, the peace of the community interrupted, houses divided and sometimes husband and wife separated, all on account of the political practice of voting for the pastor once every year," a North Carolina association charged. A Georgia minister who prided himself on holding to sanctioned Christian doctrine and rejecting conversion visions commented that "it seldom happens that a minister pastors at a church 23 years without having trouble with his members, and at the same time preach[ing] what the majority of the people in the neighborhood surely do not believe." Henry P. Jacobs, organizer of the Missionary Baptist Convention of Mississippi, discovered how the power of the pulpit was circumscribed by the authority of the pewholders. "It seems that he did not countenance all of the ways of worship practiced by his people," a black Baptist historian wrote of Jacobs's pastorates during Reconstruction. "He wanted to preach against all unnecessary customs and practices; to do that he thought it necessary to be able to make a living independent of his ministerial work." Jacobs pursued medical training in Louisville, furthering his independence. As late as the 1950s, most churches still practiced the annual call. Despite trends toward uniformity and standardization, southern Baptist churches of both races remained bastions of local traditions, "island communities" in an age that witnessed the centralization of cultural authority.[21]

Annual calls also played a significant role in preserving folk preaching styles. When asked about what influences shaped their pulpit manner, ministers often pointed out the necessity of catering to their congregants' tastes in oratory. Black clergymen practiced the old style of preaching often simply because they knew and loved the practice of chanting sermons. As a northern Baptist recorded in 1880, preachers spoke proudly of their "book within them written by God, and that when they get up to preach, God tells them what to say." A preacher might lack scriptural knowledge but claim a " 'rich 'sperience' in the Spirit. He says the Holy Spirit teaches him." One northern Baptist missionary described how the "whole argument of the preacher consisted in his own experience, interwoven with his own prophetic visions. All of which was strange, weird, vivid." In an earlier day, North Carolina Baptists acknowledged, "thunder was more enjoyed than lightning, and those who would not thunder, the people considered him not in it at all." But black Baptist associations and conventions, expressing their disapproval of black folk oratory, called for "more preaching that is teaching and less or none of that exciting carousement that is so sadly being mistaken for gospel preaching."[22]

Skilled ministers learned to speak to their varied audiences and selectively employed chanting and moaning to great effect. A sensitive observer of preaching styles found that black sermons bore little resemblance to the usual caricatures of them: "The 'mourn' will affect one in spite of himself. It makes no difference whether you be white or black, if you put yourself under the influence of an intelligent minister such as I have attempted to describe, he will make you weep or do whatsoever he will." Pulpiteers who failed to generate communal spiritual excitement faced the prospect of a meager collection at the end of the service. Those who successfully induced shouts expected a handsome monetary reward. James F. Marshall, pastor of Old Mount Zion Church in rural South Carolina, gained renown for his eloquence: "He could moan, and did. Almost invariably he made some of the people shout. If he did not moan a bit and make the people shout, his congregation felt he had not preached well." Untrained men learned their craft by imitating elders, and congregants reinforced the choice of oratorical styles. The oral tradition of black sermons passed in this manner from generation to generation. As a boy, longtime Texas minister Charley White preached to his playmates and to dolls stuck in the ground around him about hell, "how hot it was down there, with the flames licking up around you like they did around the pot when Mama was cooking in the fireplace, and all about the devil and his big pitchfork." He was simply imitating the sermons he routinely heard on Sunday afternoons: "I'd preach whatever I heard the preacher say that day." His audience of children shouted along in response.[23]

White critics of black religion abundantly demonstrated their cultural illiteracy, their inability to comprehend or appreciate orally- and musically-based forms of spiritual expression. "It is strange," one black Baptist complained, that "editors and politicians of the white race, who do not enter a Negro church and have never heard a Negro preacher deliver a sermon can so effectively point out the defects and dangers that characterize the weekly utterances of the Negro preachers." But black believers and skeptics derided their ministry just as routinely. From Reconstruction to the eve of the Civil Rights movement, the reputation of the ministry took a steep fall. Booker T. Washington, for example, startled and angered leading clerics when he publicly proclaimed that less than one-third of black ministers were intellectually or morally qualified to preach the Gospel. Less than one in twenty, he alleged, possessed any "business standing in the communities where they reside." Black Baptist officials held an equally low opinion of the practices of their rank-and-file preachers. They acknowledged the presence of trained clerics and of uncultured but "sincere" men, but condemned pulpit orators who bellowed "like an untamed animal of the Balaam specie while their thousands of followers scream like they are being stung by wasps, and shout until the building rocks in self-defense." Such men "split churches, break up homes and demoralize the communities in which they live," a black Baptist women's leader wrote. The "dilapidated, ramshackle, greasy" buildings in which they led services, she lamented, stood as "parodies on the clean, restful, sacred places" where respectable parishioners could be found.[24]

Successful ministers took pride in their importance as community spokesmen and knew that fine dress and other accoutrements of success were not begrudged them by admiring congregants. But at the same time, because of their status, established clergymen developed a reputation as Toms who played the part of the "loyal Negro" to local whites. J. L. Chestnut Jr., who would later become the only black lawyer in his town of Selma, remembered that D. V. Jemison, the pastor of the city's largest black Baptist congregation, drove the nicest car in the town and reprimanded boys who played baseball or sought other secular amusements on Sunday. "Occasionally Jemison stopped in the grocery store, and I noticed that my father and the other customers showed him a kind of deference, as if he were white—not quite but almost," Chestnut commented. Even whites in Selma bestowed the title of "Dr. Jemison" upon this divine rather than the more familiar diminutive ("uncle") customarily reserved for older black men. Jemison's cozy relations with the Selma establishment allowed him to secure large bank loans and intervene when local blacks fell afoul of the law. Jemison's post as president of the National Baptist Convention, where he became a conservative leader and expert power broker, exposed him to the underground sniping that cut the "big preacher" down to size. Chestnut himself eventually recognized that Jemison's role was to "cool off potential uprisings and to preach that blacks should clean up their own back yards rather than challenge the system. By their own example, these black leaders sent the message that to get along you go along. Any black leader who started criticizing the status quo would find no more morsels of power thrown his way by white Selma."[25]

The rise of secularized forms of black cultural and political expression left the ministry vulnerable to communal ridicule. The scheming, whoring, "jackleg" preacher, a "public hiss among the people," became a stock character in jokes and song lyrics. Ministers with a keen sense of status wrestled against the widespread suspicion that men of the cloth were hypocritical charlatans. As a rhyme passed down through generations went, "Preacher in de pulpit preachin' might well / But when he gits the money yo' kan go to hell." An ex-slave in South Carolina told his interviewer in the 1930s what he thought of religion and preachers: "I believes in churches and good folks but I don't practice them good things lak I ought to. Boss, if you take de dollar out of 'ligion and de churches, you sho' would have to hunt for them. . . . I don't see no 'ciples gwine 'bout a preachin' and doin' good, lak I has heard they once done, barefotted and askin' no pay. De preachers dese days is a ridin' in de finest automobiles and you sho' better look out for yourself, if you don't, you is gwine to git run over." Exclaimed another ex-slave, too many people "joins de church one night and goes to a dance and gits drunk de next night. . . . Dar is going to be more church folks in dat lake of fire den de Devil can stir." Song lyrics and folkloric ditties fastened on the stereotypical amorousness of the preacher:

I wouldn't trust a preacher out o' my sight
Say I wouldn't trust a preacher out o' my sight
Cause they believes in doin' too many things far in de night.

A black woman in the 1930s recalled her shock at the behavior of her pastor. "Don't you know that our preacher had his stuff, and he used to keep his eyes on me. Used to tell me all the time, 'Sister, I got my eyes on you.' I didn't say nothin' much, but I did a heap of thinkin'. You see, in them times I didn't know them preachers was running around."[26]

Blues musicians lampooned preachers for their hypocrisy, greed, and philandering. And ministers returned their fire, condemning the frequent drunkenness and malicious conjuring of the bluesmen. When the early blues popularizer W. C. Handy was growing up, he brought a guitar home to show to his father, a pious man, who responded sternly, "A guitar! One of the devil's playthings! Take it away. . . . Get it out of your hands. Whatever possessed you to bring a sinful thing like that into our Christian home? Take it back where it came from! You hear? Get!" A generation of blacks interested in the blues met (and ignored) similar rebukes from their elders.[27] The consuming attempts of preachers and bluesmen to denigrate each other highlighted the fact that they competed for the same audience of rural sharecroppers and urban working-class black men and women. Shouting preachers and blues musicians transformed the individual sorrows of everyday people into communal cries of suffering and redemption. As Albert Murray has eloquently written, Saturday night and Sunday morning served many of the same functions for working-class blacks. The countless variations on the theme of "preaching the blues" suggest how closely related were bluesmen and preachers in their ability to articulate and provide emotional release from daily tribulations.[28]

The drive to professionalize the southern clergy engaged black Baptist officials as much as it did whites. Associations, state conventions, and the National Baptist Convention passed resolution after resolution setting educational prerequisites for ministerial licensing and ordination. In the 1870s, the Alabama Colored Baptist State Convention advised that "no person should be licensed to preach who cannot read" and announced that it would "do all in its power to aid young men who desire to preach the gospel in learning to read." Black Baptist missionaries traveled the state forming churches and encouraging the spread of literacy. The "troubles" afflicting many churches, one association pronounced, "grew up out of the fact that many of those who stand up as spiritual teachers of the people, are without a proper knowledge of the things which they attempt to teach." Too many ministers, black denominationalists asserted, left their congregants unenlightened, concentrating instead on solidifying their influence in local communities. Thomas Fuller, a minister, educator, and former legislator in North Carolina and Tennessee, found only three ministers in Memphis in the early twentieth century with substantial educations. "The value of ministerial training was not appreciated," he later recalled of those years. A black Baptist association in North Carolina condemned the abundance of ill-educated men who furthered "their own glory" and created "schism and discord in our churches." To counteract their influence, the association recommended that churches refuse to license preachers who could not demonstrate an ability to "read sufficiently well to separate the truth from error." Another North Carolina association required a course of study for licentiates, including "spelling, reading, writing, arithmetic, United States history, English grammar, geography, Scripture geography, Theology," and a list of required reading of books by Baptist authors. The standard set was remarkably high given the severe limitations on black education in the South.[29]

The black press called for educated clerics who would "go to the people and teach them how to live so as to become model citizens; for to be a good citizen is a stepping stone to true Christianity." The days of "looseness and frivolity" in the pulpit would end, black Baptists believed. "The demand for upright Christian men to fill our pulpits is rapidly increasing," they hoped. Properly trained ministers would direct their people to lives energized by the desire for material accumulation and spiritual respectability. But the congregational autonomy basic to Baptist governance meant that educated pastors would not find pulpits "until the masses are lifted up to a point where they will *demand* it," a home missionary explained. The opposition to an educated ministry was "very bitter" among older preachers who were "prompted by jealousy of the more educated young men. It is easy to see that there is a fight before them."[30]

White and black denominational leaders pursued a variety of means of educating the southern ministry. Black Baptist colleges claimed an increasing share of the American Baptist Home Mission Society's energies and funds. In 1906, the four major northern missionary societies budgeted four times more funds for higher education than in 1876. The total number of missionary colleges and private secondary schools for southern blacks tripled between 1880 and 1915. In 1880, the American Baptist Home Mission Society supported eight colleges, with 852 men and 339 women enrolled. By 1892, 202 men and women taught in 13 schools owned by the mission society, with 2,219 men and 2,948 women enrolled. In 1892, 458 students in these colleges were preparing for the ministry, while over three times that number were preparing to teach. By the late nineteenth century, graduates of these institutions filled many prominent pulpits. Black Baptist associations also supported high schools, a remarkable achievement considering that as late as 1910 not a single public high school for African Americans in the region offered more than one year of schooling. Black Baptists also supported a fledgling seminary in Lynchburg, Virginia, and created a number of colleges on their own in response to the paternalistic white administrations of the missionary colleges. Black Baptist institutions performed a crucial task in cultivating the "talented tenth," a phrase coined by Henry Morehouse and later expertly employed by W. E. B. Du Bois to describe a cadre of "race leaders" among well-educated young black men and women.[31]

Important as they were, these schools served a tiny clientele. Their few hundred ministerial students represented a mere fraction of the nearly eighteen thousand men who by 1910 claimed the ministry as their calling. For most of these men, literacy was an achievement; higher training was simply out of the question. For their rank-and-file ministers, denominational leaders organized informal institutes and classes that provided some modicum of instruction and cultivated a sense of camaraderie among southern men of the cloth. In the 1870s, northern Baptists and the Southern Baptist Convention (SBC) agreed on a joint effort that resulted in the creation of 33 ministerial institutes attended by 1,119 black ministers and deacons. In Georgia, white Baptists employed one white and three black missionaries to travel in the state and conduct missionary and educational work. In the early 1880s, white Alabamans hired Charles Octavius Boothe, "one of the most pious and cultured ministers in the state," to conduct classes. He reported speaking at fifty churches and numerous Sunday schools, where he impressed upon his students that "the handling of business affairs conduces to the formation of moral character." He told his students that whites interpreted "the fact that we earn the millions and can't control the cents" as proof that "we are an inferior race."[32]

White southern Baptists condescendingly concluded that their programs to educate black clergymen would restore to them "the privileges of sane teaching, which they had formerly, when they were fellow members in the same churches with us." It was, they said, "just as honorable to evangelize and teach and train for effective service a negro in Louisiana as in Yoruba." A proper education, they argued, should reinforce the notion that "the average negro must serve . . . the white race or die. This is his mission in America and will be until all people now living shall be dead and forgotten." Ministerial education could also, they assumed, "correct the false ideas of conversion prevalent among them—to teach them that professions and ordinances do not guarantee salvation—that striking dreams and visions are not signs from Heaven—that ghosts and witches and charms have no power to help nor harm."[33]

These early endeavors at interracial cooperation in ministerial training, often short-lived and hopelessly paternalistic, nevertheless paved the way for future efforts. In the 1880s and 1890s, white southern Baptists initiated small programs that provided minimal training for ministers who lacked any theological schooling and often were marginally literate. Educated white ministers conducted these small-scale sessions for untrained preachers, including those who pastored larger urban congregations. John William Jones, a genteel Virginian and hagiographer of the Lost Cause, for example, taught white and black preachers who were, he reported, equally deficient in the "fundamental truths as we believe them" and lacking in "any notion of a connected discourse." His students extemporized from biblical texts rather than outlining formal sermons. Jones introduced elementary theology and propriety in pulpit manner to his benighted brethren.[34]

Recognizing that such local efforts were sporadic and minimally effective, in 1894 representatives of the Southern Baptist Convention, the American Baptist Home Mission Society, and black Baptist state conventions hammered out a new plan of cooperation, the Fortress Monroe agreement. The details varied from state to state, but the basic idea was to marshal the manpower of white southern Baptists and the financial capabilities of northerners to support black Baptist colleges through local committees and to conduct informal classes for untrained preachers. These "New Era Institutes" were to expose black Christians to "a sound, definite system of theology," explained one white North Carolinian, and to restore the "old-time sympathy between the two races in local communities" by "the giving to the Negroes the benefit of the guidance and instruction of the local white pastor." Leaders of these institutes lectured on topics such as the evidences of conversion and the proper use of money. Instructors emphasized "the value of good books to a minister . . . to give information; to stimulate thought; to cultivate the correct use of language, to give breadth of view, etc." Students discussed sermon outlines and heard addresses on the "qualifications, duties and obligations of ministers."[35]

The Fortress Monroe agreement also provided for the employment of black ministers to conduct New Era Institutes. Their appointments required the approval of and received funding from Baptists in both regions. In Georgia, a "General Educational Missionary" oversaw the six months of "systematic and practical instruction" on Bible study methods, theology, church history, the office of the ministry, missionary endeavors, and Christian education. The superintendent of this work recruited local trained white and black pastors as well as instructors at Atlanta Baptist College. A black tutor described his instructional program as one of teaching the art of preaching sermons that would reach down into "every man's life" and teach him "how to vote, how to bargain, how to plan, how to do any work he is called to." Because of the New Era plan, wrote John A. Whitted, pastor of a large congregation in Winston-Salem, much "sentimental and demonstrative worship gave way to intelligence and practical Christianity." The emphasis placed on advancing beyond "demonstrative worship" illustrated how whites and blacks used the institutes for similar didactic purposes.[36]

Despite the optimism of reports like John Whitted's, the Fortress Monroe agreement faltered. Black Baptists gladly accepted financial help but resisted relinquishing control over work among their own people, straining relations with northern benefactors and white southern Baptist officials. "A race feeling among the Negroes of the South has been developed," a white institute worker warned, endangering cooperative endeavors of any kind. Some white Baptists, full of their own race feeling, opposed any funding for or cooperative endeavors with African Americans, particularly those involving the direct participation of the National Baptist Convention. Even when black conciliators such as Calvin Scott Brown of North Carolina spoke before the SBC, their appearances were met with protest. Brown's pleas for more funding for schools were answered with a reminder that these institutions taught "social equality, and we cannot agree to that." White proponents of cooperative endeavors reassured skeptics that their work had "no coloring of politics, nor any so-called 'social features of the racial question'" but that they sought to train black ministers without ignoring the "tradition of our [white] people, so far as these sentiments are not contrary to those of the Gospel." But a white seminary professor privately noted the obvious problem: blacks were excluded from the premier institution for Baptist ministerial education in the region, the Southern Baptist Theological Seminary in Louisville. The policy of segregation might be politically wise, he wrote, "but the pity of it! We are willing to go into their churches and try, through the imperfect medium of a 'New Era' Institute, to instruct them, but will not let them attend the theological institution of their own denomination which we proclaim as the best on earth. It is still the old era."[37]

Racial hostilities thus continued to impede interracial religious work. Nevertheless, denominational leaders kept up cautious pleas for cooperation. Little hope for "peace and amity between the races" existed, the president of the National Baptist Convention suggested, as long as "the religious classes of each race find insuperable difficulty in cooperating in the gospel work of saving, leading, enlightening and setting Christian ideals for the masses." Under a new agreement hammered out in the early twentieth cen-

tury, the SBC funneled modest funds for missionary work through black denominational agencies as an encouragement to "racial development." This
agreement accorded with the imperatives of segregation and the ideology of
self-help. Leaders of the National Baptist Convention recognized that their
options were limited. Funds provided by the SBC came with the proviso
that only "safe" missionaries be appointed and that troublesome racial issues be avoided. No course that African American religious figures followed
would have been free from such dilemmas.[38]

The culmination of cooperation between white and black southern Baptists in ministerial training came with the opening of the American Baptist
Theological Seminary in Nashville in 1924. In debating its funding, proponents argued that black ministerial education should take place under the
supervision of southern whites, in a place where white and black students
would not mix. The National Baptist Convention, meanwhile, collected
funds for the seminary. Its leaders originally planned to build an independent institution, but this proved to be impossible. As always, white funding
was essential. Black critics of plans for the seminary accused their leaders of
"asking that the SBC (white) establish a protectorate over the so-called
'ignorant Negro Baptists' so that they may tell them when they shall and
when they shall not." O. L. Hailey, the son of an antislavery southerner and
a liaison between white and black Baptists, was responsible for convincing
the SBC to allot $50,000 to open the institution. A colleague of Hailey's
explained the importance of their work: "This is the bone that hitches in the
throat of the Southern white man, and this is the bone he must learn to
swallow. This is the southern white man's burden—not simply to give his
money to aid in Negro education, but to give himself. . . . The Negro masses
will never rise above the Negro preachers; and the Negro preachers will
never get far above the level of the masses until they acquire the white man's
ideals directly from the white man."[39]

The planners calibrated the governance of the new institution to quiet
fears that it would be wholly dominated by one race or the other. Two
boards of trustees oversaw the seminary, one with a white majority that
supervised property and financial concerns, the second with a black majority that looked after the seminary's daily functioning. The founding document stipulated that the seminary's president was to be a member of the
National Baptist Convention, but ultimate authority for governance was to
rest with whites. After its belated opening, the American Baptist Theological Seminary struggled from year to year, almost collapsing entirely in the
1930s but reopening in the middle of the decade. The SBC contributed
$10,000 annually to its maintenance. Funding from the National Baptist
Convention varied considerably from year to year but added up to less than

that provided by whites. The seminary remained a bastion of theological and social conservatism. It attracted relatively few of the ablest black theological students, because those of superior background or greater abilities (such as Martin Luther King Jr. after World War II) generally attended theological institutions or graduate schools in the North. Critics of the institution pointed out that narrowly defined theological training lacked relevance to the problems that black ministers encountered in the countryside, including illiteracy, poverty, malnutrition, domestic violence, racial harassment, and disease. Its best-known student, the Georgia sharecropper's son and civil rights activist John Lewis, led sit-ins at Nashville stores in the early 1960s during his years at the seminary. The school's administration, fearing the loss of its financial support, reprimanded Lewis. After that brief moment of turmoil, the school retreated to a relative anonymity. The seminary in Nashville never served the same seminal function in setting standards for the black ministry as did the white seminaries for the white ministry.[40]

Yet attempts to educate the black clergy did have a substantial impact on black religious culture. One longtime Texas minister believed that black southerners had "learned lots from the Christian white folks. . . . Today we have many real educated teachers, preachers, and leaders that we are not ashamed of." Black churches were as "substantial in their doctrines as any of the white peoples' churches. We believe that the Bible is God given, God sent and God revealed." Older pulpiteers complained that younger men scorned them for their lack of education. George Briggs, an "old-time" preacher, complained, "Dey wants to hear dat man preach dat can read." In fact, Briggs had been forced to take up street itinerancy. He lamented, "when I sets around de courthouse and informs men as I been doing dis evening, de Lawd has dem to drap a nickle or a dime or a quarter in my hand but He never gits dem to half of a dollar." An elderly preacher in Arkansas bemoaned how he "used to be able to go about and speak and the churches would give me something." As he aged, however, "nobody cares to pay any 'tention to me. Think you are crazy now if you say 'amen.' Don't nobody carry on the church now but three people—the preacher, he preaches a sermon; the choir, he sings a song; and another man, he lifts a collection." The role of the folk preacher was clearly on the decline.[41]

The ministry served as one of the primary avenues of social mobility for black men in the Jim Crow South. The proportion of black professional men in teaching decreased as the teaching profession was feminized, while pastoral work gained in significance for men as a route upward. Those who succeeded in educating themselves, acquiring prominent pulpits, and leading denominational organizations presented their own lives as examples of how success could be achieved despite the racial barriers to advancement. The Booker T. Washington strategy of self-help and racial uplift was personally meaningful for them. Joseph A. Booker serves as an example. Born a slave in 1859, Booker lost both of his parents when he was a child. His father had been killed for providing instruction in literacy to other slaves. Booker's grandmother raised him and taught him to read. Informal lessons from local white boys furthered his education. By the age of ten, Booker was collecting fifty cents a month from students he instructed in his home in Ashley County, Arkansas. A few years later, Booker worked his way through Branch Normal College in Pine Bluff, the first secondary school established for blacks in Arkansas. In 1881, he entered Roger Williams College in Nashville, a training ground for a number of future denominational leaders. His graduation in 1886 convinced him of the force of sheer will in advancing one's own destiny: "For many years I had struggled and battled hard against my own ignorance and poverty; against the ignorance and poverty of my own kin-people and my own race. It was impossible now, for me to forget my many difficulties in acquiring a scant living, learning a few cheap old books, and in getting some one here and there to help me master those books."[42]

After graduation, Booker worked under the auspices of the American Baptist Home Mission Society and later engaged in missionary work in cooperation with the SBC. He spent his career pastoring churches, leading denominational organizations, and promoting Prohibition and missionary work. Booker persevered in the face of criticism from both white racists and black skeptics and eventually assumed the presidency of Arkansas Baptist College in Helena, a position that at the time of his inauguration he held only on paper. As head of that institution for thirty-nine years he "held up the rewards that came from honest labor, thrift, sincerity, and truthfulness— the old-fashioned virtues that are the foundation for the best in our civilization," wrote a white home missions worker who had befriended him. He married Mary Jane Carver, the niece of National Baptist Convention president Elias Camp Morris, and later succeeded Morris as president of the convention. At Booker's funeral in 1926, a white eulogist praised him as a "mediator between the races, interposing his own life, sacrificially, devotedly, that the white man and the black man might come to understand each other better." Booker's life—his lowly childhood, struggles to achieve an education, eventual success in school, a well-chosen marriage partner, and close relationship to the local white establishment—exemplified the transition of black Baptist ministers from a Reconstruction era focus on public activism to a Washingtonian emphasis on self-help and a public demeanor of accommodation.[43]

Jordan

Lewis G. Jordan, a denominational stalwart and pioneer historian of the black Baptist church, followed a similar life path. Born of a Spanish father and black mother in Mississippi sometime in 1853, as a child Jordan worked on a farm owned by Jefferson Davis. Jordan and his mother fled their master during the war. The young contraband of war took as his new first name, Lewis, the name of a Union soldier who gave him his first full pair of clothes. After his conversion and ordination to the ministry in 1874, he pastored in Yazoo City, Mississippi, attended Roger Williams College in the early 1880s, and then moved to Texas. Jordan edited a black Baptist newspaper there and in 1888 attended the National Prohibition Convention as a delegate from the state. While in Texas he met congregants who talked of emigrating to Africa, inspiring his long-lived interest in mission work on that continent. In the 1890s, after the formation of the National Baptist Convention, he headed its Foreign Mission Board and edited the *Mission Herald*, a periodical devoted to the cause of black foreign missions. He made a number of trips to Africa and brought home young African men to attend black colleges in the United States. He also assisted black Baptist women in organizing a separate convention. In 1930, he published the first complete denominational history of black Baptists. Jordan's life experience convinced him that race advancement was possible, no matter the obstacles.[44]

Fuller

Even ministers involved in political struggles during the height of Jim Crow maintained their faith in self-help and race enterprises. More so than most of his colleagues, Thomas Fuller, for example, pursued a political career along with his ministerial occupation. Fuller was born in 1867 to devout parents; his father was a literate carpenter who was politically active during Reconstruction. In the 1880s, Fuller attended Shaw University in Raleigh, one of the premier institutions supported by the American Baptist Home Mission Society. Ordained in 1890, in the next decade he taught public school, pastored several churches, and won a state senate seat in North Carolina. He took office shortly before race riots in Wilmington and other cities ensured that his political career would be short-lived. As the only black man in the state senate, he argued against racially based disfranchisement laws, insisting that the influence of improvident or illiterate men of both races should be excised from politics (a view he shared with elite whites). He hoped that "the Anti-Kink and Anti-Black, which wily schemers of the country are dumping upon the market, will fail to destroy the identity of the race or make us ashamed that we are Negroes." As he told a group of black churchmen, "I rejoice tonight that I am a Negro." If African

Americans worked to achieve education and wealth, he assured his listeners, they would not lose their political voice. Through all the turmoil of the 1890s, Fuller preached his favorite sermon—"Work is the Law of Life"— dozens of times, sounding in the message themes drawn from Gilded Age success oratory. In typical Washingtonian spirit, he advised black Baptists that no better place existed "to cultivate race amity" than rural areas or small towns, "where the spirit of commercialism is not so pronounced nor competition along various lines not so sharp." Ignoring his own advice, he moved to Nashville in 1900, assuming pulpit duties at a large congregation. While acknowledging the ominous presence of race-baiting politicians such as Ben Tillman and scurrilous novelists such as Thomas Dixon, Fuller maintained his faith that the racial destiny of Afro-America would be realized in the Southland. Later he moved to Memphis and assumed the presidency of the Howe Institute. His close relationship with whites, however, proved fruitless in saving the school from financial collapse in the 1920s.[45]

Another exponent of the self-help philosophy, Elias Camp Morris, made *morris* his career as a ministerial orator, Republican Party stalwart, and savvy racial strategist. Born in Murray County, Georgia, in 1855, Morris apprenticed himself as a shoemaker after his parents died when he was fourteen. Following an unsuccessful stint as a minister and shoemaker in Alabama in the 1870s, he moved to Helena, Arkansas, where he was first a member and later the pastor of Centennial Baptist Church. Soon he was president of the Arkansas Colored Baptist State Convention, a delegate to the Republican national nomination convention in 1884, and the editor of a black Baptist newspaper. He assumed the presidency of the National Baptist Convention upon its founding in 1895 and held his position for twenty-five years despite uproarious battles over his increasingly autocratic tenure. In his annual addresses to the convention, he sounded the call to support "the business side of the race." Despite the difficulties of black life in the age of Jim Crow, he implored that there be "no cessation of our efforts to become taxpayers, owners of homes and constructive builders of our own fortunes." Black ministers, he asserted, should continue to deliver messages "full of hope for the ultimate triumph of Christian principles," trusting that "the matter is in the hands of a higher power." He balanced his sentiments of racial caution with a warning that black southerners would be patient for only so long. In other words, Morris and other leading black ministers exercised an "implied restraint."[46]

The ideology of uplift articulated in Morris's yearly NBC addresses was deeply rooted in nineteenth-century black thought. Free blacks in the antebellum North preached the philosophy in pulpits, newspapers, journals, and conventions. They transmitted the faith to southern blacks in large part through church work. Instances of success reinforced such optimism. Works such as William Simmons's *Men of Mark: Eminent, Progressive, Rising*, a biographical dictionary of late-nineteenth-century black men, testified to the continued vitality of such optimism. Simmons himself, an energetic black Baptist educational organizer and founder of the newly established State University in Louisville, was a prime exemplar of an eminent, progressive, and rising life, cut short by an untimely death. The ideology of improvement was malleable enough to allow black intellectuals to participate in a central part of the American cultural heritage while they decried the racist interpretation imposed on the tradition. They never fully grasped the degree to which racism—the fact that for many Americans white men's freedom depended on black men's degradation—was central to American cultural history.[47]

In the late nineteenth and early twentieth centuries, the white South closed ranks behind the social and legal norms of disfranchisement and segregation. Violence against black citizens increased in intensity and viciousness, and a secularized class of black men and women flaunted evangelical norms of public demeanor. Perceptive observers recognized that, whatever the rhetoric of racial uplift, African Americans who followed the conventional rules for upward mobility would meet against insuperable racial barriers. Clerics acknowledged and decried the poisoning of race relations in the 1890s even as they acknowledged the impotence of political antidotes. A prominent pastor in Alabama, for example, called on the "better class of men" to take hold of the politics of the country. But this same minister, presumably one of this better class, declined every offer of patronage positions "mainly because of the threats made by some of the opposite party who were opposed to colored men holding office."[48] Even sober, respectable clerics, the very personification of the white rhetoric of "conservative" and "judicious" race leaders, were not exempt from the visceral racial hatred rampant in the period. Gordon Blaine Hancock, a graduate of Benedict College in South Carolina (where he learned that "an education puts no man or woman above work"), pastored in a town near Columbia, the state capital. He led meetings of the black state convention, was a principal of a high school run by a Baptist association, and served as a statistician for the National Baptist Convention. After moving near Greenville in 1917, he delivered speeches urging rural blacks to band together to improve their condition. The rumor soon spread that he was "out to turn niggers against white folks." He learned that the Ku Klux Klan was set to "discipline" him and realized that his "standing" in the community was illusory in the face of such threats. He fled the state to attend Colgate University and later taught at Virginia Union University in Richmond. If an outstanding figure such as Hancock was vulnerable, so were other ministers with less visibility. The situation a black Baptist preacher named S. C. Garner found himself in was a case in point. After successfully farming some land in a white dominated county in Florida, Garner received threatening letters ordering him to leave. He decided to stay. More hostile letters arrived, but a local sheriff assured him that "he would be safe as any law abiding citizen of that community." Five days later he "was found by the buzzards with his body riddled with bullets." A Methodist minister stumbled across his corpse and laid him to rest.[49]

Despite their reputation for accommodationism, some ministers refused to mouth the clichés of racial harmony expected of "respectable Negroes." In his relatively safe posting in the nation's capital, for example, W. B. Johnson enjoyed a liberty of racial speech denied to many of his southern colleagues. Born in Canada, Johnson worked in the Upper South under the auspices of the ABHMS before accepting a pastorate at the Second Baptist Church in Washington, D.C. He taught math and science at Wayland Seminary in Washington, founded the National Baptist Educational Convention in 1891, and edited the short-lived but crucially important *National Baptist Magazine*. The periodical, with a circulation of about 1,500, published essays by prominent ministers and served as the approximate equivalent to the better known *A. M. E. Church Review*. In a sermon preached in Washington, D.C., Johnson praised the Republicans for their past help but added that "*the idea that the Negro is in debt to the party* is the merest rot." The Negro, he asserted, had mistakenly "narrowed down his political vision" until he could not "see salvation in any other name." This political faith, Johnson pointed out, served African Americans poorly in an age when both parties championed one or another form of Negrophobia. Johnson assailed white clerics who, chained by their "fear of the people," could not preach a "pure, unadulterated gospel." He implored them to "rise above race prejudice themselves and like true men of God, tell the people the truth." But he held few illusions that white clergymen would turn their backs on the deeply rooted strain of Euro-Christian racism: "So far as the Anglo-Saxon civilization is concerned it may be compared to the religion of Buddha, Brahmin, Confucius or Mahomet, for there is less Christianity in the Anglo-Saxon Civilization as PRACTISED than in those religions which are called heathen. Then brethren, let us preach Christianity and not Anglo-Saxon civilization."[50]

In the ensuing decades, other prominent individuals expressed openly their anger at the betrayal of African Americans by national politicians and white Christians. As one minister wrote in the *National Baptist Magazine*, black manhood was recognized only in time of war or when Negrophobia could "be used as a ladder to help some political aspirant to climb up into office." He listed some of the ways whites proposed to "solve" the race problem: "Keep the negro to himself; another is to keep him poor; another, keep him ignorant; another, degrade him; then the press must traduce and misrepresent him to the world; lynch him for every crime he is charged with, whether he be guilty or not; burn him at the stake, and another says to disfranchise him, legislate against him and another says to deport him to Africa, and another to stick him off in a state to himself." In Augusta, Georgia, William Jefferson White, editor of the *Georgia Baptist*, was forced to flee town in 1900 and 1906 because of his aggressively critical editorials. In the 1890s, his ministerial colleague Emmanuel K. Love, a stalwart in Republican politics, led the fight for more African American influence in the mission colleges, resulting in the appointment of more black faculty and trustees to Atlanta Baptist College. Love was continuing the tradition of Savannah clergymen who, during Reconstruction, articulated the visions of the freedpeople to political authorities. In Anniston, Alabama, pastor John H. Eason challenged disfranchisement laws. R. C. Judkins, pastor of the venerable Dexter Avenue Baptist Church in Montgomery, edited the *Colored Alabamian* with the slogan "Equal Rights To All, Special Privileges to None" and with stern protests against segregation and disfranchisement during his term from 1907 to 1916. In Nashville, black Baptist ministers played key roles in the streetcar boycott of 1905–6.

Rural preachers could be similarly outspoken. Lillie Chace Wyman, a correspondent for the *New England Magazine*, recorded an interview with one bitter rural clergyman, who said, "here we are together. He don't love me—of course he don't. It wouldn't be natural if he did." He continued satirically, "Do I love him? . . . Oh—I'm just lovesick for him! But I cant get any return to my affection." He told Wyman that his congregants were "bound down to suffer where they were. If there is a better country anywhere, they want to go there." Wyman reported that the minister was "perfectly fearless in expressing his political opinions, and will say to white southerners the same things about the southern situations that he says to negroes or to northerners."[51]

But much more common than the bitterness expressed by the minister interviewed by Lillie Chace Wyman was the circumspection practiced by Pastor Marshall in South Carolina, who reprimanded local blacks when they criticized whites. Of the 118 persons interviewed by Benjamin Mays, a former parishioner of Marshall's, only one could remember a pastor who was "bitter about the racial situation." Most of the interviewees reported that clergymen instructed them to obey white people and be "respectful." A

North Carolina clergyman summarized the values that he felt ministers should inculcate in their congregants: "Show our people the paramount importance of acquisitiveness. . . . Teach that frugality and economy should be handmaids of industry. Teach the people the sacredness of an obligation. Teach the importance of promptness in filling engagements. Teach the desirability of system in affairs. Teach the harmfulness of baleful habits. Teach these basal religious fundamentals." In 1903, E. C. Morris announced that the trials of black Americans were of "divine ordering," for they would compel black Christians to acquire "homes, farms, railroads, bank stocks and to enter as rapidly as possible into all the commercial interests of the country." Even W. B. Johnson interpreted disfranchisement laws as a "scourge with which God is whipping the Negro to acquire property and education." The "patient, humble Negro" of his day, he proclaimed, would give way to a "countless army of strong men, who know their rights and will contend for them."[52]

Ministers of vision knew that part of their mandate for "racial uplift" involved deconstructing the denigrating folklore of Christian racism that had seeped into black churches. Despite the white Christian cant about the supremacy of the Anglo-Saxon race, the Bible prophesied "with unfailing certainty the final commingling of men into one general brotherhood," a prominent cleric thundered. A belief in "pure Christianity," he insisted, was "the one great power that can bring the Negro people of America their full manhood rights." Robert Park, an assistant of Booker T. Washington and later a University of Chicago sociologist, witnessed a rally in which the pastor quizzed his parishioners on whether the first man was white or black. The congregants responded that Adam was white and that black was the curse of Cain. The pastor ridiculed them for swallowing this pernicious myth and preached on the verse "Of one blood God has made all nations." Park understood that this preacher was trying to "lift the 'curse' which still oppresses these humble people and takes from them sometimes the courage to struggle." Black ministers in the age of Jim Crow assured their congregants that deliverance would come. The white pharaohs of twentieth-century America, the Kentuckian William J. Simmons foresaw, would not be able to resist the plagues visited on them. He advised African Americans to "face wrong with our Gospel of deliverance. Preach it, live it, until tyranny yields; preach it, live it, until Race prejudice, ostracism, Jim crowism and Negrophobia are buried in the Red Sea of God's wrath and indignation."[53]

Ministers adapted the story of Moses and Pharaoh, a treasured narrative of deliverance from bondage, to the postbellum era. James Weldon Johnson transcribed one such sermon for his famous collection *God's Trombones*:

And the Children of Israel all lost faith,
The children of Israel all lost hope;
Deep Red Sea in front of them
And Pharaoh's host behind.
And they mumbled and grumbled among themselves:
Were there no graves in Egypt?
And they wailed aloud to Moses and said:
Slavery in Egypt was better than to come
To die here in this wilderness.
But Moses said:
Stand still! Stand still!
And see the Lord's salvation.
For the Lord God of Israel
Will not forsake his people.
The Lord will break the chariots,
The Lord will break the horsemen,
He'll break great Egypt's sword and shield,
The battle bows and arrows;
This day he'll make proud Pharaoh know
Who is the God of Israel.

As Johnson explained, "the power of the old-time preacher, somewhat lessened and changed in his successors, is still a vital force; in fact it is still the great single influence among the colored people of the United States." This influence would be tested and challenged in the early twentieth century as Jim Crow solidified, hundreds of thousands of black people migrated northward in search of better opportunities, and African American churches fought to dispel the notion that progressivism was for whites only.[54]

PART THREE

Southern Baptist Progressivism

CHAPTER SEVEN

Scientific Management in Our Church-Craft

White Southern Baptist Progressivism, 1895–1925

The woods in Alabama are full of Baptists, and we are coming out of the woods.—*Baptist World*, January 28, 1915

How in the world can the masses of our people ever be led to higher things, unless those in position to lead them are ready to speak out on important matters and lift them to higher points of view?—Edgar Young Mullins to J. W. Bailey, April 8, 1907

In 1912, Shailer Mathews, the University of Chicago theologian and administrator, appropriated the term "scientific management" from Frederick Winslow Taylor's studies of time and motion in industry for use in describing church organizations. Although southern Baptists distrusted Mathews as an avatar of theological modernism, they responded enthusiastically to the call for "the task of scientific management in our church-craft," one that would require "the discovery of every potential agent in our equipment and the development of those agents to their highest efficiency." Efficient denominations, they believed, could pursue righteous reforms and inculcate bourgeois values in Christians of the New South.[1]

Scholars have underscored the prevailing conservative orthodoxy of the major religious organizations of the Progressive Era South. Dissenters from this view have cited numerous (if scattered and often idiosyncratic) instances of southern social gospelers at work. African American religious historians have challenged the relevance of this two-party model of interpreting American Protestantism. African American churches, they point out, always have filled important social functions in black community life even while they preached a distinctive and fervent evangelicalism. Contemporary histories of social gospelers, furthermore, reject any simplistic "souls or society" schema, noting that even northern religious liberals retained evangelical notions of conversion. Still, the social gospel is closely identified with urban ministers and laypeople who placed a primary emphasis on reforming society. By definition its existence in the South could only be limited and tenuous.[2]

Social Christianity overlaps with but is not synonymous with the social gospel. Social Christianity involves envisioning a public role for Christians in reforming and regulating human institutions, without necessarily seeing this public role as primary. Among southern Baptists, there were few pure social gospelers. But denominational leaders, well-placed urban ministers, rural evangelical radicals, and women's missionary societies articulated a southern version of social Christianity that challenged the prevailing conservative orthodoxy of the Southern Baptist Convention (SBC). This chapter examines such southern Baptists as part of a broad-based progressive movement rather than judging them for their adherence to some social gospel party line.[3]

The social gospel movement and the broad currents of social Christianity deeply influenced progressivism, but progressivism also drew from sources outside of Protestant activism. Some progressives saw religion as an obstacle to rather than an instrument of reform. William James and other philosophers viewed religious phenomena primarily as an object of intellectual study. Political progressives such as Theodore Roosevelt evidenced little concern for religious sentiment beyond a bow to a Supreme Being en route to an active engagement with the world.

Churchmen of the era allied themselves with social activists for progressive change. They joined organizations of civic reform, supported restraints on corporate enterprises, advocated immigration restriction and measures of coercive assimilation, and sought to regulate (or just restrain) the behavior of the "lower orders." Religious leaders boasted of a new "muscular Christianity," placing denominationalists squarely within the corporate capitalist order. Southern religious progressives participated most fervently in the Prohibition movement, where they formed coalitions and organized single-issue pressure groups to pursue the "reign of righteousness."[4]

The experience of the white southern Baptist progressives illuminates some of the visions, and the limitations, of southern progressivism. The rhetoric exulting in the wealth of the New South coincided with fears of trusts and "mammoth combinations." The emphasis on business-mindedness among church leaders arose alongside challenges to the morality of urban-based economic dealings such as commodity speculation. Condemnations of the exploitation of laborers were accompanied by paternalistic remedies and a trust in the efficacy of individual salvation in healing social conflicts. Crusades against child labor and drink ran headlong into traditional family economies. A renewed concern for the race question eventually settled on support for segregation and disfranchisement as a means of "progress." Finally, paeans to the wholesomeness of rural life and worry for the demoralizing influence of the city sat uneasily with the drive to implant urban principles of scientific management and efficiency in rural life. Progressive activism clashed with the localist tradition of southern communities.[5]

Beginning in the 1880s and to a greater extent in the early twentieth century, the South enjoyed economic growth. The region remained relatively impoverished, but Henry Grady's vision of a New South, expressed in his boosterist paper the *Atlanta Constitution*, was not a completely meaningless myth. The growth of cities in the South was impressive, but even more so was the mushrooming of villages of 2,500 people or less. From 1880 to 1910, villages and towns in the region gained five million people, while portions of the southern countryside were depopulated. Cotton mill villages sprang up in Piedmont areas, and a rapidly growing network of rail lines transported urban possibilities of material goods and leisure activity within the range of country folk.[6]

Despite the fears of evangelical traditionalists, in urban areas church membership as a proportion of population was actually higher than in rural areas (in part simply because of the accessibility of church houses). Upwardly mobile Baptist men and women joined southerners of all faiths in seeking to make their way in villages and towns. Growing city churches constructed impressive new buildings, symbolizing the coming to consciousness of the urban evangelical middle class. Country churches, once characterized as "nurseries of pure religion," now seemed backward embarrassments. Christians in New South cities could construct "a bulwark of civic righteousness and religious conviction against which the ever-rising tides of materialism and alien immigration shall dash in vain," one denominational leader enthused.[7]

Baptist churchmen and -women in the early twentieth century personified a new era in southern religious life—the rise of a middle-class urban evangelicalism among a still predominantly marginalized class of rural believers. Long before the 1920s, when Bruce Barton's *The Man Nobody Knows* portrayed Jesus as a consummate salesman, southern denominationalists already had tapped into the language of corporate enterprise, hoping to "Christianize commerce that commerce may help us to Christianize the world," as one minister put it. Denominational activities should be "in line with the world's spirit of enterprise," another cleric insisted. T. S. Powell, a clergyman in Mississippi, argued that churches were simply business institutions "organized for the purpose of maintaining saving truths, and disseminating them through the world." Josiah Bailey, editor of the North Carolina *Biblical Recorder* and future senator for the state, suggested that businessmen in the New South would create a social order appropriate to the new age, one with the middle-class virtues of restraint, moderation, hard work, and systematic benevolence rather than the Cavalier ideals of self-display and personal honor. If this New South would be less "stately" or "exalted" than the plantation South, it would be better suited to twentieth-century social life.[8]

The growth of commercial enterprise, the progressives understood, was essential to the rebuilding of the region and the support of denominational endeavors. The corporate model could inspire the "organization and control of the total business life of the community in the service of the Kingdom of God," wrote a North Carolina minister. Americans were "taking hold of the evangelization of the world as a business proposition," he continued, and the SBC should conduct its affairs accordingly. Religious organizations should recruit the growing southern middle class in supporting endeavors created by professionalized denominational workers, he argued.[9]

In spite of, or perhaps because of, their experiences with city life, Baptist progressives recognized that their ideals faced stiff challenges in an urbanizing America. Southern "manhood and courage," Victor Masters wrote in 1910, had proved sufficient to withstand "the fiery days of poverty and distress" following the Civil War. Masters wondered whether the southern heritage would "prove itself capable of mastering and dominating for the glory of God and his Christ, the marvelous material growth which is now coming to our Southern country." In the Colonial Era, Puritan divines sounded forth their jeremiads as ritual reminders of older religious ideals to those moving forward into a more commercial society. In a similar fashion, southern Baptists warned of the "sordid" influences that came with "mammonism." "We seem to have fallen on hard times," a contentious Kentucky minister proclaimed, "when commerce has supplanted the Savior and cash is more coveted than Christ." Robert Pitt, a Virginia Baptist spokesman, hailed "material growth with gladness" but added that "if its coming should mean the quenching of greatness of spirit, God pity us." While a North Carolina minister was "proud of our factories" and rejoiced "in all the material development of our grand old commonwealth," he implored southern Christians to "insist that men are above machinery, and culture and religion more to be desired than gold and silver." The "simple democracy" of the South's social order could be tainted "through idleness and luxury," destroying the "sturdy character of the South's people," he feared.[10]

Baptist progressives expressed their fears of commercialism and mammonism in the formulaic language handed down by generations of republican hyperbole of the inevitable decline of nations because of luxury, sloth, and political or economic tyranny. Southern progressives were hardly alone in these attacks. The Ku Klux Klan of the 1920s sounded the alarm about concentrated economic power. The Klan, however, resolutely opposed progressive reforms (such as the city commission form of government), while southern religious activists spearheaded such movements. Klaverns in the Peach State reviled the prominent minister M. Ashby Jones, even though the Georgia Klan attracted numerous Baptists and Methodists (including ministers) to its ranks (and even though Jones was the son of J. William Jones, the Baptist evangelist and keeper of the flame of the Lost Cause). The Klan's attacks on commercialism bore a rhetorical similarity to that of the southern religious progressives, but they were turned to different political ends.[11]

Most southern Baptists remained confident that, in the words of one denominational official, "the fairest expression of Christ, or the spirit of Christianity, is here in our Southern country." Still, a disturbing sense that the "absorbing and threatening power" of commercialism would overwhelm the region alarmed moralists. Speaking in 1898, a North Carolina minister must have hesitated before specifically identifying men who were actively undermining the "generous ideals" of the Southland, including some of his own parishioners. He excoriated the "speculator who crowds the exchanges and gambles in futures," who cares "very little for the opinion of preachers and churches," as a visible representative of the potential corruptions of wealth. Clergymen faced vexing questions about dealing with congregants engaged in legitimate yet morally ambiguous ventures. Local churches sometimes reprimanded or excluded cotton speculators, but enthusiasts for the New South pointed out the necessity of raising capital for fledgling southern enterprises. Ministers sought advice from denominational theologians for handling these controversies. In a letter to Baptist editor Josiah Bailey, a North Carolinian asked, "How about church members gambling in cotton futures and the like? Tell us." No gambling was as "corrupting and surer in its results than cotton futures," he told Bailey. The president of a Ouachita Baptist College complained to Edgar Young Mullins about speculators who portrayed their activities as "on a level morally with the greater part of commercial transactions," ignoring the gambling inherent in futures trading.[12]

But, as markets for southern agricultural products spread into smaller towns throughout the region, this immediate concern for the moral implications of the futures trade abated. Business-minded Baptists distinguished illicit "bucket shops" from the "legitimate cotton enterprises" that built wealth in the region. But the discussion of cotton futures demonstrated that "commercialism" struck close to home. If commodities trading was to be classified as "gambling," then the very New South promoters whom the progressives most needed on their side would be excluded from individual churches.[13]

Southern Baptists remained a predominantly rural people who feared urban growth as a challenge to the evangelical foundations of American civilization. Concentrated economic power, foreign immigration, class divisions, labor conflicts, inequitable concentrations of wealth, heterogeneity in the cities—such problems compelled a rethinking of the church's role in southern society. Bourgeois evangelical values, which had gradually displaced the code of honor as prescriptive for moral behavior in the nineteenth-century South, now faced new challenges from unexpected competitors: from secularized urban businessmen and an urban proletariat. A Mississippi Baptist in 1881 found "no affinity between the plain faith of Baptists and towns in their natural state." Baptist Populists attacked cities as the centers of the financial powers strangling the small farmer. Country-life advocates in the twentieth century praised the vigor and "wholesome environment of country life." Denominational progressives, while generally urban men themselves, lamented the loss of the homogeneity of the country in the multiethnic cities. "Somehow the laboring people of the city do not seem to believe that the church is their best friend," an SBC cleric commented in 1917. It was, he concluded, "still a question whether we shall be able to cope effectively with the problems of urban life."[14]

Evangelicals across the nation feared an imminent spiritual disaster in America's cities. The struggle for the soul of the city—"where Satan's seat is"—would determine the outcome of the "battle for Christianity and civilization," the pastor of Immanuel Baptist Church in Nashville proclaimed. The urban complex was the arena for the "greatest battle ever fought" for the "preservation of our evangelical faith," where "the forces of righteousness and unrighteousness meet in hand-to-hand combat." For those accustomed to worshiping in an outdoor revival tent or in a one-room building in the countryside, the heterogeneity of urban life could be overwhelming. "If there is any one thing that the problem of the city does suggest with overwhelming force," a Baptist country-life advocate suggested, "it is the almost absolute futility and helplessness of an individual, as he confronts the apparently impervious city multitude."[15]

Important works by northern social gospelers and intellectuals (such as Josiah Strong's *Our Country* and Madison Grant's *The Passing of the Great Race*) gave prominent voice to the widespread fears of an Anglo-Saxon elite observing freedpeople in the South and an influx of immigrants from southern and Eastern Europe. Likewise, the specter of rising foreign immigration to the South (largely a figment of overheated southern evangelical imaginations) frightened those concerned with preserving regional "purity." A North Carolinian shuddered at these "swarms of foreigners," whom he thought to be "selfish and depraved as swine." A Home Mission Board publicist described for his Baptist readership the horrors arriving daily in America: "Russian nihilism, with its blood and dynamite, its no law and no God—German lager beer and rationalism—French, Irish and Italian Catholicism, with deep seated jesuitical hostility to true American institutions—these form elements of danger which must be subdued, or else they will subdue us." The rhetoric revived obsessions dating back to the Jacksonian era, and these perils seemed to be gathering force around the turn of the century. Since the North and West were already "full," a home missions advocate reasoned, new immigrants would come South, leaving the region with the "ordeal of assimilating them" and the question of "whether we will lift them to our standard or sink to theirs." Foreign immigration, a Baptist editor warned, "destroys a State's traditions and vitiates its citizenship." The SBC lamented that the "Sabbath demoralization and demon of intemperance, which sadden the hearts of Christian people all over the land," were "aided and abetted" by newcomers to America "more than any other influence in our midst."[16]

The only way to preserve national and regional purity, many Baptists came to believe, was through immigration restriction. "We can save mankind more," Victor Masters asserted, "by upholding our tradition of liberty enlightening the world, than we can by allowing the world to flood our country to the loss of its identity." The "alchemy of the gospel" was the "only power that can seize the hot and tainted elements of our immigration and merge them into the higher type of heroic Christian Americanism," an Alabama minister suggested. God blessed white people with "a great capacity for Anglo-Saxonizing other races, that is to say, raising them to the standard of their own ideals of government, society, and religion," wrote Texas denominational leader James F. Love. He warned against "race suicide" and social upheavals such as women's rights, which could yet sap "the American race, and with it American religion." The only way to save the country "from political chaos on the one hand and from religious heresy on the other," he believed, was to "at all hazard insure the predominance of the Anglo-Saxon race and evangelical Christianity in the life of the nation." The South remained the place where "Anglo-Saxon blood and American aspirations have their fullest expression and opportunity," he concluded.[17]

The evident economic inequalities of a young, growing industrial society deeply impressed men and women raised on Victorian admonitions to hard work. They recognized that some worked little and earned astronomical sums while others toiled endlessly for little recompense. Edward Bellamy, Thorstein Veblen, Henry George, and other social critics and visionaries attempted to explain and resolve this paradox. Social Darwinists justified disparities of wealth as the survival of the socially fittest. Churchmen of all denominations struggled to comprehend the class divisions of the era. Most clergymen in the nineteenth century preached that hardworking and God-fearing (white) Americans could reap the benefits of the Gospel of Wealth. Henry Ward Beecher's soothing sermons to his upscale New York congregation typified the accommodations mainstream Christians made to the corporate capitalist order.

Among many southern clerics, a deeply rooted suspicion of centralized economic power still resonated strongly. Even southern Baptists suspicious of Populism's challenge to the regional economic and racial order condemned the "grasping and greedy, oppressive and powerful" trusts. The increased number of business combinations foretold the "eclipse of democracy" and the "suspension of free government." Trusts would, the *Biblical Recorder* foresaw, "come to a hard end, whether in a tornado of socialism or in the processes of legislatures and courts." The *Recorder* warned of "Two Powerful Evils": the "Jesuit lobby" and the "corporate lobby." One represented "conspiracy for monopoly and dominion in the forms of religion," while the second produced "monopoly and dominion in the form of business. Before either of these lobbies the average politician either quails with fear or bows gratefully for favors."[18]

Southern evangelicals feared the development of a class structure in the South rivaling that which tormented the North. The widespread poverty lingering in parts of the South, progressive ministers warned, mocked the Christian message of the equality of men before God. The well-known Atlanta cleric J. B. Hawthorne eyed uneasily the "deep, yawning chasm" between capital and labor. The lords of industry deliberately worsened the condition of laborers to an intolerable point, and workers' organizations responded with "unlawful methods of retaliation," he wrote. Like most clerics of the era, Hawthorne ultimately believed that churches should act not as "partisans" but instead as "mediators" of this conflict, bringing men to a spirit of reconciliation. By "insisting on equal administration of law," churches could mitigate the inequities of an industrializing society. Baptist progressives, for example, supported stronger workmen's compensation laws even if, as one minister put it, many workplace injuries stemmed from "this reckless temper in the American people."[19]

Progressive churchmen recognized that some response to this "deep, yawning chasm" separating the social classes was necessary; the shibboleths of the Gilded Age no longer would be adequate. Frank Barnett of the *Alabama Baptist* attacked the "mammoth combinations" of Rockefeller and Carnegie. He urged his readers to resist "any effort to reduce [the people] to serfdom." From his home in Birmingham, a center of southern industry, Barnett lived closer than most Baptists to the realities of urban southern working life. He watched with dismay the recently transplanted poor whites and immigrants to the steel mills, without churches in their neighborhood, roaming the streets and filling the taverns. "With the factory," he observed, "comes ignorance and vice and a multiplying of the forces of evil." A. C. Davidson, Barnett's fellow minister in Birmingham, organized an institutional church in the city for interdenominational social services. Citing the labor economist Richard Ely for statistics on working-class wages and living conditions, Davidson pointed to the conflict between labor and capital as one of the key problems facing Christianity.[20]

But these religious progressives were certainly no crusaders for socialism. "The pursuit of dollars along the commercial highway," Barnett explained of his philosophy, "is vastly better than the pursuit of pleasure along forbidden by-ways." Still, he stands as a progressive for his recognition of the coarser side of industrial capitalism and his sympathy for regulatory controls on corporate enterprise. Barnett advocated measures such as the Pure Food and Drug Act of 1906, condemned the dangerous conditions in steel mills, proposed public supervision of industrial machinery, blamed railroad companies for overworking men and causing accidents, and publicized the evils of convict leasing. Only if believers pushed labor reforms to their "just conclusion," he wrote, would the labor movement not be "alienated from organized Christianity."[21]

Southern religious progressives generally viewed urban workers as an undifferentiated mass of irreligious men who frequented saloons and vaudeville shows rather than churches. John Gable, a minister in Birmingham, wrote of the "lawless elements" ruling the streets of this industrial city and the seven-day work weeks that hindered a proper religious life. Packed with uneducated children, sullen-looking "lintheads," and rough steelworkers, the streets of Birmingham, he suggested, powerfully reinforced the view that "cities are hopelessly corrupt and that by their very nature they are beyond the redemption of the gospel." Gable repudiated such a pessimistic conclusion but acknowledged that in a community "as scattered, as shifting, and as rapid in growth as Birmingham," the social and spiritual needs of the residents remained unmet "by the sporadic organizations which arise under our Baptist polity." Mill villages, lumber towns, and growing industrial cities like Birmingham posed unprecedented problems for southern evangelicals, who still drew the bulk of their strength from the countryside. In many places, churches simply ignored the new classes of people moving there to work. The development of a class structure in southern mill towns turned congregations into places of class bonding, increasing and reinforcing the growing social distance between the mill workers, the middle class, and the mill owners. Factory workers were too often condemned to worship in a "factory chapel" with a "third-rate preacher," a Tarboro, North Carolina, pastor acknowledged.[22]

Even those ministers who occasionally excoriated mill owners with a critique of mammonism came off as harmless gadflies. For example, a Greensboro, North Carolina, mill preacher recounted his hellfire and brimstone sermon delivered to parishioners suffering during a mill slowdown: "Hellfire is waitin' to receive the rich man who gives no thought to his soul but spends his time fillin' his storehouses with earthly goods, and you, you, the faithful, are storin' up treasures in heaven. . . . That's straight talkin', sister, but I've never been called down for it yet." But this preacher's wife astutely measured the true impact of the sermon: "I don't reckin," she commented, that the mill owners would "calculate a sermon like that'll do 'em much harm." The minister's reliance on the company for his housing (a perquisite for mill pastors) no doubt mitigated his message.[23]

As modernization slowly and incompletely transformed parts of the South, progressive ministers contributed to the formulation and articulation of a southern social Christianity. They remained evangelicals, insisting on the primacy of orthodox doctrine and a life-changing religious experience. At the same time, they rejected any exclusive choice between purely individual redemption or social salvation. Advocates of social Christianity, southern and northern, shared a vision for a righteous society and a set of campaigns by which committed Christians could employ the newfound powers of the state. Race presented a major obstacle to the progressive Christian vision, but a similar point could be made of most social gospelers of the age. Their cultural intolerance, naive optimism of the harmony of interests between classes, and reliance on moral persuasion to address significant social problems characterized the southern Baptist progressives as well. Religious and secular progressives were culturally captive to visions of an efficient and cooperative society dominated by a Protestant morality.

In the nineteenth century, personal offenses against the southern evangelical code of morals resulted in chastisement by the church, and in some cases, exclusion. Those not excluded were subject to "rebuke," a form of public humiliation that enforced communally defined standards of behavior in the democracy of the saints. Progressive churchmen replaced the practice of discipline directed at individuals with the desire to "discipline" society. The model they sketched for the relationship of Christians to contemporary society was the same one that political progressives employed to describe the ideal citizen. Christians should concern themselves equally with sanitizing social life as well as cleansing the individual soul of sin. Southern Christian progressives emphasized that the "fight for clean politics, clean civic life, is also a call for clean personal living." The twentieth-century Baptist would not "piously wash his hands of politics and the execution of the laws and the uplift of the community," one minister asserted. Ultimately, church discipline had reinforced class, race, and gender hierarchies. When churches of the era applied standards of evangelical purity to political questions, they committed themselves to a conservative vision even as they pursued reformist ideals.[24]

Leslie Gwaltney, an Alabama minister and denominational editor, remembered in his autobiography the awakenings of a social consciousness in southern religion. Typical for the religious progressives, Gwaltney questioned why any distinction should be made between "those who preached only an individualistic gospel of salvation, and those who preached that plus the salvation of society." He proposed instead that "Christians should work to eliminate from society all those things which would retard the moral and spiritual development of the people," including social ills as well as personal sins.[25]

Baptist theologians searched for a golden mean between the denuded pieties of liberal modernism in the North and the defensive conservatism of southern-style orthodoxy. Edgar Young Mullins exemplified this effort to stand astride the emerging split in American Protestantism. Mullins insisted that the proper ordering of the individual's relation with God was the "sole condition of permanent moral progress in the social sphere." His contribution to *The Fundamentals*, the original intellectual manifesto of the Fundamentalist movement, was a moderately phrased endorsement of the central doctrines of conservative evangelicalism. Yet Mullins also believed that conversion could make men agents of "social righteousness," a phrase he defined for the Baptist World Alliance in 1911 as "the destruction of those piratical forms of business which know no pity and give no quarter. It means the end of the piteous cries of overworked and pale-faced children in the factories. It means the abolition of the diseased breathing tenement and the death-infested sweat shop." By giving men and women a true vision of better lives, Christianity could inspire social justice: "Christ is the author of modern discontent in all its higher forms," he suggested. Mullins expressed conventional ideas of the virtues of "safe leaders" in labor organizations and the imminent dangers of anarchism and radicalism. But he also provided theological justification for secular organizations of social reform. This development constituted a significant advance for conservative southern theologians, who in the nineteenth century often perceived the threat of social and racial upheaval lurking behind every nostrum for change.[26]

The ideas of southern Baptist progressivism gradually spread to ministers and laypeople in the region, particularly in the larger urban churches. Churchmen in South Carolina admitted that "this social application of the Gospel has not had the emphasis in our denominational life that it should have had." Denominational leaders should not be "dumb and silent," a progressive minister proclaimed, when "the most absorbing and tremendous questions with which the minds of men are now agitated" arose for discussion. Churches should pursue in social action "the great fundamentals of justice and righteousness" and make a "direct and powerful application" of them to public life as well as private behavior. The church's call, a prominent Virginia pastor added, was to Christianize "every field of human endeavor," making all parts of human life part of God's "great social commonwealth." In an age slavishly devoted to materialism, only the church could realize an ideal of "salvation for service." He envisioned the Kingdom not as some "insubstantial ideal" but as a "City of God actually being built in the midst of a great complex social order."[27]

The most articulate exponent of southern Baptist social Christianity was Charles Spurgeon Gardner, a professor of religion and sociology at Southern Baptist Theological Seminary. Gardner was a prototypical social gospeler rather than, as was the case with most of his peers, a minister with a vague rhetorical recognition of social problems. "The supreme need today," he announced in 1914, was "the reorganization of the great central functions of the secular life." Writing much like a progressive muckraker, he described American capitalism as an "organized system of greed—a mad, selfish, unscrupulous struggle for gain, operation with but little restraint of conscience through great impersonal, 'soulless' corporations." He thought "the extension of the dominion of the Kingdom of God over these corporations" to be "one of the great religious tasks of our time." The regulatory powers of the state, he envisioned, could act as the hand of God, replacing the now failing invisible hand of classical economic theorists. Individual shortcomings could be difficult to control, he explained, "but when sin is organized into an institution or corporation, it obtains respectability." Clerics could not "deal intelligently and effectively with the individual without respect to the social group and social order of which he is a member." Gardner's students in Louisville petitioned seminary president E. Y. Mullins that social Christianity had been "too long neglected to the detriment of the church." More emphasis on the topic, they believed, would compel preachers to "become familiar with those burning social questions which are uppermost in the world consciousness of the present day."[28]

Gardner's ideas derived in large part from mainstream social gospelers such as Walter Rauschenbusch, whose seminal book *Christianizing the Social Order* presented an ideal-typical text for social gospel thought on economic justice. In *The Ethics of Jesus and Social Progress*, published in 1914, Gardner most clearly articulated his own vision of "transformed individuals in a transformed society." In this manifesto, Gardner identified the Kingdom of God as both a "subjective state of the soul" as well as an "objective social order." He asserted that "the more definitely the goal of social evolution is worked out by the students of social science, and the more adequately the concept of the Kingdom of God is grasped by the students of the gospel, the more nearly they will be found to correspond." He sketched out a postmillennial vision of Christian soldiers working in alliance with a government purified of corrupt party bosses to enforce righteous laws. For Gardner, as for many other Baptist churchmen, Woodrow Wilson appeared as an ideal symbol of the fruitful intersection of Christian ideals and the powers of the state.[29]

SBC spokesmen of the early twentieth century adopted their own versions of social Christianity. As a North Carolina minister urged, "it is time that we were beginning to consider the relation of our industrial development to the religious and social life of our people." Southern believers could not "fight intelligently the liquor traffic, the white slave traffic, the traffic in child labor and in amusements till we see that these evils have an economic basis." George McDaniel, a Virginia minister and close ally of E. Y. Mullins, synthesized the concerns of the traditionalist evangelicals and the advocates of social Christianity in 1914 when he implored SBC messengers to "mobilize our forces and march against . . . commercial greed, industrial oppression, legalized immorality and paganized philosophy."[30]

Walter Rauschenbusch and other northern social gospelers marveled at the alacrity with which their arguments, dismissed or ignored in the 1870s and 1880s, found a ready audience among twentieth-century Christians. The Federal Council of Churches, which the SBC never joined, issued its Social Creed of the Churches in 1913. The SBC organized its own Social Service Commission in 1913, a descendant of what formerly were ad hoc committees that met yearly and issued opinions on contemporary affairs. Led for some years by a former home missionary in the Southwest, SBC presidents were careful to chose commission appointees who struck a balance between social Christianity and evangelical individualism. Still, the commissioners weighed in on the side of Christian progressivism. While acknowledging the preeminence of evangelism, they suggested that denominations influence social policy "by the creation of a Christian public opinion on the wrongs and perils, the duties and possibilities, of community life." The commission's 1914 report proposed steps the church should take:

> Upon business the church must impose its ennobling restraints. It must check private greed and compose class antagonisms. It must erect the Christian standard in the marketplace, and insist that the labor of women and children be regulated in the interest of the well-being of the race, that the industrial system provide the minimum necessary working hours with the maximum of wholesome life conditions, and that the workers have a fair share in the prosperity they produce.[31]

State conventions established their own social service commissions, also balanced between advocates of social Christianity and evangelical traditionalists. The Texas commission vaguely admonished its messengers to "apply the Bible" to problems ranging from "trouble between the owners and the farm tenants of our state," to "troubles between employers and employees of labor," to the "abomination of desolation that stands in the holy place—the Sabbath—in Sunday baseball, unnecessary Sunday traveling and Sunday fairs." Its 1920 report called for open stands on "any question affecting political purity and governmental morals." Commissioners disparaged any cleric who feared being "branded by some as a 'political preacher,'" suggesting that he should "have injected into the vertebrae that supports his anatomy a strong dose of Christian courage and Baptist backbone." South Carolina Baptists charged southern believers with determining "whether or not lynching is murder, whether or not graft shall reign in the place of trust, whether or not liquor shall be handed out to our sons at every street corner contrary to law, whether or not our fair daughters shall be the prey of white slave traders and brute-like men." North Carolina Baptists specified a range of issues with which Christian reformers would need to contend, including child labor laws, temperance, and state educational standards. "It is not politics to be concerned deeply with these measures," they insisted. "It is religion."[32]

State conventions also pressed for institutionalized means of social Christianity. They concentrated resources in improving colleges, establishing orphanages, and pursuing mission work in Appalachia. Denominationalists directed southern philanthropic monies to programs expressing both traditional evangelical concerns and systematic forms of benevolence. Educational administrators relied on ministers to promote the cause of improved modern schooling. Campaigns for renovating rural school buildings and curricula took on the trappings of revival meetings. Given the weakness of public institutions in the South, religious activists played a major role in addressing real problems and in bringing churches around to an enhanced sense of social duties. Southern Baptists feared modernization, but gradually they learned to respond to it.[33]

The southern Baptist progressives' articulation and limited enactment of social Christianity depended heavily on women's activism. Before women would find their way out of the "enclosed garden" of domestic evangelicalism into the public arena demanded of progressive leaders, the heritage of conservative southern evangelical sentiment had to be overcome. As did most Protestant men of the nineteenth century ranging from the conservative James Boyce to the Unitarian Horace Bushnell, nineteenth-century southern clerics believed that women possessed a "higher and holier mission" than engaging in public deliberations. Where women were allowed out of their place, one minister exclaimed, "children are neglected and become street Arabs. . . . Marriages have become a farce; divorces are engulfing the land; skepticism and anarchy threatens to engulf church and state in one common grave." Responding to the popular notion that women's votes would cleanse civic life, the *Biblical Recorder* answered that "politics must undergo a more enduring fire than female ballots for their purification." Baptist men foresaw that groups such as the Woman's Christian Temperance Union (WCTU) would, in the name of erasing one evil (liquor), perpetrate another (female suffrage): "Of all the political ills and evils that could possibly befall the people of the South, there is not one or even a hundred combined that could equal in its enormity of evil and ruin [than] woman suffrage." Clerics implored women to preserve a "pure, gentle, sweet and elevating" home environment "in which Christ is a contest guest; a home whose brightness lingers upon a husband's face through all the business and cares of the day, and to which sons and daughters return with songs of gladness." The true woman would wield "a mightier scepter than any of her notoriety-loving sisters."[34]

The progressives complemented these visions of the true woman with arguments about how women's votes would inject morality into politics. Despite the opposition of Baptist traditionalists to the measure, progressive editors and ministers gradually came out in favor of women's suffrage. Texas Baptists welcomed it as a reform that "ought to speed up the coming of the reign of righteousness." Supporters of women's suffrage were not above playing the race card, either. They stressed the utility of women's votes in maintaining white supremacy. As Atlanta minister John White wrote, there was not a "black brute in the cane-fields of Louisiana who would not flee before the white soul of an educated woman." Education and the franchise protected women rather than defeminized them, he argued.[35]

Achieving women's suffrage within the SBC paralleled the political movement. Until 1918, southern Baptist women could neither attend SBC meetings nor vote in convention deliberations. Traditionalists connected the debate on the "woman question" to the growing disorganization and irreligion they saw in society. "If we are to disregard the plain command of the Lord in one point, where shall we stop," asked one critic of women's participation in SBC proceedings. "If we once leave common sense we can prove infant baptism, the infallibility of the Pope, the Unitarian view of God, or what not." But progressives realized that actively pious women and their allies belonged to the "progressive and missionary element in the denomination." In 1918, women were admitted to SBC meetings as delegates. Another decade passed before they would be allowed to speak in convention meetings in their own right and not have to rely on male proxies to deliver addresses.[36]

If men were somewhat recalcitrant churchgoers, women kept the evangelical flame in the home and the pew. The progressives recognized how easily this impulse could be transferred to social action. The personal service work of women was not a "substitute for salvation," an SBC report explained in 1915, but "one of the duties which accompanies salvation as a by-product of the gospel." Women's organizations, an SBC leader proclaimed, were "illustrations of efficiency without an encroachment on democracy; of cooperation with one another without sacrificing the glorious liberty and independence of the local unit."[37]

The WMU became identified with Charlotte ("Lottie") Moon, a well-bred Virginia woman and missionary in China. A much more interesting and complex character than portrayed in her various hagiographies, Moon fiercely defended specifically southern evangelical norms, while her life exemplified something very different. She began her work in the 1870s with typical conceptions of heathen degradation and the place of Americans in evangelizing the world. By the end of her career, she had adopted native dress, given hungry Chinese her own food (thus hastening her own death), and pleaded with those sending literature from home to employ a less tendentious term than "Chinese heathen." In 1901, she wrote home in support of developing a training school for female missionaries at Southern Baptist Theological Seminary. Southern women trained in the North, she reasoned, absorbed dangerous views of their extended roles. Northern missionaries believed that, as Moon put it, "they not only may but *must* do things that grate on the sensibilities of people with Southern feelings and ideals. . . . I am Southern to the core and while I admire and love many Northern people, I don't want Northern ideals of womanhood introduced into our Southern Baptist missions." Moon's letter was disingenuous. She strategically aimed her reasoning at those opposing any kind of theological education for women. But her efforts were successful, as women began matriculating at what is now named the William Owen Carver School of Social Work in the Louisville seminary. Moon's careful negotiating of gender questions was a perfect example of the balancing act performed by southern evangelical progressive women.[38]

WMU workers opened up new avenues of active piety for those longing to escape from the "enclosed garden" of nineteenth-century southern evangelical women. As Annie Armstrong, a Baltimore woman who headed the WMU from its founding until 1906, impatiently put it, "I have heard so much about the 'woman's sphere,' and her going beyond proper bounds, that I think I am beginning to feel on this point as the children do when they are told 'children should be seen and not heard.'" Women's work was, she said, "much of it hidden work, as are the springs which feed the watercourses of mighty rivers." To those who scoffed at what "sentiment" might accomplish, she answered, "it is woman's sentiment which has in the last forty years changed the codes of many states, and revolutionized the thoughts of the nation, on the subject of temperance. The creation of sentiment is as womanly as powerful."[39]

Armstrong avoided public controversy at all costs, insisting that the WMU remain an auxiliary to the activities of the SBC. Asked to take charge of services one Sunday in Oklahoma City while on a fund-raising trip, she was "much astonished" at the arrangement and even more surprised because the pastors of both churches were southerners. She refused to fill the engagements, as she steadfastly opposed women appearing in the pulpit in a ministerial role. She preferred to "help in a work without appearing publicly" and avoid "being a target for criticism." The growth of her organization, she felt, had not caused activists to lose "one iota of womanliness, but [to] gain in all that goes to make up a rounded Christian character." The success of the WMU pointed to women's "competency and business sense in managing new lines of missionary effort."[40]

Much like their Methodist counterparts, WMU leaders adopted "community uplift" as a principal rather than a peripheral theme. Early in its history the WMU created its own Personal Service Committee, part of a shift from the nineteenth-century individualistic ethos to the Progressive Era stress on social action. At the beginning of anti-child-labor campaigns, Baptist women in North Carolina appealed for fewer work hours so that children's lives "be not completely stunted and crushed mentally, morally, and physically." In order to meet the needs of "the unlovely people about us"—factory children, cotton mill women, mountain women, and blacks— South Carolinians advocated active measures from evangelical women to alleviate "poverty, ignorance, disease, and crime." North Carolinians in 1919 urged pious women to acquaint themselves with state and federal laws pertaining to the employment and health of women and children and "endeavor to eradicate all social evils as far as possible." They endorsed "child labor and temperance legislation, welfare work, prison reforms, social service centers, [and] every activity of this kind." Women's religious progressivism peaked in the years during World War I. The national WMU set as its agenda support for "those forces in our country which make for righteousness: patriotism working toward universal and permanent peace, prohibition, Sabbath observance, the sacredness of the home, the effort toward a more general re-establishment of the family altar, and the crusade against poverty, disease, illiteracy, vice, and crime." By including the staples of Protestant moral fervor along with more contemporary social ills, the WMU articulated a social consciousness that strode out in advance of the male progressives in the SBC.[41]

Progressives in the SBC and the WMU threw themselves into a varied set of reform efforts in the early twentieth century. They fought against "white slavery" and prostitution, campaigned for restrictions on child labor, Sunday amusements, and immigration quotas. They acted on their missionary impulse to bring the light of civilization to Appalachia and rejuvenate country life with innovative ideas of farm management and rural church growth. Most importantly and effectively, they joined in the crusade for Prohibition. All these campaigns intermingled evangelical imperatives with social and political concerns. The obstacles these activists faced illustrated the conflict between their urban religious ideology and the rural constituency that they led. Their idea of a progressive New South clashed with the reality of a region still dominated by staple-crop economies and of impoverished social regions that resisted outside agents of change.

The widespread use of child labor in the emerging cotton mill industries demanded the attention of southern religious progressives. The early campaign against child labor met opposition from businessmen of the New South. Entrepreneurs such as Richard Edmonds, a Baptist layman and editor of the Baltimore *Manufacturer's Record*, accused progressive crusaders of blocking an industrial revitalization of the region and suggested that children were learning useful skills in the factories. Progressive southern Baptists rejected these familiar arguments, pointing out that the child labor problem was even worse than known because parents and mill owners often failed to report underage workers to state labor bureaus. In 1902, at least twelve thousand children under twelve worked in southern factories. Mills faced overwhelming economic pressures from their competitors to lower labor costs. Southern religious progressives initially suggested that compulsory education would remedy these problems. Barring that, they implored, "all the manhood and womanhood" of the South should demand that states protect young people through enforceable legislation.[42]

The progressives extended the dominion of the state to the rule of the patriarch in the home. They called for the abolition of child labor for those under sixteen while condemning factory workers and mill employees for their supposed profligacy and tyrannical control over their young ones. Frank Barnett, editor of the *Alabama Baptist*, effectively publicized the abuse of children in the mills, which attracted thousands of white families to company villages. It was, he charged, a type of slavery "worse than anything the old South ever knew." Such practices ensured "the lowering of the wage scale and the swelling of the army of the unemployed." He demanded that "our pulpits should not be silent on this great stigma on our civil life." *Alabama Baptist* periodical covers portrayed pathetic images of grimy, sooted children coming off a heartlessly lengthy work shift, and columns by Alexander McKelway, regional progressive crusader, filled in readers on legislative progress on this issue. Barnett hoped to mobilize a public sentiment that would compel "the enactment of laws for the protection of the helpless children." Opposition to such measures "as represented by capital invested in factories and other fields of child labor," could be formidable, he acknowledged, but "not so mighty as Christian sentiment, when . . . awakened and massed." To the argument that such legislation would cripple fledgling southern industries, he countered that business carried out "at the expense of decency, morality, and humanity ought not only to be hurt, but wounded unto death." Responding to Barnett's pleas, the SBC in 1910 urged "Christian employers and Christian citizens generally to put forth such effort as shall abolish all abuse of childhood throughout the Southern states."[43]

The southern anti-child-labor movement faltered due to the difficulties of endorsing decisive federal action. While seemingly a clear moral imperative, the crusade raised complicated issues of how far the state could regulate private family decisions. Without a nationwide, uniform policy, the humanitarians pointed out, industries would simply migrate to cheap-labor areas just as the cotton mill industry moved from New England to the South. Southern businessmen countered that mill workers themselves depended on wages from each family member to make ends meet. The resistance of southern cotton mill workers to child labor restrictions was especially frustrating. The objects of progressive benevolence seemed to act in ways contrary to their own interests.[44]

By contrast, southern churchmen found a safe and widely supported entrance into the public realm in their advocacy of state enforced alcohol restriction. The Prohibition crusade signaled a major shift in southern Baptist attitudes toward the relationship of the state and personal morality.

Many southerners grew up in homes where whiskey drams were considered "not dangerous or deleterious" and when "it was common for their ministers to take their drinks." Jeremiah Jeter, an influential Virginia Baptist through the nineteenth century, wrote that if a church member could use intoxicating drinks with moderateness, then he felt unable "by any law of God or man to condemn him." Jeter fell out with temperance organizations because of the divisions they created in local churches. Even in homes that practiced teetotalism, the idea that any central government should enforce dry laws seemed an infringement of basic individual liberties. And those sympathetic to the Prohibition Party reminded their fellow churchmen that religious associations should not be partisan.[45]

Nineteenth-century southern Christians generally trusted in moral suasion in the form of earnest preaching and firm church discipline as the remedy for human moral deficiencies. Many southern Baptists fought bitterly against Prohibition, insisting that church and state "should be kept as far apart as the poles" and opposing moral legislation as "an interference with personal liberty." The *Biblical Recorder*, the North Carolina state Baptist newspaper, voiced the common sentiment that a sermon or lecture against drink was "more far-reaching and surer in its effects than a campaign speech" and warned that Prohibition would require "a practical constabulary occupation of the country."[46]

As early as the 1880s, however, the tide was turning. Denominationalists learned that "*public sentiment*" was inadequate and increasingly invoked the "aid of the strong arm of the law in banishing" the "blighting presence" of alcohol. The prominent Texas Baptist B. H. Carroll fought tirelessly for Prohibition. "On this question which thus concerns every single vital interest of the people individually and collectively, socially and intellectually, civilly and politically, financially, morally and religiously, how can I remain silent?" he asked one congregation. J. B. Cranfill, a state denominational figure, appeared on the national Prohibitionist ticket in the 1880s, as did SBC president Joshua Levering of Maryland. "Whatever good may have been accomplished in the past through the agency of temperance societies," Alabama Baptists declared in 1887, "the opinion now seems to prevail that deliverance must come through legal enactment." Mixing older moralism with the newer political emphases, Mississippi Baptists in 1887 invoked "the family, the school, the church, the law and the ballot box . . . in removing this curse from the earth." The SBC passed its first temperance resolution in 1886, pledging its "influence in the exercise of our rights as citizens of this free country, socially, morally, religiously and in all other proper ways," to eradicate liquor. Tennessee Baptists condemned the saloon as the "breathing hole of the devil, the concrete representation of hell on earth, the breeding place of anarchy and crime, the nest of treason, the fertile soil of infidelity, the nursery of everything that degrades and destroys, the hotbed of every vice, the friend and ally of evil, the enemy of all good, the deadliest foe of the home, the bitterest opponent of the churches."[47]

The Prohibitionist platform gathered strength with the urbanization of Christians in the region, especially of their key ministerial figures. When drinking was confined to backwoods homes, it could easily be avoided by sober Christians, who excluded such offenders from their churches. In cities, where public drinking establishments were evident to everyone and open to anyone, control of alcohol obviously required more than just prayer and church disciplinary proceedings. It necessitated the coercive hand of the state. Bernard Spilman, a devoted Sunday school organizer, grew up in a small North Carolina town. Upon moving to Louisville to attend seminary in the 1890s, he was shocked to see stores and saloons open on Sunday. "All that was new to me," he remembered. "I saw SIN raw and rank for the first time in my life."[48]

Confronted with the ubiquity of "sin"—defined as disorderly social behavior—men like Spilman realized that moral exhortation was inadequate. They stumped from their pulpits and in civic meetings for local option, alcohol-free zones, state dry laws, and finally, for the Eighteenth Amendment. The Baptist progressives worked more closely with temperance organizations than did their nineteenth-century forebears. In the 1890s, J. B. Hawthorne, an Atlanta cleric, welcomed the coming of the WCTU until he sensed that Frances Willard, its public representative, was "pressing women into the gospel ministry, as preachers and leaders." By the early twentieth century, although the ax-wielding antics of Carrie Nation and other temperance celebrities still elicited fears of public disorder, the way was opening for groups such as the WCTU to work with conservative church organizations. Alabama minister A. B. Crumpton assumed the presidency both of the Alabama Baptist State Convention and the Alabama Anti-Saloon League, while editors of the state denominational newspaper sought federal legislation to prevent liquor from being transported across state lines. As an Alabama Baptist declared of the campaign, "we believe in a Christianity that will make a man march up to the polls and vote for the right."[49]

Ministers throughout the South engaged in high profile campaigns to eliminate alcohol, prostitution, and other social ills from their communities through both moral shaming and legislative enactments. Many churches declared it the duty of members to vote the Prohibition ticket "and to aid the cause in every conceivable way in influence and work," as one Mississippi congregation declared in 1884. Feeling that it was his duty to "take part in shaping the destinies of our country," one layman wrote to denominational newspaper to announce, "I will not defile myself by voting for any more whiskey guzzlers." Exulting in the passage of a dry law in his Virginia county, the pastor of a prominent church there privately wrote, "this is my victory the Lord has given." And J. C. Massee of Raleigh's Tabernacle Baptist Church spearheaded a citywide campaign to eliminate alcohol and prostitution. The governor of Mississippi, who was also a member of the First Baptist Church in Jackson, signed into law the state's Prohibition measure. Baptist home missions worker Arthur J. Barton served on the national committee of the Temperance League, while Benjamin F. Riley, a pastor and college professor in Alabama, worked to organize the Negro Anti-Saloon League in Texas, where he cooperated with prominent African Americans such as Kelly Miller. In his work with the Anti-Saloon League, Riley avoided the standard racial argument for Prohibition, that drunken blacks raped white women. Riley's refusal to fan the fires of racism in this way, however, was rare even among the southern religious progressives. [50]

Southern progressives recognized control of alcohol as a complex problem requiring not only individual purification but also enforceable and systematic legislative remedies. Partial solutions such as dispensaries (state-run and regulated alcohol stores), the southern progressives came to understand, legitimized rather than limited the liquor trade. As one activist argued, there was "nearly as much evil" in the "union of the State with the saloon as there was in connection of church and state." The licensing system provided saloons with a legal right to "corrupt, debauch, and kill" under the "sanction and protection of the commonwealth." The tax revenues generated by dispensaries, a benefit often pointed out by their proponents, provided no comfort to the Prohibitionists. God forbid that a "Christian community would debauch its manhood to supply its treasury," South Carolina Baptists concluded of this argument. [51]

Prohibition linked evangelical zeal with sophisticated pressure group campaigning and united the variety of constituencies making up southern progressivism—bureaucrats, good government reformers, humanitarians, and evangelicals. Southern religious activists demonstrated that Christian sentiment organized into sophisticated moral campaigns could achieve righteous reforms. [52]

The complexities of race and politics posed a serious obstacle to churchmen, for southern Baptist progressivism followed the pattern of the national movement in another way: in its racism. The *Biblical Recorder* initially refused to support the state temperance movement for fear that the issue might split the white vote, paving the way for renewed "Negro domination" in politics. "Since the gates of Eden closed on Adam and Eve," the *Recorder* opined, "no greater calamity has befallen a people than that which was thrust upon the stricken South" by black suffrage. In Charlotte in the 1880s, when even the support of African American ministers could not sway their constituents to ban drink, the failure of the local option campaign seemed to confirm fears about the obstacle to Prohibition presented by the black vote.[53]

To clear the way for reform, progressives endorsed efforts to eliminate black suffrage. "So long as the Negro is a citizen," the *Recorder* remarked in 1898, on the eve of a constitutional convention which disfranchised black men in the state, "North Carolina will not make much political progress." Black voting "gives us forebodings of insurrection and bloodshed," the editor warned. Some Baptist progressives countered that disfranchisement clauses would be counterproductive. "Often while we are trying to enact laws to put the negro at a disadvantage," an Alabama minister reasoned, "we unwittingly do exactly the opposite." But many other progressives insisted that the reins of power should "remain forever in the hands and under the control of white men." As a Baltimorean declared, the South was "not so much a solidarity against the North as against the Negro."[54]

By eliminating black political influence and lessening the chances of incendiary social situations (such as white women and black men in close contact), disfranchisement and segregation would, Baptist progressives believed, invigorate the reform agenda. The elimination of the Negro vote, a Georgia minister later crowed, allowed for the "emancipation of the white voter. Now, at last, he can go to the polls and vote for men and measures such as he approves, without the fear that once oppressed him. . . . He is no more to be frightened by his party leaders back into his bondage." After disfranchisement in North Carolina, the *Biblical Recorder* exulted that "the battle for the supremacy of the white race now leads—as we all hoped and prayed—into a battle for the supremacy of the right-minded members of that race. To lose this second battle will be to forfeit all the benefits of the first." While whites might "continue to resent the occasional appointment of a negro to office," the *Recorder* concluded, they would "no longer mistake this for Negro Domination and make it the central idea of their campaign." Elections could now be sober civic rituals rather than besotted civic parties for unruly voters "treated" by the candidates. The solution to the race question, these progressives suggested, lay in the exercise of "Christian sympathy and patience, and not upon political passion and vengeance." Of course the solution also relied upon disfranchisement, which, for all its progressive trappings, was in fact driven by passion and vengeance. And disfranchisement did little to mitigate race baiting practiced by a new generation of politicians, including Hoke Smith and Cole Blease.[55]

Disfranchisement and the mushrooming of the Prohibition movement were intimately connected. Both pursued an agenda cleansed of the corruption that the progressives commonly associated with the "lower level of both races," as Atlanta minister John E. White expressed it. "The white man's liquor and the white man's blood make a hellish combination in a black man," a well-known minister in Texas thundered. He was, he pointedly added, not as concerned to save "the negro's hide" as to preserve "the white man's soul. If we wantonly destroy the negro, we destroy our own souls." The southern temperance movement exploited fears of unleashing the "drunken Negro" on helpless white women. Even those who admitted the progress of African Americans since emancipation foresaw such dreadful possibilities. "As the inferior race increases in intelligence and wealth the friction between the two races becomes greater and more difficult to prevent race conflict," Alabama Baptists explained. They considered it "wisdom on our part in order to preserve our civilization . . . to use every means to keep whiskey from the negro. . . . Our women in the rural districts live in constant fear for their personal safety."[56]

Such a specter played itself out for a riveted viewing public in *Birth of a Nation*, the cinema version of Thomas Dixon's novels *The Clansman* and *The Leopard's Spots*. Dixon, originally a minister widely noted for his vibrant oratory on social Christianity, found his real niche in racist historical fiction. In *Birth of a Nation*, blacks "drunk on wine and power" assume political airs, insult whites on the streets, and attack a southern belle, forcing her to jump off a cliff to save herself. Dixon's imagery paralleled that espoused by northern reformers, who imagined that drunken and anarchic immigrant men menaced respectable women in northern cities. Some southern Baptists were critical of Dixon not for his racism per se but for his refusal to robe white supremacy in paternalistic garb. The *Alabama Baptist* believed that the greatest crime had been perpetrated not by Dixon's pandering to southern racist sentiment but by those who had "forced the southern people to resort to such methods in sheer self-defense." Those who held the race card could still outbid the progressives' more tentative hand.[57]

The progressives targeted another group for benevolence, the "mountaineers," a people deemed to need "uplift" as much as the freedpeople. The Appalachian region, home to people "of the most unmixed Anglo-Saxon stock," according to national mythology, saw an intensive missionizing campaign conducted by all the major southern denominations in the late nineteenth century. The Presbyterians beat other groups to the field, but the SBC was not far behind. The region was full of independent Baptist churches, a legacy of antimissionism. Denominational leaders expressed a special responsibility to Appalachian people but at the same time felt distant from them. They were "our contemporary ancestors," according to early scholars of the region, but at the same time they were "other," a foreign people. As a Virginia Baptist historian explained, home missionaries "came as part of a larger movement to colonize the people of the Southern Appalachians. Along with the development of mines, coke furnaces, and railroads, came the educated minister, the church budget, Sunday schools, and missionary societies." In the denominational imagery, the mountaineers were naturally and profoundly religious but were also considered to be destitute of religious education, naturally prone to feuding and family violence, and inclined to drunkenness and bootlegging. Churchgoers in the mountains were members of small congregations who met in simple structures and encouraged emotional responses to long, improvised sermons by preachers who were skilled in oral traditions but usually illiterate. The faithful practiced a physically tactile and vocally emotive style of worship once more characteristic of southern evangelicalism in general. They laid on hands, washed each other's feet, and hugged each other. Unaccompanied singing, spontaneous testimony, and chanted sermonizing characterized most services. The churches generally resisted any incorporation into larger denominational structures. Even churches ostensibly missionary in orientation often remained independent of the national denominations.[58]

As they worked in the mountains, SBC home missionaries understood their mission as one akin to evangelizing among the freedpeople. It was a work of acculturation of as well as evangelization to a group very distinct and separate from mainstream white culture. Albert E. Brown, superintendent of mountain missions for the Home Mission Board of the SBC, best expressed this view. A native of Asheville, North Carolina, where his father had been president of Mars Hill College, Brown's theological education trained him in the language of religious progressivism. Teachers in missionary schools, including Brown, emphasized the image of "sturdy" and naturally pious mountain people who awaited assistance in "development." The purpose of his schools, he said, was to bring to its "fullest and best self-expression" the southern population that was of "the most unmixed Anglo-Saxon stock." Denominational workers were to teach the gospel of respectability as well as the ethic of bourgeois production and consumption to mountain folk, to "induce a desire for better things, to stimulate them to establish schools, to erect better houses of worship, to promote Sunday-schools, and to elevate them to a higher plane of life."[59]

Those who served in Appalachia vividly depicted the problems they faced. John H. Spencer summarized what he found in his days preaching in the Kentucky hills: "The preachers, like the people, were very illiterate, and most of the churches were anti missionary, both in theory and practice. The people generally were very poor and improvident, but cheerful and contented in their poverty. The worst feature I saw among them was that the women performed most of the labor while the men devoted their time to hunting and rude sports." The fact that he viewed the men as lazy and the women as oppressed with men's tasks demonstrated how deeply bourgeois gender conceptions dominated the southern evangelical consciousness. The missionaries also found the Calvinism deeply ingrained in mountain belief to be inimical to progressive notions of development. The trust in the "sweet hope" of grace, freely afforded to unworthy recipients by God's Spirit, stifled notions of self-improvement and missionary work. It would be no easy task "to line up the great mass of Baptists in the cause of missions after generations of indifference and hostility," one missions worker acknowledged. Mountain exhorters avoided denominational meetings because "they did not wish to associate with high-salaried manicured preachers."[60]

Southern Baptists supported approximately forty-five mountain mission schools, ranging from institutions like Mars Hill College in North Carolina, which accepted students for relatively advanced study, to small private academies that taught the rudiments of reading and writing. Home Mission Board workers recruited talented younger preachers who hungered for education and shipped them off to schools, colleges, and seminaries. Many of these men returned to work in their home counties. Because of such work, Albert Brown proudly announced in the 1920s, "the moral tone has greatly improved, crime has lessened, feuds have disappeared," while Appalachian women now boasted washbowls and other conveniences denoting "advanced ideas of home life." But denominational organizations made limited inroads in the backwoods. In the early twentieth century, the folklife movement began to valorize (and market) Appalachian customs such as quilting. Highland musicians drew the attention of folklorists interested in preserving a "dying way of life." Tourists found in the mountains relief from the urban life. But SBC workers, progressive missionaries of the New South, remained advocates of assimilationism.[61]

The period during the First World War witnessed a great flourishing of religious progressivism across the denominations. Baptist churchmen, always in but not quite of the larger national movement, joined in the crescendo of Protestant excitement even while remaining self-consciously separate from the large interdenominational ventures of the era. The sectional chauvinism of southern Baptists mixed uncomfortably with their dreams of global Christianization. The internationalist visions of the progressives bore little relevance to the SBC constituency of small churches in rural settings with part-time preachers who exhorted traditional evangelical themes.

As World War I intensified, anger with Germany gradually gelled into support for Wilson's declaration of war. The *Baptist World*, an organ of the progressives, insisted to religious pacifists that the Christian duty was not "to attempt to enforce a millennial state of society upon a pre-millennial age of sin and selfishness." Early in 1917, as anti-German sentiment rose markedly, the Virginia *Religious Herald* proclaimed that "there could scarcely come to the world a calamity so deep, so dire, so dreadful, or so extended as the triumph of German arms." While acknowledging the dangers of the "hateful spirit of militarism," southern Baptists were certain of who held the "prime responsibility for the awful slaughter." Evangelical progressives felt philosophically vindicated by the war. Here, they said, was the result of the poisonous mixture of Prussian militarism with German philosophy. The aggression of the Germans was the natural result of the intellectual fruits of higher criticism, "atheistic evolution," and other continental theological heresies. At the root of Germany's "great and efficient military and social organizations," American evangelicals asserted, "is her philosophy, her scheme of life, her theory of society, her apotheosis of the state, with its submergence of individual freedom, and . . . her open and shameless abandonment of the eternal distinctions between right and wrong."[62]

Visions of the waxing of democratic Christianity throughout the western world induced a heady euphoria among American Protestants across the sectarian spectrum who saw their own principles writ large on the world political canvass. As seminary professor William Owen Carver explained, the utter failure of the amoral balance-of-power system left the "Christianization of international relationships" as the crucial imperative of postwar diplomacy. The democracy of Baptist church polity suited postwar desires for expanding human freedom, he suggested. Characteristic of the new epoch would be the "rise of democracy, of self-determination, of the direct access of the soul to God, and of the autonomy of nations and individuals." Finally released from the horrors of the war and now charting a course between a resurgent papacy and an insurgent Bolshevism, Europeans needed "simple, elementary, democratic forms of Christianity." America itself would be nothing but a "bedlam of socialism and anarchy" without evangelicalism. Even Russia, another minister proclaimed, lay in wait to hear the Gospel from the apostles of spiritual democracy. "The majority of her people are white people, and the white race is particularly responsive to the spiritual, democratic message of the New Testament," he explained.[63]

Protestant spokesmen in the early twentieth century proposed a series of ecumenical ventures to unite American Christians in efficiently carrying out the work of benevolence and evangelization. In 1908, they established the Federal Council of Churches to provide an official forum for cooperative endeavors. The Student Volunteer Movement, the brainchild of John Mott and Robert Speer, enlisted enthusiastic young people for missionary service under the slogan, "the evangelization of the world in this generation." The ambitious goal necessitated cooperation between the myriad organizations conducting mission work. Much of this Protestant enthusiasm found expression also in the social gospel movement. Religious activists lobbied for political and social reforms through the auspices of interdenominational agencies.[64]

Much of the rhetoric of the movement for Christian cooperation resonated with the southern Baptist progressives. "Is it not possible," Robert H. Pitt of the Virginia *Religious Herald* asked, "for Christian denominations to unite in the discharge of great common Christian tasks without surrendering or compromising their distinctive tenets?" But Pitt's stance drew fire from denominational stalwarts, who defended SBC separatism. "This is the Baptist day," Texan J. B. Gambrell proclaimed, and the believers should "keep the New Testament faith and order to the front and keep ourselves free to deliver our message unembarrassed." Gambrell's arguments carried the day, as delegates to the SBC refused to join in interdenominational ventures such as the Federal Council of Churches.[65]

The denouement of this debate came in 1919. In that year Protestants devised plans for the Interchurch World Movement, which called for the major participating denominations to centralize fund-raising and recruitment for worldwide mission projects. Representatives from the movement implored the SBC to flow with the "mighty currents" that were moving "toward co-operating for practical ends and applying business principles to the conduct of Christian enterprises." SBC officials informed the movement organizers in response that the convention had long since expressed its views on "unionism" and that in any case the denomination itself lacked any authority to devise a single policy for all independent Baptist congregations. Some denominational spokesmen reached a point of hysteria concerning this "unionism." J. B. Gambrell, for example, lambasted the idea as "a cheap and cheapening propaganda conducted on lines of convenience, expedience, and economy. The community church is urged to save money, rather than to uphold the truth." The program was, he predicted, "the forerunner of a vast apostasy from the faith of the Gospel." And M. E. Dodd, a denominational conservative, defiantly proclaimed that "the world shall not crucify our convictions upon a cross of unionism, nor will we sell our principles for thirty pieces of popular praise."[66]

The deflation of wartime idealism was swift and severe for southern Baptists as for virtually all Protestant groups. The savagery and brutality of World War I called into question how such a catastrophe could "usher in the reign of righteousness" after all. Southerners soon found other ominous social developments also occupying their attention. J. O. Alderman, a prominent North Carolinian, worried about those affected by "new experiences in war and new thoughts from foreign touch," suggesting the pervasive fears among whites about black soldiers who might encounter opportunities unsuited to their place at home, where they were in a permanently inferior racial caste. Even some of the progressives retreated significantly from their position of relative toleration once they saw social gospelers actually implement some of their ideas (such as the involvement of the Federal Council of Churches with the steel strike of 1919). Home missions advocate Victor Masters reminded his readers that "deeper and of more importance than securing justice between different sections of society is to bring men of every class in right relations with God and men." In the 1920s, Masters grew increasingly hostile to social Christianity, doggedly opposing "modernism" in any form and persecuting denominational progressives. Those suspicious of Protestant progressivism reminded their believers that "the world needs theology more than it needs sociology."[67]

During and after World War I, southern Baptists outlined two distinct visions of the future of American evangelicalism. Edgar Mullins best expressed the progressives' ideal of the gradual diffusion of a democratic Christianity. "The law of gravitation," he confidently predicted, was "scarcely more inevitable in its workings than the drift of the nations towards Christ's ideal—the recognition of mutual rights and cooperation instead of imperialism and domination." But conservatives and Fundamentalists foresaw a far bleaker future. Even deeper than the conflict between political systems in World War I, they believed, lay the struggle for the future of Bible-based Christianity. "When men ask for the bread of life," the Virginia Baptist convention reminded its churches, "we must not hand them a treatise on eugenics or a Liberty Bond." John Porter, a Kentucky Baptist Fundamentalist, pointed out that the course of nations "disproves the claim of universal progress." Porter's book *Evolution—A Menace* presaged the pessimistic, beleaguered southern evangelical mentality of the 1920s, the kind of "mind of the South" acutely described and savagely parodied by W. J. Cash and H. L. Mencken. Even the successes of evangelical sentiment, such as Prohibition, dimmed for these observers in the shadow of insidious intellectual and cultural dangers such as evolution and higher criticism. Many southern believers argued that an overemphasis on the social ideal explained the decline of churches. As one conservative but representative pamphleteer put it, "programs, propaganda, moral issues, universal peace all grow tiresome because they do not satisfy; but the story of Jesus always meets the fiercest cravings of a restless world."[68]

In the 1920s, denominational conservatives perceived that they had lost the culture war to preserve an America dominated by a conservative Protestant morality. But they in fact had won the struggle to define their own denomination. In future years, voices for progressive change often went unheard.[69]

CHAPTER EIGHT

The Holy Spirit Come to Us and Forbid the Negro Taking a Second Place

Black Southern Baptists in the Age of Jim Crow

We must as a denomination work out our own salvation.—*National Baptist Magazine*, July 1896

After Reconstruction, African Americans found in church work an outlet for their social energies, entrepreneurial skills, and political ambitions. They preached the equality of souls before God and challenged white supremacist thought, as had their forebears who were enslaved preachers. Critics charged ministers of the race with complicity in the white dominated order. This view acknowledged the powerlessness of churches to stem the tide of institutionalized American racism but failed to recognize that black spiritual leaders made choices within a constricted range of possibilities.[1]

Black Baptists formulated their own version of southern religious progressivism, one that incorporated social gospel notions and drew from free-floating concepts of uplift, rationality, and efficiency. They employed a rhetoric drawn from nineteenth-century evangelicalism and twentieth-century sociology. "We believe that it is the divine plan that all races of men shall eventually enter into the social movements that are to perfect human society," one minister proclaimed.[2] African American churchmen accommodated themselves to the realities of white supremacy while battling the racial mythologies that undergirded the order. By the end of the period that witnessed the rise of segregation and disfranchisement and the lynchings of scores of black Americans, they suffered from disillusionment but soldiered on. In the 1920s they entered a period of relative political dormancy until the flowering of the Civil Rights movement. White southern Baptist progressivism was defeated from within; black Baptist progressivism was defeated from without. The black Baptist story during the era of Jim Crow, then, is not one of triumph but of struggle, of small victories hard won and even harder kept.

By 1906, the Baptist faith was firmly entrenched as the dominant institutional expression of African American religious culture. Baptists in that year numbered 2,2261,607 men and women, 60 percent of black churchgoers, an increase of nearly one million from the total listed in 1890. In addition, a number of churchgoers expected and waited for conversion but were not officially listed on church rolls. Most black Baptist churches were affiliated with the National Baptist Convention (NBC), with about 10 percent connected with various Primitive Baptist groups, Freewill Baptists, and other smaller sects. In 1906, black Baptists counted 18,534 church organizations, 17,832 church buildings, and 17,478 Sunday schools. By 1916, the black Baptist fold numbered around three million (about 60 percent of whom were women). The next largest African American denomination, the African Methodist Episcopal (AME) Church, totaled about 495,000 members. By then the NBC was the third largest religious organization in the country.[3]

Despite their great numbers, black Baptist churchmen faced formidable obstacles in their organizational work. AME churches boasted more trained ministers, a less impoverished set of congregants, and a denominational structure ideally suited for organized endeavors. AME bishops such as Daniel Payne and Henry McNeal Turner acquired national recognition that exceeded that of their Baptist counterparts. Black Baptist churches were most often poor, isolated, and rural. They generally met in small, decrepit buildings rented by the congregation, supplied by a local landlord, or donated by local whites. Even the relatively wealthier congregations, which included the small black professional and middle classes, were made up primarily of men and women who worked as tenants and sharecroppers, domestic servants, day laborers, gardeners, cooks, and janitors.[4]

Recognizing their numerical strength but financial and social weaknesses, officials of the National Baptist Convention sought to ensure a measure of self respect and to secure needed white funds and assistance for missionary organizations, publishing endeavors, and educational work. The men and women active in this work in the Jim Crow era recognized that the political and social disfranchisement of black Americans from the 1880s to World War I demanded new strategies for "race advancement." If they remained overly optimistic about the imminent acceptance of successful African Americans, they shared this naïveté with nearly all racial liberals of their day. Black clergymen, the president of the NBC assured his colleagues, were not the "theoretical leaders of the race made by the newspapers and magazines," but the "real, practical leaders . . . who have by the spirit of tolerance and perseverance, kept peace between the two conspicuous races in this country."[5]

Black Baptists offered their hand of cooperation to whites North and South even while warning their supporters that the time of self-sufficiency was at hand. "Brethren, when are we going to cease begging and whining at the white man's feet for help?" a National Baptist Convention organizer asked. The self-help ideal presented the "most profitable and substantial" program for black Americans; it "develops strength of character, rounds out manhood and utilizes all the latent forces in one's being," another NBC supporter argued. E. C. Morris, president of the convention, repeatedly stressed that "no color or racial lines" existed in "the kingdom of grace" but that "race distinctiveness" remained a fundamental social reality. He preached tirelessly that black churchgoers should keep alive the "spirit of progress" that had seized the race. They should "own, control or manage" denominational agencies, "newspapers, dry goods stores, grocery stores, farms, factories, or any other enterprise necessary to develop the business side of the race." A Texas minister in 1886 urged black Christians to profit by their "past mistakes and blunders," that is, to concentrate less on politics and more on "the acquisition of education and property," the "elements of power and respectability."[6]

Churchmen embraced the call of hard work, thrift, temperance, and practical education as the best way to ensure the progress of the race. Black Americans, they said, could achieve success in America as defined by whites—social mobility through individual competition. Collective racial self-help would come through individual striving, while racial solidarity would enhance the black individual's success—or so ran the logic common among black Victorians. The church, of necessity, would be at the center of this race advancement. "Our banks, our insurance companies, our mercantile establishments, our fair associations, and similar corporations have been compelled to use the Negro church as a foundation stone upon which to stand until they could stand alone," a minister explained. When Booker T. Washington spoke of the primary importance of temperance and frugality and W. E. B. Du Bois sang the praises of the savings bank and of the talented tenth, black Baptists heard a language consonant with their own vision of the striving of the race.[7]

Black Baptists pleaded with white churchmen during the late nineteenth century, the "nadir of race relations," to administer Christian antidotes to the poison of racism. N. C. Bruce of Shaw University, a mission college in Raleigh, implored his white brethren to preach that blacks were not the "wicked, low, contemptible, lustful, womanhood destroyers, lazy, obtrusive, menacers to civilization whom scribblers, reporters, stump orators and often the entire press have represented the Negroes to be, if not all along, certainly at every recurring Southern re-election for many years." Bruce assured whites that "no people on earth" were "so docile, so patient and law-abiding" as Negroes. How much more patience could be expected of them, black Baptists in Texas wondered, when black soldiers fresh from the Spanish-American War were "chased, dragged through the streets and shot down." Yet they too advised their constituents to unite with the "better class of white citizens" to "suppress lawlessness." As "the true exponent of all moral law," the ultimate solution to the race problem lay in the churches, E. C. Morris argued. No true recognition of the rights of black Americans would come until "a moral sentiment has been created among the people to grant those rights." The Christian church had failed the test; it remained "asleep in many places and is not fully awake now." Morris prophesied that black religious leaders would inspire white Americans to recognize the moral imperative of race equality. Little did he realize how long it would take for the slumbering moral consciences of white Christians to be roused to the point of action.[8]

For white southern Baptists, by contrast, there was no American dilemma but merely a "Negro problem" that could be managed successfully by judicious whites. To give "undue prominence" to the Negro, the *Biblical Recorder* suggested, "encourages his encroachments upon our social structure. . . . No degree of culture or learning or experience can raise him to the dignity of a white man." Whites should "mercifully, religiously, and patriotically" protect their "dignity, supremacy and social status." Teaching African Americans to be "reliable and industrious" farmers would do more to solve the race problem than all the anguished discussions conducted by "newspapers, debaters, and teachers." To white critics, black Baptists lacked "clear, judicious" leaders, and a "spirit of unreasoning racism" poisoned their meetings. "The only way to manage the Negro is to manage him," the *Biblical Recorder* summarily concluded.[9]

Even racial "liberals" among white southern Baptists were, at best, paternalists who proffered "patience, persuasiveness, and helpfulness" as the answer to the race problem. Benjamin Riley, a southern Baptist concerned with the race issue, condemned the white racial attitude as "one of the boldest and basest travesties of modern Christianity." He blasted the southern pulpit for remaining "amazingly silent" on black-white relationships, "a vital, burning question in the South," and for bowing to a Negrophobia worsened by a "hostile press and by charlatan politicians." Riley's book *The White Man's Burden*, published in 1910, outlined the familiar southern liberal view that blacks were held down by the force of circumstance rather than by innate nature. But Riley also argued that the Negro needed "the most rudimentary training in morals alongside sufficient mental instruction to enable him to apply these principles." Riley's colleague E. Y. Mullins, who admitted black ministerial students for informal tutoring at Southern Baptist Theological Seminary, traced the "difficulty" of the race problem to the "visionaries and radicals among the negroes and also among the white people of the North." The *Baptist World*, a mouthpiece for white Baptist progressives, insisted that racial harmony was effected more by men such as J. L. M. Curry, conservative head of the Southern Education Board, than by films such as *Birth of a Nation*, which were "condemned and deprecated by right-thinking people, North and South." Exemplifying the conservative temperament at work, a Texan wrote that while Thomas Dixon's popular novel *The Clansman* appealed to his "hot southern blood," works such as Booker T. Washington's *Up From Slavery* exerted a "stronger appeal" to his "regenerated soul."[10]

While not silent on the evil of lynching, white southern churchmen argued strictly from law and order, almost deliberately disavowing any sympathy for the victims of mob action. Lynching, they said, hindered proper law enforcement and incited animal excitements among the mob. Both the Bible and the laws denounced "murder under the guise of lynching," yet it was "practiced almost under the shadow of pulpits, and yet who ever heard a sermon in denunciation of it?" asked B. F. Riley. "Riots in the name of race-hatred," the *Biblical Recorder* warned, were "more than likely to bring forth other riots in the name of class-hatred." Lynching was the "best expression of anarchy" and the "repudiation of our country and our civilization," it concluded. Even while condemning the vicious white-initiated racial conflagration that engulfed Atlanta in 1906, Georgia Baptists hoped that "good Negroes" would assume responsibility for the crimes that supposedly instigated riots. A Christian should be a "conservative force in his community, a temperate man in all things," the *Christian Index* advised, "and so a savior of his people from the control of their passions."[11]

Racial "liberalism" among white southern Baptists was actually racial conservatism: the belief that African Americans were human souls, that they would benefit from evangelization, that inflammatory films and literature would only worsen the race problem, and that the "best" white people united with "judicious" race leaders could best oversee a racial truce. The Negro should "await in patience the normal development of his race with the march of time," a white Baptist progressive wrote some sixty-six years after the Emancipation Proclamation. To force social equality "would not only demand a Communistic program which Americans would not tolerate, but it would be the saddest injury which could be inflicted upon the negro race."[12]

Even while pleading for the "best class" of white southerners to declaim the most egregious forms of racism, black churchmen despaired of the complicity of their "white brethren" in prejudice. White Americans, they understood, assumed the Negro was "predestined to fill an inferior place" and stood ready at all times "by means fair or foul" to "constrain him to be content in" second-class citizenship. Racial conflict remained "almost wholly the problem of the white Christians," while "the patience to see it solved" lay with black churchmen. Yet white Christians were failing to live up to their professed creed, cultivating instead "class and race antipathy" and destroying "the feeling of that common brotherhood, which should permeate the soul of every Christian believer." Whites transmitted their "senseless prejudice" to succeeding generations, and "by an oppression worse than that from which we were lately delivered, they fetter and burden and wither our manhood and womanhood, blind to all we have contributed toward the wealth and power of the American people," W. B. Johnson thundered. Johnson understood that successful African Americans could be (and were) targeted by whites bent on teaching a lesson about the "place" of the Negro in the South, a bitter reality understood by few of his fellows.[13]

Black Baptists responded to the coming of Jim Crow in the 1890s with shock and protests. As the laws spread through the South, they gradually resigned themselves to make self-help work as a catalyst for race advancement. Black clergymen in 1899 pleaded with southern governors to suppress race antagonisms. The ostensibly neutral disfranchisement clauses were in fact written with the "skillfully planned purpose and intention of systematically and lawfully disfranchising the Negroes in this state," black Alabamans pointed out. Jim Crow laws, E. C. Morris argued, represented the response of frightened whites to the advancement of the race, one that would in time shame their authors. Once the Negro came "into contact with the schoolhouse and the Church, and began to be more and more a man, there sprang up a unanimous action in the South to deprive him of those rights," he pointed out. Southern racism would compel African Americans to fall back on their own resources. In the meantime, he concluded, black churchmen should contend for rights "in a cool, dispassionate way."[14]

These pleas for rights obviously availed little. "The Holy Ghost can not work around the ballot box," a white Atlantan told his black colleagues. C. S. Brown, a Virginia minister, was involved in local political affairs, particularly the cause of Prohibition. But he warned his fellow black Baptists "greatly excited over political matters" that political solutions to racial problems would not be forthcoming: "The political condition of the Negro in the South could not be worse; the blame rests alone upon the States; the remedy is righteousness. The election of Mr. Taft or Mr. Bryan will not produce the millennium dawn."[15]

Inferior conditions on segregated trains and in black schools as a result of Jim Crow laws especially frustrated black churchmen. In train coaches, dignified ministers discovered how little their clerical collar meant when placed over black skin. Ministers traveling to convention meetings in the 1880s and 1890s witnessed train companies capitulating with increasing frequency to the informal rules of segregation enforced by hostile white passengers. A North Carolina missionary, for example, helplessly watched his baggage and Bible tossed out the door into a water hole on the Roanoke and Tar River Railroad, a line renowned for its "cruelly intolerable and savagely inhumane" treatment of Negroes. Black Baptist organizations insisted that separate train coaches should either be equal or else nonexistent. While separate coach laws themselves were "wise," a black minister in Texas noted, "discriminations in service are wrong." National Baptist Convention officials in 1907 described Jim Crow cars as "close akin to the slave pen of the last generation" and insisted that "objectionable and offensive persons ride together without regard to race." Whites failed to grasp that "the class lines in our race are as deeply drawn and as rigidly observed as the class lines in the race to which they belong," argued Nannie Burroughs, a black Baptist women's leader. Burroughs later rejected "separate and equal" as the euphemism that it was. But many African Americans accepted segregated public facilities as the lesser of the many evils they faced. As an ex-slave expressed it, "some of my color don't like that about the Jim Crow law, but I say if they furnish us a nice comfortable coach I would rather be with my own people. And I don't care to go to the white folks' church."[16]

The practices of lynching and other direct assaults on black bodies were legion in the period from 1890 to 1920. Local newspapers documented this violence in unassumingly gruesome detail, the perpetrators sometimes posing with the charred remains of body parts as souvenirs. Numerous other murders likely went unrecorded; southern state governments exerted little effort to collect information on such matters. Black Baptist spokesmen decried the practices of racial violence as relentlessly as they were practiced. "Even in the rudest period of civilization, good men condemned lynching," a minister noted in 1894, remarking that "then, as now, lynching was done in the name of virtue, and under the cover of religion." The black publishing entrepreneur Richard Henry Boyd disputed the common notion that lynching arose because of the prevalence of unconvicted rapists, a view he called an "empty, hollow, meaningless farce." Extralegal violence against African Americans would stop wherever "the good white people elect that it shall cease," he argued. If Negroes would act "respectably" in public and southern officials assume responsibility to maintain law and order, the excuses that justified extralegal violence would be exposed as false, Boyd concluded. "The eyes of the people are upon us," a North Carolina Baptist told a group of ministers, "and as the leaders of our race, . . . it becomes every one of us . . . to do all in their power to restrain the lawless element in our race."[17]

The violence waged against African Americans did not go unanswered, however. Voices of protest arose. Probably the best known of these was Sutton E. Griggs, a Texas-born minister, pastor in several states, and author of the didactic novel *Imperium in Imperio*. The book, published in 1898, is the story of a well-educated black man, Belton, who leads a student insurrection at a dining table at his college, Stowe University (a stand-in for Roger Williams University in Nashville, where Griggs attended school). Belton's revolt showed that "the cringing, fawning, sniffing, cowardly Negro which slavery left, had disappeared, and a new Negro, self-respecting, fearless, and determined in the assertion of his rights was at hand." As the story continues, Belton encounters racism firsthand as he is defrauded of an office by a white electoral board, attacked on a train traveling to Louisiana, and witness to a lynching. Frustrated at the lack of job opportunities, he temporarily joins a black revolutionary plot, aiming to establish a separate black state in Texas, only to betray the plan at the last minute. Griggs also authored *The Hindered Hand* (1905), a novel commissioned as a response to the white supremacist fiction of Thomas Dixon. Griggs's several self-published novels cost him financially. He avoided using the novelistic conventions normally reserved for black characters, which left him with virtually no white readership.[18]

As pastor of the black East First Baptist Church in Nashville from 1901 to 1908, Griggs helped to organize a streetcar boycott, publicized instances of police brutality, participated in the Niagara Movement (the immediate predecessor to the NAACP), and initially supported the formation of the NAACP in 1909. Later in his life, however, Griggs resigned himself to an accommodationist position. In 1912, he accepted a pastorate at the Tabernacle Baptist Church in Memphis, where he spent the next twenty years organizing welfare leagues and associations and building an institutional church. In his published sermons and essays, including titles such as *Building Our Own: A Plea for a Parallel Civilization*, he preached the conservative racial politics that he had rejected earlier in his life. When his church indebtedness reached a crisis point in the late 1920s, whites failed to come to his aid, forcing the congregation into bankruptcy. The Church of God in Christ, a fledgling Pentecostal denomination begun by former Baptist minister Charles Harrison Mason, purchased the building. Castigated as a "white man's Negro," Griggs died in Nashville as a bitter and broken man.[19]

The rhetoric of the younger Griggs and Richard H. Boyd in Nashville (discussed later in this chapter) was remarkable given the cautiousness of much of the black Baptist leadership. Many churchmen established close ties to the conservative Booker T. Washington machine, acting as his lieutenants in convention politics. As Washington explained in a letter to President Theodore Roosevelt, "with the exception of a few extreme radicals" (including Griggs), black Baptists were "kindly" to the Republican administration. In 1908, E. C. Morris lined up his convention forces to defeat a resolution that condemned the court-martial of black soldiers in Brownsville, Texas, who had defended themselves with firearms against assaults by local white citizens. Washington wrote to President Roosevelt that Morris had taken "a firm stand against" the resolution "and his hands were held up by the strong men of the convention." Black Baptist historian Lewis Garnett Jordan corresponded with Washington, the "Wizard of Tuskegee," concerning attempts to foil the Niagara Movement, while Richard Boyd served as vice president of the National Negro Business League, an organization controlled by Washington. NBC men shared with the Tuskegeean not only a penchant for behind-the-scenes political maneuvering but also a talent for articulating the most optimistic interpretation of racial politics in the darkest moments of southern racism.[20]

NBC leaders also generally aligned themselves in public support of the policy associated with Washington's life—"industrial education." As Tuskegee Institute garnered the lion's share of white philanthropic dollars aimed at black institutions, Washington carried on a public debate with critics such as W. E. B. Du Bois, who charged him with capitulating to second-class citizenship. The distinction between the two men's philosophies can be overdrawn. Du Bois affirmed the value of institutions such as Tuskegee in providing practical occupational training for young black men and women (though as the years progressed he grew embittered at the overemphasis on the Tuskegee model in educational philanthropy). Initially, Du Bois simply insisted that industrial training should not represent the only option available for young black students. Later, Du Bois and others lambasted the devious means by which the Wizard of Tuskegee controlled whites' purse strings.[21]

At black Baptist meetings, Washington defended his record as a race spokesman. He pleaded that the commonly held notion that industrial education was a "synonym for limited development" was false. Washington underscored the difficulty of giving "a man much culture when he has no house to live in" or making a "good Christian out of a hungry man." Ministers in the National Baptist Convention sustained a careful rhetoric of praise for Washington. Even educators and administrators who worked in black Baptist colleges, which emphasized biblical study, reiterated the value of practical workaday training. Bernard Tyrrell, who taught at a fledgling black Baptist seminary in Lynchburg, Virginia, praised the South as the "natural home" for the Negro, but added that the Negro "could never own it and have a home until he can build a home." He advised black southerners not to "forsake the farm," where they could work out their "own salvation of independence without fear or trembling" rather than become "appendages to independent and influential white men."[22]

Despite the general public consensus, an undercurrent of dissent ran through black discussions of industrial education. In his days as principal of Arkansas Baptist College, E. C. Morris, Washington's friend and ally, avoided any exclusive emphasis on artisanal training, suggesting that the "magic forces of the present age" would not "tolerate . . . old-time methods of plodding along." Ministers who were educated in northern Baptist-supported institutions were hardly candidates for rejecting the model of classical Christian higher education. Sutton Griggs blasted the racial politics associated with Washington as "that which pleased the Southern white man, because it proscribed the Negro." Griggs believed that the race had not accepted this policy but "contended for all that other men contended for." Grigg's sometime ally Richard Boyd, while serving as a vice president of Washington's National Negro Business League, condemned the "false theory of education" that placed the "ability to do skilled labor above the high arts of reason and the noble graces of manhood." National Baptist Convention meetings routinely entertained both Washington and his major public critic, Du Bois, on the platform, and they both enjoyed lavish praise in the black Baptist press and pulpit. [23]

There is thus little reason to imagine a chasm between supporters of the northern-born scholar Du Bois and those who championed the southern-born pragmatist Washington. For, whatever their position on this specific debate, black Baptists applied the American gospel of success to the race problem. Through industrial education, classical higher learning, race enterprises, and the assistance of sympathetic whites, they suggested, black Americans would advance. They assumed that education and the accumulation of property and wealth would dissolve the color line. With the population and property of African Americans increasing, the tendency of the age inevitably favored the "obliteration of race distinctions." "Accomplished Negroes" would find an honored place in society: "Colored Millionaires will not suffer much from prejudice." Charles Walker, a sometimes controversial minister in Georgia and New York, called for less attention to "politics and parties, and more attention to race pride; race unity; race confidence. More interest in race enterprises, the accumulation of property and homes." The progress of southern Negroes, Walker believed, would uplift the race in America and in the motherland.[24]

Redeeming the race from the scourge of alcohol also energized black Baptists, who joined in this Progressive Era crusade. Respectable whites blamed social conflagrations such as the Atlanta Riot of 1906 on low-down men who sold liquor to blacks, who then committed crimes. In fact, rumors and street fracases instigated by whites, not black criminal activity, ignited this riot; but this made little impression on white churchmen. The Atlanta mob scene arose out of that "worst liquor-cursed section of the city," Decatur Street, a Georgia Baptist paper reminded its readers. Black Baptist leaders agreed that the black "criminal class largely comes from saloons run by white men to teach the Negro lessons in carnality." Benjamin F. Riley, the white Alabama Baptist minister who spoke for the black temperance movement in Texas, argued that the two races would rise and fall together—and drink would cause the fall. Drink, he continued, was "a common enemy to all alike and all must fight it or ruin will come to all." The basis for the "so-called negro problem" was liquor, he concluded. "Ignorance, poverty, vagrancy, demoralization, debauchery, divorcement, lawlessness and criminality" emerged from saloons, the center for the "debasement of both races."[25]

The rise of temperance among black Baptists followed a similar trajectory as it did among whites. Black churchmen and women gradually incorporated a wider application of Christian principles to social problems. In the nineteenth century, individual churches assumed drinking to be a matter for moral discipline rather than social activism. "No person who keeps a barroom will be allowed to do so," on the penalty of forfeiting their membership in the church, the First African Baptist Church of Richmond resolved in 1877. Urban black churches zealously enforced their purity, disciplining and excluding drinkers at nearly every conference. The wife of one black Baptist minister remembered that "bad white folks" who ran a whiskey still, "where you could git three gallons of liquor for a silver dollar," near their home fought her husband because he preached messages that galled "both makers and drinkers. Him 'dured persecution for de Lord's sake." But as was the case with whites, local pastors often resisted involvement in the temperance crusade. A missionary in Georgia recounted how the moderator of a state association announced that he drank whiskey and meant to continue. Another pastor held dances where shootings disgraced respectable

Christians. Even worse, in this area there were "women who call themselves preachers, and drink whiskey just like the men. . . . Just such things I meet when I am out in the dark places among our people."[26]

In the early twentieth century, denominational leaders such as this Georgia missionary took up Prohibition in earnest. The time had passed, North Carolina Baptists proclaimed, when churchgoers could assume that "internal tranquility, preaching once a month, communion once in three or six months, and a plenty of shouting going on" constituted "gospel order." The Progressive Era church should instead measure itself by its contribution to "the salvation and civilization of the world." E. R. Carter's congregation in Atlanta invited white female temperance organizers to advocate Prohibition. Most black Baptist organizations by the early twentieth century supported state-sanctioned alcohol restriction. They saw it as part of a broader campaign to acculturate blacks to American life. "Intemperance" in all its forms, they argued, dragged down the race:

> It is intemperance of speech that leads us to talk more than we act. It is intemperance of conduct that renders our demeanor unpolished and unbecoming. It is intemperance of feeling that stands in the way of moral improvement. It is intemperance of passion that leads to physical wreck and open scandal. It is intemperance of appetite that leads us to spend too large a part of our income for costly dainties and rich food. It is intemperance that leads us to smoke up and drink up the largest part of our income.

But the black temperance activists served as only junior partners to the larger white movement. The Prohibition campaign was as segregated as the other crusades of the Progressive Era.[27]

Black Baptist women in the Jim Crow era pursued evangelization among and moral uplift for African American women. They organized themselves under the dynamic direction of Nannie H. Burroughs, a figure once forgotten by chroniclers of black life but now resurrected by the work of historian Evelyn Brooks Higginbotham. Black churchwomen joined their male counterparts in serving as advocates of bourgeois values and for the "politics of respectability." Black Baptist men (like their white counterparts) understood scripture to mandate separate, distinct, and subordinate roles for women. In the early twentieth century, Baptist men admitted that women could direct complex enterprises of religious benevolence; but they still fought any ideas of women serving in roles of pastoral authority or denominational leadership.

Black Baptist women in the late nineteenth century laid the groundwork for Progressive Era leaders. William J. Simmons, a minister, historian, and denominational organizer, afforded women important positions of leadership in the American National Baptist Convention, a predecessor to the National Baptist Convention. As president of a black college in Louisville, he aided women such as Mary V. Parrish (formerly Cook), wife of the prominent cleric C. H. Parrish, in acquiring educations and assuming positions of authority. The women encouraged by Simmons promoted individual success, racial solidarity, and the cultivation of female virtues. At the inaugural meeting of the organization in 1886, Lucy Wilmot Smith, historian for the group, recounted how black women had contended with "repression, limitation and servitude." She advised that women should remain on the farm, practice careful domestic habits, and cultivate profitable domestic trades such as beekeeping. For her, individual success and racial solidarity were intertwined. The following year, her colleague Mary Parrish explained how the freedom of Baptist theology and polity required that "free men cannot conscientiously shut the doors against those [customarily] limited in privileges and benefits." When the "vitalizing principles" of Baptists permeated Christianity, she envisioned, "women will become free." This freedom, however, would not require radical reformulation of gender roles. There was "no necessity" for women to "step over the bounds of propriety, or to lay aside modesty, to further the work."[28]

Building on the efforts of her predecessors, Virginia Broughton, a widely traveled missionary in the nineteenth century, organized women's groups and preached respectable spirituality. A graduate of Fisk University, Broughton served under the Woman's American Baptist Home Mission Society for twenty years. Throughout her tenure, she encountered staunch opposition from local pastors, who "looked with disdain upon a criticism that came from a woman." They uneasily eyed the "growing popularity" of women's societies, viewing them as a threat to "their own positions of power and honor." Men lingered in the back of churches during women's meetings, listening for "some cause to condemn our teaching, as being false doctrine." Although "we were given a good shaking and thrashing," she concluded in her memoirs, her message had taken "root too deeply in the hearts of women ever to be uprooted."[29]

Broughton faced an even more tenacious challenge from Holiness believers, a group with whom she initially sympathized. Holiness congregations afforded expanded opportunities for "women of the spirit" to lead churches, but Broughton drew back from the dangerous implications of Holiness spiritualism and affirmed the practice of restrained piety. She rejected one kind of expanded role for women, the preaching and exhorting common in Holiness groups, but affirmed another, the work of benevolence in women's missionary societies, the religious equivalent of the black women's club movement of the urban South. She led the battle in women's groups for "intelligent worship" and the "Bible plan of church government in the discipline of members, in supporting churches, and in preaching and teaching the gospel." She succeeded in combating Holiness dissension, by her own account, only because of a "fresh anointing of the Holy Spirit," an explanation mimicking Holiness theology itself. She quieted "much of the growing confusion in the ranks of her Bible women" who, like Broughton, "desired to follow the Lord wholly" but also remain orthodox Baptists. With her victories, she finally felt delivered from this "bitterest persecution of all her experiences," a trial that seemed a "direct aim at her earthly existence." The strength she and her cohorts drew from these struggles motivated them in preaching the gospel of self-help and self-discipline: "The common evil practices of intemperance in beer drinking, tobacco using, excessive eating and dressing, and the desecrating customs of using church houses for fairs, festivals and other worldly amusements were all strongly condemned by our Bible women, while righteousness, holiness, purity and all the kindred graces of Christianity were upheld and emphasized."[30]

Nannie Burroughs, the founder and corresponding secretary of the Woman's Auxiliary to the National Baptist Convention, followed the path first trod by Lucy Smith, Mary Cook, Virginia Broughton, and others; but she blazed her own trail more determinedly in the direction of gender separatism in religious work. Nannie Burroughs's cooperation with Annie Armstrong, the corresponding secretary of the white Woman's Missionary Union of the SBC, aided her in forming a similar organization for black women. Armstrong worked with Richard Boyd and Burroughs to distribute devotional literature to black Baptist churches, and she persuaded the SBC to contribute $1,800 a year toward the salary for mission work among black women. "You have no idea of how . . . thankful I am that God is allowing us this opportunity to help to elevate the colored woman as well as to assist the work in Africa," Armstrong wrote to James Frost, secretary of the Sunday School Board. "It will prove to the colored people that we are anxious to help them," she believed. The "life long acquaintance" of southern whites with their black servants furnished "the most favorable of opportunities" for the uplift of black women, she told an assembly of white women. Northern women entertained unrealistic expectations about missionary work, she alleged: "There may be more romance in it to those at a distance," but there were "larger possibilities in it for us." Despite Armstrong's penchant for paternalistic language, which normally riled Nannie Burroughs, the two women maintained a good working relationship. If Burroughs had drawn the line at paternalistic rhetoric, work with any white agencies at all would have been virtually impossible.[31]

In 1900, with the assistance and advice of Armstrong, northern Baptists such as the venerable missionary Joanna Moore and sympathetic men in the National Baptist Convention, Burroughs's plan for a Woman's Convention, an auxiliary to the National Baptist Convention, came to fruition. She met the predictable resistance from convention churchmen with a determined and appealing rhetoric. She spoke movingly of the "righteous discontent" and "burning zeal" motivating pious women of the race. Women's groups would be the "dynamic force in the religious campaign at the opening of the twentieth century," she predicted. She finally garnered approval for a separate national organization that linked missionary societies in individual churches and associations. The Woman's Convention collected funds for the missionary programs of the convention and for its own independent endeavors, and by 1909, it had raised nearly $63,000 and operated the only educational institution in the country owned by black women.[32]

Nannie Burroughs formulated a "feminist theology," as historian Evelyn Brooks Higginbotham has lucidly explained, that both supported and redefined Progressive Era notions of gender roles. Typically for Christian women of this time, Burroughs cited biblical verses to sanctify women's role in the home. But Burroughs's emphasis on domesticity in no way contradicted her actively developed social conscience. She reinterpreted Genesis to demonstrate that women were men's equal in creation and that Christ had ensured their "enfranchisement from the degradation of paganism." Black Baptist women believed "with a conviction that cannot soon be uprooted," she announced in 1903, "that the masses of our sisters must hear the gospel of industry and heed its blessed principles before they can be morally saved." She urged convention workers to teach "virtue of simple, sober, unostentatious living," a job with which a generation of early-twentieth-century white female social workers also busied themselves. Burroughs's seemingly conservative rhetoric was not so restrictive when viewed from the context of black women's working lives. They normally toiled at low-paying and often degrading jobs while attempting to raise families, care for other relatives, and support their local churches.[33]

In the twentieth century Burroughs became an increasingly vocal advocate of an activist racial politics. She urged black Baptists to cooperate with the NAACP, the Southern Sociological Congress, and other groups working for progress in race relations. She excoriated Negro caricatures in popular culture and history books and implored schools in black districts to transmit a history that would stir race pride. She advised black families to teach their children to "give their lives to redeem the race." Racial segregation could be fought not only through protests against its unjustness, she asserted, but also through "soap and water, hoes, spades, shovels and paint." The black church remained too distant from everyday problems, she alleged: "We do not need to take up our time getting happy and telling our experience of grace." Her intensely practical mind and zeal for uplift left little room for emotionally expressive spirituality. Burroughs took comfort in the fact that God might be "preparing to smite this merciless nation because of her sins," but she held only a slender hope that Christian zeal would "burn away" race prejudice. "The mob is now setting fire to Negro tenements, but that fire is going to spread, and it will reach the mansions before many years," she warned in 1908. On the one hand she acknowledged that black Americans needed white friends to defend them because "we are not often so situated that we can speak for ourselves," but on the other, she lashed out at the complicity of the "good white people" in racial oppression. The "peculiar silence" of the so-called friends of the Negro had "emboldened our enemies, until they attack us with impunity," she charged. Burroughs was so outspoken that the Wilson administration placed her under surveillance during World War I for her critique of racism at a time when the U.S. forcibly squelched internal dissent.[34]

Burroughs merged private piety and racial uplift in her role as founder and head of the National Training School for Women and Girls in Washington, D.C. Opened in 1909, valued at $15,000, and funded originally by money raised from black women across the country, Burroughs cultivated a financial base that ensured the school's relative autonomy from the political infighting plaguing the NBC. After the school's founding, northern Baptist women funded a new building named after the Baptist home missionary Mary Burdette. Burroughs maintained that the institution should remain free from the control of the NBC. North Carolina black Baptist men countered in 1917 that "no body of women can exist independently of the church, and line out an independent program conflicting with the plans of the denomination." But Burroughs and her convention followed precisely this course in raising money for the Training School. Burroughs successfully saved the school from the feuding that split the NBC in 1915 by incorporating it separately from the denominational organization and placing a majority of women on the Training School's trustee board.[35]

Burroughs ran the Training School in a fashion similar to Hampton and Tuskegee, stressing practical skills and strict discipline. The curriculum inculcated moral values alongside vocational training. The morning routine resembled that of a military institute: "The bed lines must be spotless, the room must be clean in every crack and crevice; Every student must keep herself clean from skin out." Students who failed tests of personal hygiene sometimes were denied diplomas. The required courses prepared pupils for the occupations open to them, domestic service in particular. To criticisms that the curriculum overly emphasized such vocational training, Burroughs responded that women in service jobs "give more and attend services better than any other class of laborers." The influence of young women trained in habits of bourgeois housekeeping would overcome the baser influences dragging down black life, Burroughs believed, radiating the school's influence throughout America.[36]

In her work with the National Training School, Burroughs combined the roles of the feminine moralist concerned with preserving womanly virtue, the black educator obsessed with garnering philanthropic support, and the urban social worker seeking to uplift the lives of impoverished and ill-educated women. Like the other long-lived black stalwart of the century, W. E. B. Du Bois, Burroughs lived to see the beginnings of the Civil Rights movement. She died during the freedom rides of 1960–61. Unlike Du Bois, she maintained her faith in America, remaining active in race work for nearly sixty years.

Richard Henry Boyd was another unsung hero of the urban black middle class during the early Jim Crow years. He moved to Nashville around 1895, the year of Booker T. Washington's "Atlanta Exposition Address." He died just after the violence of the "Red Summer" of 1919. During these dispiriting years, Boyd transformed a fledgling Sunday school enterprise into the largest black publishing house in the nation. Late in his life, a rancorous dispute within the National Baptist Convention set the stage for his present reputation as being one party in a schism that split the chronically divided black church. But Boyd's entire career, not just this one episode, merits attention.

Born a slave and educated at Bishop College in Marshall, Texas, Boyd came of age just when political options for ambitious black men closed down. His main religious endeavor, the National Baptist Publishing Board (established in 1896), exemplified Booker T. Washington's philosophy of using the resources of the insular black community as well as outside white assistance to create a thriving business. Boyd's other enterprises, including a stake in a publishing company and a bank, also demonstrated the self-help philosophy in action. At the same time, Boyd fought the imposition of Jim Crow openly and publicly, helping to organize a black boycott of streetcars and publishing (together with his son) the *Nashville Globe*, a newspaper that tirelessly promoted race enterprises. Richard H. Boyd's story shows that the supposed dichotomy between accommodationism and militancy breaks down on close inspection. Boyd combined separatism as an ideology with cooperation as a practice.

Boyd complemented his ideological emphasis on black independence with business and legal acumen. The force of his own personality as a "witty and resourceful debater, trained by a long and hard contest in Texas Conventions," won over ministers formerly skeptical of the publishing board idea. He "foresaw possibilities which even the most far-visioned of his brethren failed to see at first," a colleague remembered of his work. In 1896, Richard Boyd secured a charter for the National Baptist Publishing Board, placing it under the control of a self-perpetuating board of nine men (effectively shielding it from denominational dictates). Boyd was also named the secretary-treasurer of the Home Mission Board of the NBC, the primary recipient of funds from white Baptists for aiding missionary work. Boyd promoted the National Baptist Publishing Board as a thriving enterprise and an instrument of black cultural expression. White religious literature, he pointed out, reinforced racist stereotypes. When northern Baptist publications, for example, depicted angelic white figures in heaven and demonic black figures guarding the gates to hell, children would naturally assume "that the latter belong to an inferior creation." White denominational publishers sold material to their own churches, he added, making their "invasion" of the Negro market unjustified.[37]

The publishing houses for the Southern Baptist Convention (the Sunday School Board) and the National Baptist Convention (the National Baptist Publishing Board) both operated from Nashville. The railroads extending out of this growing center for education and publishing reached wide and diverse markets, including rapidly growing strongholds of the Baptist faith such as Mississippi and Texas. Boyd's tact and personal skills secured the aid of James M. Frost, secretary of the white Sunday School Board. Together the two men introduced successful business methods into their respective denominations, meeting the opposition to their efforts by stressing the necessity of the "development" and "uplifting" of their people. The two entrepreneurs worked in buildings just a few blocks apart in downtown Nashville, and they developed a successful working relationship. The city dubbed the "Athens of the South" served Richard Boyd's purposes ideally.[38]

The relationship between the heads of the two agencies exemplified how white and black southern Baptists could cooperate on specific projects even within the segregated southern religious world. Frost offered funds, technical advice, printing presses, and literature to Boyd's publishing firm. Most white southern Baptists viewed racial separatism as a way to contain black autonomy. Boyd, however, interpreted separatism as the basis for true independence. At the beginning of his association with James Frost, according to

Boyd's account, some black denominationalists predicted that the white board would subsume the black publishing effort. But Frost never dictated "what to preach or where to preach," and helpfully aided black endeavors. While some religious bodies acted as if "Negro Baptists have no rights that should be respected by them," white southern Baptists dealt "on principles of equality and manhood" with independent black brethren, Boyd proclaimed in 1899. He suggested that white northern Baptists should learn this lesson:

> The National Baptist Convention has a right to own and control its own business enterprises, to maintain, on a larger scale, distinctive educational institutions, and in the exercise of this priestly prerogative, no band of white brethren anywhere should undertake to embarrass or molest them. With the recognition of these rights and corresponding brotherly treatment, our white brethren will find in the constituency of the National Baptist Convention *ardent friends* and *loyal supporters*.[39]

In January of 1897, Boyd's presses set in type the first series of Sunday school lessons, authored mostly by white and black Sunday school writers. With assistance from James Frost, Boyd sold his publications to churches throughout the country. Starting with virtually nothing in the mid-1890s, by 1906 the publishing board had accumulated a business valued at $160,152. By 1910, the board's presses pumped out over eleven million pieces of literature each year and employed over 150 black workers. By 1915, the board reported a cumulative total of over $2,500,000 worth of business. Boyd plowed back into the enterprise his yearly profits. He set up subsidiary companies to supply churches with pews, benches, hymnbooks, pulpits, choir robes, and children's dolls. His enterprise held together the diffuse and loosely organized National Baptist Convention.[40]

Boyd was loath to cede any personal control over his multifaceted enterprises, and disputes over the quasi-independence of his agency disrupted NBC meetings. Facts that dribbled out about Boyd's management of his properties were disturbing. Boyd had taken out mortgages and borrowed money against the publishing board's property, using the funds to help finance his other ventures. His family was encumbered with personal mortgages on property that officials of the National Baptist Convention claimed as the denomination's own. Copyrights on Sunday school commentaries were in Boyd's own name and were binding for twenty-eight years, meaning that Boyd profited personally by selling religious literature to churches. Challenged to transfer his copyrights to the denomination, Boyd responded that he legally spawned the board as a private enterprise affiliated with but not controlled by the convention.[41]

The wrangling for control of the publishing board began in earnest in 1905 and dragged on over the next ten years. At the annual meeting in Chicago in 1915, NBC officials sought to establish the legal authority of the denomination over Boyd's firm (and over the Home Mission Board, which Boyd used as a publicity agency). After failing to interrupt the regular convention meeting, Boyd reconvened his supporters at a different Chicago church. Boyd's forces took all the publishing board records and with them the "members who declared that the secretary's argument in defense of his claim that the Publishing House was his own private property was a perfectly just and reasonable one." Boyd also claimed the $10,000 contributed by whites to the black Home Mission Board, setting off another legal tussle.[42]

The basic issue in the dispute involved who would exercise ultimate authority over the publishing house. "Shall the Baptists of this country own and control that which they, through their principal organization, have founded and built up, or shall its control be left to a few to be used for personal gain?" asked E. C. Morris, Boyd's chief rival. An arbiter hired to untangle the legal knot determined that the various black Baptist agencies of the convention held property "in trust, for the uses and benefit" of the NBC. The legal counsel suggested that the organization create an executive board to transact denominational business, and Morris soon incorporated the original convention.[43]

The Boyd faction in this dispute (those who supported the independence of the publishing firm) argued that the fiction of incorporation simply masked the personal control of the convention's agencies by E. C. Morris and his minions. Since the publishing board showed financial stability, whereas other denominational agencies never established a secure funding base, Morris allegedly wanted to exploit Boyd's own efforts for his own personal gain. Boyd contended that he stood for the "ancient doctrine" that Baptist conventions were merely voluntary associations from which individuals and groups could withdraw. He accused the Morris faction of pursuing a "strong centralization form of government, a permanent organization with the property rights vested in a central body." Boyd objected to turning the denomination into a modern nonprofit corporation, a move that would, in his view, wrest away the crown jewel of his business empire. As the legal entanglement worsened, the disputants demanded that ministers and churches choose sides. As a result, Boyd's son, Henry Allen Boyd, was not allowed a seat in the Alabama Colored Baptist State Convention. When the National Baptist Convention supporters attempted to issue literature through the auspices of northern agencies, Boyd blasted them for "going to a publishing society that does not even employ a colored man to wash spittoons."[44]

At the request of some of the black disputants, white churchmen in 1918 attempted to referee the fray. O. L. Hailey, a white Baptist who was instrumental in the opening of the black American Baptist Theological Seminary in Nashville, headed the committee of arbiters. Hailey discovered that many white southern Baptists held "no sympathy with the effort to help the Negro," and he wrote privately to a colleague that publicizing the controversy "in its true colors would tend to confirm these brethren in their prejudice against the negroes." Hailey responded to these skeptics by asserting that "the present World situation is calling for us to take care of the Negro." White southerners would "need the help of the Negro in the next period. And while we have them with us, we ought to help them that they may be ready to stand with us when the testing time comes, as it is destined to come soon." Hailey's committee, which favored the Morris faction's philosophy of denominational control of all agencies, failed in its conciliation efforts. The schism grew deeper as each separate convention developed constituent churches and agencies. Some black critics of the reunification committee questioned why whites should be trusted to resolve this dispute when blacks were "lynched and burned right under some of these white commissioners nose and not one word spoken or protest uttered against it." Such evils, these allies of Boyd's suggested, were "more dangerous and damnable than all the dissension the race can create among themselves."[45] The two main contenders in the publishing board battle, Richard H. Boyd and Elias C. Morris, died in the early 1920s, leaving behind them the unfortunate legacy of this bitter legal split.

Boyd's position with the publishing board assured him a high profile among Nashville blacks and afforded him a significant political voice. In the 1890s, Boyd had warned his fellow citizens and ministers to "carefully guard" their interests lest politicians "turn the hand backward on the political dial [by] a quarter of a century." Like many African Americans, Boyd could accept separate and equal and could have probably reconciled himself to separate and incidentally unequal, but he could not abide separate and deliberately, systematically, and egregiously unequal. Boyd stood for racial peace but added that "peace from the Negro point of view does not mean quiet submission to all forms of injustice, oppression, and violence."[46] And Boyd practiced what he preached. When Nashville began enforcing laws requiring segregated streetcars, which provided inferior accommodations for blacks, Boyd helped to organize a boycott. He must have known the risks involved, for in Augusta, Georgia, in 1898, after blacks led a successful fight against a similar measure, a round of violence against the city's black citizens ensued. When the *Georgia Baptist*, the black state denominational newspaper, reprinted stories of the outrages, angry whites formed a mob and attacked the editor, William Jefferson White, a man half white and extremely light skinned. Despite such potential results, Boyd implored black Nashvillians to "buy buggies and start to trim their corns, darn their socks, wear solid shoes, and walk." The *Nashville Globe*, edited by Boyd's son, publicized the boycott, and Boyd's fellow Nashville Baptist ministers Sutton Griggs and Edward Isaac urged black Nashvillians who had "express wagons" to make them available for transport. Boyd also joined with black businessmen in creating the Union Transportation Company and loaned the basement of his publishing house for the generator that powered the company's trolleys. The venture eventually failed, however, because its steam-driven vehicles proved unable to negotiate Nashville's hills. A tax imposed by the city on streetcars of the type used by the company finished off the undercapitalized endeavor. The boycott and the company both collapsed in 1906, but Boyd firmly established himself as an important voice in Nashville affairs.[47]

Boyd also became an important personage in black Nashville through the National Negro Doll Company. Although Marcus Garvey and the United Negro Improvement Association are often credited with popularizing black dolls, Richard H. Boyd pioneered the marketing of dolls to black consumers. The figurines were one way, he said, that black "personality and individuality" would not be "submerged" in the white world. Boyd's opinion was reinforced while he was shopping for Christmas toys for his children: he could find no black figures that were not gross Negro caricatures. An advertisement for the products of the National Negro Doll Company (which ran in the *Nashville Globe*, other black newspapers, and Boyd's Sunday school publications) conveys Boyd's sense of cultural respect. His figures, the publicity copy stated, would not be "made of that disgraceful and humiliating type that we have been accustomed to seeing black dolls made of. They represent the intelligent and refined Negro of today, rather than that type of toy that is usually given to the children, and as a rule used as a scarecrow. These toys are placed in the city and at the disposal of the people that they may teach their children how to look upon their people." Shortly after the founding of the company, the National Baptist Convention called on its members to remove the "flaxen-haired, blue eyed Caucasian dolls from the homes of every self-respecting Negro."[48]

Another of Boyd's Nashville ventures was the One Cent Savings Bank and Trust Company, begun in partnership with local black businessmen who provided banking facilities for black depositors. Citing the failure of the Freedmen's Bank during Reconstruction, Boyd insisted that his institution would practice fiscal conservatism over a period of years to protect clients. His bank was not created "for the purpose of investing and accumulating money for the stockholders," he said, but rather "for the purpose, first, of restoring confidence in the already industrious colored citizens and training young men in financial dealings." The bank assumed a slow-growth posture. Some of his partners dissented from his conservative policies. They began their own bank with looser restraints on investing and lending. But Boyd's cautious strategy paid off. His institution persevered through difficult years while other Nashville banks, white and black, became insolvent.[49]

Boyd's two roles—religious entrepreneur and race spokesman—were evident in his public positions. On the one hand, he was fully capable of embracing accommodationist slogans. "The Southern white man has many peculiarities," he admitted, and "frightens too easily at the 'social equality' ghost, of which most Negroes never dream." But the southern white man nevertheless gave "the industrious Negro the very best opportunity to make money with which to buy property, and to speculate in legal business ventures." On the other hand, in both the *Nashville Globe* and the *National Baptist Union-Review* (a denominational newspaper he edited), Boyd launched forthright attacks on southern racism, maintaining his stance even when Sutton Griggs resigned himself to a conservative version of racial separation. Responding to an article in the Georgia *Christian Index* (a white denominational newspaper) in 1917, which suggested that blacks had been "well managed" in the South, Boyd bristled, "we do not like the idea of being 'managed.'" The migration of blacks to the North was, he exulted, a "great religious movement. God's hand in it is visible." The so-called "Negro problem," he said, was the result of the perpetration of "mob violence, starvation wages, peonage, shameful educational neglect, Jim Crow laws, enforced segregation, miscarriage of justice in the courts, brutal police relations, inadequate housing, . . . disfranchisement, [and] mistreatment of our women and girls by a vicious element."[50]

Boyd's son, Henry Allen Boyd, worked with his father and eventually became his business successor. In 1906, Henry Allen Boyd and three other local businessmen founded the *Nashville Globe* and, later, the Globe Publishing Company. Henry Boyd took daily editorial charge of the paper, while his father's money (and frequent advertisements for National Baptist Publishing Board literature) bankrolled it. From its founding until its demise in 1960, the *Globe* provided an invaluable record of Nashville's black world-within-a-world, a community that went largely unrecorded by whites. By the late 1920s, some 20 percent of Nashville's black families subscribed. The *Globe* promoted black businesses of all kinds, from tiny barber shops to successful undertakers. But the *Globe* not only represented the Washingtonian ideal of self-help, it also provided a forum for local black protest thought. It publicized police abuses against blacks, demanded that more black faculty be added to the rolls at Fisk University, and protested changes in local electoral law that diluted the black vote. A stalwart in Republican Party politics locally, Henry Boyd was instrumental in obtaining money for a land grant for what later became Tennessee State University. He protested the pittance blacks received for teacher education through the Peabody Fund and directed a campaign to build a black YMCA.[51]

In the 1920s, after the death of his father, Henry Allen Boyd put out the *National Jubilee Melody Book*, a hymnal that was one of the first to record the nineteenth-century slave spirituals. Thomas Andrew Dorsey, a founding father of gospel music, published many of his compositions through the National Baptist Publishing Board before later moving on to more commercial presses. After a long and productive career, Henry Allen Boyd died in 1958, leaving considerable stock in the Citizen's Bank to his daughter. The Boyd legacy in Nashville was a long-lived one.[52]

Though a relatively obscure figure in black history, Richard H. Boyd waged in pragmatic and businesslike ways the battle that W. E. B. Du Bois fought in the pages of his essays—to define how to be a Negro and an American and to maintain that "double consciousness" in constant and fruitful tension. Boyd trusted in the promise that the long night of Jim Crow would turn into a new morning of freedom, if one kept the faith.

The participation of black soldiers in World War I, the mass pilgrimage of hundreds of thousands of African Americans to northern cities, and the race riots stemming in part from the migration, all demanded the attention of the nation's largest black religious group. The hopes first raised and then crushed by the illusory opportunities for racial progress during and after the First World War demonstrated again how difficult it would be to breach the defenses of American racism.

Many of the issues facing African Americans had been brewing for decades, including the question of African emigration. The case for quitting America and pursuing a racial destiny elsewhere rang out most passionately in the words of Henry McNeal Turner of the AME church, a former Reconstruction legislator, able church organizer, and fiery racial rhetorician. While black Baptists at local levels occasionally took up camp in Turner's ideological army, few denominationalists (at least at a national level) espoused Turner's views. Despite the fact that "enthusiastic reformers" might advocate emigration, it was nothing more than a "wildcat scheme that every thinking Negro will discourage," a black Baptist paper argued. Even those men and women who dedicated their lives to missionary work considered Africa a continent "bound in heathen darkness." In the early nineteenth century missionaries had proposed to accomplish the task of civilization while living permanently in their stations and preparing the way for future emigrants to come. By the late nineteenth century, however, few of the black apostles of American Christianity considered emigration as part of their calling. When the African peoples who the black missionaries served called them "white men," the notion that Africa was "home" must have seemed particularly far-fetched. They aided instead in the immigration of a number of young African men for education in black institutions. Some of these students used their knowledge in organizing anticolonial rebellions back home and in forming independent African churches, challenging the prerogatives of the black Americans who converted them.[53]

Far more compelling for most black Christians than African emigration was migration to another Promised Land, the North. The mass exodus of blacks from the South during World War I discomfited black denominational leaders. For a generation, white and black religious conservatives drilled their folk in the mantra that the South represented the "best hope" for the African American. Before the mass movement, black Baptists uneasily eyed younger urban migrants who rejected southern rural life: "The old church in which mother and father worshipped is allowed to go down and the farm slip back into the hands of the white man. They go North to make their fortunes; many of them return moral and physical wrecks." One minister suggested that "it would be better if our people could be taught that culture, manhood and self-respect will grow in any clime, and by proper application the Negroes can work out their salvation here." Migrants heading northward should at least acquire practical skills first in southern schools of industrial education, he advised. Too many young people, he warned, "choose to be dudes. They seem to think that a standing-collar, a fine coat and a keen toed pair of shoes, make a gentleman. . . . Young men and women who might become useful to their race . . . have no higher aspiration than to dress up and look fine." Young people in the cities, as black Baptist leaders portrayed them, too often were "drunkards, gamblers and midnight prowlers." North or South, the "salvation" of the Negro lay in "his industry and obedience to law." Such advice, of course, would be hard to follow in the face of the racial pressures and economic incentives that both pushed black people out of the South and pulled them to northern industrial centers.[54]

For a more creditable assessment of which region offered the "best hope," black congregants usually listened instead to relatives and friends who had made the northward trek. Many clergymen who urged their congregants to remain in their southern homes eventually found themselves on a northern-bound train. As the flood tide of southern refugees moved northward, black

Baptists praised the "hand of God leading us out of persecution," and forecast that migration would continue so long as African Americans were "segregated, our women lynched, our men flayed alive and burned at the stake and the courts used with partiality against us." At the same time they depicted the dangers awaiting those moving to northern cities:

> Do you see the thousands of boys and girls of our race coming from the slums of the cities, degenerate children, who hear nothing but vulgarity in its worst form. . . . Look at the number of idle boys of our race at the depots, standing at the corners of the streets in front of hotels, begging to carry baggage and to sell papers. . . . Look at the men standing in front of the barrooms, sitting on the barrels with bloated eyes. . . . Look at the chain gangs and penitentiaries. . . . What a sad picture.[55]

Nannie Burroughs articulated for many women this mixed assessment of the migration. She understood the movement as a healthy rebuke to a generation of racial oppression but worried about the fate of the "modest, industrious, honest" country girl of the past. Enticed by the lures of urban life, the country girl had a "hungering and thirsting for finery. Her city cousin visits her occasionally and sows the seed of restlessness and discontent that is seldom ever satisfied until the girl makes her way to some city, unprepared for the new life, and is lost in the great whirl." Yet Burroughs also keenly understood the forces inducing urbanization. By the 1910s, the Woman's Convention employed sociological analyses in explaining the urbanization of its constituency, moving gradually away from pietistic platitudes.[56]

The shortage of immigrant labor in the North during World War I not only created an increase in job opportunities for blacks in northern industrial centers, it also extended a golden opportunity to blacks to bargain for better conditions in the South. Black ministers in local areas learned to maneuver within these cracks in the wall of Jim Crow. If black southerners desired to "better their present condition" by migrating, "now is the time to do so," North Carolina Baptists advised in 1916. A black Baptist association in 1920 demanded that whites provide better wages and public accommodations for black employees, since the humiliations blacks experienced were "driving thousands of our people away from the South. . . . The Negro is looking for better things now, and it seems that he will have them, if he has to go after them." Even the racial conciliator Richard Carroll, a minister of mixed ancestry who worked closely with the SBC, used the migration as a bargaining chip. "Our Southern white men have called meetings on the boll weevil and it is now up to them to call a meeting on the negro and say what they will do for them if they will stay in the South," he informed a white readership in a South Carolina newspaper. At the same time he assured his readers of his continued "hope" for the region: "If I thought there was no change coming I would leave the South myself."[57]

Optimism about the benefits of the migration faded rapidly after the war. Race riots raged in northern cities, and a nationwide recession reduced wages and cost recent migrants their jobs, tarnishing the image of the northern promised land. A Texas black Baptist noted ruefully in 1921 that Negroes had been "fooled" into thinking that conditions were markedly better in the North than in the South. Since the war, he said, "irreconcilables and radicals" (by which he meant men such as Marcus Garvey) had "felt divinely called to solve race problems in a way different from God's way as outlined in His Bible." The Texan retreated back to the familiar faith that the best people of both races could work out a racial compromise. But the task would be difficult, he conceded: "In a Democracy like ours, much time and patience should be exercised in bringing the common people to the necessary standards of self-government." Whites talked of "ignorant Negroes," one embittered black Baptist wrote, while ignoring white immigrants who were "anarchists, godless and characterless, as dangerous as is a suppressed volcano, . . . knowing nothing of American ideas, and caring less; ignorant of the constitution and ready to haul down the American flag that their red flag may float in instead."[58]

Black Baptists' reactions to World War I resembled their responses to segregation and disfranchisement, from conciliatory rhetoric to embitterment and resignation. At the beginning of the Great War, black Baptists echoed Du Bois's advice to prove their valor in combat and loyalty at home. World War I was, they said, a "splendid opportunity for the Negro to reacquaint the American people with the kind of patriotism which the Negro as Americans possess." Focusing on racial issues during the war would not be expedient. "Let us not stop to cavil over our domestic grievances and discrimination," advised a group of North Carolinians in 1917. "This is our country in spite of the pet phrase of the political demagogue to the contrary," Georgia Baptists asserted. The Wilsonian ideal of self-determination moved some to envision a better future after the Armistice. "Autocracy will not be destroyed and universal liberty established," E. C. Morris announced during the war, "until the black and the white Americans march shoulder to shoulder into the gates of Berlin, or drive the Hun back there." In the meantime, he advised, patience and quietism remained the wisest course.[59]

But black churchmen soon learned how little the war would foster progress in race relations. A show of loyalty to the country, they feared, once again had proved to be a faulty strategy. At first denominational leaders had seized on the war as an opportunity for straightforward talk on race prejudice. "We feel keenly the unnecessary, unjust and unpatriotic discrimination, Jim Crowism and segregation forced upon our race," one women's convention resolved during the war. Yet even at the height of postwar optimism, the same racial dilemmas remained unresolved. A North Carolina educator detected a "subtle propaganda" leading to the bountiful funds extended to institutions of industrial education "under the pretext of the training of the hand or of the education of the Negro servilely" and the small sum earmarked for the "education of Negroes as statesmen." Race leaders should inform whites of their discontent "without cringing the suppliant knee or the FAWNING LIP," he insisted.[60]

By the early 1920s, black churchmen and -women retreated to their familiar position of imploring that African Americans simply wanted an equal chance. As a group of Alabamans put it in 1921, "our aim is to attain race equality, not social equality but race equality." Even while decrying the "compulsions of unjust laws and the restrictions of an unrighteous domination," a black denominational newspaper nonetheless saw "the practical establishment of Christianity" as the only answer to prejudice. Churches should stand "first of all for spiritual religion, for personal regeneration," and secondarily for "patriotism, education, industry and other phases of sociology," it suggested.[61]

Black Baptists in Virginia in 1921 expressed much of the strained optimism, as well as the frustration, that black Americans felt as Jim Crow remained solidly in place after the war. The president of the Virginia Baptist convention urged blacks to play their part in "the great work of making America American," to unite Negroes with native whites to restrict immigrants and exile residents of questionable loyalty. But Carter Woodson, a pioneer scholar of African American history and sociology present at the same meeting, assessed the situation more realistically. He pointed out that black Americans who fought in the war often bore the brunt of racial attacks for their efforts. That African Americans had shown themselves "loyal" counted for little when in northern cities layoffs disproportionately affected black employees and in the South white supremacists remained firmly in control. The rise of the "lily-white" Republicans destroyed hopes in the traditional party of the African American. The Virginians, once associated with a rhetoric of cooperation, adopted a new motto indicative of the move to separatism: "Faith in Self, Self Help, Negro Control of Negro Institutions, Negroes Only Safe and Efficient Teachers for Negroes." Contrary to earlier hopes, Nannie Burroughs admitted, racial solidarity and individual advancement would not necessarily mitigate racial oppression. "Everybody is an expert on the Race Question," she scoffed, "and everybody feels as if he has the only solution for it." The object of black Baptist organizations must be "to uneducate the Negro in many things in which he has been educated. . . . Our job is to make people believe in themselves."[62]

In the 1920s, the black Baptist constituency was in great flux. The migration to the North challenged churches to assimilate southern migrants. It was also a period of great creativity for black religious culture. Thomas Andrew Dorsey, himself a migrant from Georgia to Chicago, tested out the new sounds that later blossomed into black gospel music. Storefront holiness churches revived black religious expressive styles, in direct rebuke to a generation of exhortation for "intelligent worship." The cultural creativity was not matched by a similarly rejuvenated period of religio-political activism, however. The black Baptist constituency still was plagued by its abject poverty, the virulent racism of 1920s America, and the factionalism that paralyzed denominational politics. The promised land appeared so distant as to be barely discernible, while more years of wandering in the wilderness darkened future prospects.[63]

Religion, Race, and Culture in the South

This book has illuminated commonalities in the experiences of white and black Baptists while also highlighting their mutual antagonisms in the white supremacist South. Evangelicalism in the region arose in biracial worship settings—in rural one-room church houses, camp meetings, and larger urban congregations. This biracial aspect of worship, already explored by historians of the antebellum era, has not yet been incorporated sufficiently into studies of postbellum southern Protestantism. The racial separation of churches after the Civil War did not preclude intriguing parallels and interactions between white and black believers in belief and practice, sometimes at an institutional level, often in ways unacknowledged.

During Reconstruction, churches became one center of political and social struggles pitting white versus black. The political resistance to Reconstruction among white southerners, the clarion call to battle against Yankee faith, quickened the rebuilding of white southern religious institutions. The interracial cooperation evidenced in the establishment of a few black churches could not mitigate the contentious struggle for political power between the fragile biracial Reconstruction coalition and the increasingly confident Redeemers. Southern Democrats benefited from political support among the white ministerial elite, who preached to their constituents of God's plan to "redeem" the South from "political-religionism" and "fanaticism"—their terms for white northern missionaries and the politics of biracial democracy.

Black Baptist organizers, temporarily

enthused by the possibilities presented by Reconstruction, soon recognized that Anglo-Americans would not reject their own deeply rooted racism. In the era of Jim Crow, black churches sustained the spirit of African Americans in a region dedicated to their subjugation and humiliation. The work of black Christian leaders, sometimes overtly political but more often not, pursued the same goals that energized black political activity during Reconstruction. Their work was considered politically conservative—accommodationist, in African American historical terms. But their work was also conservative in the more positive sense—it conserved a people's spirit.

White and black Baptists struggled through many of the same ambivalent, contradictory responses to modernization. Denominational leaders, most often educated in the colleges and seminaries of the New South, brought the "task of scientific management" into their "church-craft." They centralized denominational procedures, built educational institutions, introduced Victorian notions of public decorum to rural farmers and wage laborers, and taught their congregations about the virtues of sobriety and propriety. Yet their Baptist constituency kept alive into a new era venerable spiritual practices of rural southern evangelicalism—ring shouts, chanted sermons, shape-note and lined out singing, footwashing, dramatic conversions, and communal baptisms. Modernization came slowly and erratically to the South—and the same might be said for southern religious cultures. "Folkways" and modern ways, rural customs and urban innovation existed side by side, lending a far greater variety to southern evangelical practice than has commonly been recognized.

In the interwar years, the South came under withering scrutiny. Among the national intelligentsia, political leaders, journalists, and racial reformers, the region came to stand for all that was backward, downtrodden, and self-defeating in America. H. L. Mencken memorably savaged the region in "The Sahara of the Bozart." W. J. Cash's *Mind of the South* described southern religion with as much acerbity. New black voices in politics and literature condemned the South's racial past and celebrated the escape of so many African Americans to presumably better lives in the North. Southern evangelicals, increasingly marginalized from the national culture, spent these years on the defensive, their customs condemned as relics of barbarism.

During these same years, however, millions of white and black people migrated out of the region and, after World War II, transplanted southern evangelical cultures onto new soil. White and black gospel music found its way into the world of American popular music. And southern white and black religious traditions, once revived and politicized by a new generation of leaders, gradually reemerged and fueled some of the most important political movements of recent times, including the Civil Rights movement and that of the New Religious Political Right.

Black Americans drew from their own rich religious traditions during the Civil Rights movement. The exact relationship between the church and the movement varied. In urban centers such as Montgomery and Atlanta, religious activists and the people in the pews inspired heroic acts of nonviolent civil disobedience. In rural areas, especially in Mississippi, churches disappointed movement activists time and time again, accepting payoffs from local landlords in exchange for closing their doors to organizing meetings. Regardless of the role of the institutional churches, the expressive culture of black worship, maintained against a generation of stern admonition for "intelligent worship," emboldened the common men and (especially) women who peopled the front lines in the nonviolent war against Jim Crow. Martin Luther King Jr. expressed his appreciation for the traditions of black expressive culture—the hymns, humor, jokes, food, and spirituality—which had sustained his people through generations of oppression. He was also keenly aware that the church often bore little relevance to the everyday concerns of the congregants. King's upbringing in an emotionally expressive congregation, together with his training in the social gospel, came together in the Civil Rights movement.

More obscure are the roots of the New Religious Political Right in the white southern religious traditions. Beginning in the 1920s, as Fundamentalism "moved south" and went underground, conservative southern ministers, increasingly swayed by the pessimistic doctrine of premillennialism, taught a generation of people about the meaning of events in this world. They witnessed a secularizing America in which a Manichaean struggle between good and evil raged. They prophesied that this cataclysmic battle would culminate in a time of tribulation and an eventual triumphant return of Christ. After decades of this training and a generation of upward mobility, this version of biblical literalism emerged from the shadows into the political limelight in the antiabortion crusade, Ronald Reagan's presidential campaigns, and most recently in the Christian Coalition. The ambivalent relationship that southern Fundamentalists in the 1920s held toward the nation continues to bedevil the contemporary conservative evangelicals, who cannot fully decide whether America is, or can be, a "Christian nation."

Beginning in the late 1970s and culminating in the early 1990s, the nation's largest Protestant denomination underwent the same furious internal battle for the "soul of the convention" that nearly every American Protestant group fought earlier in the century. White southern Fundamentalists staged a conservative coup d'état in the Southern Baptist Convention in the 1980s, through more than a decade of bitter political battles, re-crimination, and purges. The "moderates" in the SBC, dominant in the years since World War II, argued that the denomination should put aside overly stringent theological litmus tests in favor of church growth. Rela-tively conservative in politics and theology but amenable to some social change, these moderates represented the legacy of the white southern Bap-tist progressivism detailed in chapter seven of this work. The current crop of Fundamentalists have politicized the Landmarkist-influenced rural tra-ditions that earlier had defeated southern Baptist progressivism. The con-temporary Fundamentalist leaders of the SBC are politically astute and technologically literate men, but they represent a tradition deeply rooted in white southern belief. Their victory, however, will be a Pyrrhic one: the Southern Baptist Convention itself is now well on its way to a schism, as moderates form protodenominational groups. And the culture war pro-moted by the Fundamentalist leaders, with its implicitly racially loaded content, ultimately will have limited appeal in an increasingly pluralistic society.

Denominations as institutions were ideally suited to American social life in the nineteenth and early twentieth century. But the rise of parachurches, the decline of the older mainstream denominations, and analyses that dem-onstrate how the rate of membership growth declines when "sect" becomes "church" all raise questions about the future of denominations. As the South enters a more pluralistic era, its Protestant evangelical hegemony will erode gradually. But the racial interactions that have given southern religion its distinctive character will continue to shape America's religious land-scape. Southerners, white and black, will remain two people divided by a religious heritage with common internal struggles and millennial dreams.

NOTES

Abbreviations Used in Notes

AB	*American Baptist*
ABHMS	American Baptist Home Mission Society
ABHS	Samuel Colgate Library, American Baptist Historical Society, Rochester, N.Y.
BHMM	*Baptist Home Mission Monthly*
BR	*Biblical Recorder* (N.C.)
BW	*Baptist World* (Ky.)
CABMC *Report*	Consolidated American Baptist Missionary Convention
CI	*Christian Index* (Ga.)
CWR	*Christian Watchman and Reflector*
ESB	Lynn May et al., eds., *Encyclopedia of Southern Baptists* (Nashville, 1958), vols. 1 and 2
Narratives	George Rawick, ed., *The American Slave: A Composite Autobiography*, 41 vols. (Westport, Conn., 1972–79). Individual volumes of the narratives will be referred to by state (e.g., *Texas Narratives*), with the series, part, volume number, page, and name of interviewee following.
NBC	National Baptist Convention
NBC *Journal*	The annual journal of the proceedings of the National Baptist Convention. I have simply noted the year and the page and omitted other publishing information.
NBM	*National Baptist Magazine*
RH	*Religious Herald* (Va.)
SBC	Southern Baptist Convention
SBC *Annual*	Annual Proceedings of the Southern Baptist Convention
SBHLA	Southern Baptist Historical Library and Archives, Nashville, Tenn.
SBTS	James P. Boyce Library, Southern Baptist Theological Seminary, Louisville, Ky.
SSB	Library of the Sunday School Board of the Southern Baptist Convention, Nashville
WFU	Z. Smith Reynolds Library, North Carolina Baptist Historical Commission, Wake Forest University, Winston-Salem, N.C.
WMU	Woman's Missionary Union, Auxiliary to the Southern Baptist Convention
Woman's Convention *Journal*	The annual journal of the proceedings of the Woman's Convention, Auxiliary to the National Baptist Convention

Unless noted otherwise, church, association, state convention, and national convention minutes were consulted on microfilm at the Southern Baptist Historical Library and Archives in Nashville, Tennessee. I have omitted specific details of publication for the meetings, as they are most easily consulted under the name of the organization. I have instead simply included the name of the organization, an abbreviated title such as *Proceedings* or *Minutes*, the year, and the appropriate page numbers. For local Baptist associations, I have included the name of the state in parenthesis. For example: New Hope Missionary Baptist Association (North Carolina) *Minutes*, 1919, 36.

Introduction

1. A few of the standard works that both established southern religious history as a field and outlined its major interpretive themes include John B. Boles, *The Great Revival, 1787–1805: The Origins of the Southern Evangelical Mind* (Lexington, Ky., 1972); Donald G. Mathews, *Religion in the Old South* (Chicago, 1977); Samuel S. Hill Jr., *Southern Churches in Crisis* (New York, 1967); Samuel S. Hill Jr., ed., *Religion and the Solid South* (Nashville, 1972); and Kenneth Bailey, *Southern White Protestantism in the Twentieth Century* (New York, 1964).

Some important recent works that focus on white and black believers and religious organizations include John B. Boles, ed., *Masters and Slaves in the House of the Lord: Race and Religion in the American South, 1740–1870* (Lexington, Ky., 1988); Katharine L. Dvorak, *An African-American Exodus: The Segregation of the Southern Churches, 1865–1871* (Brooklyn, N.Y., 1991); Randy Sparks, *On Jordan's Stormy Banks: Evangelicalism in Mississippi, 1763–1877* (Athens, Ga., 1994); and Daniel Stowell, "Rebuilding Zion: The Religious Reconstruction of the South, 1863–1877" (Ph.D. diss., University of Florida, 1994).

Two important studies on gender and southern religion are Jean Friedman, *The Enclosed Garden: Women and Community in the Evangelical South, 1830–1900* (Chapel Hill, 1985), and Ted Ownby, *Subduing Satan: Religion, Recreation, and Manhood in the Rural South, 1865–1920* (Chapel Hill, 1990). The relationship of gender and religion appears to be the next major research area for studies in southern religion.

The study of African American religious history has become a vital and rapidly growing field. Older works of importance include W. E. B. Du Bois, *The Negro Church* (Atlanta, 1903); Carter G. Woodson, *The History of the Negro Church* (Washington, 1921); Benjamin Mays, *The Negro's God, as Reflected in His Literature* (New York, 1938); and E. Franklin Frazier, *The Negro Church in America* (New York, 1964). Frazier's work should be contrasted to Melville Herskovits, *The Myth of the Negro Past* (Boston, 1941). Most works addressing the debate between Frazier and Herskovits on the origins of African American religious practices have stressed how black Christians synthesized European beliefs and practices with African conceptions of ritual.

The 1960s and 1970s witnessed an outpouring of seminal scholarly work on African American religion, especially the religion of the slaves. See for example, Albert Raboteau, *Slave Religion: The "Invisible Institution" in the Antebellum South* (New York, 1978); Eugene Genovese, *Roll, Jordan, Roll: The World the Slaves Made* (New York,

1974); Edmund Wheeler, *Uplifting the Race: The Black Minister in the New South, 1865–1902* (Lanham, Md., 1983); Gayraud Wilmore, *Black Religion and Black Radicalism: An Interpretation of the Religious History of the Afro-American People* (Maryknoll, N.Y., 1983); and Mechal Sobel, *Trabelin' On: The Slave Journey to an Afro-Baptist Faith* (Westport, Conn., 1979). For more recent works, see Margaret Washington Creel, *"A Peculiar People": Slave Religion and Community-Culture Among the Gullahs* (New York, 1988), and Sylvia Frey, *Water From the Rock: Black Resistance in a Revolutionary Age* (Princeton, N.J., 1991).

Four particularly outstanding studies on material closely related to this work are James Melvin Washington, *Frustrated Fellowship: The Black Baptist Quest for Social Power* (Macon, Ga., 1986); William Montgomery, *Under Their Own Vine and Fig Tree: African-American Religion in the South, 1865–1900* (Baton Rouge, 1993); Evelyn Brooks Higginbotham, *Righteous Discontent: The Women's Movement in the Black Baptist Church, 1880–1920* (Cambridge, Mass., 1993); and James Campbell, *Songs of Zion: The African Methodist Episcopal Church in the United States and South Africa* (New York, 1995). Taken together, these works have provided provocative new directions for the study of postbellum African American religious history.

The best overall historiographical survey of material on southern religion is John B. Boles, "The Discovery of Southern Religious History," in *Interpreting Southern History: Historiographical Essays in Honor of Sanford W. Higginbotham*, ed. John B. Boles and Evelyn Thomas Nolen (Baton Rouge, 1987), 510–48. A convenient and comprehensive bibliography of material up to 1985 may be found in James Lippy, ed., *Bibliography of Religion in the South* (Macon, Ga., 1985). For black religion in particular, consult the bibliography of Ethel Williams and Clifton Brown, *The Howard University Bibliography of African and Afro-American Religious Studies, With Locations in American Libraries* (Wilmington, Del., 1977). For a guide to material from the American Baptist Historical Society, a major resource for this work, see Lester Scherer and Susan Eltscher, *Afro-American Baptists: A Guide to the Records in the Library of the American Baptist Historical Society* (Rochester, N.Y., 1985). Another crucial reference work for primary source materials on the religious culture of African Americans is Eileen Southern and Josephine Wright, eds., *Afro-American Traditions in Song, Sermon, Tale, and Dance, 1600s–1920: An Annotated Bibliography of Literature, Collections, and Artworks* (New York, 1990).

2. Interview in Frederick L. Gwynn and Joseph L. Blotner, *Faulkner in the University: Class Conferences at the University of Virginia, 1957–1958* (Charlottesville, 1959), quoted in Charles Wilson, "William Faulkner and the Southern Religious Culture," in *Faulkner and Religion*, ed. Doreen Fowler and Ann Abadie (Jackson, Miss., 1991), 27–28.

3. The fullest analysis of Dixon may be found in Joel Williamson, *The Crucible of Race: Black / White Relations in the American South Since Emancipation* (New York, 1984). The novels used for the screenplay of *The Birth of a Nation* were Thomas Dixon, *The Leopard's Spots: A Romance of the White Man's Burden—1865–1900* (New York, 1902), and *The Clansman: An Historical Romance of the Ku Klux Klan* (New York, 1905). For an analysis of *Birth of a Nation*, see Michael Rogin, " 'The Sword Became a Flashing Vision': D. W. Griffith's *The Birth of a Nation*," in *Ronald Reagan, the Movie, and Other Episodes in Political Demonology*, ed. Michael Rogin (Berkeley, 1987), 120–235.

4. Excerpts from both kinds of sermons are quoted in Richard C. Goode, "The Godly

Insurrection in Limestone County: Social Gospel, Populism, and Southern Culture in the Late Nineteenth Century," *Religion and American Culture: A Journal of Interpretation* 3 (Summer 1993): 155–70.

5. On Washington, see Louis Harlan, *Booker T. Washington: The Making of a Black Leader, 1865–1901* (New York, 1972), and *Booker T. Washington: The Wizard of Tuskegee, 1901–1915* (New York, 1983). Sutton Griggs's works include *Imperium in Imperio* (Cincinnati, 1889), and *The Hindered Hand: Or, the Reign of the Repressionist* (Nashville, 1905). On Nannie Burroughs, see Brooks Higginbotham, *Righteous Discontent*, and Evelyn Brooks, "Nannie Burroughs and the Education of Black Women," in *The Afro-American Woman: Struggles and Images*, ed. Sharon Harley and Rosalyn Terborg-Penn (Port Washington, N.Y., 1978). For more on African American everyday resistance to the structures of Jim Crow, see Robin D. G. Kelley, " 'We Are Not What We Seem': Rethinking Black Working-Class Opposition in the Jim Crow South," *Journal of American History* 80 (June 1993): 75–112.

6. John Boles, "Evangelical Protestantism in the Old South: From Religious Dissent to Cultural Dominance," in *Religion in the South*, ed. Charles Reagan Wilson (Jackson, Miss., 1985), 13–34; Samuel S. Hill Jr., *The South and the North in American Religion* (Athens, Ga., 1980); David Edwin Harrell Jr., ed., *Varieties of Southern Evangelicalism* (Macon, Ga., 1981). For work on slave religion, see note 1 above and Charles Joyner, *Down By the Riverside: A South Carolina Slave Community* (Urbana, Ill., 1984). For work on postbellum black religion, see note 1 above, Clarence Walker, *A Rock in a Weary Land: The African Methodist Episcopal Church during the Civil War and Reconstruction* (Baton Rouge, 1978), and Stephen Angell, *Bishop Henry McNeal Turner and African-American Religion in the South* (Knoxville, 1992). For social gospel influences in southern religion, see Ralph Luker, *The Social Gospel in Black and White: American Racial Reform, 1885–1912* (Chapel Hill, 1991), and William Link Jr., *The Paradox of Southern Progressivism, 1880–1930* (Chapel Hill, 1992).

7. Helpful summaries of the relevant statistics can be found in Robert Baker, *The Southern Baptist Convention and Its People, 1607–1972* (Nashville, 1974); Leroy Fitts, *A History of Black Baptists* (Nashville, 1985); Montgomery, *Under Their Own Vine and Fig Tree*, 105–8; Brooks Higginbotham, *Righteous Discontent*, 6–8; and Edward Ayers, *The Promise of the New South: Life After Reconstruction* (New York, 1992), 498–500.

8. This summary of Baptist background comes primarily from Baker, *The Southern Baptist Convention and Its People*, 15–57; W. W. Barnes, "Baptists," in *Encyclopedia of Southern Baptists*, ed. Clifton Allen et al. (Nashville, 1958), 1:135–41; Clarence C. Goen, *Revivalism and Separatism in New England, 1740–1800: Strict Congregationalists and Separate Baptists in the Great Awakening* (New Haven, Conn., 1962); Robert G. Torbet, *A History of the Baptists* (Valley Forge, Pa., 1963); and Rhys Isaac, *The Transformation of Virginia, 1740–1790* (Chapel Hill, 1982).

9. Isaac, *The Transformation of Virginia*; Mathews, *Religion in the Old South*; Jon Butler, *Awash in a Sea of Faith: The Christianization of the American People* (Cambridge, Mass., 1990); Nathan Hatch, *The Democratization of American Christianity* (New Haven, Conn., 1989); Patricia Bonomi, *Under the Cope of Heaven: Religion, Society, and Politics in Colonial America* (New York, 1986).

10. For quotation from the Home Mission Society, see Robert Baker, ed., *A Baptist*

Source Book, With Particular Reference to Southern Baptists (Nashville, 1966), 106–8. For the role of slavery in other denominational splits, see Clarence C. Goen, *Broken Churches, Broken Nation: Denominational Schisms and the Coming of the American Civil War* (Macon, Ga., 1985); David Bailey, *Shadow on the Church: Southwestern Evangelical Religion and the Issue of Slavery, 1783–1860* (Ithaca, N.Y., 1985); Anne Loveland, *Southern Evangelicals and the Social Order, 1800–1860* (Baton Rouge, 1980); Donald G. Mathews, *Slavery and Methodism: A Chapter in American Morality, 1780–1845* (Princeton, N.J., 1965); Sparks, *On Jordan's Stormy Banks*; and Mitchell Snay, *Gospel of Disunion: Religion and Separatism in the Antebellum South* (Cambridge, Mass., 1993).

11. A full explanation of the differences between the "society" method and the "denominational" method may be found in Robert Baker, *Relations Between Northern and Southern Baptists*, 2nd ed. (Ft. Worth, Tex., 1954), and "The American Baptist Home Mission Society and the South, 1832–1894" (Ph.D. diss., Yale University, 1947). For a detailed statistical breakdown of attendees at the 1845 organizational meeting of the SBC and a conclusive analysis on the importance of the defense of slavery, see Robert G. Gardner, *A Decade of Debate and Division: Georgia Baptists and the Formation of the Southern Baptist Convention* (Macon, Ga., 1995).

12. The activities of elite ministerial leaders of the antebellum era are described and analyzed in E. Brooks Holifield, *The Gentlemen Theologians: American Theology in Southern Culture* (Durham, N.C., 1978), and Loveland, *Southern Evangelicals and the Social Order*. A parallel process of "respectability" through church architecture among Georgia's Methodists is documented in Chris Owen, "By Design: The Social Meaning of Methodist Church Architecture in Nineteenth-Century Georgia," *Georgia Historical Quarterly* 75 (Summer 1991): 221–53.

13. Bertram Wyatt-Brown, "The Antimission Movement in the Jacksonian South: A Study in Regional Folk Culture," *Journal of Southern History* 36 (November 1970): 501–29; Cecil Lambert, *The Rise of the Antimission Baptists: Sources and Leaders, 1800–1840* (New York, 1980).

14. The fullest account of Landmarkist doctrines can be found in James E. Tull, *A History of Southern Baptist Landmarkism in the Light of Historical Baptist Ecclesiology* (1960; reprint, New York, 1980). An attempt to place Baptist Landmarkism within the interdenominational tradition of Protestant primitivism can be found in Richard T. Hughes and C. Leonard Allen, *Illusions of Innocence: Protestant Primitivism in America, 1630–1875* (Chicago, 1988). See also Nathan Hatch, *The Democratization of American Christianity* (New Haven, Conn., 1989). The best interpretive history of Landmarkism is Marty Beall, "James Robinson Graves and the Rhetoric of Demagogy: Primitivism and Democracy in Old Landmarkism" (Ph.D. diss., Vanderbilt University, 1990).

15. This brief "moment" and its rapid eclipse are documented and provocatively analyzed in Boles, "Evangelical Protestantism in the Old South," and Mechal Sobel, *Trabelin' On*, and *The World They Made Together: Black and White Values in Eighteenth-Century Virginia* (Princeton, N.J., 1987). On the mingling of the cultures of honor, paternalism, and evangelicalism among the planters, see Edward Crowther, "Holy Honor: Sacred and Secular in the Old South," *Journal of Southern History* 58 (November 1992): 619–36. The transformation of evangelicalism into support for paternalism apparently began in the late eighteenth century and took hold in the nineteenth. See

Allan Gallay, "Planters, Slaves, and the Great Awakening," in *Masters and Slaves in the House of the Lord: Race and Religion in the American South, 1740–1870*, ed. John B. Boles (Lexington, Ky., 1988).

16. H. Shelton Smith, *In His Image, But . . .: Racism in Southern Religion, 1780–1910* (Durham, N.C., 1972). The quotation from Nat Turner is reprinted in Willie Lee Rose, ed., *Documentary History of Slavery in North America* (New York, 1976), 132. The best account of Denmark Vesey's religious role and the white response to this aborted rebellion may be found in Creel, *"A Peculiar People,"* 150–64.

17. For information on the First African Baptist Church of Savannah (and the First Bryan Baptist Church in Savannah, the equally important church that split from it in the 1830s), see James Simms, *The First Colored Baptist Church in North America* (Philadelphia, 1888). A "rival" history published for the same occasion but presenting a different interpretation of the church's history is Emmanuel K. Love, *History of the First African Baptist Church, from its organization, January 20th, 1788, to July 1st, 1888: including the centennial celebration, addresses, sermons, etc.* (Savannah, 1888).

18. A growing body of scholarship documents black participation in white-run antebellum churches. For Baptists in particular, see Larry James, "Biracial Fellowship in Antebellum Baptist Churches," 37–57, and Randy Sparks, "Religion in Amite County, Mississippi," 58–80, both in *Masters and Slaves in the House of the Lord: Race and Religion in the American South, 1740–1870*, ed. John B. Boles (Lexington, Ky., 1988); and Frederick Bode, "The Formation of Evangelical Communities in Middle Georgia: Twiggs County, 1820–1861," *Journal of Southern History* 60 (November 1994): 711–48. Also see Kenneth Bailey, "Protestantism and Afro-Americans in the Old South: Another Look," *Journal of Southern History* 41 (November 1975): 451–72, and "The Post–Civil War Racial Separations in Southern Protestantism: Another Look," *Church History* 47 (December 1977): 453–73.

19. This discussion of the meaning of slave religion is based primarily on Genovese, *Roll, Jordan, Roll*, and Raboteau, *Slave Religion*.

20. *Texas Narratives*, supp. series 2, pt. 3, vol. 4, 1266 (Anderson Edwards).

21. See Richard Carwardine, *Evangelicals and Politics in Antebellum America* (New York, 1993); Snay, *Gospel of Disunion*; Eugene Genovese, *The Slaveholders' Dilemma: Freedom and Progress in Conservative Southern Thought, 1820–1860* (Columbia, S.C., 1992); and Loveland, *Southern Evangelicals and the Social Order*.

22. H. Shelton Smith, *In His Image*, 173–80, suggests that state Baptist conventions in the Lower South supported secession, while those in the Upper South were more hesitant. Even in the Lower South, however, division occurred. In South Carolina, Richard Furman received votes to serve as president of the secession convention, and in Alabama, Basil Manly Sr. prayed at the formative meeting of the Confederate States of America. But their Baptist colleagues in South Carolina and Virginia, James Boyce and John A. Broadus, argued against secession. For the positions of these men, see J. A. Broadus to Miss Cornelia Talieferro, January 22, 1861, in *Life and Letters of John A. Broadus*, ed. Archibald T. Robertson (Philadelphia, 1901), 181; and Basil Manly Sr. Diary, entry for February 9, 1861, in Manly Family Papers, reel 6, SBHLA. For a fuller analysis, see Paul Harvey, "The Civil War and the Public World of White Southern Baptist Ministers," in *Religion and the American Civil War*, ed. Charles Reagan Wilson and Harry S. Stout (forthcoming), and Beth Barton Schweiger, "The Transformation of

Southern Religion: Clergy and Congregations in Virginia, 1830–1895" (Ph.D. diss., University of Virginia, 1994). Sidney Romero, *Religion in the Rebel Ranks* (Lanham, Md., 1983), 94–95, 163, shows that Baptists made up about two-thirds of the colportage force in the army. Drew Gilpin Faust, "Christian Soldiers: The Meaning of Revivalism in the Confederate Army," *Journal of Southern History* 53 (February 1987): 63–90, provides the single best source for interpreting the meaning of evangelical Protestantism in the Confederate Army. See also Gardiner H. Shattuck Jr., *A Shield and Hiding Place: The Religious Life of the Civil War Armies* (Macon, Ga., 1987).

23. See David W. Blight, *Frederick Douglass' Civil War: Keeping Faith in Jubilee* (Baton Rouge, 1987); Leon F. Litwack, *Been in the Storm So Long: The Aftermath of Slavery* (New York, 1979), 450–71; Lawrence Levine, *Black Culture and Black Consciousness: Afro-American Folk Thought From Slavery to Freedom* (New York, 1977), 3–80; Dvorak, *An African-American Exodus*; and Montgomery, *Under Their Own Vine and Fig Tree*, chapter 2.

24. George Marsden, *Fundamentalism and American Culture: The Shaping of Twentieth-Century Evangelicalism, 1870–1925* (New York, 1980). For a look at how northern-bred Fundamentalism "moved South" in the interwar years, see William Robert Glass, "The Development of Northern Patterns of Fundamentalism in the South" (Ph.D. diss., Emory University, 1991).

25. For a contrasting look at the political implication of white southern and black southern religion in the era of the Civil Rights movement, see Andrew Manis, *Southern Civil Religions in Conflict: Black and White Baptists and Civil Rights, 1947–1957* (Athens, Ga., 1987), and David Chappell, *Inside Agitators: White Southerners in the Civil Rights Movement* (Baltimore, 1993).

26. Dickson Bruce, *And They All Sang Hallelujah: Plain-Folk Camp-Meeting Religion, 1800–1845* (Knoxville, 1974); Michael W. Harris, *The Rise of Gospel Blues: The Music of Thomas Andrew Dorsey in the Urban Church* (New York, 1992); Bruce A. Rosenberg, *Shall These Bones Live? The Art of the American Folk Preacher* (Urbana, Ill., 1985); and Walter Pitts, *Old Ship of Zion: The Afro-Baptist Ritual in the African Diaspora* (New York, 1993), all document and analyze the spread of folk preaching styles throughout the country. James N. Gregory, *American Exodus: The Dust Bowl Migration and Okie Culture in California* (New York, 1989); Ellen Rosenberg, *The Southern Baptists: A Subculture in Transition* (Knoxville, 1989); and Nancy T. Ammerman, *Baptist Battles: Social Change and Religious Conflict in the Southern Baptist Convention* (New Brunswick, N.J., 1990), all discuss southern Baptists' feelings of marginalization and responses to it. For a look at the way southern cultural forms, especially music, have penetrated American life, see Bill Malone, *Southern Music, American Music* (Lexington, Ky., 1979).

Chapter 1

1. *CI*, February 23, 1865; *BR*, May 4, 1870; resolution from Big Hatchie Baptist Association, November 1865, reprinted in *CI*, November 9, 1865.

2. For an account of the early history of the Sunday School Board, see James Marion Frost, *Sunday School Board History and Work* (Nashville, 1914), and Robert Baker, *The Southern Baptist Convention and Its People, 1607–1972* (Nashville, 1974), 294–96.

3. Basil Manly Sr. to Basil Manly Jr., February 10, 1861, in Manly Family Papers, reel

1, folder 125, SBHLA; SBC *Proceedings*, 1863, 54; North Carolina Baptist State Convention *Minutes*, 1861, 22; Baptist General Association of Virginia *Minutes*, 1861, 15–16; Waco Baptist Association (Texas) *Minutes*, 1864, 22; Edgefield Baptist Association (South Carolina) *Minutes*, 1864; Daniel Stowell, "Rebuilding Zion: The Religious Reconstruction of the South" (Ph.D. diss., University of Florida, 1994), 65.

See also "Report on Religious Instruction of Colored People," Alabama Baptist State Convention *Minutes*, 1863, Appendix; Texas Baptist State Convention *Minutes* 1862, 6, and 1863, 6; and Edwin L. Cliburn, *In Unbroken Line: A History of the First Baptist Church of Thomaston, Georgia, from Its Beginnings at Bethesda to Its One Hundred Fiftieth Anniversary* (Thomaston, Ga., 1979), 121. The congregation of the First Baptist Church of Thomaston resolved that "in this great struggle for all that is dear to us as a people, we have the approving smiles of Him who rules at His will the destinies of nations."

4. Basil Manly Jr. to parents, July 13, 1863, in Basil Manly Sr. Papers, folder 5, SBHLA.

5. Stowell, "Rebuilding Zion," 30–45; W. Harrison Daniel, *Virginia Baptists, 1860–1902* (Bedford, Va., 1987), 16; Minutes of the Central Baptist Church, Nashville, Tenn., February 16, 1862, and July 10, 1864; Lynn E. May, *The First Baptist Church of Nashville, Tennessee, 1820–1970* (Nashville, 1970), 100–105; " 'They Can Never Both Prosper Together': Black and White Baptists in Antebellum Nashville, Tennessee," *Tennessee Historical Quarterly* 38 (Fall 1979): 296–307; T. S., "Letter from Nashville," *CWR*, May 6, 1875.

6. Minutes of the Carrollton Baptist Church, Carroll County, Miss., June 1864; Minutes of the Bethany Baptist Church, Burnt Corn, Ala., September 30, 1865; Daniel, *Virginia Baptists*, 6–9; Tennessee church minutes quoted in Stowell, "Rebuilding Zion," 21; J. H. Spencer, "Autobiography," unpublished typewritten manuscript, in J. H. Spencer Papers, folder 13, SBHLA, 138. See also "Letter from Kentucky," *CWR*, April 9, 1868.

7. Richard Andrew Fox, handwritten sermon delivered in early 1865, in Richard Andrew Fox Papers, folder for 1865, Virginia Historical Society, Richmond, Virginia; Stowell, "Rebuilding Zion," 68–69; William Hatcher, *Along the Trail of Friendly Years* (New York, 1910), 112; L. R. Mills, "My Recollections of Dr. Wingate," in Lansing Burrows Papers, box 10, folder 232, SBHLA.

8. J. H. Spencer, "Autobiography," 138–67; D. P. Berton to Basil Manly Sr., November 7, 1866, in Basil Manly Sr. Papers, folder 7, SBHLA.

9. Charleston Baptist Association *Minutes*, 1865, 8; E. A. C., "The Signs of the Times," *South Carolina Baptist*, April 20, 1866; *South Carolina Baptist*, June 29, 1866; Charles Manly to parents, March 27, 1862, Manly Family Papers, reel 1, folder 149; Charles Manly to Basil Manly Jr., July 15, 1867, in Manly Family Papers, reel 2; Charles Manly, untitled speech delivered at Confederate Memorial Exercises, Lexington, Va., June 4, 1904, in Manly Family Papers, reel 4, folder 735, all in SBHLA; *CWR*, June 29, 1865.

10. Lansing Burrows, "The Fall of Richmond," copy of handwritten speech delivered in Louisville, 1875, in Lansing Burrows Papers, box 9, folder 196, SBHLA.

11. Charles Manly to Basil Manly Jr., September 25, 1866, in Manly Family Papers, reel 2, folder 179, SBHLA; G. F. Williams to John A. Broadus, February 10, 1866, in

John A. Broadus letter file, SBTS. Accounts of the physical and emotional "destitution" of churches from SBC *Proceedings*, 1867, 44–46, Austin Baptist Association (Texas) *Minutes*, 1872, 10–11, Carey Baptist Association (Alabama) *Minutes*, 1866, and Shelby Baptist Association (Alabama) *Minutes*, 1866; Alabama Baptist State Convention *Minutes*, 1866, n.p.; Report from Alabama Baptist State Convention, in *Christian Index and Southwestern Baptist*, December 17, 1868; Central Baptist Association (Mississippi) *Minutes*, 1867, 111; Report of First Baptist Church, Charleston, in Charleston Baptist Association *Minutes*, 1864, 38, and in Robert Baker, *Adventure in Faith: The First Three Hundred Years of the First Baptist Church of Charleston, South Carolina* (Nashville, 1972).

12. Statistics from Stowell, "Rebuilding Zion," 15–30, 322–26.

13. *BR*, November 17, 1869, August 9, 1871.

14. *BR*, January 5, 1876; *CI*, February 23, 1865.

15. *Christian Index and Southwestern Baptist*, January 2, 1868; D. P. Berton to Basil Manly Jr., September 28, 1866, Basil Manly Sr. Papers, folder 7, SBHLA; "Letter from South Carolina," *CWR*, February 4, 1869.

16. *RH*, May 3, 1866 (J. L. Reynolds); *RH*, October 19, 1865.

17. *RH*, June 3, 1869; W. Wilkes, "Religious Schism and Defection," *Alabama Baptist*, January 5, 1875. See also *CWR*, July 18, 1867, and *Christian Index and Southwestern Baptist*, August 4, 1870 (George Brewer). For discussions of reunion, see *RH*, July 7, 1870 ("Pacificator"), and SBC *Proceedings*, 1870, 19–22.

18. *South Carolina Baptist*, July 19, 1867, July 10, April 10, 1868 (W. B. Carson); *RH*, March 5, 1868 (J. J. D. Renfroe); Daniel Hollis, *A History of the First Baptist Church, Jacksonville, Alabama, 1836–1986* (Jacksonville, Ala., 1987); B. F. Riley, *A Memorial History of the Baptists of Alabama: Being An Account of the Struggles and Achievements of the Denomination from 1808 to 1923* (Philadelphia, 1923), 175.

19. *RH*, January 3, 1874; David Butler, "The Victory—Rejoice," *CI*, November 19, 1874.

20. *CWR*, July 2, 1866; *South Carolina Baptist*, September 27, 1867.

21. *BR*, December 7, 1887; "Why Not Dissolve the Convention," *RH*, April 4, 1885; *BR*, June 19, 1891.

22. *RH*, November 19, 1865; Fair River Baptist Association (Mississippi) *Minutes*, 1884, 17; *CI*, June 7, 1888. For a fuller discussion of the history of southern Baptist women, see Catherine Allen, *A Century to Celebrate: History of Woman's Missionary Union* (Birmingham, 1987).

23. *Baptist Record*, May 19, 1881 (Mrs. Jenny Beauchamp).

24. SBC *Annual*, 1882, 38, 1885, 34; J. J. D. Renfroe, "The Woman Question," *RH*, June 4, 1885; *Baptist Record*, August 9, 1888; *BR*, April 21, 1886 ("Virginia"); 4th Annual Meeting of the Woman's Missionary Societies, from Sketch and Constitution of the Woman's Missionary Societies, May 1887 to May 1888, 3–4, microfilm copy; WMU organizational meeting, May 11, 1888, Richmond, Va., microfilm copy; and Constitution of WMU, 1888, microfilm copy, all in SBHLA.

25. Allen, *A Century to Celebrate*, 337.

26. *Home and Foreign Journal*, August 1870, 15 (J. P. Shaffer).

27. Home Mission Board Minutes, Atlanta, March 12, 1883, in Home Mission Board Papers, reel 1, SBHLA; SBC *Annual*, 1892, Appendix A, Home Mission Board Report; *ESB*, 1:646.

28. Allen, *A Century to Celebrate*, 117; *CI*, June 5, 1884 ("Cleia").

29. *BR*, June 15, 29, 1881.

30. Basil Manly Sr. to Basil Manly Jr., August 6, 1860, in Manly Family Papers, reel 1; T. E. Skinner to John Broadus, July 11, 1863, typewritten copy of letter in Basil Manly Sr. Papers, folder 3; Basil Manly Jr., "To the Baptists of the Confederate States," July 3, 1863, typewritten copy in Basil Manly Sr. Papers, folder 3; and D. H. Gwathmey to Basil Manly Jr., April 29, 1863, all in SBHLA; Stowell, "Rebuilding Zion," 226, 231, 238.

31. SBC *Proceedings*, 1870, 33; Minutes of the Home Mission Board of the SBC, January 12, 1885, Home Mission Board Papers, reel 1, SBHLA; *Our Home Field*, August 1888, 5; "Report on Kind Words," SBC *Annual*, 1885, reprinted in Robert Baker, ed., *Baptist Source Book, with Particular Reference to Southern Baptists* (Nashville, 1966), 148–50; C. A. Anderson, "The Southern Publication Board," *Western Recorder*, April 17, 1890; West Tennessee Baptist Convention *Proceedings*, 1874, 12. See also "Report from Chowan Association," *BR*, May 25, 1870.

32. *ESB*, 1:512; SBC *Proceedings*, 1892, Sunday School Board Report, 64. Relevant portions of the debate about the formation of the Sunday School Board are reprinted in Baker, ed., *Baptist Source Book*, 145–55. Unlike the northern American Baptist Publication Society, which remained an independent benevolent organization financed by interested individual participants, the southern Sunday School Board was specifically created as a denominational agency to do the bidding of the Southern Baptist Convention. See Robert Baker, "The American Baptist Home Mission Society and the South, 1832–1894" (Ph.D. diss., Yale University, 1947).

33. Baker, ed., *Baptist Source Book*, 165–68; Frost, *Sunday School Board History and Work*, 81–83; *ESB*, 2:1318, 1339.

34. For a discussion of SBC religious literature and "programmed piety," see Bill Leonard, *God's Last and Only Hope: The Fragmentation of the Southern Baptist Convention* (Grand Rapids, Mich., 1990).

35. *ESB*, 2:1256–57.

36. *BR*, August 7, 1895. For a concise analysis of evangelicals and modernity, see Grant Wacker, "Uneasy in Zion: Evangelicals in Postmodern Society," in *Evangelicalism and Modern America*, ed. George Marsden (Grand Rapids, Mich., 1984), 17–28.

37. Charles Manly to Jane Manly, March 8, 1866, Manly Family Papers, reel 2, folder 180, SBHLA.

38. Basil Manly Jr. to parents, August 3, 7, December 7, 1865, in Manly Family Papers, reel 2, folder 177; Basil Manly Jr. to parents, April 1, 1867; and Basil Manly Jr. to Charles Manly, November 28, 1870, in Manly Family Papers, reel 1, all in SBHLA. Basil Manly Jr. generally wrote letters to his family in his own shorthand. I have spelled out the words that he abbreviated or otherwise shortened. Thaddeus Stevens articulated the views of the Radicals in the House of Representatives. He advocated taking land from planters who supported the Confederacy and redistributing it to freedmen.

39. Basil Manly Jr. to Parents, July 25, 1866, in Basil Manly Sr. Papers, folder 7, Basil Manly Jr. to Charles Manly, April 2, 1868, in Manly Family Papers, reel 1, both in SBHLA.

40. The story of Manly's ministry to enslaved people in his church in South Carolina comes from Larry Tise, *Proslavery: A History of the Defense of Slavery in America, 1701–1840* (Athens, Ga., 1987), 305–6. An analysis of the role of South Carolina

ministers in formulating proslavery doctrine may be found in Creel, *"A Peculiar People,"* chapter 5.

41. Basil Manly Sr. Diary, entry for February 9, 1861, in Manly Family Papers, reel 6; Basil Manly Sr. to Mary Jane Shorter, February 21, 1863, in Manly Family Papers, reel 2, folder 157; Basil Manly Sr. to Jane, June 8, November 8, 1865, Manly Family Papers, reel 1; Basil Manly Sr. to children, November 7, 1867, in Basil Manly Sr. Papers, folder 8, all in SBHLA.

42. See John Storey, "The Negro in Southern Baptist Thought" (Ph.D. diss., University of Kentucky, 1968); Rufus B. Spain, *At Ease in Zion: Social History of Southern Baptists, 1865–1900* (Nashville, 1967); and John Edward Hughes, "A History of the Southern Baptist Convention's Ministry to the Negro, 1845–1904" (Th.D. diss., Southern Baptist Theological Seminary, 1971), for a complete exposition of the views expressed by white southern Baptists toward blacks in the period.

43. *CWR*, June 4, 1868.

44. See John B. Boles, ed., *Masters and Slaves in the House of the Lord: Race and Religion in the American South, 1740–1870* (Lexington, Ky., 1988), for a series of closely researched case studies on whites and blacks in antebellum churches.

45. Report from North Carolina Baptist State Convention in *BR*, June 5, 1867; Edgefield Baptist Association *Minutes*, 1865, 9; Daniel, *Virginia Baptists*, 77–78; Yazoo County Baptist Association (Mississippi) *Minutes*, 1869, 8.

46. Basil Manly Sr. quoted in Stowell, "Rebuilding Zion," 79; Minutes of the Wake Forest Baptist Church, July 1865; Minutes of the First Baptist Church of Abbeville, South Carolina, July 25, 1866; Edgefield Baptist Association *Minutes*, 1866, 8; *BR*, June 5, 1867; Baptist General Association of Virginia *Minutes*, 1866, n.p.; *RH*, October 19, 1865. See also B. B. Williamson, *History of Livingston First Baptist Church Sesquicentennial, 1834–1984* (Livingston, N.C., 1984), 39–40, and H. Shelton Smith, *In His Image, But . . .: Racism in Southern Religion, 1780–1910* (Durham, N.C., 1972), 226–29.

47. Charleston Baptist Association *Minutes*, 1866, 12–13. The story of the Richmond church is detailed in Mechal Sobel, *Trabelin' On: The Slave Journey to an Afro-Baptist Faith*, 2nd ed. (Princeton, N.J., 1987), 208–10.

48. See SBC *Proceedings*, 1866, for the white southern version of the story. For a moderate northern account, see *CWR*, April 5, 1866. For an account that considers the various sides, including the version of events understood by abolitionists and blacks, see James M. Washington, *Frustrated Fellowship: The Black Baptist Quest for Social Power* (Macon, Ga., 1986), 65–70.

49. W. P. Price, *Sixty Years in the Life of a Country Village Baptist Church, Dahlonega, Georgia, 1839–1897* (Atlanta, 1897), n.p., copy in SBHLA.

50. Daniel Hollis, *A History of the First Baptist Church, Jacksonville, Alabama, 1836–1986* (Jacksonville, 1987); Daniel, *Virginia Baptists*, 76; Chronicles of the First Baptist Church, Tuscaloosa, Alabama, November 20, 1865, and July 2, 1866, typewritten from original, in SBHLA; E. T. Winkler, "The Color Line," *Alabama Baptist*, June 10, 1880. See also Minutes of the First Baptist Church of Carrollton, Mississippi, January 1867 and April 1870.

51. "Religious Instruction of the Colored People," Liberty Baptist Association (Alabama), 1865, 1868, handwritten notes, SBHLA; Goshen Baptist Association quoted in William Montgomery, *Under Their Own Vine and Fig Tree: The African-American*

Church in the South, 1865–1900 (Baton Rouge, 1993), 109; Bethlehem Baptist Association (Alabama) *Minutes*, 1866, Appendix D; Edgefield Baptist Association *Minutes*, 1871, 3.

52. Quoted from Daniel Stowell, " 'The Negroes Cannot Navigate Alone': Religious Scalawags and the Biracial Methodist Episcopal Church in Georgia, 1866–1876," in *Georgia in Black and White: Explorations in the Race Relations of a Southern State, 1865–1950*, ed. John Inscoe (Athens, Ga., 1994), 65.

53. "Report on the Colored Population," Texas State Baptist Convention *Minutes*, 1866, 6; Waco Baptist Association *Minutes*, 1865, 4–5; Austin Baptist Association *Minutes*, 1866, 9, 1868, 10, and 1873, 9. See also Charles Rankin, "The Rise of Negro Baptist Churches in the South Through the Reconstruction Period" (Th.D. diss., New Orleans Baptist Theological Seminary, 1955).

54. "Religious Instruction of the Colored People," Alabama Baptist State Convention *Minutes*, 1866, Appendix, 11.

55. Record of debate at the North Carolina Baptist State Convention in *RH*, May 30, 1867 (R. M. Young).

56. SBC meeting report in *BR*, June 2, 1869; *Christian Index and Southwestern Baptist*, May 13, 1869.

57. "Our Chastisement," *CI*, January 5, 1865; "Report on Colored Population," Columbus Baptist Association (Mississippi) *Minutes*, 1866, 13; *BR*, December 12, 1866 (W. H. J.); E. T. Winkler quoted in H. Shelton Smith, *In His Image*, 253. See also *RH*, April 4, 1867, for Jeremiah Jeter's analysis of the "chastening" of the South by northern administrators. Jeter also added, however, that the North had "no just grounds for their procedure against us."

58. *RH*, September 3, 1874; E. T. Winkler, "Baccalaureate Address," June 16, 1878, in E. T. Winkler Papers, folder 1, SBHLA; *BR*, September 9, 1874; Mississippi Baptist State Convention *Minutes*, 1879, 47.

59. Report of Jeremiah Jeter on the American Baptist Home Mission Society meeting, in Baptist General Association of Virginia *Minutes*, 1865, 16–17; *Christian Index and Southwestern Baptist*, February 17, 1866 (I. T. Tichenor); *BHMM*, January 1884, 11 (W. W. Landrum); *CI*, December 2, 1880; *South Carolina Baptist*, February 28, 1868; *CI*, January 6, 1876 (W. J. Northen). See also *Christian Index and Southwestern Baptist*, September 2, 1869 (J. J. D. Renfroe).

60. L. Q. Gwaltney to John A. Broadus, January 27, 1866, in Broadus letter files, SBTS; *BR*, May 23, 1877.

61. *RH*, January 4, 1883 (W. B. Carson); "What We Owe the Colored People," *Alabama Baptist*, November 4, 1886; John A. Broadus quoted in *BHMM*, April 1883, 82–84.

62. See also G. S. Anderson, "Colored Evangelization," speech read before Alabama State Baptist Convention, in *Alabama Baptist*, April 1, 1886; *South Carolina Baptist*, December 20, 1867; H. H. Tucker's letter quoted in Emmanuel K. Love, *History of the First African Baptist Church, from its organization, January 20th, 1788, to July 1st, 1888: including the centennial celebration, addresses, sermons, etc.* (Savannah, 1888), 322.

63. Claude Bowers, *The Tragic Era: The Revolution after Lincoln* (New York, 1929). The "reunion" of North and South is compellingly explored in Nina Silber, *The Romance of Reunion: Northerners and the South, 1865–1900* (Chapel Hill, 1993).

64. *RH*, September 9, 1866.

65. Minutes of the Sandy Run Baptist Church, December 1869, quoted in Wade W. Bridger, *From the Wilderness to the Hilltop: A History of Sandy Run Baptist Church* (Gastonia, N.C., 1973); E. T. Winkler in *CWR*, January 4, 1872.

66. For an authoritative interpretation of Reconstruction and a scathing examination of the older myths of the "tragic era," see Eric Foner, *Reconstruction: America's Unfinished Revolution* (New York, 1992).

67. J. L. Johnson, *Autobiographical Notes* (privately printed, 1938), 252–53. *separation language*

68. *BR*, February 1, 1905; SBC *Annual*, 1891.

Chapter 2

1. *AB*, June 16, 1868 (Sister Lynch), June 25, 1867, May 4, 1869.

2. William Montgomery has estimated the black Baptist population at the end of the war as somewhere between 150,000 and 400,000. This number includes those who were officially enrolled in a white congregation, an independent black congregation, or were counted by local missionaries. No very good statistics on the numbers of black Baptists exist until the 1890s. See William Montgomery, *Under Their Own Vine and Fig Tree: The African-American Church in the South, 1865–1900* (Baton Rouge, 1993), 105–8. See also Bureau of the Census, *Religious Bodies, 1906*, vol. 1 (Washington, D.C., 1910), 137–39; Evelyn Brooks Higginbotham, *Righteous Discontent: The Women's Movement in the Black Baptist Church, 1880–1920* (Cambridge, Mass., 1993), 6; and Gregory Wills, *Democratic Religion: Freedom, Authority, and Church Discipline in the Baptist South, 1785–1900* (New York, forthcoming), 136–38. The page numbers from Wills are cited from the manuscript version that I consulted in the course of research. Quotation from Matthew Gilbert, "Colored Churches: An Experiment," *NBM* 1 (January 1894): 165.

3. W. P. Price, *Sixty Years in the Life of a Country Village Baptist Church, Dahlonega, Georgia, 1837–1897* (Atlanta, n.d.); Beth Barton Schweiger, " 'Lives are the Words of God': Clerical Authority and Popular Religion in Virginia, 1830–1910," paper presented to the American Historical Association, December 30, 1991 (copy in my possession); W. Harrison Daniel, *Virginia Baptists, 1860–1902* (Bedford, Va., 1987), 67–93.

4. *RH*, October 19, 1865 (Jeter); January 24, 1867 (Andrew Broaddus).

5. Rappahannock Baptist Association quotation from Stowell, "Rebuilding Zion: The Religious Reconstruction of the South, 1863–1877" (Ph.D. diss., University of Florida, 1994), 135; Charles Manly to Basil Manly Jr., May 28, 1866, in Manly Family Papers, reel 2, folder 179, Basil Manly Sr. Diary, entry for June 24, 1866, in Basil Manly Sr. Papers, folder 6, both in SBHLA; *AB*, February 25, 1868, October 19, 1869 (Prince Murrell); "Alabama News," *Christian Index and Southwestern Baptist*, October 1, 1868. See also letter from reader printed in *Alabama Baptist*, February 3, 1876.

6. Montgomery, *Under Their Own Vine and Fig Tree*, 88; Howard Rabinowitz, *Race Relations in the Urban South, 1865–1900* (Chicago, 1978), 199, 204; A. W. Pegues, *Our Baptist Ministers and Schools* (Springfield, Mass., 1892), 264–66; Walter Brooks, "The Life of Walter Brooks," in *The Washington World*, January 30, 1931, clipping in Una Roberts Lawrence Papers, box 2, folder 32, SBHLA; [Hampton Institute and Works Progress Administration], *The Negro in Virginia* (Hampton Institute, 1940), 251.

7. History of Gillfield Baptist Church (Petersburg, Virginia) from Gillfield Church

records, microfilm, SBHLA, and from Mechal Sobel, *Trabelin' On: The Slave Journey to an Afro-Baptist Faith*, 2nd ed. (Princeton, N.J., 1987), 190, 206–7; Minutes of the Gillfield Baptist Church, Petersburg, Virginia, September 20, 1869.

8. Mechal Sobel, " 'They Can Never Both Prosper Together': Black and White Baptists in Antebellum Nashville, Tennessee," *Tennessee Historical Quarterly* 38 (Fall 1979): 296–307; Rabinowitz, *Race Relations in the Urban South*, 204.

9. Emmanuel K. Love, *History of the First African Baptist Church of Savannah, Georgia, from its organization, January 20th, 1788, to July 1, 1888: including the centennial celebration, addresses, sermons, etc.* (Savannah, 1888), 58; Montgomery, *Under Their Own Vine and Fig Tree*, 276–77.

10. Charles Corey, *A History of Richmond Theological Seminary With Reminiscences of Thirty Years' Work Among the Colored People of the South* (Richmond, 1895), 72; Montgomery, *Under Their Own Vine and Fig Tree*, 93, 101; Rabinowitz, *Race Relations in the Urban South*, 204; Spelman information from Brooks Higginbotham, *Righteous Discontent*, 32.

11. Frederick Bode, "The Formation of Evangelical Communities in Middle Georgia: Twiggs County, 1820–1861," *Journal of Southern History* 58 (November 1994): 735; Shiloh Baptist Church petition quoted in Charles Horace Hamilton and John Ellison, *The Negro Church in Rural Virginia* (Blacksburg, Va., 1930); Stowell, "Rebuilding Zion," 146, 177; N. H. Pius, *An Outline of Baptist History: A Splendid Reference Work for Busy Workers* (Nashville, 1910), 53; Tichenor quoted in Katharine L. Dvorak, *An African-American Exodus: The Segregation of the Southern Churches, 1865–1871* (Brooklyn, N.Y., 1991), 70; Rabinowitz, *Race Relations in the Urban South*, 200–203; Robert L. Hall, "Tallahassee's Black Churches, 1865–1885," *Florida Historical Quarterly* 58 (October 1979): 191.

12. Zelia S. Evans and J. T. Alexander, *The Dexter Avenue Baptist Church, 1877–1977* (Montgomery, Ala., 1978); *South Carolina Baptist*, July 31, 1868; *Texas Narratives*, supp. series 2, vol. 2, pt. 1, 450 (Sylvester Brooks); *Texas Narratives*, supp. series 2, pt. 2, vol. 3, 769 (Harrison Cole); *Texas Narratives*, supp. series 2, pt. 9, vol. 10, 4055–46 (Alice Wilkins); Minutes of the Carrollton Baptist Church, Carrollton, Mississippi, December 1867; J. A. Whitted, *History of the Negro Baptists of North Carolina* (Raleigh, 1908), 34–35. For other accounts of white-black cooperation in Texas, see *Texas Narratives*, supp. series 2, vol. 3, pt. 2, 703 (Henry Childers). See also G. W. S., "Colored People of America and Africa," *CWR*, July 15, 1869.

13. Information on David Graham from Eric Foner, *Freedom's Lawmakers: A Directory of Black Officeholders During Reconstruction* (New York, 1993), 89; information on the use of household production and the cost of lots of land for churches from Sharon Ann Holt, "Making Freedom Pay: Freedpeople Working for Themselves, North Carolina, 1865–1900," *Journal of Southern History* 60 (May 1994): 249–51; "Letter from Beaufort," *AB*, July 30, 1867.

14. Montgomery, *Under Their Own Vine and Fig Tree*, 52–53; Armstead L. Robinson, "Plans Dat Comed From God: Institution Building and the Emergence of Black Leadership in Reconstruction Memphis," in *Toward a New South: Studies in Post–Civil War Southern Communities*, ed. Orville Vernon Burton and Robert C. McMath Jr. (Westport, Conn., 1982), 73–74; Kathleen C. Berkeley, " 'Colored Ladies Also Contributed': Black

Women's Activities From Benevolence to Social Welfare, 1866–1896," in *The Web of Southern Social Relations: Women, Family and Education*, ed. Walter Fraser Jr., R. Frank Saunders Jr., and Jon L. Wakelyn (Athens, Ga., 1985), 182–201; Orville Vernon Burton, *In My Father's House Are Many Mansions: Family and Community in Edgefield, South Carolina* (Chapel Hill, 1985), 249, 256; *AB*, November 24, 1868 ("W").

15. Teague quote in Wills, *Democratic Religion*, 141; *Texas Narratives*, supp. series 2, vol. 5, pt. 4, 1640 (William Hamilton); *Texas Narratives*, supp. series 2, vol. 5, pt. 4, 1799 (Scott Hooper).

16. Baptist State Convention, Colored, of North Carolina, *Proceedings*, 1870, 7; Roanoke Missionary Baptist Association (North Carolina) *Minutes*, 1868, 11, 1870, 5, 1872, 5–6; *AB*, September 3, 1867.

17. *Texas Narratives*, supp. series 2, pt. 7, vol. 8, 3062–63 (Lu Perkins); *AB*, December 4, 1866, March 26, 1867, February 18, 1868.

18. *Texas Narratives*, supp. series 2, vol. 5, pt. 4, 1648–51 (Pierce Harper); Edgefield Baptist Association (South Carolina) *Minutes*, 1871, quoted in Burton, *In My Father's House Are Many Mansions*, 250; Dvorak, *An African-American Exodus*, 89; *Arkansas Narratives*, orig. series 2, vol. 9, pt. 4, 68; *South Carolina Narratives*, orig. series, vol. 2, pt. 2, 121 (Brawley Gilmore); *Arkansas Narratives*, orig. series 2, vol. 9, pt. 3, 258–61 (Harriet Hill).

19. *Texas Narratives*, supp. series 2, vol. 8, pt. 7, 3342 (Steve Robertson); *Oklahoma Narratives*, supp. series 1, 99–102. See also David James Merrill, "At a Negro Meeting," *Zion's Herald* 73 (September 18, 1895): 594.

20. *Florida Narratives*, orig. series, vol. 17, 209–10 (Edward Lycurgas); Hall, "Tallahassee's Black Churches," 194; Mary Allan-Olney, *The New Virginians*, vol. 2 (Edinburgh, 1880), 148–50; Sir George Campbell, *White and Black: The Outcome of a Visit to the United States* (London, 1879), 330; *South Carolina Narratives*, orig. series, vol. 3, pt. 4, 159 (Mack Taylor); Philip Bruce quoted in John Blassingame, *Long Memory: The Black Experience in America* (Oxford, 1982), 107.

21. Resolution of First Baptist Antioch Association, 1868, quoted in Patrick Thompson, *History of Negro Baptists in Mississippi* (Jackson, 1898), 44; Report of the "Committee on the State of the Country," CABMC *Report*, 1872, 17–18.

22. Foner, *Freedom's Lawmakers*, introduction, 228; Pegues, *Our Baptist Ministers and Schools*, 526–37; Heard quoted in Dvorak, *An African-American Exodus*, 128.

23. Ira Berlin et al., eds., *Free At Last: A Documentary History of Slavery, Freedom, and the Civil War* (New York, 1992), 310–12.

24. Robert Eugene Perdue, *The Negro in Savannah, 1865–1900* (New York, 1973), 37–47; Foner, *Freedom's Lawmakers*, 109–10; James Simms, *The First Colored Baptist Church in North America* (1888; reprint, New York, 1969), 141.

25. Simms, *The First Colored Baptist Church in North America*, 141, 151–52; Perdue, *The Negro in Savannah*, 37–47; "Travels in Georgia," *CWR*, May 16, 1867; Foner, *Freedom's Lawmakers*, 6, 110, 196; U.S. Senate, *Testimony Taken by the Joint Select Committee to Inquire into the Conditions of Affairs in the Late Insurrectionary States*, 42nd Congress, 2nd sess., Georgia Testimony, vol. 7, pt. y, p. 615; House Miscellaneous Documents, 40th Congress, 3rd sess., no. 52, p. 9; Montgomery, *Under Their Own Vine and Fig Tree*, 157–63.

26. Foner, *Freedom's Lawmakers*, 22, 116; Pegues, *Our Baptist Ministers and Schools*, 66–68, 280; Williams Simmons, *Men of Mark: Eminent, Progressive, Rising* (Louisville, Ky., 1887), 707–12.

27. Howard Rabinowitz, "Holland Thompson and Black Political Participation in Montgomery, Alabama," in *Southern Black Leaders of the Reconstruction Era*, ed. Howard Rabinowitz (Urbana, Ill., 1982), 249–80; Allen Woodrow Jones, "Alabama," in *The Black Press in the South, 1865–1979*, ed. Henry Lewis Suggs (Westport, Conn., 1983), 23–64; Foner, *Freedom's Lawmakers*, 32.

28. Northwestern and Southern Baptist Convention *Minutes*, 1866, n.p.; E. H. Lipscombe, "Our Masters," *African Expositor*, January 1883; Simmons's speech from American National Baptist Convention *Journal*, 1886, quoted in Pegues, *Our Baptist Ministers and Schools*, 446; CABMC *Report*, 1879, 10; Virginia Baptist State Convention *Minutes*, 1879, 24. For more information on the Exodusters, see Nell Irvin Painter, *Exodusters: Black Migration to Kansas After Reconstruction* (New York, 1977).

29. Elizabeth Banks, "The American Negro and His Place," *Nineteenth Century* 46 (September 1899): 463; N. H. Pius, *An Outline of Baptist History*, 62; *CWR*, November 23, 1865 (B.); Charles Dudley Warner, *On Horseback: A Tour in Virginia, North Carolina, and Tennessee* (Boston, 1889), 7–10; H. S. Bennett, "The Religion of the Negro," *Independent*, July 15, 1875, 12–13; *Texas Narratives*, supp. series 2, vol. 8., pt. 7, 3103 (Louvinia Young Pleasant); Benjamin Mays, *Born to Rebel: An Autobiography* (New York, 1971), 13–17. See also *Texas Narratives*, supp. series 2, vol. 7, pt. 8, 2952 (Isaiah Norwood). For close examinations of black political leadership in specific local areas, which stress the importance of institutions other than the church, see Thomas Holt, *Black Over White: Negro Political Leadership in South Carolina During Reconstruction* (Urbana, Ill., 1977).

30. *AB*, July 28, 1870 (Rufus Perry); *AB*, March 23, 1869 (Charles Satchell), August 11, 1870, May 4, 1869 (William Troy).

31. *AB*, July 20, 1869 (M. Wright), July 6, 1869, May 4, 1869 (William Troy).

32. Virginia Baptist State Convention *Minutes*, 1868, 14; Joseph B. Earnest, "The Religious Development of the Negro in Virginia" (Ph.D. diss., University of Virginia, 1913), quoted in Montgomery, *Under Their Own Vine and Fig Tree*, 110–12; Virginia Baptist State Convention *Minutes* quoted in CABMC *Report*, 1871, 13.

33. Statistics from Stowell, "Rebuilding Zion," 161; quotation from Missionary Baptist State Convention of Texas *Minutes*, 1885, 5.

34. Montgomery, *Under Their Own Vine and Fig Tree*, 100–115; J. M. Carroll, *A History of Texas Baptists* (Dallas, 1923), 228–39, 346, 349; Frenise Logan, *The Negro in North Carolina, 1867–1894* (Chapel Hill, 1964), 164–65; George Tindall, *South Carolina Negroes* (Columbia, S.C., 1952), 186–89; Edward Freeman, "Negro Baptist History," *Baptist History and Heritage* 4 (1969), 89–100.

35. Ronald E. Butchart, *Northern Schools, Southern Blacks, and Reconstruction: Freedmen's Education, 1862–1875* (Westport, Conn., 1980), 69, 74–75; CABMC *Report*, 1869, 9. For more information, see Washington, *Frustrated Fellowship: The Black Baptist Quest for Social Power* (Macon, Ga., 1986), and Montgomery, *Under Their Own Vine and Fig Tree*, 227.

36. *AB*, September 15, 1868; CABMC *Report*, 1869, 16; *AB*, September 29, 1868, August 11, 1870 (H. H. White), June 8, 1869. The full story can be traced in Wash-

ington, *Frustrated Fellowship*, 95–100. Douglass's views on black independence and black abolitionism are discussed in William McFeely, *Frederick Douglass* (New York, 1991), 104–82, and Waldo Martin, *The Mind of Frederick Douglass* (Chapel Hill, 1984).

37. Missionary Baptist Convention of the State of Georgia *Minutes*, 1875, 17–20; *AB*, February 17, 1870; Montgomery, *Under Their Own Vine and Fig Tree*, 227.

38. Montgomery, *Under Their Own Vine and Fig Tree*, 189; Ed Crowther, "Interracial Relations Among White and Black Baptists in Alabama, 1865–1890," paper delivered at Southern Historical Association meeting, November 1994 (copy in my possession); Jeter quoted in *AB*, July 30, 1867. See also *Baptist Record* (Mississippi), May 27, 1880 (J.A.H.).

39. *AB*, September 22, 1868; CABMC *Report*, 1877, 28–33; *National Baptist*, January 11, 1883 (Gregory); February 1, 1883 (J. L. Dart).

40. William C. Turner, "African American Education in Eastern North Carolina: American Baptist Mission Work," *American Baptist Quarterly* 12 (December 1992): 299–308.

41. Robert Baker, "The American Baptist Home Mission Society and the Freedmen, 1832–1880" (Ph.D. diss., Yale University, 1947); James McPherson, *The Abolitionist Legacy: From Reconstruction to the NAACP* (Princeton, N.J., 1975).

42. Information on Shaw from Turner, "African American Education in Eastern North Carolina," 290–308; W. E. B. Du Bois, *The College-Bred Negro American* (Atlanta, 1910), 13–16; and McPherson, *The Abolitionist Legacy*, 170–75. The article by Turner comes in a series of historical articles on black Baptist colleges that collectively constitute the single most accessible source to the history of black Baptist education in this period. See "Pursuit of the Promise: American Baptists and Black Higher Education," parts 1 and 2, *American Baptist Quarterly* 11 (December 1992); 12 (March 1993). Quotation from Lipscombe, "Our Masters," *African Expositor*, January 1883; *African Expositor*, January 1884.

43. Information on Roger Williams from Eugene Teselle, "The Nashville Institute and Roger Williams University: Benevolence, Paternalism, and Black Consciousness, 1867–1910," *Tennessee Historical Quarterly* 41 (Spring 1982): 360–79.

44. Teselle, "The Nashville Institute and Roger Williams University," 369, 372–73; McPherson, *The Abolitionist Legacy*, 284–90; Faye Wellborn Robbins, "A World-Within-a-World: Black Nashville, 1880–1915" (Ph.D. diss., University of Arkansas, 1980), 39–40, 67–61, 120–21.

45. For a critique of the ideology of uplift, see Kevin Gaines, *Uplifting the Race: Black Leadership, Politics, and Culture in the Twentieth Century* (Chapel Hill, 1996).

46. Baptist Missionary State Convention of Texas *Minutes*, 1887, n.p.

47. General Baptist State Convention of Texas *Minutes*, 1894, 20–32. For more on Bishop and Guadalupe, see Michael Heintze, *Private Black Colleges in Texas, 1865–1954* (College Station, Tex., 1985), 40–70, 129–32, and Montgomery, *Under Their Own Vine and Fig Tree*, 249–51.

48. Circular letter to black Baptists in Virginia quoted in the 1st Annual Session, General Association of Virginia *Proceedings*, 1899, n.p.

49. See Washington, *Frustrated Fellowship*, 160–70, and Lewis G. Jordan, *Negro Baptist History, U.S.A.* (Nashville, 1930), 120–32, for accounts of the controversy and formation of the National Baptist Publishing Board.

50. C. Durham, "Negroes and the Publication Society," and T. M. Pittman, "Dissenting View," *BR*, January 8, 1890; Edmund Brawley, ed., *The Negro Baptist Pulpit* (Philadelphia, 1890); Washington, *Frustrated Fellowship*, 170; *BR*, February 5, 1890; *CI*, February 6, 1890.

51. P. F. Morris, "Excerpts to Dr. E. K. Love's Article in the Last Issue of the Magazine," *NBM*, April 1897, 327–30; Jordan, *Negro Baptist History*, 250; E. M. Brawley, "The Duty of Negro Baptists, In View of the Past, the Present, and the Future," in *The Negro Baptist Pulpit*, ed. E. M. Brawley (Philadelphia, 1890), 297–98.

52. L. C. Garland, "Why We Should Use the Sunday School Literature Published at Nashville, Tennessee," *NBM*, September 1901, 352–57; American National Baptist Convention *Journal*, 1893, 36; E. C. Morris, "The Demand for a Baptist Publishing House," *NBM*, January 1894, 18–20.

53. Missionary Baptist Convention of Georgia *Minutes*, 1897, 35–45, 52–53; Montgomery, *Under Their Own Vine and Fig Tree*, 246–48; Quote from 1896 in Jordan, *Negro Baptist History*, 122–23; Emmanuel K. Love quoted in Edward Freeman, *The Epoch of Negro Baptists and the Foreign Mission Board, National Baptist Convention, Inc.* (Kansas City, Mo., 1953), 87.

54. For more detail on all these groups, see Washington, *Frustrated Fellowship*.

55. John A. Whitted, *A History of the Negro Baptists of North Carolina* (Raleigh, 1908), 25.

56. The work of the Lott Carey group, especially in the area of foreign missions, is summarized and analyzed in Sandy Dwayne Martin, *Black Baptists and African Missions: The Origins of a Movement, 1880–1915* (Macon, Ga., 1989).

57. E. C. Morris, *Sermons, Addresses, Reminiscences* (Nashville, 1901), 17, 102. The reference to "all things leading to mutual progress" comes from Booker T. Washington's famous address at the Atlanta Exposition of 1895, in Booker T. Washington, *Up From Slavery* (New York, Airmont Books edition, 1967), 150.

Chapter 3

1. Solomon L. M. Conser, *Virginia After the War: An Account of Three Years' Experience in Reorganizing the Methodist Episcopal Church in Virginia at the Close of the Civil War* (Indianapolis, 1891), 39–40.

2. Mary Allan-Olney, *The New Virginians*, vol. 2 (Edinburgh, 1880), 196; Stephen Powers, *Afoot and Alone: A Walk From Sea to Sea by the Southern Route* (Hartford, Conn., 1886), 31–32, 81; *Florida Narratives*, orig. series, vol. 17, 353 (Willis Williams).

3. T. S. Powell, *Five Years in South Mississippi* (Cincinnati, 1889), 8, 33, 47, 111.

4. See Lawrence Levine, *Highbrow / Lowbrow: The Emergence of Cultural Hierarchy in America* (Cambridge, Mass., 1986), and Nina Silber, *The Romance of Reunion: Northerners and the South, 1865–1900* (Chapel Hill, 1993).

5. For more on the Primitives, see Cecil Lambert, *The Rise of the Anti-Mission Baptists: Sources and Leaders, 1800–1840* (New York, 1980), and Bertram Wyatt-Brown, "The Anti-Mission Movement in the Jacksonian South: A Study in Regional Folk Culture," *Journal of Southern History* 36 (November 1970): 501–29. On the anti-Whiggish notions of nineteenth-century plainfolk Baptists, see Richard Carwardine, *Evangelicals*

and Politics in Antebellum America (New Haven, Conn., 1993). Cranfill's story from J. B. Cranfill, *Dr. J. B. Cranfill's Chronicle: A Story of Life in Texas, Written By Himself About Himself* (New York, 1916), 92.

6. A. J. Holt, *Pioneering in the Southwest* (Nashville, 1923), 1–35, 46–47, 55–69, 72–73, 76–79, 80–87, 89–120.

7. *Baptist Standard*, June 8, 1893 (J. L. Walker); "Laodicean Spirit," *Baptist Standard*, August 1, 1912 (J. B. Gambrell); *Baptist Standard*, August 9, 1906 (E. G. Townsend); Victor Masters, "The Country Church and New World Conditions," *Home and Foreign Fields*, July 1920, 7–9; Victor Masters, "Home Missions and the Country Church," in *The Home Mission Task*, ed. Victor Masters (Atlanta, 1914), 313, 323.

8. Figures from Mississippi Baptist State Convention *Minutes*, 1892, 54.

9. Antioch Baptist Church, 1898, Rules of Decorum, p. 285, Antioch Record Book, 1891–1913, Virginia Baptist Historical Society, University of Richmond, Richmond, Virginia; Gregory Wills, *Democratic Religion: Freedom, Authority and Discipline in the Baptist South, 1785–1900* (New York, forthcoming), 60–64. The page numbers from Wills are cited from the manuscript version that I consulted in the course of research. *Alabama Baptist*, April 14, 1887; Ted Ownby, "Mass Culture, Upper-Class Culture, and the Decline of Church Discipline in the Evangelical South: The 1910 Case of the Godbold Mineral Well Hotel," *Religion and American Culture* 4 (Winter 1994): 107–32.

10. Mrs. Hight C. Moore, "Woman's Widening Work," address before Woman's Missionary Union, 1920, in *Kind Words*, May 1, 1921, 8; Lansing Burrows, "Woman's Position in the Church," manuscript of sermon delivered June 1872, in Lansing Burrows Papers, box 3, folder 55, sermon no. 148, SBHLA. See also Morton Bryan Wharton, *Famous Women of the New Testament: A Series of Popular Lectures Delivered at the First Baptist Church of Montgomery* (New York, 1890).

11. *BR*, November 22, 1893; W. M. Jones, "McDowell County as a Mission Field," *BR*, October 12, 1898; W. Harrison Daniel, *Virginia Baptists, 1860–1902* (Bedford, Va., 1987), 97–99; Ownby, "Mass Culture, Upper-Class Culture," 114; Alva Crumpton, *The Days of Our Years* (Reidsville, Ga., 1977), 35; Tom Terrill and Jerrold Hirsch, eds., *Such As Us: Southern Voices of the Thirties*, 3rd ed. (Chapel Hill, 1987), 52; Victor I. Masters, *Country Church in the South, Arranged to Meet the Needs of Mission Study Classes and also of the General Reader* (Atlanta, 1916), 40.

12. Rules of Decorum of Bethel Baptist Church, Lafayette County, Mississippi, 1890, copy consulted in Oxford Public Library, Oxford, Mississippi; Rules of Decorum of the Shiloh Baptist Church, Prince George County, Virginia, 1890, Shiloh Baptist Church Records, SBHLA.

13. Jeremiah Bell Jeter, *The Recollections of a Long Life* (Richmond, 1891; reprint, New York, 1980), 83; W. C. Tyree, "Religious Liberty and Doctrinal Looseness," *BR*, November 18, 1903. For contrasting views on discipline, see Wills, *Democratic Religion*, 36, who provides the best "internalist" analysis of discipline, and Frederick Bode, "The Formation of Evangelical Communities in Middle Georgia: Twiggs County, 1820–1861," *Journal of Southern History* 60 (November 1994): 711–48, who emphasizes that "the ideal of benevolence and the practice of discipline allowed the evangelicals of rural middle Georgia to universalize individual behavior into a paradigm for *social* righteousness. . . . An offense like intoxication was more than a sin. It was also a violation of the

standards that evangelicals had set for their own communities and the larger society." Discipline was, he says, an effective way to place constraints on idiosyncratic behavior and thus to promote "the discipline required of a market society."

14. Minutes of the Chappawasmic Primitive Baptist Church, Virginia, November 16, 1889, copy in Virginia Historical Society, Richmond, Virginia; Wills, *Democratic Religion*, 183; Minutes of the United Baptist Church, Murfreesboro, Tennessee, March 1888; Lawrence Edwards, ed., *Minutes of Davis Creek Baptist Church* (n.p., 1978), March 1878, March 1, 1884, July 1890, March 1, 1907, copy in SBHLA.

15. Minutes of the Shiloh Baptist Church, Lafayette County, Mississippi, August 2, 1902; Minutes of the Oxford Baptist Church, Oxford, Mississippi, 1893, 1894, passim; Shelby Baptist Association (Alabama) *Minutes*, 1868, 153; B. H. Carroll, *Sermon on the Dance* (Dallas, 1877); Minutes of the Penfield Baptist Church quoted in Edward Ayers, *Vengeance and Justice: Crime and Punishment in the Nineteenth-Century South* (New York, 1984), 181; Mississippi *Baptist Record* quoted in Ownby, "Mass Culture, Upper-Class Culture," 122; case of Ira Reid quoted in Wills, *Democratic Religion*, 255.

16. Ownby, "Mass Culture, Upper-Class Culture"; Edgar Young Mullins to J. E. Lucas, March 25, 1903, in Mullins letterpress books, SBTS.

17. Daniel, *Virginia Baptists*, 95–105.

18. Minutes of the Carrollton Baptist Church, Carrollton, Mississippi, February 27, 1876; *RH*, November 1, 1866; final quotation from William Link, *The Paradox of Southern Progressivism* (Chapel Hill, 1992), 32.

19. *BR*, March 18, 1896 (R. D. Cross); John S. Hardaway, "Church Discipline," *BR*, August 10, 1898; Chowan Baptist Association (North Carolina) *Minutes*, 1875, n.p.; Shelby Baptist Association (Alabama) *Minutes*, 1861, 107, 1890, n.p.; Alabama Baptist State Convention *Minutes*, 1881, n.p.; Edgefield Baptist Association (South Carolina) *Minutes*, 1907, 11; Report from Flat River Association from *BR*, August 29, 1877; Minutes of the Wake Forest Baptist Church, December 15, 1880; *CI*, August 5, 1886; B. J. W. Graham, *A Ministry of Fifty Years* (Atlanta, 1938), 42–50; R. J. Tabor, "History of Churches Composing the Concord Baptist Churches," 1909, typed manuscript found in microfilm reel of Shiloh Baptist Church records, Bernice, Louisiana, in SBHLA.

20. Figures from E. P. Alldredge, ed., *Southern Baptist Handbook, 1923, In Two Parts* (Nashville, 1924).

21. Arthur Gordon, "Church Building," in *The Home Mission Task*, ed. Victor Masters (Atlanta, 1914), 246; *BR*, February 7, 1912; *Baptist World*, January 13, 1916, 9; Alldredge, ed., *Southern Baptist Handbook*, chapters 1–3; Victor Masters, "Land Tenure and the Country Churches," *The Home Field*, November 1914, 11–12.

22. Alldredge, ed., *Southern Baptist Handbook*, 100–107; *BW*, December 28, 1916; Bernard Spilman, "Journal," in Bernard Spilman Papers, box 3, folder 1, SBHLA; *BR*, March 18, 1896 (R. D. Cross).

23. Charles Horace Hamilton and William Edward Garnett, *The Role of the Church in Rural Community Life in Virginia* (Blacksburg, Va., 1923), 22, 44, 60–61, 68, 102–9. For an analysis of the huge number of rural church studies done in the early twentieth century, see James Madison, "Reformers and the Rural Church, 1900–1950," *Journal of American History* 73 (December 1986): 645–98. Madison's analysis supports the argument in this chapter: "The resistance of rural Americans was quieter and more private than that of most rebellions. Many rural churchgoers resisted the diagnosis and advise of

outside agents of change in the simplest manner possible: they continued as they had—attending the same church, singing the same hymns, listening to the same Scriptures and sermons. . . . Often their communities and churches persisted despite the objections of several generations of reformers. Rural churches and rural people changed in twentieth-century America, but only slowly and largely because of forces beyond the influence of those trying hardest to reform them" (668).

24. John E. White, "The Backward People in the South," *Our Home Field*, May 1909, 15–17. See also *CI*, April 5, 1900. For an analysis of rhetoric about mountain whites and the "discovery" of Appalachia as a "strange region inhabited by peculiar people," see Henry Shapiro, *Appalachia On Our Mind: The Southern Mountains and Mountaineers in the American Consciousness, 1870–1920* (Chapel Hill, 1978).

25. Landmarkism as a theological program is explained clearly in James E. Tull, *A Study of Southern Baptist Landmarkism in the Light of Historical Baptist Ecclesiology* (1960; reprint, New York, 1980). Robert T. Handy, "Biblical Primitivism in the American Baptist Tradition," in *The American Quest for the Primitive Church*, ed. Richard T. Hughes (Urbana, Ill., 1988), puts Landmarkism within the context of Protestant primitivism, as do Richard T. Hughes and C. Leonard Allen in *Illusions of Innocence: Protestant Primitivism in America, 1830–1875* (Chicago, 1988). The best interpretation of Landmarkism as a social movement in nineteenth-century Protestantism may be found in Marty Beall, "James Robinson Graves and the Rhetoric of Demagogy: Primitivism and Democracy in Old Landmarkism" (Ph.D. diss., Vanderbilt University, 1990).

"Ecclesiastical squatter sovereignty" phrase from *Alabama Baptist*, January 4, 1883; "Eastern hotbeds of indifferentism" from A. H. Autry, "An Indictment of the Southern Baptist Convention," clipping in W. C. Taylor's Album of Mission Methods, ca. 1907, SBHLA. See also J. F. Love, "Missions on the Frontier," in *The Home Mission Task*, ed. Victor Masters (Atlanta, 1914), 260–62.

26. *RH*, March 28, 1896; Handy, "Biblical Primitivism in the American Baptist Tradition," 145; Beall, "James Robinson Graves and the Rhetoric of Demagogy," 217, 230; *BR*, May 4, 1870; Minutes of the Leigh Street Baptist Church, November 26, 1866, copy in Virginia Baptist Historical Society, University of Richmond, Richmond, Virginia.

27. *Christian Index and Southwestern Baptist*, January 13, 1870; W. C. Taylor, ed., newspaper clipping in "Album of Mission Methods," SBHLA; J. A. Scarboro, *The Bible, the Baptists, and the Board System* (Fulton, Ky., 1904), 253–54, 285, 385; E. Y. Mullins to Clarence Barbour, May 3, 1919, in Mullins letterpress books, SBTS.

28. SBC *Annual*, 1905, 43–45, recounts the efforts of the Landmarkers in that year to change the basis of representation in the convention from a financial one to a numerical one. Landmarkers described the "money basis" as the "lowest and most unscriptural" basis for cooperative efforts; convention leaders responded that money was simply a necessary component of carrying on the convention's activities. M. P. Metheny, "Annual Address," in General Association of Landmark Baptists *Minutes*, 1917, n.p.; General Association of Arkansas Baptists *Minutes*, 1919, 26.

29. The vast literature on Populism is too voluminous to cite here. Some of the best works on the subject include Lawrence Goodwyn, *The Populist Moment: A Short History of the Agrarian Revolt in America* (New York, 1978); Robert C. McMath Jr., *Populist*

Vanguard: History of the Southern Farmers' Alliance (Chapel Hill, 1975); Bruce Palmer, *"Man Over Money": The Southern Populist Critique of American Capitalism* (Chapel Hill, 1980); and Barton C. Shaw, *The Wool-Hat Boys: A History of the Populist Party in Georgia, 1892 to 1910* (Baton Rouge, 1984). An excellent historiographical overview of the subject may be found in Richard L. Watson Jr., "From Populism through the New Deal: Southern Political History," in *Interpreting Southern History: Historiographical Essays in Honor of Sanford W. Higginbotham*, ed. John B. Boles and Evelyn Thomas Nolen (Baton Rouge, 1987), 308–90. See also the section on Populism in Edward Ayers, *The Promise of the New South: Life After Reconstruction* (New York, 1992).

30. *Alabama Baptist*, March 1, 1888 (P. S. Montgomery); S. M. Adams, "Politics and Religion," *Alabama Baptist*, May 9, 1889. See also Scott Hershey, "Our Washington Letter," *Alabama Baptist*, July 17, 1890.

Goodwyn, *The Populist Moment*; McMath, *Populist Vanguard*; and Keith Lynn King, "Religious Dimensions of Agrarian Protest in Texas, 1870–1908" (Ph.D. diss., University of Illinois at Urbana-Champaign, 1985), provide numerous examples of the ways in which Populists used the language of evangelicalism. See also Wayne Flynt, "Southern Baptists: Rural to Urban Transition," *Baptist History and Heritage* 16 (January 1981): 24–34; Richard Goode, "The Godly Insurrection in Limestone County: Social Gospel, Populism, and Southern Culture in the Late Nineteenth Century," *Religion and American Culture: A Journal of Interpretation* 3 (Summer 1993): 155–69; and James Green, *Grass Roots Socialism: Radical Movements in the Southwest, 1895–1943* (Baton Rouge, 1978).

31. *Baptist Record*, June 13, 1888; *CI*, October 17, 1895 (J. B. Hawthorne).

32. *BR*, January 20, 1886 (A. B. L. Hurley), October 19, 1892; *Alabama Baptist*, September 3, 1891, March 22, 1900; Watson quote in S. Paul Raybon, "Stick By the Old Paths: An Inquiry into the Southern Baptist Response to Populism," *American Baptist Quarterly* 11 (September 1992): 231–45.

33. J. A. Stradley, "Live in Peace," *BR*, July 11, 1890; "Preachers in Politics," *BR*, April 27, 1892; *CI*, June 13, 1892; *Alabama Baptist*, October 6, 1892; E. B. Teague, "Despondency," *CI*, November 3, 1892; *Alabama Baptist*, April 7, 1892; Raybon, "Stick By the Old Paths," 239; *CI*, August 18, 1892. See also Frederick Bode, *Protestantism and the New South: North Carolina Methodists and Baptists in Political Crisis, 1894–1903* (Charlottesville, 1975).

34. For more on Holiness and Pentecostalism, see Edith L. Blumhofer, *Restoring the Faith: The Assemblies of God, Pentecostalism, and American Culture* (Urbana, Ill., 1993), and Robert Mapes Anderson, *Vision of the Disinherited: The Making of American Pentecostalism* (New York, 1982). For a southern version of the story, see John Lawrence Brasher, *The Sanctified South: John Lakin Brasher and the Holiness Movement* (Urbana, Ill., 1994), and Brian Keith Turley, " 'A Wheel Within a Wheel': Southern Methodism and the Georgia Holiness Association" (Ph.D. diss., University of Virginia, 1994).

35. Ethel Hilliard quoted in Allen Tullos, *Habits of Industry: White Culture and the Transformation of the Carolina Piedmont* (Chapel Hill, 1989), 249; *BR*, October 14, 28, 1896; Edwin L. Cliburn, *In Unbroken Line: A History of the First Baptist Church of Thomaston, Georgia, from Its Beginnings at Bethesda to Its One Hundred Fiftieth Anniversary* (Thomaston, 1979), 293.

36. "Delusions and Fallacies of the Higher Life Doctrine," *BR*, March 28, 1896; J. J.

Landsell, sermon preached in Roxboro, North Carolina, reprinted in "Sanctification," *BR*, February 27, 1884; J. F. Love, "The Causes of the Sanctification Schism," *BR*, April 19, 1899. For other examples of how Baptists explained the Holiness phenomenon, see W. C. Tyree, "Religious Liberty and Doctrinal Looseness," *BR*, November 18, 1903, and John S. Hardaway, "Church Discipline," *BR*, August 10, 1898.

37. *South Carolina Baptist*, October 11, 1867; Alabama Baptist State Convention *Minutes*, 1893, 3; *BR*, September 22, 1875; *RH*, September 1, 1870; SBC *Annual*, 1896, 17; Powell, *Five Years in South Mississippi*, 60–68. See William Hatcher, *Along The Trail of Friendly Years* (New York, 1910), 294, for a typically romanticized account of an older preacher's young days on the revival circuit. For a look at the origins of the camp meetings and the quickly organized efforts to tame and commercialize them, see Paul Conkin, *Cane Ridge: America's Pentecost* (Madison, Wisc., 1990); John B. Boles, *The Great Revival, 1787–1805: The Origins of the Southern Evangelical Mind* (Lexington, Ky., 1972); and R. Laurence Moore, *Selling God: American Religion in the Marketplace of Culture* (New York, 1994), 71–77.

38. Report of the Committee on Evangelism, SBC *Annual*, 1905, 35–40.

39. *RH*, November 26, 1875, March 5, 1885.

40. Report of the Committee on Evangelism, SBC *Annual*, 1908, 10–11; *RH*, November 26, 1875.

41. *BR*, November 15, 1893.

42. Tuskegee Baptist Association (Alabama) *Minutes*, 1905, 17; Powell, *Five Years in South Mississippi*, 37; *South Carolina Baptist*, August 22, 1867 (R. F.).

43. Mississippi Baptist State Convention *Minutes*, 1905, 44–45; John A. Broadus, "Syllabus as to hymnology," printed for use in classes in homiletics, 2nd ed., 1892, found in C. M. Thompson Papers, SBHLA.

44. *BR*, June 9, 1886; *Alabama Baptist*, November 2, 1893.

45. *BR*, June 7, 1893; *Alabama Baptist*, June 7, 1877.

46. William Walker, *The Southern Harmony*, ed. Glenn Wilcox (1854; reprint, Los Angeles, 1966); Mary Collins Green, *First Baptist Church Spartanburg: A History* (Spartanburg, 1983); Dana J. Epstein, *Sinful Tunes and Spirituals: Black Folk Music to the Civil War* (Urbana, Ill., 1977); Harry Eskew, "Southern Baptist Contributions to Hymnody," 19 (January 1984): 27–35; Hugh McElrath, "Turning Points in the Story of Baptist Church Music," *Baptist History and Heritage* 19 (January 1984): 4–16; Harry Eskew, "Use and Influence of Hymnals in Southern Baptist Churches Up To 1915," *Baptist History and Heritage* 21 (July 1986): 21–30.

47. Basil Manly Jr., *The Choice: A New Selection of Approved Hymns for Baptist Churches* (Louisville, Ky., 1891), 2; Eskew, "Use and Influence of Hymnals in Southern Baptist Churches." Hymn lyrics from *Southern Baptist Hymnal* (Nashville, 1954). For a fuller discussion of the metaphors employed by gospel hymns, see Sandra S. Sizer, *Gospel Hymns and Social Religion: The Rhetoric of Nineteenth-Century Revivalism* (Philadelphia, 1978).

48. W. J. McGlothlin, *A Vital Ministry: The Pastor of Today in the Service of Man* (New York, 1913), 136.

49. *South Carolina Baptist*, May 8, 1868 (G.).

50. Aquila Peyton Diary, March 12, 1860, copy in Virginia Historical Society, Richmond, Virginia.

51. Minutes of the Leigh Street Baptist Church, Richmond, Virginia, February 6, 1905, copy in Virginia Historical Society, Richmond, Virginia; Lynn May, *The First Baptist Church of Nashville, Tennessee, 1820–1970* (Nashville, 1970), 176–77; Minutes of the Citadel Square Baptist Church, Charleston, South Carolina, July 5, 1897, April 4, 1898.

52. *BR*, June 7, 1893; B. H. Carroll, "Church Music," February 12, 1874, manuscript in B. H. Carroll Papers, reel 1, SBHLA; "When the Choir Sings," *BR*, February 26, 1898; *BR*, November 15, 1893.

53. "Report of State Board of Missions," Alabama Baptist State Convention *Minutes*, 1893, 3; J. W. Morgan, "Criticisms of the Convention," *BR*, January 3, 1912.

54. Minutes of the Columbia Baptist Church, Columbia, South Carolina, March 13, 1870, March 16, 1874. For a critique of the pew rent system, see *BR*, November 13, 1867.

55. Minutes of the Wake Forest Baptist Church, Winston-Salem, North Carolina, December 15, 1875, February 12, 1884, January 1885; Minutes of the Yockanookany Baptist Church, Attala County, Mississippi, November 1915.

56. For discussions of the agent system, see *BR*, November 17, 1869; SBC *Annual*, 1879, 29; and Home Mission Board Report, SBC *Annual*, 1884, Appendix A, xix–xx.

57. John F. Johnson, *Minutes of the Baptist Church of Christ at Greensboro, 1846–1897*, ed. John W. Brannon (University, Miss., 1985), minutes for November and December 1893; *BR*, November 29, 1893; Home Mission Board Report, SBC *Proceedings*, 1884, xix–xx; W. A. Hobson to E. Y. Mullins, January 14, 1914, in Mullins letter files, SBTS.

58. G. W. Hyde, "The Report on Plan of Work," 22, 6th Annual Meeting of Woman's Missionary Societies, held in Memphis, Tennessee, May 10–13, 1889, microfilm copy in SBHLA.

59. Catherine Allen, *A Century to Celebrate: History of the Woman's Missionary Union* (Birmingham, 1987), 119, 123–24; [Woman's Missionary Union], *W. M. U. Manual of Methods: Reference Book for Missionary Organizations* (Baltimore, 1917), 239.

60. Tennessee Baptist State Convention *Minutes*, 1919, 25.

61. Tuskegee Baptist Association (Alabama) *Minutes*, 1919, 13.

62. Quotation from W. J. McGlothlin, "Our Present Denominational Situation" (Nashville, n.d.), in SBHLA pamphlet collection, no. 969. The progress of the campaign may be followed in the SBC *Annual* from 1919 to 1922. The clearest narrative of the campaign's history is in James R. Thompson, *Tried as By Fire: Southern Baptists and the Religious Controversies of the 1920s* (Macon, Ga., 1982), 15–21.

63. Brooks Hays, "Reflections on the Role of Baptists in Politics and the Future of America," *Baptist History and Heritage* 17 (July 1970): 170.

Chapter 4

1. Myrta L. Avary, *Dixie After the War: An Exposition of The Social Conditions Existing in the South, During the Twelve Years Succeeding the Fall of Richmond* (1906; reprint, New York, 1969), 203–5. In a similar passage, Philip Bruce, in *The Plantation Negro as Freeman: Observations on His Character, Condition, and Prospects in Virginia* (New York, 1889), 106–7, wrote that it was "this desire to give full rein to all the promptings of their

religious fervor that causes the system of government that distinguishes the Baptist denomination to be considered with so much favor by the individuals of the race."

2. *BHMM*, April 1886, 90–91.

3. NBC *Journal*, 1909, 34, 1907, 86. See also L. C. Simon, "The Real Value of Christian Organization," address before Louisiana Baptist Convention, reprinted in *National Baptist Union*, November 21, 1908, 1.

4. *BHMM*, July 1884, 174; *Texas Narratives*, supp. series 2, pt. 8, vol. 9, 3798–99 (Bill and Ellen Thomas); *South Carolina Narratives*, orig. series, pt. 3., vol. 3, 5.

5. See Rhys Isaac, *The Transformation of Virginia, 1740–1790* (Chapel Hill, 1982), for an analysis of early southern evangelical worship customs in Virginia. See Lawrence Levine, *Black Culture and Black Consciousness: Afro-American Folk Thought From Slavery to Freedom* (New York, 1977); Mechal Sobel, *The World They Made Together: Black and White Values in Eighteenth Century Virginia* (Princeton, N.J., 1987); and Theophus H. Smith, *Conjuring Culture: Biblical Formations of Black America* (New York, 1994), on the complex intertwining of white and black folk spiritualities.

6. For two of numerous examples of this point, see *RH*, June 6, 1867, and B. F. Riley, *History of Baptists of Alabama, from the Time of the First Occupation of Alabama in 1808 until 1904 . . .* (Birmingham, 1908). The dual image of the "faithful slave" and the barbarous freedman is explored in Leon F. Litwack, *Been in the Storm So Long: The Aftermath of Slavery* (New York, 1979). For the continuation of this dual view into the 1890s and early twentieth century, see Joel Williamson, *Rage For Order: Black-White Relations in the American South Since Emancipation* (New York, 1988).

7. *RH*, April 11, 1901. William Hatcher, in *John Jasper: The Unmatched Negro Philosopher and Preacher* (New York, 1908), 170–73, relates his own account of being moved by Jasper's sermon.

8. Walter Hines Page, "Religious Progress of the Negroes," *Independent*, September 1, 1881, 6–7; *Harper's Weekly*, November 24, 1880, 749; Orra Langhorne, "Southern Sketches," *Southern Workman*, October 1891, 34; Eliza Frances Andrews, *The War-Time Journal of a Georgia Girl, 1864–1865* (New York, 1908), 89; Lydia Austin Parrish, *Slave Songs of the Georgia Sea Islands* (New York, 1942), 55. See also *National Baptist*, March 1, 1883, 5, 132; B. F. Riley, *History of the Baptists of Alabama*, 169–70; and D. F. L. Leach, "The Freedmen on the Plantations," *CWR*, May 1, 1873, for similar accounts.

9. William Montgomery, *Under Their Own Vine and Fig Tree: The African-American Church in the South, 1865–1900* (Baton Rouge, 1993), 283, 293; James Bryce, *The American Commonwealth* (New York and London, 1888), 520–21; Richard Carroll, "Negroes on the Coast of South Carolina," *Savannah Tribune*, April 22, 1911. See also Henry Deedes, *Sketches of the South and West, or, Ten Months Residence in the United States* (London, 1869), 157, and George R. Stetson, *The Southern Negro As He Is* (Boston, 1877), 8–9.

10. *RH*, November 30, 1882, January 5, 1888 (E. Harrison).

11. *BHMM*, February 1881, 27–29 (R. Agnes); *Savannah Tribune*, May 14, 1898; Kenansville Eastern Missionary Baptist Association (North Carolina) *Minutes*, 1913, 16.

12. H. L. Morehouse, "Plantation Life of the Colored People," *BHMM*, March 1894, 95; Michael W. Harris, *The Rise of Gospel Blues: The Music of Thomas Andrew Dorsey in the Urban Church* (New York, 1992), 19.

13. William Wells Brown, *My Southern Home; or, The South and Its People* (Boston, 1880; reprint, New York, 1969), 196–97; *BHMM*, February 1881, 27–29; [Phi], "Our Washington Letter," *CWR*, May 4, 1882. See also Ernest Abbot Hamlin, "Religious Tendencies of the Negro," *Outlook* 3 (December 21, 1901): 1075.

14. H. T. Kealing, "A Race Rich in Spiritual Content," *Southern Workman*, January 1904, 41–44; *Savannah Tribune*, August 10, 1912; A. W. Pegues, *Our Baptist Ministers and Schools* (Springfield, Mass., 1892), 18.

15. Daniel Alexander Payne, *Recollections of Seventy Years* (Nashville, 1888); Missionary State Baptist Convention of Texas *Proceedings*, 1882, n.p. For a brilliant extended discussion of the tortured issue of respectability, see James Campbell, *Songs of Zion: The African Methodist Episcopal Church in the United States and South Africa* (New York, 1995), 32–63.

16. *Texas Narratives*, supp. series 2, pt. 5, vol. 6, 2259 (Ann Ladly), and supp. series 2, pt. 2., vol. 3, 946 (Jane Cotton).

17. This description comes from Peter Goldsmith, *When I Rise Cryin' Holy: African-American Denominationalism on the Georgia Coast* (New York, 1989), 100–110.

18. Walter Pitts, *Old Ship of Zion: The Afro-Baptist Ritual in the African Diaspora* (New York, 1993).

19. F. M. Davenport, "The Religion of the American Negro," *Contemporary Review*, September 1905, 369–75. W. D. Siegfried, in *A Winter in the South, and Work Among the Freedmen* (Newark, N.J., 1870), notes the practice of setting one's self aside during the days of conversion; Contributors' Club, "Certain Beliefs and Superstitions of the Negro," *Atlantic Monthly* 67 (August 1891), quoted in *The Negro and His Folklore in Nineteenth-Century Periodicals*, ed. Bruce Jackson (Austin, Tex., 1967), 286–88; W. C. Gannett, "The Freedmen at Port Royal," *North American Review* 101 (July 1865): 1–28. For an incisive analysis and description of conversion experiences as rites of passage see Zora Neale Hurston, *The Sanctified Church* (Berkeley, 1981), 85–90.

20. *Texas Narratives*, supp. series 2, pt. 8, vol. 9, 3798–99 (Bill and Ellen Thomas), and supp. series 2, pt. 2, vol. 3, 860–61 (Preely Coleman).

21. Melville Herskovits, *The Myth of the Negro Past*, 2nd ed. (Boston, 1958), 252–53.

22. Harris, *The Rise of Gospel Blues*; Robert Palmer, *Deep Blues* (New York, 1981); and Jon Michael Spencer, *Blues and Evil* (Knoxville, 1993), provide some of the most compelling discussion of the relationship between the blues and African American spirituality.

23. See Clifton Johnson, ed., *God Struck Me Dead*, and Howard Snyder, "The Ordination of Charlie," *Atlantic* 127 (March 1921): 338–42.

24. Charley White, *No Quittin' Sense* (Austin, Tex., 1967), 134.

25. For more on this point, see Mechal Sobel, *Trabelin' On: The Slave Journey to an Afro-Baptist Faith*, 2nd ed. (Princeton, N.J., 1987); Margaret Washington Creel, *"A Peculiar People": Slave Religion and Community-Culture Among the Gullahs* (New York, 1988); Sheila Walker, *Ceremonial Spirit Possession in Africa and Afro-America: Forms, Meanings, and Functional Significance for Individuals and Social Groups* (Leiden, England, 1972); and Robert Hood, "Ghosts and Spirits in Afro Cultures: Morrison and Wilson," *Anglican Theological Review* 73 (Summer 1991): 297–313. Sterling Stuckey presents the centrality of the African tradition in his controversial work *Slave Culture and the Foundations of Black Nationalism* (New York, 1987). A great deal of anthropolog-

ical literature on spirits and possessions in traditional African religions is available. For a useful introduction, see Geoffrey Parrinder, *African Traditional Religion*, rev. ed. (Westport, Conn., 1970).

26. *South Carolina Narratives*, orig. series 1, pt. 3, vol. 3, 254 (Amy Perry); *Texas Narratives*, supp. series 2, pt. 5, vol. 6, 2033–34 (Mary Ellen Johnson). For an analysis of low-church worship that explains how liturgy ("filled") worship finds its way into low churches that practiced extemporized ("unfilled") worship, see Paul K. Conkin, *The Uneasy Center: Reformed Christianity in Antebellum America* (Chapel Hill, 1995), 185–209.

27. Rossa B. Cooley, *School Acres: An Adventure in Rural Education* (1930; reprint, Westport, Conn., 1970), 151. See also Joseph Holloway, ed., *Africanisms in American Culture* (Bloomington, Ind., 1990).

28. *BHMM*, February 1881, 27–29 (R. Agnes); Minutes of the Gillfield Baptist Church, September 20, 1869; Alfred Pinkston, "Lined Hymns, Spirituals, and the Associated Lifestyle of Black People in the United States" (Ph.D. diss., University of Miami, 1975). See also Contributors' Club, "Certain Beliefs," quoted in Jackson, *The Negro and His Folklore*, 286–88.

29. Theodore Rosengarten, ed., *All God's Dangers: The Life of Nate Shaw* (New York, 1974), 332–34, 410–11.

30. Report on "Religious Instruction of the Colored People," Alabama Baptist State Convention (white) *Proceedings*, 1868, 11; *CWR*, April 1, 1880. See also *RH*, July 1, 1875 (J. W. Patterson), and *Savannah Tribune*, May 14, 1898.

31. Zora Neale Hurston, *Dust Tracks on a Road* (Philadelphia, 1942), 275, 280, and *The Sanctified Church*, 83.

32. Lillie Barr, "Three Months on a Cotton Plantation," *Independent*, June 30, 1881, 1–2; W. C. Gannett, "The Freedman at Port Royal," *North American Review* 101 (July 1865): 1–28. Barr was on St. John's Island, South Carolina. See William L. Andrews, ed., *Sisters of the Spirit: Three Black Women's Autobiographies of the Nineteenth Century* (Bloomington, Ind., 1986), for the stories of Lee and Elaw.

33. Barr, "Three Months on a Cotton Plantation"; Minutes of the Gillfield Baptist Church, August 17, September 7, 1868; Woman's Baptist State Convention of North Carolina *Minutes*, June 1900, 9. For more on African secret societies, see Creel, *"A Peculiar People,"* chapters 1–2.

34. *AB*, February 15, August 18, 1868.

35. Missionary Baptist Convention of Louisiana and Mississippi *Minutes*, 1877, 34. For an extended analysis of church mothers, see Cheryl Townsend Gilkes, "The Roles of Church and Community Mothers: Ambivalent American Sexism or Fragmented African Familyhood?" *Journal of Feminist Studies in Religion* 2 (Spring 1986): 41–59.

36. Rosengarten, ed., *All God's Dangers*, 410–11.

37. *Oklahoma Narratives*, supp. series 1, 194–96 (Lewis Jenkins); Philip Bruce, *The Plantation Negro as Freeman: Observations on His Character, Condition, and Prospects in Virginia* (New York, 1899), 105. For a similar description to that of Bruce, see O. W. Blacknall, "The New Departure in Negro Life," *Atlantic Monthly* 52 (November 1883): 684. See also *Texas Narratives*, supp. series 2, pt. 9, vol. 10, 4263, and supp. series 2, pt. 2, vol. 3, 769 (Harrison Cole).

38. *South Carolina Narratives*, orig. series 1, pt. 3, vol. 3, 108–11 (Easter Lockhart);

Texas Narratives, supp. series 2, pt. 8, vol. 9, 3798–99 (Bill and Ellen Thomas); *Florida Narratives*, vol. 17, 192 (Cindey Kinsey); *Texas Narratives*, supp. series 2, pt. 7, vol. 8, 3043 (Ellen Payne).

39. Stetson, *The Southern Negro As He Is*, 9–10; Cooley, *School Acres*, 151.

40. *African Expositor*, January 1883, 1; W. H. Brooks, "Experiences in Louisiana," *National Baptist*, June 9, 1881, 364.

41. Stetson, *The Southern Negro As He Is*, 8–9; Rupert Sargent Holland, ed., *Letters and Diary of Laura Towne* (New York, 1969), 20; Frances Butler Leigh, *Ten Years on a Georgia Plantation* (London, 1883), 60; Francis D. Gage, "Religious Exercises of the Negroes of the Sea Islands," *Independent*, January 15, 1863, 6; *BR*, January 5, 1871; F. M. Davenport, "The Religion of the American Negro," *Contemporary Review*, September 1905, 369–75; *BHMM*, February 1881, 27–29. See also Maria Waterbury, *Seven Years Among the Freedmen* (Freeport, N.Y., 1971), 195.

42. Du Bois, *The Souls of Black Folk* (1903; reprint, New York, 1989), 8, 135; Cooley, *School Acres*, 148.

43. "A Summer on a Southern Plantation," *Independent*, December 11, 1879, 3–4; Charles Horace Hamilton and John Ellison, *The Negro Church in Rural Virginia* (Blacksburg, Va., 1930), 24–25.

44. O. W. Blacknall, "The New Departure in Negro Life," *Atlantic Monthly* 52 (November 1883): 684; Frederick Burrill Graves, "Southland Studies," *Zion's Herald*, February 22, 1893, 57. For accounts of revivals at black colleges, see David Levering Lewis, *W. E. B. Du Bois: Biography of a Race, 1868–1919* (New York, 1993), 176, and Campbell, *Songs of Zion*, 276.

45. Howard Snyder, "A Plantation Revival Service," *Yale Review* 10 (October 1920): 168–80; John Bennett, "A Revival Sermon at Little St. Johns," *Atlantic* 98 (August 1906): 256–68. See also Nathan Irvin Huggins, *Harlem Renaissance* (New York, 1971), 133–36.

46. These accounts come from Portia Smiley, "The Foot-Wash in Alabama," *Southern Workman*, May 1896, 101–2; J., "The Ceremony of 'Foot-Wash' in Virginia," *Southern Workman*, April 1896, 82; Charles Edwards, "A Scene from Florida Life," *MacMillan's Magazine* 50 (August 1884): 265–70; and Mary E. Penniston, "Flatwoods: A Black-Belt Study," *Southern Workman*, November 1914, 630–35. See also *CWR*, March 29, 1866.

47. Note on funerals in *Southern Workman*, January 1897, 18–19; Susan Showers, "A Weddin' and a Buryin' in the Black Belt," *New England Magazine* 18 (June, 1898): 478–83; Hatcher, *John Jasper*, 38; and Charles H. Corey, *A History of Richmond Theological Seminary With Reminiscences of Thirty Years' Work Among the Colored People of the South* (Richmond, 1895). See also H. P. Jacobs quoted in Patrick Thompson, *History of Negro Baptists in Mississippi* (Jackson, 1898), 108.

48. Note on funerals in *Southern Workman*, January 1897, 18–19. See also Robert Hood, "Ghosts and Spirits in Afro Cultures," and the sections on rituals of death and funerals in Creel, *"A Peculiar People,"* and Sobel, *Trabelin' On*, 196–200.

49. Yvonne Chireau, "Conjure and Christianity: Religious Elements of African-American Occultism" (copy of unpublished paper, in my possession), 3; *South Carolina Narratives*, orig. series, pt. 1, vol. 2, 322 (Will Dill), and orig. series, pt. 2, vol. 2, 99 (Janie

Gallman). Chireau's work, forthcoming as a book, may be found in her "Conjuring: An Analysis of African-American Folk Beliefs" (Ph.D. diss., Princeton University, 1994).

50. *Texas Narratives*, pt. 1, vol. 2, 32 (Jacob Aldrich); D. F. L. Leach, "The Freedmen on the Plantations," *CWR*, May 1, 1873.

51. *Texas Narratives*, supp. series 2, pt. 1, vol. 2, 16–19. See also Chireau, "Conjure and Christianity," 11, 20, and Orishatukeh Faduma, "The Defects of the Negro Church," in *American Negro Academy, Occasional Papers, No. 10* (Washington, 1904; reprint, New York, 1969), 5.

52. T. L. Robinson, "The Colored People of the United States," *Leisure Hour* 38 (1889), 54–59.

53. *Texas Narratives*, supp. series 2, pt. 9, vol. 10, 4151 (Wayman Williams), supp. series 2, pt. 6, vol. 7, 2812 (Leo Mouton), and supp. series 2, pt. 2., vol. 3, 515 (Vinnie Brunson). See also *South Carolina Narratives*, orig. series, pt. 1, vol. 2, 236 (Dinah Cunningham).

54. *AB*, June 25, 1867.

55. *Harper's Weekly*, November 24, 1880, 749; Joseph B. Earnest, *The Religious Development of the Negro in Virginia* (Charlottesville, 1914), 152; Harris, *The Rise of Gospel Blues*, 19–22. See also T. O. Fuller, *History of the Negro Baptists of Tennessee* (Memphis, 1936), 231–32.

56. Cooley, *School Acres*, 154–55; William E. Barton, "Recent Negro Melodies," *New England Magazine*, n.s., 19 (February 1899): 707–19; Lillie B. Chace Wyman, "Colored Churches and Schools in the South," *New England Magazine*, n.s., 31 (February 1891): 787; D. L. Gore, "The Negro Race," *The Home Field*, July 1911, 21.

57. H. L. Morehouse, "Plantation Life of the Colored People," *BHMM*, March 1894, 95; *BHMM*, August 1882, 225.

58. "Studies in the South," *Atlantic*, October 1882, 479; "A Summer on a Southern Plantation," 3–4; Contributors Club, "Certain Beliefs," quoted in Jackson, *The Negro and His Folklore*, 286–88; Orra Langhorne, "Southern Sketches," *Southern Workman*, October 1891, 34.

59. *Texas Narratives*, supp. series 2, pt. 9, vol. 10, 4293 (Fannie Yarbrough); *North Carolina Narratives*, orig. series, pt. 1, vol. 14, 269 (Squire Dowd).

60. Mary Allan-Olney, *The New Virginians*, vol. 2 (Edinburgh, 1880), 238–45; Elizabeth Kilham, "Sketches in Color: IV," *Putnam's Monthly* 15 (March 1870): 304–11; Herskovits, *Myth of the Negro Past*, 223.

61. *National Baptist Union*, November 21, 1908, 7.

62. Quoted in Jon Michael Spencer, *Black Hymnody: A Hymnological History of the African-American Church* (Knoxville, 1992), 80, 84. These paragraphs on black Baptist hymnody come primarily from Spencer's very detailed and informative study.

63. Harris, *The Rise of Gospel Blues*, 171–73; Spencer, *Black Hymnody*, 87–88; Levine, *Black Culture and Black Consciousness*; George Ricks, *Some Aspects of the Religious Music of the United States Negro: An Ethnomusicological Study with Special Emphasis on the Gospel Tradition* (New York, 1977); Jon Michael Spencer, *Protest and Praise: The Sacred Music of Black Religion* (Minneapolis, 1994).

64. See Cheryl Sanders, *Saints in Exile: The Holiness-Pentecostal Experience in African American Religion and Culture* (New York, 1996), 15–16, 19–20.

65. James Henry Eason, *Sanctification Versus Fanaticism* (Nashville, 1899), 57; J. A. Whitted, *A History of the Negro Baptists of North Carolina* (Raleigh, 1908), 5, 51.

66. White, *No Quittin' Sense*, 128–30.

67. *South Carolina Narratives*, orig. series 1, pt. 1, vol. 2, 53–54 (Anne Bell).

68. Rosengarten, ed., *All God's Dangers*, 198. Eugene Genovese, *Roll, Jordan, Roll: The World the Slaves Made* (New York, 1972), explains the dual role of slave religion. Benjamin Mays, *The Negro's Church* (New York, 1933), and E. Franklin Frazier, *The Negro Church in America* (New York, 1964), depict the black church as a force for accommodationism, while more recent works such as Evelyn Brooks Higginbotham's *Righteous Discontent: The Women's Movement in the Black Baptist Church, 1880–1920* (Cambridge, Mass., 1993) and Theophus H. Smith's *Conjuring Culture* present a more positive assessment.

69. Hamilton and Ellison, *The Negro Church in Rural Virginia*, 3; [Hampton Institute], *The Negro in Virginia* (New York, 1940), 262.

70. See Taylor Branch, *Parting the Waters: America in the King Years, 1954–1963* (New York, 1988); Lewis Baldwin, *There is a Balm in Gilead: The Cultural Roots of Martin Luther King, Jr.* (Minneapolis, 1991); and David Garrow, *Bearing the Cross: Martin Luther King, Jr., and the Southern Christian Leadership Conference* (New York, 1987), for analyses of how King reconciled the Fundamentalism and emotionalism of the black southern church with the liberal Protestant teachings he received in northern seminaries and universities.

Chapter 5

1. S. L. Morgan to Hight Moore, June 27, 1917, in Hight C. Moore Papers, box 3, folder 20; William Owen Carver Diary, entry for January 1, 1893, in William Owen Carver Papers, box 1, folder 10, both in SBHLA.

2. Quoted in Tom Terrill and Jerrold Hirsch, eds., *Such As Us: Southern Voices of the Thirties* (Chapel Hill, 1978), 159.

3. E. Brooks Holifield, *The Gentlemen Theologians: American Theology in Southern Culture, 1795–1860* (Durham, N.C., 1978); Anne Loveland, *Southern Evangelicals and the Social Order, 1800–1860* (Baton Rouge, 1980); Donald G. Mathews, *Religion in the Old South* (Chicago, 1978); and Nathan Hatch, *The Democratization of American Christianity* (New Haven, Conn., 1989).

4. Jeremiah Bell Jeter, *The Recollections of a Long Life* (Richmond, 1891; reprint, New York, 1980), 52–54.

5. Basil Manly Jr. to Charles Manly, October 8, 1869, in Manly Family Papers, reel 4, SBHLA; *ESB*, 2:817–18.

6. James Frost, Journal for 1872, in James Marion Frost Papers, box 36, SSB.

7. George Blount Diary, entry for July 26, 1868, in George Blount Papers, folder 4, SBHLA; *South Carolina Baptist*, May 8, 1868 (I. H. Goss); Otis Webster Yates, *A Country Boy Used By the Lord* (New York, 1979), 25; J. M. Carroll, "The Story of My Life," typewritten manuscript in J. M. Carroll Papers, Texas Baptist Historical Library, Southwestern Baptist Theological Seminary, Ft. Worth, Texas, reprinted in *Texas Baptist History* 6 (1986): 44–45, 82–83; J. B. Cranfill, *Dr. J. B. Cranfill's Chronicle: A Story*

of *Life in Texas, Written by Himself about Himself* (New York, 1916), 166–80. See also John Sampey, *Memoirs of John Sampey* (Nashville, 1947).

8. Edwin Hansford Rennolds, "Autobiography," 52–54, typewritten manuscript in E. H. Rennolds Sr. Papers; William Owen Carver Diary, entries for July 4, 1894, and July 30, 1896, in Carver Papers, box 11, both in SBHLA.

9. "Call to Ministry," *RH*, October 6, 1910; *BR*, February 1, 1892 (J. M. White). See also Lansing Burrows, "God's Agency in Secular Matters," manuscript of sermon preached July 1873, in Lansing Burrows Papers, box 4, folder 91, sermon 223.

10. John Broadus, *Sermons and Addresses* (Baltimore, 1886), 201; A. W. Duncan license in A. W. Duncan Papers, SBHLA; ordination practice of Leigh Street Baptist Church from Minutes of the Leigh Street Baptist Church, Richmond, Virginia, June 23, 1890, Virginia Historical Society, Richmond.

11. George Blount Diary, 1875, in George Blount Papers, folder 4, SBHLA; Joseph Martin Dawson, *A Thousand Months to Remember* (Waco, Tex., 1964), 23–25.

12. D. W. P., "Letter from Tennessee," *CWR*, January 5, 1882; John T. Oakley, "Fifty Years in the Ministry," typewritten manuscript of articles originally written for the *Carthage Courier*, comp. and ed. by William F. Oakley and Rosalee Oakley, March 1979, copy in John T. Oakley Papers, SBHLA.

13. Broadus, *Sermons and Addresses*, 202; Fair River Baptist Association (Mississippi) *Minutes*, 1878, 8; Lansing Burrows, "An Educated Ministry, the Need of the Future," manuscript of sermon preached February 1875, in Lansing Burrows Papers, box 7, folder 141, sermon 331, SBHLA; Tennessee Baptist State Convention *Anniversary*, 1895, n.p. See also B. H. Carroll, sermon preached in San Antonio, Texas, January 28, 1900, reprinted in *Christian Education: A Sermon* (Waco, Tex., 1900), 13–29, for his call to evangelical colleges to stir up the "Sons of Zion . . . against the Sons of Greece."

14. *BR*, October 5, 1892; *Alabama Baptist*, October 19, 1884; Central Baptist Association (Mississippi) *Minutes*, 1890, 6.

15. Austin Baptist Association (Texas) *Minutes*, 1890, 14; B. J. W. Graham, *A Ministry of Fifty Years* (Atlanta, 1938).

16. John Broadus, *Memoir of James Petigru Boyce, D.D., L.L.D., late president of the Southern Baptist Theological Seminary* (New York, 1893), 255.

17. James P. Boyce, "An Inaugural Address," reprinted in Robert Baker, ed., *A Baptist Source Book, With Particular Reference to Southern Baptists* (Nashville, 1966), 132–36. Information on Boyce's life comes from Broadus, *Memoir of James Petigru Boyce*, and *ESB*, 1:182–83.

18. J. J. Porter to T. T. Eaton, June 6, 1896, in Eaton letter files, box 6, SBTS; John Broadus to Basil Manly Jr., 1859, typewritten transcript of letter found in William H. Whitsitt Papers, Virginia State Library, Richmond, Virginia.

19. Basil Manly Jr. to Charles Manly, April 27, 1868, Manly Family Papers, reel 1, SBHLA; [illegible] Porter to James P. Boyce, August 1, 1867, in Boyce letter files, SBTS.

20. *ESB*, 2:1269; "looseness and isms" from F. H. Kerfoot to E. Y. Mullins, February 10, 1900, in Mullins letter files, SBTS. Full details of the history of the seminary can be found in William Mueller, *A History of Southern Baptist Theological Seminary* (Nashville, 1959).

21. E. Y. Mullins to J. H. Farmer, March 23, 1907, in Mullins letter files, SBTS. For a look at the development of theological education in the nineteenth century, see Glenn T. Miller, "God, Rhetoric, and Logic in Antebellum American Theological Education," in *Communication and Change in American Religious History*, ed. Leonard Sweet (Grand Rapids, Mich., 1993), 165–84, and Mark Noll, "The Evangelical Enlightenment and the Task of Theological Education," in ibid., 270–300.

22. Bernard Spilman, "Journal," manuscript in Bernard Spilman Papers, box 3, folder 1, SBHLA. The suggestion that by 1920 congregations of 200 or more members in small-town or urban settings rarely considered untrained men for pulpit openings comes from an extensive survey of local church histories deposited in SBHLA. It should be understood that ministerial "training" often consisted of one or two semesters at one of the seminaries or an extension course from a Baptist college.

23. *ESB*, 2:1423. For Toy's statement, see *RH*, December 11, 1879, as reprinted in Baker, ed., *A Baptist Source Book*, 169–72. The *Religious Herald* supported Toy, but only weakly: "If the Bible tells us that all Scripture is given by the inspiration of God, but gives us no explanation of the mysterious process by which divine truth is communicated through human channels, is that not one of the secret things which belong not to us, and which we had better not meddle with?" *RH*, March 4, 1880.

24. T. T. Eaton to Edgar Allen Forbes, February 7, 1905, in Eaton letter files, box 6, SBTS; *BR*, September 16, 1885; "new theology" from A. Justice to Edgar Young Mullins, April 10, 1900, in Mullins letter files, and Frost letter from J. M. Frost to T. T. Eaton, March 27, 1906, in Eaton letter files, box 6, both in SBTS. For an example of Landmarkist criticism of the seminary, see W. T. Amis to William Owen Carver, March 5, 1903, in Carver Papers, folder for 1903, SBHLA. For defenses of orthodoxy at the seminary, see A. T. Robertson, "Presuppositions of New Testament Criticism," *Baptist Argus*, August 8, 1907. For reassurances on the compatibility of evangelicalism and science, see also George McDaniel, "What Is the Truth About the Bible and Science?," 9–10, Pamphlet 801 in Pamphlet Collection, SBHLA. For the most liberal expression of southern Baptist thought on higher criticism, see A. J. Dickinson, "Higher Criticism," *RH*, November 21, 1906.

25. Whitsitt's position is summarized in William H. Whitsitt, *A Question in Baptist History* (Louisville, Ky., 1896).

26. V. P. Armstrong to T. T. Eaton, March 14, 1898, in Eaton letter files, box 7; H. O. Hurley to Eaton, March 12, 1898, T. T. Eaton Papers, box 7; Hugh C. Smith (Martinsville, Virginia) to Eaton, April 8, 1899, in Eaton letter files, box 7, 1899 correspondence; G. H. [Easter?] to Eaton, May 23, 1897, in Eaton letter files, box 7; B. J. Davis to Eaton, September 21, 1896, Eaton letter files, box 6; collection of associational resolutions against Whitsitt in Eaton letter files, box 1, all in SBTS; John Oakly to W. O. Carver, February 8, 1897, in Carver Papers, folder for 1897, SBHLA.

27. W. H. Whitsitt, "The Whitsitt Controversy—1896–99," typewritten manuscript in William H. Whitsitt Papers, reel 37, Virginia State Library, Richmond, Virginia; Charles Manly to Bro. Julius, March 23, 1898, in Manly Family Papers, reel 8, SBHLA; *RH*, February 16, 1899; B. H. Carroll, "A Word in Passing on the Seminary Issue," typewritten manuscript, September 9, 1897, in B. H. Carroll Papers, reel 1, SBHLA. A full account of the Whitsitt affair may be found in *ESB*, 2:1496, and Charles Briggs, "The Whitsitt Controversy: A Study in Denominational Conflict" (Th.D. thesis,

Southern Baptist Theological Seminary, 1972). Whitsitt originally received the support of the trustees of the seminary, who characterized him as "demanding of those in charge of the departments of instruction the utmost patience in research and the greatest discretion in utterance, to foster, rather than repress, the spirit of earnest and reverent investigation."

28. R. H. Pitt to E. Y. Mullins, August 21, 1899, in Mullins letter files, folder for 1899, and J. S. K. to Mullins, August 12, 1899, in Mullins letter files, SBTS; E. Y. Mullins, "Our Seminary's Ideals," *BR*, October 18, 1899; Mullins, "The Seminary Endowment Needs Pressing," *Alabama Baptist*, November 10, 1909; Mullins to Henry Watterson, December 27, 1911, Mullins letterpress books, SBTS.

29. W. R. L. Smith to Mullins, October 27, 1901, and E. Y. Mullins to C. S. Gardner, May 4, 1907, in Mullins letterpress books, SBTS; Mullins to William Owen Carver, September 17, 1907, in William Owen Carver correspondence, SBHLA; Mullins to Cornelius Woolfolk, November 7, January 7, 1911, in Mullins letterpress books; W. H. Jones to E. Y. Mullins, February 18, 1901, and J. R. Sampey to Mullins, August 21, 1903, in Mullins letter files, all in SBTS.

30. C. M. Thompson, notebook for course in Homiletics at SBTS, Spring 1896, in C. M. Thompson Papers, SBHLA.

31. *BW*, April 27, 1916; B. G. Parker to E. Y. Mullins, February 20, 1918, in Mullins letter files, SBTS. Samuel Haber, in *The Quest for Authority and Honor in the American Professions, 1750–1900* (Chicago, 1991), discusses the importance of the camaraderie and collegiality between men with professional aspirations that developed in graduate professional schools, including seminaries, of the time. A few of the better-known works by Southern seminary professors of the time include E. Y. Mullins, *The Axioms of Religion: A New Interpretation of the Baptist Faith* (Philadelphia, 1908); William Owen Carver, *The Course of Christian Missions: A History and an Interpretation* (New York, 1932); and John Broadus, *Treatise on the Preparation and Delivery of Sermons*, 17th ed. (New York, 1891). Broadus's work was widely used in courses on preaching in seminaries.

32. W. J. McGlothlin, *A Vital Ministry: The Pastor of Today in the Service of Man* (New York, 1913), 184; Mullins, *Axioms of Religion*, 16; Mullins to M. Ashby Jones, March 9, 1910, Mullins letterpress books, SBTS. See also *Alabama Baptist*, September 9, 1908.

33. Baptist General Convention of Texas *Annual*, 1915, 114–16; Leonard Doolan to W. O. Carver, January 20, 1908, in Carver Papers, folder for 1908, SBHLA.

34. This discussion of the relationship between evangelicalism and public life in the nineteenth century is based most directly on Donald G. Mathews, "The Second Great Awakening as an Organizing Process," *American Quarterly* 21 (Spring 1969): 23–43. See also Hatch, *The Democratization of American Christianity*; Ronald Walters, *The Anti-Slavery Appeal: American Abolitionism Before 1830* (New York, 1976); Samuel S. Hill Jr., *The South and the North in American Religion* (Athens, Ga., 1980); Ernest R. Sandeen, *The Roots of Fundamentalism: British and American Millenarianism, 1800–1930* (Chicago, 1970); George M. Marsden, *Fundamentalism and American Culture: The Shaping of Twentieth-Century Evangelicalism, 1870–1925* (New York, 1980); and Timothy P. Weber, *Living in the Shadow of the Second Coming: American Premillennialism, 1875–1925* (New York, 1979). For fuller explanations of the literature of Christian sentimental Victorianism, particularly autobiographies, memoirs, doggerel, and gospel hymns, see Colleen

McDannell, *The Christian Home in Victorian America* (Bloomington, Ind., 1986), and Sandra S. Sizer, *Gospel Hymns and Social Religion: The Rhetoric of Nineteenth-Century Revivalism* (Philadelphia, 1978). The best analysis of concepts of afterlife in revival preaching may be found in Jon Butler, *"Softly and Tenderly Jesus is Calling": Heaven and Hell in American Revivalism* (New York, 1991). For more on Moody, see James Gilbert, *Perfect Cities: Chicago's Utopias of 1893* (Chicago, 1991).

35. For a sample of Boyce's theology, see James Petigru Boyce, *James Petigru Boyce: Selected Writings*, ed. Timothy George (Nashville, 1989); description of "straight" Calvinism from *Our Home Field*, February 1889, 6; "inclined to Arminianism" from J. H. Spencer, "Autobiography," unpublished typewritten manuscript, in J. H. Spencer Papers, folder 13, SBHLA, 92.

36. E. Y. Mullins, "The Meaning of Religion," *RH*, May 1, 1919; Mullins to I. N. Penick, March 4, 1910, in Mullins letter files, SBTS.

37. Edgar Young Mullins, *Christianity at the Crossroads* (Nashville, 1924), 262; Mullins to Charles R. Shepherd, September 8, 1917, in Mullins letterpress books, SBTS; *Alabama Baptist*, April 15, 1908 (review of Mullins, *Axioms of Religion*), and *Alabama Baptist*, January 23, 1907 (editorial on the "New Theology"). See also Edgar Young Mullins, *Why is Christianity True? Christian Evidences* (Philadelphia, 1905), *The Christian Religion in Its Doctrinal Expression* (Nashville, 1917), and *Axioms of Religion*.

38. W. R. L. Smith to William Owen Carver, September 14, 1899, in Carver Papers, folder for 1899, SBHLA; *Alabama Baptist*, July 1, 1880; *Baptist Standard*, August 5, 1912, January 3, 1902.

39. Z. T. Cody, "Are Baptist Calvinists," *BW*, April 12, 1911; Mullins, *Axioms of Religion*, 5. See also Robert Kendall, "The Rise and Demise of Calvinism in the Southern Baptist Convention" (M.A. thesis, University of Louisville, 1973).

40. *CI*, April 25, 1867; John Broadus to E. Y. Mullins, January 27, 1894, in Archibald T. Robertson, ed., *Life and Letters of John Albert Broadus* (Philadelphia, 1901), 417; E. Y. Mullins to W. L. Fick, April 11, 1908, in Mullins letterpress books, SBTS; *Alabama Baptist*, August 6, 1878; B. H. Carroll, "The Way to World Peace," in *The River of Life*, ed. J. B. Cranfill (Nashville, 1928), 158–93. To the degree that there existed a consensus among SBC spokesmen on the subject, most were "amillennialists"; that is, most SBC theologians rejected any particular vision of the precise timing and nature of Christ's Second Coming. See Pamela Colbenson, "Millennial Thought Among Southern Evangelicals" (Ph.D. diss., Georgia State University, 1980), and Hester O'Neal, "Millennialism in Southern Baptist Thought" (Th.D. thesis, Southwestern Baptist Theological Seminary, 1981).

41. For two examples of critiques of the decline of Calvinism and rise of sentimental imagery in preaching, see *BR*, April 30, 1890, and *CI*, September 5, 1872. The critique of contemporary sermonizing comes from J. B. Hawthorne, untitled typewritten manuscript of sermon delivered before SBC on May 7, 1886, in Convention Sermon Collection, SBHLA, and Commencement Address of W. A. Montgomery, reprinted in *RH*, July 3, 1884.

42. *Alabama Baptist*, February 9, 1910; *BW*, October 6, 1910, 17; *Our Home Field*, February 1906, 1.

43. [Illegible] to William Owen Carver, April 24, 1907, in Carver correspondence,

SBHLA; C. W. Carter to E. Y. Mullins, May 21, 1910, and Edward C. Applegarth to E. Y. Mullins, June 2, 1903, in Mullins letter files, SBTS.

44. Jeter, *The Recollections of a Long Life*, 19–25; W. T. Tardy, *Trials and Triumphs: An Autobiography*, ed. J. B. Cranfill (Marshall, Tex., 1919), 27. See also *CWR*, November 14, 1867.

45. Basil Manly Sr. to son, February 10, 1865, in Manly Family Papers, reel 1, folder 125, SBHLA; Diary of J. L. M. Curry, May 22, 1877, quoted in Jerry Windsor, "Preaching Up a Storm from 1839 to 1889," *Alabama Baptist Historian* 29 (January 1993): 13–24; *RH*, April 5, 1900; F. M. Jordan, *Life and Labors of F. M. Jordan* (Raleigh, 1899), 322–23. See also Rufus Weaver, "The Outlook for Orthodoxy," *BW*, March 3, 1910.

46. J. M. White, "Methods in Church Work," *BR*, March 3, 1894; McGlothlin, *A Vital Ministry*, 39. See also W. F. Felix, untitled typewritten manuscript of sermon delivered before SBC on May 12, 1905, 8, in Convention Sermon Collection, SBHLA, and J. J. D. Renfroe, "Stand by the Old Symbols of the Faith," lecture on preaching to ministerial students, in *Alabama Baptist*, January 8, 1885.

47. B. J. W. Graham, *A Ministry of Fifty Years* (Atlanta, 1938), 101–2. John William Jones, who carried the torch of the Lost Cause from the 1860s to the 1890s, also conducted numerous ministers' institutes and left accounts for them. See, for example, *Alabama Baptist*, May 15, 1889.

48. George William Gardner, "A Chronicle in the Life of a Young Baptist Pastor in the Early 1880s," entry for February 4, 1883, typewritten manuscript of diary, comp. and ed. by John Kemp Durst; William Owen Carver Diaries, entry for December 22, 1895, and November 20, 1896, in Carver Papers; J. H. Spencer, "Autobiography," 186; Lansing Burrows, "Farewell Sermon," Lansing Burrows Papers, box 10, folder 218, all in SBHLA.

49. J. H. Spencer, "Autobiography," 135–60.

50. Minutes of the Wake Forest Baptist Church (North Carolina), January 1865, January 1874; *RH*, September 5, 1867 (G. T. Wilburn); Austin Baptist Association *Minutes*, 1864, 6, 1865, 6; G. F. Williams, Report from Alabama Baptist State Convention in *The Home and Foreign Journal*, December 1868, 29. See also Daniel Hollis, *A History of the First Baptist Church, Jacksonville, Alabama, 1836–1986* (Jacksonville, Ala., 1987), and T. E. Skinner to John A. Broadus, October 12, 1865, in John Broadus correspondence, SBTS.

51. *Home and Foreign Journal*, June 1870, 7 (E. L. Compere); R. S. Duncan, *Life Story of R. S. Duncan*, ed. Wiley Patrick (Kansas City, Mo., 1910), 63. For other examples of rural preachers who encountered this sentiment, see *BR*, April 25, 1877; T. S. Powell, *Five Years in South Mississippi* (Cincinnati, 1889), 138–45; and *RH*, September 5, 1867 (G. T. Wilburn).

52. George Blount Diary, entries for March 31, May 5, 12, April 27, 1875, in George Blount Papers, folder 4, SBHLA.

53. W. H. Rich to E. Y. Mullins, July 4, 1901, in Mullins letter files, SBTS; Minutes of the Shiloh Baptist Church, Prince George County, Virginia, March 1890.

54. Mildred Bobo and Catherine Ryan Johnson, *The First Baptist Church of Huntsville, Alabama: The First 175 Years, 1809–1984* (Huntsville, Ala., 1985); William Owen Carver Diary, February 6, 1895, in Carver Papers, SBHLA.

55. Minutes of the Clear Creek Baptist Church, Lafayette County, Mississippi, May 1891, October 1891; *BR*, November 14, 1906; Hight C. Moore, "Twigs of Balsam," typewritten manuscript of autobiography, in Hight C. Moore Papers, box 1, folder 11, SBHLA.

56. Annual call figures from E. P. Alldredge, ed., *Southern Baptist Handbook, 1923* (Nashville, 1924), 64–70. See also Powell, *Five Years in South Mississippi*, 89–91.

57. R. J. Tabor, "History of Churches Composing the Concord Baptist Churches," 1909, on microfilm reel of Shiloh Baptist Church Records, Bernice, Louisiana, SBHLA; *BR*, November 26, 1884.

58. O. V. Sholars to E. Y. Mullins, February 5, 1904, in Mullins letter files, SBTS; William Thomas Tardy, *The Man and the Message* (Marshall, Tex., 1920), 49–50; W. L. A. Stranburg to E. Y. Mullins, May 1, 1903, in Mullins letter files, SBTS.

59. John Lipscomb Johnson, *Autobiographical Notes* (privately printed, 1938), 180; Charles Harris Nash to William Owen Carver, June 14, 1906, in Carver correspondence, folder for 1906, SBHLA.

60. Quoted in Allen Tullos, *Habits of Industry: White Culture and the Transformation of the Carolina Piedmont* (Chapel Hill, 1989), 211; William Harrison Williams, "Charge of Ordination of Ministers," handwritten notes in William Harrison Williams Papers, WFU.

61. E. Y. Mullins to E. M. Poteat, November 16, 1885, in Mullins letter files, folder for 1885–98, SBTS.

62. "The Pastoral Relation," *South Carolina Baptist*, November 30, 1866; Tardy, *Trials and Triumphs*, 80. See also Graham, *A Ministry of Fifty Years*, 132.

63. B. F. Riley, "Lectures to Ministerial Students," *Alabama Baptist*, May 5, 1887. The classic analysis of southern honor in the antebellum years is Bertram Wyatt-Brown, *Southern Honor: Ethics and Behavior in the Old South* (New York, 1982).

64. E. P. West, "The Blight of Modernism in Religion," *Baptist Standard*, February 6, 1908; *Baptist Standard*, August 1, 1912; Powell, *Five Years in South Mississippi*; General Baptist Convention of Texas *Annual*, 1901, 28; George McDaniel, *A Memorial Wreath* (Dallas, 1921), 82; Elridge Hatcher, "The Country Church—Its Ideals, Problems, and Future," *Home and Foreign Fields*, June 1918, 8–9.

Chapter 6

1. See Edmund Wheeler, *Uplifting the Race: The Black Minister in the New South, 1865–1902* (Lanham, Md., 1986), for an excellent exploration of the lives of leading ministers in the postwar era.

2. Henry L. Morehouse, "Negro Baptist Ministers," *Home Mission Echoes*, February 1903, 11, and "Plantation Life of the Colored People," *BHMM*, March 1894, 96. U.S. census figures reached similar conclusions. Census takers estimated that there were 12,159 black Baptist ministers in 1890 and nearly 18,000 by 1910. See U.S. Department of Commerce, Bureau of the Census, *Negro Population, 1790–1915* (Washington, D.C., 1918), 526; William Montgomery, *Under Their Own Vine and Fig Tree: The African-American Church in the South, 1865–1900* (Baton Rouge, 1993), 312; and Evelyn Brooks Higginbotham, *Righteous Discontent: The Women's Movement in the Black Baptist Church, 1880–1920* (Cambridge, Mass., 1993), 41.

3. Ira De A. Reid, *The Negro Baptist Ministry: An Analysis of Its Profession, Preparation and Practices: Report of Survey Conducted by the Joint Survey Commission of the Baptist Inter-Convention Committee* (Nashville, 1951), 88–104; Ralph Felton, *These My Brethren: A Study of 570 Negro Churches and 1542 Negro Homes in the Rural South* (Madison, N.J., 1950), 58–70; Harry V. Richardson, *Dark Glory: A Picture of the Church Among Negroes in the Rural South* (New York, 1947).

4. W. E. B. Du Bois, *The Souls of Black Folk* (New York, 1903), 134; *Georgia Narratives*, supp. series 1, pt. 1, vol. 3, 300 (John Harris); E. C. Morris, *Sermons, Addresses, Reminiscences* (Nashville, 1901), 135; final quotation from Montgomery, *Under Their Own Vine and Fig Tree*, 322.

5. *South Carolina Narratives*, orig. series, pt. 1, vol. 2, 324 (Thomas Dixon); *South Carolina Narratives*, orig. series, pt. 1, vol. 12, 94 (George Briggs); *Arkansas Narratives*, orig. series 2, pt. 3, vol. 9, 206 (Dr. D. B. Gaines).

6. *Texas Narratives*, supp. series 2, pt. 8, vol. 7, 2952 (Isaiah Norwood), and vol. 9, 3636 (James Smith).

7. Howard Snyder, "The Ordination of Charlie," *Atlantic* 127 (March 1921): 338–42; Minutes of the Gillfield Baptist Church, August 3, June 2, 1868.

8. New Hope Missionary Baptist Association (North Carolina) *Minutes*, 1911, 16; *Savannah Tribune*, September 26, 1896; Charley White, *No Quittin' Sense* (Austin, Tex., 1969), 106.

9. Minutes of the Springfield Baptist Church, Augusta, Georgia, May 20, 1885, March 14, 1886, December 23, 1888.

10. *National Baptist Union-Review*, February 18, 1919, 9; Emmanuel K. Love, *History of the First African Baptist Church, from its organization, January 20th, 1788, to July 1st, 1888: including the centennial celebration, addresses, sermons, etc.* (Savannah, 1888), 104.

11. Love, *History of the First African Baptist Church*, 58; Benjamin Mays, *Born to Rebel: An Autobiography* (New York, 1971), 14–15.

12. Alabama Colored Baptist State Convention *Journal*, 1903, n.p.; *Southern Workman*, June 1879, 66, February 1879, 14 (Harriet Beecher Stowe from Florida).

13. Old Eastern Missionary Baptist Association (North Carolina) *Minutes*, 1913, Appendix; Charles Hamilton and John Ellison, *The Negro Church in Rural Virginia* (Blacksburg, Va., 1930), 17–25; *Georgia Narratives*, supp. series 1, pt. 1, vol. 3, 283 (John Harris). See also *Texas Narratives*, supp. series 2, pt. 4, vol. 2, 4 (Frank Adams).

14. For the full text of the New Era agreement, see Keith Louis Harper, "Southern Baptists and Social Christianity, 1890–1920" (Ph.D. diss., University of Kentucky, 1991), Appendix, 200–220. A. L. Bassett, "Going to Housekeeping in North Carolina," *Lippincott's Magazine* 28 (August 1881): 205–8, describes fund-raising raffles in churches with Bibles as prizes. Love, *History of the First African Baptist Church*, 147, explains his fund-raising techniques at his church.

15. *The Journal and Guide*, October 31, 1914, quoted in miscellaneous Negro newspapers on microfilm, reel 2, 596–97; Orville Vernon Burton, *In My Father's House Are Many Mansions: Family and Community in Edgefield, South Carolina* (Chapel Hill, 1986), 256; Mays, *Born to Rebel*, 15; O. W. Blacknall, "The New Departure in Negro Life," *Atlantic Monthly* 52 (November 1883): 685. See also Richard De Baptiste, "Ministerial Education," *NBM*, October 1896–January 1897, 240–47.

16. Minutes of the Gillfield Baptist Church, Petersburg, Virginia, July 20, September 21, 1868, April 5, November 1, 1869.

17. Minutes of the Springfield Baptist Church, Augusta, Georgia, January 23, 1881, November 16, December 21, 1887, January 16, 1901.

18. James Simms, *The First Colored Baptist Church in North America* (Philadelphia, 1888; reprint, New York, 1969), 152–53; *Savannah Tribune*, February 7, 1914.

19. Missionary Baptist Convention of Mississippi and Louisiana *Minutes*, 1870, n.p.; Mays, *Born to Rebel*, 15.

20. *Georgia Narratives*, supp. series 1, pt. 1, vol. 3, 283 (John Harris); W. T. Hewetson, "The Social Life of the Southern Negro," *Chautauquan* 26 (December 1897): 295–304; Trent River Oakley Grove Missionary Baptist Association *Minutes*, 1917, n.p.; *National Baptist Union*, June 12, 1909, 4.

21. Middle District Missionary Baptist Association *Proceedings*, 1917, 14; *Savannah Tribune*, May 14, 1898; A. W. Pegues, *Our Baptist Ministers and Schools* (Springfield, Mass., 1892), 280. See also Wake Baptist Association (North Carolina) *Minutes*, 1886, 8. "Island communities" comes from Robert Wiebe, *The Search For Order: America, 1877–1920* (New York, 1967).

22. *CWR*, April 1, 1880; *CWR*, August 13, 1868 ("Heart"); D. N. Vassar, "Improvement in Preaching," *Home Mission Echoes*, March 1898, 14; Hope Missionary Baptist Association (North Carolina) *Minutes*, 1896, 14; Middle Baptist Association (North Carolina) *Minutes*, 1919, 19. See also T. L. Robinson, "The Colored People of the United States," *Leisure Hour* 38 (1889): 54–59.

23. H. T. Kealing, "The Colored Ministers of the South—Their Preaching and Peculiarities," *AME Church Review* 1 (1884): 139–44; Mays, *Born to Rebel*, 14; White, *No Quittin' Sense*, 33. Felton, in *These My Brethren*, documents the continued importance even after World War II of the congregants' demand for good folk preaching. Bruce A. Rosenberg, *Can These Bones Live: The Art of the American Folk Preacher* (Urbana, Ill., 1970; reprint, 1988), is a sensitive exploration of the craft of the folk preachers free of the biases that have marred older studies.

24. *Savannah Tribune*, October 13, 1906 (D. W. Cannon of Beth-Eden Baptist Church); *Christian Union*, August 14, 1890, in Louis Harlan, ed., *The Papers of Booker T. Washington* (Urbana, Ill., 1974), 9: 72–73; Booker T. Washington, "The Religious Life of the Negro," *North American Review* 181 (1905): 20–23; Executive Board and Corresponding Secretary of the Woman's Convention, Auxiliary to the National Baptist Convention, *Report* (n.p., [1915]), 49.

25. J. L. Chestnut Jr., and Julia Cass, *Black in Selma: The Uncommon Life of J. L. Chestnut, Jr.* (New York, 1990), 38–41, 46–48. See also Nancy Bullock Woolridge, "The Negro Preacher in American Fiction Before 1900" (Ph.D. diss., University of Chicago, 1945), and C. Harold Woodell, "The Preacher in Nineteenth-Century Southern Fiction" (Ph.D. diss., University of North Carolina, Chapel Hill, 1974).

26. Elijah P. Marrs, *Life and History of Elijah P. Marrs* (Louisville, Ky., 1885), 35; Folklore quotation from J. Mason Brewer, ed., *American Negro Folklore* (Chicago, 1968), 36; *South Carolina Narratives*, orig. series 1, pt. 3, vol. 3, 44 (James Johnson); *Texas Narratives*, supp. series 2, pt. 6, vol. 7, 2838–39 (Calvin Moye); Tom E. Terrill and Jerrold Hirsch, eds., *Such As Us: Southern Voices of the Thirties* (Chapel Hill, 1978), 223.

See also Lawrence Levine, *Black Culture and Black Consciousness: Afro-American Folk Thought From Slavery to Freedom* (New York, 1977), 326.

27. W. C. Handy, *Father of the Blues: An Autobiography*, ed. Arna Bontemps (New York, 1941), 10.

28. Levine, *Black Culture and Black Consciousness*, explains the functions of the preachers and the bluesmen in the oral tradition of African Americans, as do Albert Murray, *Stomping the Blues* (New York, 1976), and James H. Cone, *The Spirituals and the Blues* (New York, 1972). The best recent analysis of blues and black spirituality is Jon Michael Spencer, *Blues and Evil* (Knoxville, 1993).

29. Alabama Colored Baptist State Convention *Minutes*, 1874, 16; Missionary Baptist Convention of Georgia *Minutes*, 1878, 35; Thomas O. Fuller, *Twenty Years of Public Life: North Carolina–Tennessee, 1890–1910* (Nashville, 1910), quoted in David M. Tucker, *Black Pastors and Leaders: Memphis, 1819–1972* (Memphis, 1975), 63; Johnston District Baptist Association (North Carolina) *Minutes*, 1893, 9–10. For other examples of ordination resolutions, see Hope Missionary Baptist Association (North Carolina) *Minutes*, 1896, 14, and Wake Baptist Association (North Carolina) *Minutes*, 1898, 32. See also D. W. Phillips, "Letter from Tennessee," *Christian Watchman*, February 15, 1877. I am indebted to Montgomery, *Under Their Own Vine and Fig Tree*, 105–25, for this discussion.

30. *Savannah Tribune*, November 27, 1897; NBC *Journal*, 1902, 29; *BHMM*, February 1881, 27–29 (R. Agnes Wilson); Tuskegee Miscellaneous Negro Newspapers on microfilm, reel 6, p. 93 [name of newspaper unknown], 1917; O. W. Blacknall, "The New Departure in Negro Life," *Atlantic Monthly* 52 (November 1883): 684–85; *Home Mission Echoes*, May 1894, 10 (Mary Traver). See also J. J. Spelman, "Need of an Educated Ministry Among the Colored People of the Mississippi Valley," *BHMM*, September 1883, 187–90.

31. James MacPherson, *The Abolitionist Legacy: From Reconstruction to the NAACP* (Princeton, N.J., 1975), 143–45; Brooks Higginbotham, *Righteous Discontent*, 24, 90.

32. Statistics from Daniel Stowell, "Rebuilding Zion: The Religious Reconstruction of the South, 1863–1877" (Ph.D. diss., University of Florida, 1994), 277; information about Boothe from Ed Crowther, "Interracial Cooperative Missions Among Blacks By Alabama's Baptists, 1868–1882" (unpublished paper, in author's possession), 10–15, and Charles Octavius Boothe, *The Cyclopedia of Colored Baptists in Alabama* (Birmingham, 1895), 265.

33. SBC *Annual*, 1910, 53–54; Emerson Ricks, "The Imperative Call of Southern Baptists," *BR*, April 13, 1904; "The Mission of the Negro in America," *BR*, August 20, 1902; *Alabama Baptist*, May 15, 1879. See also Baptist Educational and Missionary Convention of North Carolina *Proceedings*, 1901, 10–13.

34. George N. Scales, "The Gospel and the Negroes," *National Baptist Union*, June 11, 1904, 5; *Our Home Field*, March 1889 (J. W. Jones).

35. *BR*, August 17, 1892; SBC *Annual*, 1904, 164–67; final quotation from Harper, "Southern Baptists and Social Christianity," 220.

36. Harper, "Southern Baptists and Social Christianity," 215–17; A. L. Winslow, "The Growing Demand for Educated Men and Women Among the Colored People," *NBM*, April 1898, 553–57; J. A. Whitted, *A History of the Negro Baptists of North*

Carolina (Raleigh, 1908), 68. See also William Anthony Avery, "Better Education for New Rural Ministers," *Southern Workman*, October 1920, 458–67.

37. *CI*, May 17, 1894; Report of the Home Mission Board, SBC *Annual*, 1901, 143–44; *BR*, July 13, 1904 (Joe Spruill); *Alabama Baptist*, September 21, 1904 (A. J. Barton); W. J. McGlothlin to William Owen Carver, November 5, 1901, in William Owen Carver Papers, folder for 1901 letters, SBHLA. See also *BR*, September 14, August 17, 1904, and November 25, 1903 (C. G. Wells).

38. NBC *Journal*, 1903, 24; SBC *Annual*, 1904, Home Mission Board Report, 164–67, and 1905, 5–8. For similar sentiments, see Victor Masters, "Death Silences Voice of Gifted Prophet of Racial Good Will," newspaper clipping in Una Roberts Lawrence Papers, box 2, folder 2, and Una Roberts Lawrence, "Joseph Albert Booker—Mediator," typewritten manuscript in Lawrence Papers, box 1, folder 21, both in SBHLA; NBC *Journal*, 1904, 24–30.

39. *RH*, September 6, 1906; *National Baptist Union-Review*, January 25, 1919; C. C. Brown, "A Suggested Solution to the Race Problem," *The Home Field*, April 1916, 5–8. For information on O. L. Hailey see "O. L. Hailey, by a Lifelong Acquaintance," typewritten manuscript in Lawrence Papers, box 3, folder 4, and O. L. Hailey to E. C. Dargan, March 8, 1913, in E. C. Dargan Papers, box 1, folder 3, both in SBHLA; SBC *Annual*, 1914, 25–26; *ESB*, 1:43.

40. For a summary of the criticisms directed at black theological education, see Reid, *The Negro Baptist Ministry*, 88–104. Reid points out the problems created by the multiple governing bodies of the school.

41. *Texas Narratives*, supp. series 2, pt. 6, vol. 7, 2734 (A. M. "Mount" Moore); *South Carolina Narratives*, orig. series, pt. 1, vol. 2, 92 (George Briggs); *Arkansas Narratives*, orig. series, pt. 4, vol. 9, 293 (Needham Love).

42. Joseph A. Booker, "Autobiography of Jos. A. Booker," typewritten manuscript, 2, in Lawrence Papers, box 1, folder 21, SBHLA.

43. Una Roberts Lawrence, "Joseph Albert Booker—Mediator," typewritten manuscript, 7–9, in Lawrence Papers, box 1, folder 21, SBHLA; Booker, "Autobiography of Jos. A. Booker," 5–10, 29–39; *Home and Foreign Fields*, March 1926, 1.

44. Una Roberts Lawrence, "The Boy Who Was Named for His Coat and Pants," in Lawrence Papers, box 5, folder 16, SBHLA; Lewis G. Jordan, *On Two Hemispheres: Bits from the Life Story of L. G. Jordan* (n.p., [1935]). Jordan's work at writing a history of black Baptists culminated in his book *Negro Baptist History, U.S.A.* (Nashville, 1930). Though not an interpretive work, his book provides a great deal of useful documentation and contains reprints of articles and black Baptist reports that would otherwise be unavailable.

45. Quotations from John Blassingame, *Long Memory: The Black Experience in America* (New York, 1982), 96; Fuller, *Twenty Years in Public Life*, 108. See also the discussion of Fuller's life in Tennessee in David M. Tucker, *Black Pastors and Leaders: Memphis, 1819–1972* (Memphis, 1972), 55–70.

46. Montgomery, *Under Their Own Vine and Fig Tree*, 229; Pegues, *Our Baptist Ministers and Schools*, 354–56; NBC *Journal*, 1908, 33; Morris, *Sermons, Addresses, Reminiscences*, 135–37; Peter Paris, *The Social Teachings of the Black Churches* (Philadelphia, 1985).

47. William J. Simmons, *Men of Mark—Eminent, Progressive, Rising* (Louisville, Ky.,

1887). For more information on State University, see Lawrence Williams, *Black Higher Education in Kentucky, 1879–1930: A History of Simmons University* (Lewiston, 1987). For excellent discussions of the complicated interplay of hope, ideology, experience, and disillusionment among black exponents of the ideology of improvement, see Patrick Rael, "African American Thought in the Antebellum North" (Ph.D. diss., University of California, Berkeley, 1995), and James Campbell, *Songs of Zion: The African Methodist Episcopal Church in the United States and South Africa* (New York, 1995). For recent explorations of the dependence of white manhood and republicanism on racial ideologies, see David Roediger, *The Wages of Whiteness* (London, 1991), and Eric Lott, *Love and Theft: Blackface Minstrelsy and the American Working Class* (New York, 1994).

48. Pegues, *Our Baptist Ministers and Schools*, 153. The pastor was Iverson Dawson.

49. See Raymond Gavins, *The Perils and Prospects of Southern Black Leadership: Gordon Blaine Hancock, 1884–1970* (Durham, N.C., 1977), and *Savannah Tribune,* April 28, 1917 (reprint from *Tampa Bulletin*).

50. W. B. Johnson, "Citzenship, Suffrage, and the Negro," in *The Scourging of a Race, and Other Sermons and Addresses* (Washington, D.C., 1904), 59–72; W. B. Johnson, "The Church as a Factor in the Race Problem," in *Sparks From My Anvil: Sermons and Addresses* (Lynchburg, Va., 1899), 42–44; W. B. Johnson, "The Great Commission," *NBM*, July 1894, 186–91. For information on the *NBM*, see Penelope Bullock, *The Afro-American Periodical Press, 1838–1909* (Baton Rouge, 1981).

51. William Waring, "The Negro Preacher of the Twentieth Century," *NBM*, October 1899, 23–26; J. H. Van Lue, "The Negro Problem in the United States," *NBM*, August–October 1898, 153, 158; David Levering Lewis, *W. E. B. Du Bois—Biography of a Race, 1869–1919* (New York, 1992), 255; Pegues, *Our Baptist Ministers and Schools*, 319, 526; Allen Woodrow Jones, "Alabama," in *The Black Press in the South, 1865–1979*, ed. Henry Lewis Suggs (Westport, Conn., 1983), 23–64; Lillie B. Chace Wyman, "Colored Churches and Schools in the South," *New England Magazine*, n.s., 31 (February 1891): 785–96.

52. Mays, *Born to Rebel*, 15–16; *Savannah Tribune*, November 27, 1897; Union Baptist Association (North Carolina) *Minutes*, 1914, 20; NBC *Journal*, 1903, 24; W. B. Johnson, *The Scourging of a Race*, 1–17; W. B. Johnson, "National Perils," sermon delivered October, 1889, in *Sparks From My Anvil: Sermons and Addresses* (Lynchburg, Va., 1899), 18–22.

53. William Waring, "The Negro Problem of the Twentieth Century," *NBM*, October 1899, 23–26; Robert Park, "The Money Rally at Sweet Gum," *Southern Workman*, October 1913, 537–46; C. H. Parrish, *Golden Jubilee of the General Association of Colored Baptists in Kentucky* (Louisville, Ky., 1915), 15. See also Johnston Baptist Association (North Carolina) *Minutes*, 1915, 21–22.

54. James Weldon Johnson, *God's Trombones: Seven Negro Sermons in Verse* (New York, 1927), 51, 2.

Chapter 7

1. Shailer Mathews, *Scientific Management in the Churches* (Chicago, 1912); Amos Clary, "Our Acres of Diamonds," *The Home Field*, December 1912, 11–12. See Susan Curtis, *A Consuming Faith: The Social Gospel and Modern American Culture* (Baltimore,

1991), for a fascinating analysis of Mathews. For the kind of books from Mathews that particularly troubled evangelical conservatives, see Shailer Mathews, *The Faith of Modernism* (New York, 1924).

2. For an articulation of the "two-party" model, see Ferenc Szasz, *The Divided Mind of Protestant America, 1880–1930* (Tuscaloosa, Ala., 1982), and Jean Miller Schmidt, *Souls or the Social Order: The Two-Party System in American Protestantism* (Brooklyn, N.Y., 1991).

For more on black evangelicalism and its relationship to the social gospel, see Gayraud Wilmore, *Black Religion and Black Radicalism: An Interpretation of the Religious History of the Afro-American People*, 2nd ed. (Maryknoll, N.Y., 1983), and Peter Paris, *The Social Teachings of the Black Churches* (Philadelphia, 1985). For an encyclopedic study of social gospel ideas, see Donald Gorrell, *The Age of Social Responsibility: The Social Gospel in the Progressive Era, 1900–1920* (Macon, Ga., 1988).

3. C. Vann Woodward, *Origins of the New South, 1877–1913* (Baton Rouge, 1951), 450, found little evidence of any social Christianity in the South. But since then a plethora of studies have demonstrated otherwise. A few of the important studies of the social gospel in the South include John Patrick McDowell, *The Social Gospel in the South: The Woman's Home Mission Movement in the Methodist Episcopal Church, South, 1886–1939* (Baton Rouge, 1982); Wayne Flynt, "Alabama White Protestantism and Labor, 1900–1914," *Alabama Review* 25 (July 1972): 192–217, and "Dissent in Zion: Alabama Baptists and Social Issues," *Journal of Southern History* 35 (November 1969): 523–42; and John Lee Eighmy, *Churches in Cultural Captivity: A History of the Social Attitudes of Southern Baptists*, 2nd ed., ed. Samuel Hill (Knoxville, 1987). John Storey, *Texas Baptist Leadership and Social Christianity, 1900–1980* (College Station, Tex., 1986), argues that though the white southern Baptists lacked a strong social gospel tradition many ministers nevertheless expressed a "social Christianity." See also Louis Keith Harper, "Southern Baptists and Social Christianity, 1890–1920" (Ph.D. diss., University of Kentucky, 1991). Older studies that stressed how the social gospelers ignored racial problems in the South have now been supplanted by Ralph Luker, *The Social Gospel in Black and White: American Racial Reform, 1885–1912* (Chapel Hill, 1991), who abundantly documents the transition in religious racial thought from the educational and uplift efforts of the postbellum period to the social settlement movement of the early twentieth century.

William Link, *The Paradox of Southern Progressivism* (Chapel Hill, 1992), argues that the heavy participation of southern evangelicals in the prohibition movement played a vital role in providing the "ideational glue" for progressive-minded white religious southerners to attack a broad array of southern social problems ranging from child labor to health problems. Link also stresses that progressives relied on bureaucratic and technocratic models for reform that clashed with the localist ethic of southern communities.

4. See William James's *The Varieties of Religious Experience: A Study in Human Nature* (New York, 1902), a work that was very influential in the thinking of Edgar Young Mullins. On muscular Christianity, see Gail Bederman, "The Women Had Charge of the Church Work Long Enough': The Men and Religion Forward Movement of 1911–1912 and the Masculinization of Middle Class Protestantism," *American Quarterly* 41 (September 1989): 432–61. On the country life projects and the social gospel's view of

the rural church, see James Madison, "Reformers and the Rural Church, 1900–1950," *Journal of American History* 73 (December 1986): 645–98.

5. For more on "social Christianity," see Eighmy, *Churches in Cultural Captivity*; Storey, *Texas Baptist Leadership and Social Christianity*; Patricia Martin, "Hidden Work: Baptist Women in Texas, 1880–1920" (Ph.D. diss., Rice University, 1988); and Harvey Newman, "The Role of Women in Atlanta's Churches, 1865–1906," *Atlanta Historical Journal* 24 (1980): 17–30. I am using the concepts of "efficiency" and "uplift" in the way the Progressives did, as described in Samuel Haber, *Efficiency and Uplift: Scientific Management in the Progressive Era, 1890–1920* (Chicago, 1964). For a parallel in the world of educational reform to the argument presented here, see William Link, *A Hard Country and a Lonely Place: Schooling, Society, and Reform in Rural Virginia, 1870–1920* (Chapel Hill, 1986).

6. For statistics suggesting that the South was actually growing faster than other parts of the country, see Gavin Wright, *Old South, New South: Revolutions in the Southern Economy Since the Civil War* (New York, 1986). For the New South rhetoric, see Paul M. Gaston, *The New South Creed: A Study in Southern Mythmaking* (New York, 1970).

7. Edward Ayers, *Southern Crossing: A History of the American South* (New York, 1994), 37; *BW*, March 11, 1909.

8. William Hatcher, "Housekeeping For Our Neighbor," in *The Home Mission Task*, ed. Victor Masters (Atlanta, 1914), 90; *Our Home Field*, March 1896, 4; T. S. Powell, *Five Years in South Mississippi* (Cincinnati, 1889), 47; *Alabama Baptist*, May 4, 1900; *BW*, February 3, 1910. For short but penetrating analyses of this development, see Wayne Flynt, "Southern Baptists: Rural to Urban Transition," *Baptist History and Heritage* 16 (January 1981): 24–34, and "The Impact of Social Factors on Southern Baptist Expansion, 1800–1914," *Baptist History and Heritage* 17 (July 1982): 20–32. For a general discussion and critique of the widespread adoption of the language and methods of corporate enterprise by Protestant church organizations, see Ben Primer, *Protestants and American Business Methods* (Ann Arbor, Mich., 1979), 65–154.

9. Edwin M. Poteat, "Religion and Money," address delivered at SBC, 1908, copy in Home Mission Board Papers, SBHLA; *BW*, May 6, 1915. See also J. W. Morgan, "Criticisms of the Convention," *BR*, January 3, 1912, and *Alabama Baptist*, January 4, 1900.

10. Victor Masters, "Southern Problems for Southern Baptists" (Atlanta, 1910), 7, pamphlet in Home Mission Board Papers, SBHLA; *Baptist Standard*, May 19, 1910 (Victor Masters); Victor Masters, "A New Problem in the South," *Alabama Baptist*, May 4, 1910; John W. Porter, "Monarchy of Money," *RH*, November 11, 1906; *RH*, February 4, 1909; *BR*, January 16, 1901; A. J. Moncrief, "What Shall the South Do With Her Increasing Wealth," *BR*, May 4, 1910. See also Edwin M. Poteat, "Spiritual Needs of the South," *BW*, December 21, 1916, and Livingston Johnson, "State Missions and Statecraft," *BR*, June 26, 1912. For an analysis of the jeremiad, see Perry Miller, *Errand in the Wilderness* (Cambridge, Mass., 1958).

11. For a penetrating analysis of how the attack on "commercialism" could be used for the ends of a "reactionary populism," see Nancy MacLean, *Behind the Mask of Chivalry: The Making of the Second Ku Klux Klan* (New York, 1994).

12. B. D. Gray, "Work of the Home Mission Board," address delivered to SBC, May

14, 1904, pamphlet found in Una Roberts Lawrence Papers, box 10, folder 30, SBHLA; Forrest Smith Papers, handwritten sermons, delivered at Louisburg, North Carolina, 1898–99, in WFU; *BR*, November 11, 1903 (A. D. Hunter); J. W. Conger to Mullins, November 25, 1903, in Mullins letter files, SBTS. See also J. A. Hendricks to Edgar Young Mullins, January 19, 1900, in Mullins letter files, SBTS; "Futures," *BR*, March 21, 1894.

13. *Alabama Baptist*, August 15, 1906; *CI*, March 1, 1906.

14. *Baptist Record*, February 10, 1881; Victor Masters, "The City in Kingdom Strategy," *Home and Foreign Fields*, August 1917, 16–17; Masters, "A New Problem in the South"; Charles Duke, "The Risen Lord and His Struggling Church," typewritten manuscript of sermon delivered before SBC on May 16, 1917, in Convention Sermon Collection, SBHLA.

15. Rufus Weaver, "The Problem of the City," 12–13, pamphlet in Home Mission Board Papers, SBHLA; Rufus Weaver, "The Needs of the City," in *The Home Mission Task*, ed. Victor Masters (Atlanta, 1914), 295–305; SBC *Annual*, 1907; Victor Masters, "Shall Southern Baptists Save Their Cities," *BW*, November 3, 1910.

16. For the classic early social gospel statement on fears for the future of an Anglo-Protestant America, see Josiah Strong, *Our Country: Its Possible Future and Present Crisis* (New York, 1885), and Madison Grant, *The Passing of the Great Race; Or, the Racial Basis of European History*, 4th ed. (New York, 1921). Quotations from *BR*, August 26, 1885; J. S. Dill, "Missions in the Southern States: A Great Danger and a Great Demand" (Baltimore, 1894), 2–3, and Victor Masters, "A Study of Southern Baptist Home Missions by the Editorial Secretary V. I. Masters" (Atlanta, 1909), 17–21, Home Mission Board pamphlets, both in Home Mission Board Papers, SBHLA; *BR*, July 18, 1894; and SBC *Annual*, 1883, 29.

17. Victor Masters, "As to the Restriction of Immigration," *Home and Foreign Fields*, March 1917, 20–21; *Alabama Baptist*, September 25, 1907, 4 (James D. Gwathmey); *Our Home Field*, January 1907, 19–20; J. F. Love, *The Mission of Our Nation* (New York 1912), 42, 64–65, 107–8; J. F. Love, "Missions on the Frontier," in *The Home Mission Task*, ed. Victor Masters (Atlanta, 1914), 266. See also SBC *Annual*, 1916, Appendix, 12; W. D. Knight, *Missions in Principle and Practice* (Nashville, 1929), 163–64; John Dixon, "Present-Day Immigration a Challenge to Christianity," *Our Home Field*, October 1906, 8–9; and "America or Anarchy," *Home and Foreign Fields*, January 1920, 2–4.

18. *BR*, April 5, 1899, October 22, 1902; "Two Powerful Evils," *BR*, April 7, 1897.

19. Thomas W. O'Helley, "Equality," typewritten manuscript of sermon delivered before SBC on May 14, 1913, in Convention Sermon Collection, SBHLA; *CI*, July 5, 1894; *Alabama Baptist*, May 28, 1905; "The Church in Relation to the Toiling Class and the Lost," *BW*, February 11, 1915; *BW*, January 5, 1911, 16–17.

20. *Alabama Baptist*, January 21, 1901, October 18, 1900, October 30, 1907, October 28, 1908; Flynt, "Alabama White Protestantism and Labor," 197, 205, 215. See also Frances Hazmark, "The Southern Religious Press and the Social Gospel Movement" (M.A. thesis, Lanier University, 1979).

21. *Alabama Baptist*, October 30, 1907; Flynt, "Alabama White Protestantism and Labor," 197, 205, 215.

22. *Alabama Baptist*, October 18, 1900, February 21, 1906 (John Gable); Braxton

Craig, "The Gospel and the Factory," *BR*, March 28, 1890. See also *Alabama Baptist*, February 4, 1903.

23. Tom Terrill and Jerrold Hirsch, eds., *Such As Us: Southern Voices of the Thirties* (Chapel Hill, 1978), 167–68. For a look at the vital religious life of the millworkers that was sustained even in company-run churches, see Liston Pope, *Millhands and Preachers: A Study of Gastonia* (New Haven, Conn., 1942), and Jacquelyn Dowd Hall et al., *Like a Family: The Making of a Southern Cotton Mill World* (Chapel Hill, 1987), 145–50.

24. *BW*, January 2, 1913, December 14, 1916. The best analyses of the origins, function, rise, and decline of church discipline may be found in Gregory Wills, *Democratic Religion: Freedom, Authority, and Discipline in the Baptist South, 1785–1900* (New York, forthcoming), and Ted Ownby, *Subduing Satan: Religion, Recreation, and Manhood in the Rural South, 1865–1920* (Chapel Hill, 1990). Wills presents the clearest explanation of the various kinds of discipline: "rebuke," "suspension," and "exclusion" or "excommunication."

25. Leslie L. Gwaltney, *Forty of the Twentieth; or, The First Forty Years of the Twentieth Century* (Birmingham, 1940), 124, 146–47.

26. "Transformed individuals in a transformed society" comes from C. S. Gardner, "Thy Kingdom Come," typewritten manuscript of sermon delivered before SBC on May 17, 1911, 12, in Convention Sermon Collection, SBHLA. For Mullins's contributions to a defense of evangelicalism, see his articles in R. A. Torrey et al., eds., *The Fundamentals: A Testimony to the Truth* (Chicago, 1910). Quotations from Edgar Young Mullins, *Axioms of Religion: A New Interpretation of the Baptist Faith* (Philadelphia, 1908), 204, 210, and "Lord of the Intellect," address to the Baptist World Alliance, reprinted in *RH*, September 7, 1911.

27. Edgefield Baptist Association (South Carolina) *Minutes*, 1919, 16; *RH*, May 6, 1920, November 8, 1917; J. E. Hicks, "God's Program," *RH*, December 7, 14, 1911.

28. Charles S. Gardner, *The Ethics of Jesus and Social Progress* (New York, 1914), 112; Gardner, "Thy Kingdom Come," 12; C. S. Gardner, "Shall America Be a Christian Nation?," *The Home Field*, February 1915, 8–10; petition from students to Mullins, February 21, 1910, in Mullins letter files, SBTS.

29. Gardner, *The Ethics of Jesus and Social Progress*, 7, 74, 84, 112; Part II, chapters 3 and 4; Walter Rauschenbusch, *Christianizing the Social Order* (New York, 1912).

30. J. W. Morgan, "Criticisms of the Convention," *BR*, January 3, 1912; George W. McDaniel, "Southern Baptists at Kadesh-Barnea," typewritten manuscript of sermon delivered before SBC on May 13, 1914, 10, in Convention Sermon Collection, SBHLA. See also William Louis Poteat, "The Relation of Baptists to Social Questions," address before Baptist World Congress, reprinted in *RH*, August 10, 1905.

31. SBC *Annual*, 1914, 37–38.

32. General Baptist Convention of Texas *Annual*, 1915, 26–26, 1920, 28; Greenville Baptist Association (South Carolina) *Minutes*, 1912, n.p.; *BR*, February 11, 1903. See also Mississippi Baptist State Convention *Minutes*, 1910, 52–53.

33. On orphanages and other forms of benevolence, see Hight C. Moore, "Day Well Spent With Orphans," Raleigh *News and Observer*, Sunday, April 17, 1904, in Hight C. Moore Papers, box 3, folder 1, SBHLA, and Harper, "Southern Baptists and Social Christianity." See Henry Shapiro, *Appalachia on Our Mind: The Southern Mountains and*

Mountaineers in the American Consciousness, 1870–1920 (Chapel Hill, 1978), esp. 32–58, for a discussion of the motivations behind missionary work in the region. For a look at the work of R. C. Buckner, a Texas Baptist successful at directing philanthropic money from wealthy ranchers and oil men into benevolent enterprises, see David Murrah, *C. C. Slaughter: Rancher, Banker, Baptist* (Austin, Tex., 1981).

34. Waco Baptist Association (Texas) *Minutes*, 1891, 18; *BR*, February 28, 1894, September 30, 1885; Newman, "The Role of Women in Atlanta's Churches," 17 (quoting J. B. Hawthorne).

35. "The Bible and the Feminist Movement," *BW*, March 25, 1915; General Baptist Convention of Texas *Annual*, 1920, 78; *CI*, December 1, 1904 (J. E. White, reprint of speech given before SBC). For a full recounting of the varied opinion on the issue, see Bill Sumners, "Southern Baptists and Women's Right to Vote, 1910–1920," *Baptist History and Heritage* 12 (January 1977): 45–57. The best studies of the women's suffrage movement in the South are Glenda Gilmore, *Gender and Jim Crow: Women and the Politics of White Supremacy in North Carolina, 1896–1920* (Chapel Hill, 1996), and Marjorie Spruill Wheeler, *New Women of the New South: The Leaders of the Woman Suffrage Movement in the Southern States* (New York, 1993).

36. *Baptist Standard*, August 3, 1916, 24 (G. W. Paschal); Mullins to Kathleen Mallory, September 27, 1917, in Mullins letterpress books, SBTS; SBC *Annual*, 1917, 37.

37. SBC *Annual*, 1915, 30–31; *Baptist Standard*, July 13, 1916, 10. See also Maude McLure, "W.M.U. Training Schools As Seen By the Principal," *BW*, May 14, 1908.

38. Moon to James M. Frost, undated letter in James Marion Frost Papers, box 23, folder 6, SSB; Moon to R. J. Willingham, November 7, 1901, in Mullins letter files, SBTS. For an analysis of the symbology of Moon and her central role in contemporary fund-raising efforts, see Irwin Hyatt, *Our Ordered Lives Confess: Three Nineteenth-Century American Missionaries in East Shantung* (Cambridge, Mass., 1976), and Paul Harvey, "The Politicization of White and Black Southern Baptist Missionaries, 1880–1930," *American Baptist Quarterly* 13 (September. 1994): 204–20.

39. See Jean Friedman, *The Enclosed Garden: Women and Community in the Evangelical South, 1830–1900* (Chapel Hill, 1985), for a fascinating argument about why women's religious associations were so relatively slow to develop in the South compared to their northern sisters. Annie Armstrong to T. P. Bell, July 8, 1893, in Frost Papers, box 1, folder 1A, SSB; WMU *Report*, 1894, 10, 1896, 9, SBHLA.

40. Annie Armstrong to J. M. Frost, October 6, 1906, in Frost Papers, box 15, folder 10a, and Armstrong to T. P. Bell, December 13, 1893, both in SSB; WMU *Report*, 1893, 10, SBHLA.

41. WMU (North Carolina), *Report*, 1919, 22, 93; WMU (South Carolina) *Minutes*, 1912, 39–40. See also WMU (North Carolina) *Minutes*, 1895, 15; Annie Armstrong, "Mission Methods," *Foreign Mission Journal*, October 1897, 152–53; and SBC *Annual*, 1917, 90. For more information on southern Baptist women and progressivism, see Gregory Vickers, "Models of Womanhood and the Early Woman's Missionary Union," *Baptist History and Heritage* 24 (January 1989): 41–53, and "Southern Baptist Women and Social Concern, 1910–1929," *Baptist History and Heritage* 23 (October 1980): 3–12; Catherine Allen, *A Century to Celebrate: A History of the Woman's Missionary Union* (Birmingham, 1987); and Martin, "Hidden Work."

42. "Factory Problem?" *BR*, October 4, 1899; *BR*, November 8, 1899 (T. H. Briggs);

BR, September 24, 1902; *BR*, May 12, 1897; "Child Slaves of the Factories," *BR*, February 15, 1899; *BR*, April 12, 1899.

43. *Alabama Baptist*, August 27, October 8, 1902, February 6, 13, July 3, 1907; Flynt, "Alabama White Protestantism and Labor," 204–5; SBC *Annual*, 1910, 46–47.

44. See Pope, *Millhands and Preachers*, and Hall et al., *Like A Family*. See William A. Leuchtenburg, *Franklin D. Roosevelt and the New Deal, 1932–1940* (New York, 1963), for information on J. W. Bailey's attempt to organize a coalition of Democratic and Republican congressmen into an anti–New Deal party.

45. J. B. Cranfill, *Dr. J. B. Cranfill's Chronicle: A Story of Life in Texas, Written by Himself about Himself* (New York, 1916), 284; Jeremiah Bell Jeter, *Recollections of a Long Life* (Richmond, 1891; reprint, New York, 1980), 37, 83; *RH*, November 1, 1866; *CI*, December 8, 1892.

46. Edgefield Baptist Association (South Carolina) *Minutes*, 1908, 13–14; J. L. Johnson, *Autobiographical Notes*, 108; *BR*, March 21, 1894; "Constabulary occupation" quote from Link, *Paradox of Southern Progressivism*, 311.

47. Waco Baptist Association (Texas) *Minutes*, 1877, 12; B. H. Carroll, untitled address on Prohibition, in B. H. Carroll Papers, reel 12 (sermon no. 615), SBHLA; Alabama Baptist State Convention *Minutes*, 1887, 43; Mississippi Baptist State Convention *Minutes*, 1887, 29; SBC *Annual*, 1886, 33; Tennessee Baptist State Convention *Twenty-Seventh Anniversary*, 1901, 35. See also Austin Baptist Association (Texas) *Minutes*, 1885, 6, and General Baptist Convention of Texas *Minutes*, 1886, 9.

48. Bernard Washington Spilman, "Journal," 98, typewritten manuscript from hand-written notes, 1939, in Bernard W. Spilman Papers, box 3, folder 1, SBHLA.

49. *RH*, February 21, 1901; Daniel Lee Cloyd, "Prelude to Reform: Political, Economic, and Social Thought of Alabama Baptists, 1877–1890," *Alabama Review* 31 (January 1978): 48–64; *Alabama Baptist*, October 6, 1909, 8.

50. John Thomas, ed., *The Minutes of Pleasant Prospect Baptist Church, Montgomery County, Mississippi, 1883–1980*, June 21, 1884, typewritten manuscript in SBHLA; *Alabama Baptist*, November 6, 1884 (John C. Orr); John L. Pollard Diary, entries for January 4 and 9, 1901, in Clark Family Papers, Virginia Historical Society, Richmond, Virginia; Richard Aubrey and Nannie Pitts McLemore, *The History of the First Baptist Church of Jackson, Mississippi* (Jackson, 1976); James H. Timberlake, *Prohibition and the Progressive Movement, 1900–1920* (New York, 1964); Terry Lawrence Jones, "Benjamin Franklin Riley: A Study of His Life and Work" (Ph.D. diss., Vanderbilt University, 1975), chapter 4.

51. Quoted in Link, *Paradox of Southern Progressivism*, 111; Greenville Baptist Association (South Carolina) *Minutes*, 1910, 21.

52. Link, *Paradox of Southern Progressivism*, 96, argues that the evangelical prohibitionists "launched an ambitious crusade to remake folkways through an unprecedented exertion of public power. The antisaloon campaign became a successful model of publicity and pressure group organization."

53. "The Negro As Obstacle," *BR*, October 6, 1897; Janette Thomas Greenwood, *Bittersweet Legacy: The Black and White "Better Classes" in Charlotte, 1850–1910* (Chapel Hill, 1994), 104–10.

54. *BR*, September 28, October 26, 1898; "An Alarming Condition," *Alabama Baptist*, February 13, 1907 (W. B. Crumpton, reprinted from *Montgomery Advertiser*);

"Black or White," *Baltimore Baptist*, reprinted in *Alabama Baptist*, November 28, 1899. See also *BR*, July 25, 1890, October 2, 1895, and *Alabama Baptist*, April 11, 1901.

55. *CI*, November 12, 1908, 6; *BR*, February 4, 1903, December 3, 1902; Victor I. Masters, "The Home Mission Task" (Atlanta, 1910), 10–11, pamphlet in Home Mission Board Papers, SBHLA. See also J. F. Love, "The Supremacy of the Anglo-Saxon Race," address before the North Carolina Baptist State Convention, reprinted in *BR*, December 1, 1907.

56. John E. White, "Prohibition: The New Task and Opportunity of the South," *South Atlantic Quarterly* 7 (April 1908): 130–42; William T. Tardy, *The Man and the Message* (Marshall, Tex., 1920), 186; Montgomery Baptist Association (Alabama) *Minutes*, 1911, 22.

57. Thomas Dixon, *The Clansman: An Historical Romance of the Ku Klux Klan* (New York, 1905), and *The Leopard's Spots: A Romance of the White Man's Burden—1865–1900* (New York, 1902); *Alabama Baptist*, November 7, 1901, 1, June 11, 1902, 7.

58. Lynn C. Dickerson, "The Baptists of the Cumberland Mountains," *Appalachian Heritage* 3 (Spring 1975): 60, quoted in Deborah Vansau McCauley, *Appalachian Mountain Religion: A History* (Champaign-Urbana, Ill., 1995), 204; Albert E. Brown quoted in *The Home Mission Task*, ed. Victor Masters (Atlanta, 1914), 210. See also William Gooddell Frost, "Our Contemporary Ancestors in the Southern Mountains," *Atlantic Monthly* 83 (March 1899): 311–19. For more on the history and culture of religion in the mountains, see James L. Peacock and Ruel W. Tyson Jr., *Pilgrims of Paradox: Calvinism and Experience Among the Primitive Baptists of the Blue Ridge* (Washington, D.C., 1989).

59. John E. White, "The Southern Highlands," in *The Home Mission Task*, ed. Victor Masters (Atlanta, 1914), 231; Albert E. Brown, quoted in *The Home Mission Task*, 210; SBC *Annual*, 1885, Appendix A, xi. See also Victor Masters, "Mountain Mission Schools of the SBC," *Alabama Baptist*, August 18, 1909; *BR*, May 2, 1900; and *Our Home Field*, May 1907, 31.

60. J. H. Spencer, "Autobiography," unpublished typewritten manuscript, in J. H. Spencer Papers, folder 13, SBHLA, 182–83; "The Georgia Mountain Preacher," *BW*, June 5, 1916. See also "Needed Changes in the Policy of the Home Mission Board," *BR*, September 2, 1903.

61. See Harper, "Southern Baptists and Social Christianity," 161–64, 211–12; Mabel Swartz Withoft, *Oak and Laurel: A Study of the Mountain Mission Schools of Southern Baptists* (Nashville, 1923), 16, 139; Wayne Flynt, "Southern Baptists and Appalachia: A Case Study of Modernization and Community," *CrossRoads: A Journal of Southern Culture* 2 (Fall 1993/Winter 1994): 63–64.

62. *BW*, February 9, 1915; *RH*, January 13, 1916, May 24, March 15, 1917, March 7, September 17, 1918.

63. William Owen Carver, *Missions in the Plan of the Ages* (New York, 1908); William Owen Carver, "The Outlook for World Missions," *Home and Foreign Fields*, October 1918, 5–6; E. Y. Mullins, "The Call of Europe to Southern Baptists," pamphlet, n.d., 6–14, original in Pamphlet Collection, SBHLA; Mullins to Funk & Wagnalls Co., September 22, 1916, in Mullins letterpress books, SBTS; *RH*, October 3, 1918; M. E. Dodd, *The Democracy of the Saints* (Nashville, 1924), 75.

64. See Primer, *Protestants and American Business Methods*.

65. *RH*, October 30, 1913 (debate between R. H. Pitt and J. B. Gambrell).

66. *BW*, May 1, 1919; J. B. Gambrell, *Baptists and Their Business* (Nashville, 1916), 104; M. E. Dodd's sermon reprinted in *RH*, May 29, 1919; M. E. Dodd, *The Democracy of the Saints* (Nashville, 1924), 25–26, 53. See also James F. Love, *The Union Movement* (Nashville, 1918), 65–67, 106, 111, 114. For a fuller explication of the SBC response to the union movement, see James J. Thompson Jr., *Tried as By Fire: Southern Baptists and the Religious Controversies of the 1920s* (Macon, Ga., 1982), 3–28.

67. J. O. Alderman to L. G. Frazier, April 10, 1919, in J. O. Alderman Papers, WFU; Masters, ed., *The Home Mission Task*, 14–16; John W. Porter, "The Baptist Debt to the World," typewritten manuscript of sermon delivered before SBC on May 12, 1915, in Convention Sermon Collection, SBHLA.

68. E. Y. Mullins, *Faith in the Modern World* (Nashville, 1910); Baptist General Association of Virginia *Minutes*, 1917, 120–22; John W. Porter, *Evolution—A Menace* (Nashville, 1922), 67; George Wood, "A Case of Misdirected Energy" (Macon, Ga., 1919), pamphlet found in George Blount Papers, folder 8, SBHLA.

69. For a look at the future conservatism of the SBC, see Edward L. Queen II, *In The South the Baptists are the Center of Gravity: Southern Baptists and Social Change, 1930–1980* (Brooklyn, N.Y., 1991); Ellen Rosenberg, *The Southern Baptists: A Subculture in Transition* (Knoxville, 1989); Nancy T. Ammerman, *Baptist Battles: Social Change and Religious Conflict in the Southern Baptist Convention* (New Brunswick, N.J., 1990); and David T. Morgan, *The New Crusades, The New Holy Land: Conflict in the Southern Baptist Convention, 1969–1991* (Tuscaloosa, Ala., 1996). These four authors provide different but complementary perspectives on the continued conflict between progressives and traditionalists in the denomination.

Chapter 8

1. A balanced assessment may be found in William Montgomery, *Under Their Own Vine and Fig Tree: The African-American Church in the South, 1865–1900* (Baton Rouge, 1993). The charge of the "deradicalization" of the church may be found in Gayraud Wilmore, *Black Religion and Black Radicalism: An Interpretation of the Religious History of the Afro-American People*, 2nd ed. (Maryknoll, N.Y., 1983), 187–227; Theophus Smith, *Conjuring Culture: Biblical Formations of Black America* (New York, 1994), emphasizes the enduring Africanness of the African-American church.

2. J. R. L. Diggs, "The Negro as a Social Scientist," *NBM*, September 1901, 343. See also *National Baptist Union-Review*, April 12, 1919 (L. L. Campbell). For more on the black church's response to social issues, see W. E. B. Du Bois's classic *The Negro Church: Report of a Social Study Made under the Direction of Atlanta University* (Atlanta, 1903); Carter G. Woodson, *The History of the Negro Church* (Washington, D.C., 1921); Joseph R. Washington, *Black Religion: The Negro and Christianity in the United States* (Boston, 1964); E. Franklin Frazier, *The Negro Church in America* (New York, 1964); Wilmore, *Black Religion and Black Radicalism*, and Albert Raboteau, *A Fire in the Bones: Reflections on African-American Religious History* (Boston, 1995).

3. Bureau of the Census, *Religious Bodies, 1906*, vol. 1 (Washington, D.C., 1910), 137–39; Bureau of the Census, *Religious Bodies, 1916*, part 1, vol. 1 (Washington, D.C., 1919), 121–28; Montgomery, *Under Their Own Vine and Fig Tree*, 105–8.

4. See Clarence Walker, *A Rock in a Weary Land: The African Methodist Episcopal*

Church During the Civil War and Reconstruction (Baton Rouge, 1982); Stephen Ward Angell, *Bishop Henry McNeal Turner and African-American Religion in the South* (Knoxville, 1992); and James Campbell, *Songs of Zion: The African Methodist Episcopal Church in the United States and South Africa* (New York, 1995).

5. NBC *Journal*, 1905, 23. See also Peter Paris, *The Social Teachings of the Black Churches* (Philadelphia, 1985).

6. J. H. Eason, *Sanctification versus Fanaticism* (Nashville, 1899), 98–99; NBC *Journal*, 1902, 22, 27; E. C. Morris, "Negro Baptists—Retrospective and Prospective," *NBM*, October 1897, 439, 444, and "The Negro's Work for the Negro," *The Baptist World Alliance, Second Congress, Philadelphia, June 19–25, 1911* (Philadelphia, 1911), 286–90; Morris, address before National Baptist Convention in 1897, reprinted in E. C. Morris, *Sermons, Addresses, Reminiscences* (Nashville, 1901), 69–77; see also ibid., 36–40, 111, 114. Missionary Baptist Convention of Texas *Minutes*, 1886, 46–50. See also Harvey Johnson, "A Fraternal Letter," *NBM*, January 1896, 16–18; *National Baptist Union-Review*, June 21, 1902.

7. C. T. Walker, "The Negro Church as Medium for Race Expression," in *The New Voice in Race Adjustments*, ed. A. M. Trawick (New York, 1914), 50–54. For more on the general currents of black thought in the early twentieth century, see David Levering Lewis, *W. E. B. Du Bois: Biography of a Race, 1868–1919* (New York, 1993), and August Meier, *Negro Thought in America, 1880–1915: Racial Ideologies in the Age of Booker T. Washington* (Ann Arbor, Mich., 1963).

8. *BR*, August 15, 1890; Isaac D. Chapman, "The Future Hope of the Negro, Despite Great Obstacles," *NBM*, April 1898, 566; Texas Baptist State Sunday School Convention *Minutes*, 1900, 54–56, copy in ABHS; C. H. Parrish, *Golden Jubilee of the General Association of Colored Baptists in Kentucky* (Louisville, Ky., 1915), 15; *National Baptist Union*, November 21, 1908, 4; NBC *Journal*, 1907, 28–34; E. C. Morris, "The Church as a Factor in Solving the Race Problem in America," *NBM*, April 1899, 185–87.

9. *BR*, March 19, 1902, September 16, 1903; *BHMM*, July 1899, 264; *BR*, May 11, 1904. See also *Alabama Baptist*, May 17, April 26, 1900.

10. B. F. Riley, "Our Attitude to the Negro," *BW*, March 1, 1917, 5; *BW*, August 5, 1915 ("Uneeda Hunch"); SBC *Annual*, 1915, 48–50; Benjamin F. Riley, *The White Man's Burden: A Discussion of the Interracial Question with Special Reference to the Responsibility of the White Race to the Negro Problem* (Birmingham, 1910); E. Y. Mullins to O. H. Van Norden, January 12, 1907, in Mullins letterpress books, SBTS; *BW*, May 27, 1915; *Baptist Standard*, November 27, 1902 (J. B. Cranfill).

11. *Alabama Baptist*, March 1, 1894; John Broadus, article in *Courier Journal*, September 27, 1886, reprinted in *Life and Letters of John Broadus*, ed. Archibald T. Robertson (Philadelphia, 1901), 352–54; *BR*, October 10, 1906; *CI*, October 4, September 6, 1906.

12. Joel Williamson, *A Rage for Order: Black / White Relations in the American South Since Emancipation* (New York, 1986); W. H. Knight, *Missions in Principle and Practice* (Nashville, 1929), 165.

13. *National Baptist Union-Review*, July 19, 1902; NBC *Journal*, 1912, 33–36, 1904, 30; Morris, *Sermons, Addresses, Reminiscences*, 36–40; W. B. Johnson, "The Church as a Factor in the Race Problem," in *Sparks From My Anvil: Sermons and Addresses* (Lynchburg, Va., 1899), 43.

14. NBC *Journal*, 1899, 63–65; Alabama Colored Baptist State Convention *Proceedings*, 1896, 26–29; Morris, *Sermons, Addresses, Reminiscences*, 119; NBC *Journal*, 1907, 30–32.

15. Baptist State Educational and Missionary Convention of North Carolina *Minutes*, 1899, 20–21; Lott Carey Baptist Foreign Mission Convention *Proceedings*, 1908, n.p.

16. Roanoke Missionary Baptist Association *Minutes*, 1895, 9; General Missionary Baptist Convention of Mississippi *Minutes*, 1895, reprinted in Patrick Thompson, *History of Negro Baptists in Mississippi* (Jackson, 1898); *National Baptist Union-Review*, April 12, 1919 (L. L. Campbell); NBC *Journal*, 1907, 78–79; Woman's Convention *Journal*, 1902, 18–20; *Arkansas Narratives*, orig. series 2, pt. 6, vol. 10, 35. For a careful study of the rise of segregated train travel that puts great emphasis on how the black "better class" tried to use the class card to trump the race card, see Patricia Minter, "The Codification of Jim Crow: The Origins of Segregated Railroad Transit in the South, 1865–1900" (Ph.D. diss., University of Virginia, 1994).

17. J. T. Brown, "The Bible's Attitude Towards Lynching," *NBM*, January 1894, 8; *National Baptist Union*, June 28, 1902; Old Eastern Missionary Baptist Association *Minutes*, 1911, 14. Among the many books on lynching and racial violence, a particularly illuminating volume is Fitzhugh Brundage, *Lynching in the New South: Georgia and Virginia, 1880–1930* (Urbana, Ill., 1993).

18. Sutton E. Griggs, *Imperium In Imperio* (1899; reprint, New York, 1969), and *The Hindered Hand; Or, the Reign of the Repressionist* (Nashville, 1905).

19. Sutton E. Griggs, *Wisdom's Call* (Nashville, 1911), and *Building Our Own: A Plea for a Parallel Civilization* (Memphis, 1923). For more information on Griggs, see Lester Lamon, *Black Tennesseans, 1900–1930* (Knoxville, 1977), 12–14; Edward Ayers, *Southern Crossing: A History of the American South, 1877–1906* (New York, 1995), 44, 93, 223; and Faye Wellborn Robbins, "A World-Within-A-World: Black Nashville, 1880–1915" (Ph.D. diss., University of Arkansas, 1980), 271–72.

20. Booker T. Washington to President Theodore Roosevelt, letter reprinted in *Booker T. Washington Papers* (Urbana, Ill., 1972–1989), 9: 337; Morris, *Sermons, Addresses, Reminiscences*, 96; L. G. Jordan to Emmett Scott, in *Booker T. Washington Papers*, 8: 521.

21. Lewis, *W. E. B. Du Bois*, demonstrates the capacity of ministers to straddle the fence in the debate and also illustrates Washington's great skill at holding ministers in line through means fair and foul. See also Louis Harlan, *Booker T. Washington: The Wizard of Tuskegee, 1901–1915* (New York, 1983).

22. Booker T. Washington, "Why Push Industrial Education in the South," *NBM*, July 1898, 166–67; Bernard Tyrrell, "Watchman, What of the Night," *NBM*, April 1894, 89–95. See also H. P. Cheatham, "Educational Work for the Negroes," *BHMM*, November 1898, 371–74; Texas Baptist State Sunday School Convention *Minutes*, 1900, 15.

23. E. C. Morris, "Industrial Education," *NBM*, January 1896, 11–14; Speech of Sutton Griggs to the Woman's Convention, Auxiliary to the NBC, *Journal*, 1903, 316–17; *National Baptist Union*, November 22, 1902. See also R. H. Bowling, "God's Hand in the History of the American Negro," *NBM*, May 1901, 274.

24. P. H. Collier, "The Future of the Negro in the United States," *NBM*, October 1895, 210–14; Morris, *Sermons, Addresses, Reminiscences*, 163; Charles T. Walker, *The*

Negro Problem: Its Scriptural Solution, Sermon Delivered at Tabernacle Baptist Church, Augusta, Georgia, Sunday June 4, 1893 (Augusta, Ga., 1893), 12–16. See also Johnson, "The Religious Status of the Negro," in *Sparks From My Anvil: Sermons and Addresses* (Lynchburg, Va., 1899), 12–17.

25. *CI*, editorial reprint in *Alabama Baptist*, October 3, 1906; NBC *Journal*, 1904, 158–66; "The Saloon and Demoralization," *Alabama Baptist*, March 10, 1909; *Alabama Baptist*, April 21, 1909 (B. F. Riley).

26. Minutes of the First African Baptist Church, Richmond, Virginia, December 4, 1877, copy in Virginia State Library, Richmond, Virginia; *South Carolina Narratives*, orig. series 1, vol. 3, pt. 3, 39; *Home Mission Echoes*, December 1902, 1 (S. E. De-Lamotta).

27. Roanoke Missionary Baptist Association (North Carolina) *Minutes*, 1914, 6; Samuel Vass, "Temperance is the Problem," *NBM*, October 1899, 73; *National Baptist Union-Review*, January 4, 1919, 3.

28. Lucy Smith, "The Future Colored Girl," American National Baptist Convention *Minutes and Addresses*, 1886, 68–74; Mary Cook, "Women's Place in the Work of the Denomination," American National Baptist Convention *Journal and Lectures*, 1887, 45–56.

29. Virginia Broughton, *Twenty Years' Experience of a Missionary* (Chicago, 1907), 30–35.

30. Broughton, *Twenty Year's Experience of a Missionary*, 34, 79–82. For stories of black women's clubs, see Maude T. Jenkins, *The History of the Black Woman's Club Movement in America* (Ed.D. diss., Columbia University, 1984), and Janette Thomas Greenwood, *Bittersweet Legacy: The Black and White "Better Classes" in Charlotte, 1850–1910* (Chapel Hill, 1994). See William Andrews, ed., *Sisters of the Spirit: Three Black Women's Autobiographies of the Nineteenth Century* (Bloomington, Ind., 1986), for the autobiographies of black female holiness exhorters.

31. NBC *Journal*, 1902, 58–60; Annie Armstrong to James M. Frost, January 26, 1897, in James Marion Frost Papers, box 3, SSB; Annie Armstrong to J. M. Frost, July 19, 1892, in Frost Papers, box 1, folder 1, SSB; WMU *Report*, 1895, 14, 1897, 15–20. See also Jacqueline Jones, *Soldiers of Light and Love: Northern Teachers and Georgia Blacks, 1865–1873* (Chapel Hill, 1980).

32. Statistics from W. B. Johnson, "The Story of Negro Baptists," *National Baptist Union*, January 30, 1909; Burroughs quote from NBC *Journal*, 1900, 196–97.

33. Woman's Convention *Journal*, 1902, 12, 1903, 27–28, 43–46, 1905, 344–45, 1911, 73–74. For more on black women's working lives, see Jacqueline Jones, *Labor of Love, Labor of Sorrow: Black Women, Work, and the Family from Slavery to the Present* (New York, 1985). For more on Burroughs's feminist theology, see Evelyn Brooks, "The Feminist Theology of the Black Baptist Church," in *Class, Race and Sex: The Dynamics of Control*, ed. Amy Swendlow and Hanna Lessinger (Boston, 1983), 31–59; and Evelyn Brooks, "Nannie Burroughs and the Education of Black Women," in *The Afro-American Woman: Struggles and Images*, ed. Sharon Harley and Rosalyn Terborg-Penn (Port Washington, N.Y., 1978), 97–108.

34. *Fifteenth Annual Report of the Executive Board and Corresponding Secretary of the Woman's Convention, Auxiliary to the National Baptist Convention* [Nashville, 1915], 50–52; Woman's Convention *Journal*, 1908, 264–65, 273; 1911, 42–44; 1903, 316–17.

35. Woman's Convention *Journal*, 1909, 286–92; Union Baptist State Convention of North Carolina *Proceedings*, 1917, 26–27.

36. Woman's Convention *Journal*, 1909, 286, 1930, 5. Elizabeth Lasch-Quinn argues that the conservative nature of industrial education has been overstated and that vocational training of the kind offered by Tuskegee and its imitators was part of the broader trend away from classical curricula, which characterized progressive educational thought in the late nineteenth century. See Elizabeth Lasch-Quinn, *Black Neighbors: Race and the Limits of Reform in the American Settlement House Movement, 1890–1945* (Chapel Hill, 1993).

37. L. G. Jordan, *Negro Baptist History, U.S.A.* (Nashville, 1930), 250; Report of the Publishing Board and the Home Mission Board, NBC *Journal*, 1900.

38. See Don H. Doyle, *Nashville in the New South, 1880–1930* (Knoxville, 1985), 116–17, for a discussion of the variety of publishing enterprises centered in Nashville. See also Jordan, *Negro Baptist History*, 240–60.

39. SBC *Annual*, 1897, Appendix B, 74; [National Baptist Publishing Board], *Twelfth Annual Report of the Home Mission Board, Together With Eleventh Annual Report of the National Baptist Publishing Board for the Fiscal Year Ending August 31, 1907* (Nashville, 1907); NBC *Journal*, 1899, 42–43; *National Baptist Union*, July 19, 1902.

40. W. B. Johnson, "The Story of Negro Baptists," *National Baptist Union*, January 30, 1909; Leroy Fitts, *A History of Black Baptists* (Nashville, 1985), 83. For more information on Boyd, see Henry Lewis Suggs, ed., *The Black Press in the South, 1865–1979* (Westport, Conn., 1983), 313–55.

41. The confusing facts of the publishing board's relationship to the NBC are set out in Jordan, *Negro Baptist History*, 247–50, though Jordan was hardly an impartial observer to the controversy (he was in the anti-Boyd faction). See also Richard H. Boyd, *A Story of the National Baptist Publishing Board. The Why, How, When, Where, and By Whom It Was Established* [Nashville, n.d.].

42. See Fitts, *A History of Black Baptists*, 89–98, for a detailed account of the dispute. Jordan, *Negro Baptist History*, 127, 135.

43. "Statement of the Causes of Confusion," NBC *Journal*, 1915, 33–34. Morris's speech was interrupted by a court injunction, which halted the convention's proceedings and caused chaos on the floor of the convention. Morris's speech was later continued after the court allowed the convention to continue its business and after Boyd had staged a walkout. *Lawyers Opinion Defining the Relation of the National Baptist Convention to the National Baptist Publishing Board and Its Other Boards*, 1915, copy in SBHLA.

44. NBC of America *Journal*, 1916, 61–135, gives Boyd's side of the controversy. See also *National Baptist Union-Review*, April 12, July 26, 1919.

45. Edgar Young Mullins to O. L. Hailey, January 8, 1919, in Mullins letterpress books, and O. L. Hailey to Edgar Young Mullins, February 8, 1918, in Mullins letter files, both in SBTS; SBC *Annual*, 1918, 67–69; M. F. R. Chapman, "The Baptist Difference as Seen by a Texan," *National Baptist Union-Review*, April 5, 1919.

46. Quoted in Lester Lamon, *Black Tennesseans, 1900–1930* (Knoxville, 1977), 1; *National Baptist Union*, December 6, 1902.

47. See Glenn Eskew, "Black Elitism and the Failure of Paternalism in Postbellum Georgia: The Case of Bishop Lucius Henry Holsey," *Journal of Southern History* 58

(November 1992): 637–66, who cites the *Augusta Chronicle*, June 3, 5, 1900; and Robbins, "A World-Within-A-World," 212–13. For more on the outcome of the boycott, see Lamon, *Black Tennesseans*, 12–14; Doyle, *Nashville in the New South*, 116–20; and Robbins, "A World-Within-A-World," 126–27, 212–13, 249–50.

48. *National Baptist Union*, October 24, December 19, 1908; Samuel Shannon, "Tennessee," in *The Black Press in the South, 1865–1979*, ed. Henry Lewis Suggs (Westport, Conn., 1983), 332; NBC *Journal*, 1911, 165.

49. Christopher M. Scribner, " 'Nashville Offers Opportunity': *The Nashville Globe*, and Business as a Means of Uplift," *Tennessee Historical Quarterly* 54 (Spring 1995): 58; Lamon, *Black Tennesseans*, 12–14, 184–85; Robbins, "A World-Within-a-World," 249–50.

50. *National Baptist Union*, June 20, 1908; *National Baptist Union-Review*, July 28, 1917.

51. See Samuel Shannon, "Tennessee," 313–55, and Scribner, "Nashville Offers Opportunity," for more information on Henry Allen Boyd and the *Nashville Globe*.

52. See Robbins, "A World-Within-a-World," 249–50, and Michael W. Harris, *The Rise of Gospel Blues: The Music of Thomas Andrew Dorsey in the Urban Church* (New York, 1992), for information on Dorsey's connections with A. M. Townsend and other figures in Baptist music publishing.

53. Morris, *Sermons, Addresses, Reminiscences*, 103; *National Baptist Union*, May 24, 1902. On Turner's supporters, see Baptist Educational and Missionary Convention of North Carolina *Minutes*, 1894, 16–17. See also Donald Roth, " 'Grace Not Race': Southern Negro Church Leaders, Black Identity, and Missions to West Africa, 1865–1919" (Ph.D. diss., University of Texas, Austin, 1975). One account of a black Baptist missionary being called a white man by native Africans is C. C. Boone, *Congo As I Saw It* (New York, 1927). See also Angell, *Henry McNeal Turner*; George Shepperson, *Independent African: John Chilembwe and the Origins, Setting, and Significance of the Nyasaland Native Rising of 1915* (Edinburgh, 1958); and Campbell, *Songs of Zion*.

54. Virginia Baptist State Sunday School Convention *Minutes*, 1899, n.p.; *National Baptist Union*, November 17, 1906; New Hope Missionary Baptist Association *Minutes*, 1896, 14; *National Baptist Union*, November 21, 1908; Woman's Convention *Journal*, 1915, 202. See also West Roanoke Association (North Carolina) *Minutes*, 1914, 12, and Shiloh Baptist Association (North Carolina) *Proceedings*, 1908, 23.

55. NBC, Unincorporated, *Journal*, 1917, Appendix, 10, 123; *National Baptist Union-Review*, April 14, 1917, 13 (Resolution of Woman's First District Baptist Association); Missionary Baptist Convention of Georgia *Minutes*, 1901, 155–56. For more on the church and migration, see James R. Grossman, *Land of Hope: Chicago, Black Southerners, and the Great Migration* (Chicago, 1989), 156–60.

56. Woman's Convention *Journal*, 1907, 23–25, 1915, 200–204; Alabama Colored Baptist State Convention *Journal*, 1910, 116–18.

57. Old Eastern Missionary Baptist Association (North Carolina) *Minutes*, 1916, 26; Zion Missionary Baptist Association (North Carolina) *Minutes*, 1920, 20–21; Richard Carroll, "Races Should Agree," *The State* (Columbia, S.C.), July 6, 1917, newspaper clipping in Una Roberts Lawrence Papers, box 2, folder 2, SBHLA.

58. Missionary Baptist General Convention of Texas *Annual*, 1921, 100 (speech of L. L. Campbell, president of the convention); *National Baptist Union-Review*, April 12,

1919. See also W. B. Johnson, "National Perils," sermon delivered October, 1889, in *Sparks From My Anvil: Sermons and Addresses* (Lynchburg, Va., 1899), 18–22.

59. Georgia Baptist Missionary Convention, 1917, as reported in *Savannah Tribune*, April 28, 1917; SBC *Annual*, 1918, 57. See also Union Baptist State Convention of North Carolina *Proceedings*, 1917, 26–27, and Charles T. Walker, *The Colored Man for the Twentieth Century* (New York, n.d.).

60. *National Baptist Union-Review*, April 14, 1917, 13 (Woman's First District Baptist Association), and February 1, 1919; Roanoke Missionary Baptist Association (North Carolina) *Minutes*, 1919, 10–13.

61. C. T. Hayes, "Response to Welcome," Alabama Colored Baptist State Convention *Journal*, 1921, 123; *National Baptist Union-Review*, April 12, 1919.

62. Virginia Missionary Baptist State Convention *Annual*, 1921, 10–15; Virginia Baptist State Convention *Minutes*, 1928, 1. For more on Woodson, see Jacqueline Goggin, *Carter G. Woodson: A Life in Black History* (Baton Rouge, 1993).

63. See Nancy MacLean, *Behind the Mask of Chivalry: The Making of the Second Ku Klux Klan* (New York, 1994), and William J. Harris, "Etiquette, Lynching, and Racial Boundaries in Southern History: A Mississippi Example," *American Historical Review* 100 (April 1995): 387–410.

Colgate University, 190
Coliseum Place Baptist Church (New Orleans), 35–36
Colored Alabamian, 192
Commodity speculation, 201–2
Confederacy, 17, 18, 19, 21, 29, 32, 141, 266–67 (n. 22)
Conjure, 126–27
Conser, Solomon, 77
Consolidated American Baptist Missionary Convention (CABMC), 62–65
Cooley, Rossa, 117, 122, 123, 129
Cooperationists, 68–70
Corey, Charles, 49
Cotton mills, 160–61, 199, 214–15
Cranfill, James B., 78, 141, 216
Crumpton, A. B., 217
Cultural captivity thesis, 4, 10. *See also* Southern religious history
Curry, Jabez Lamar Monroe, 24, 39, 157, 231

Dancing, 83–84
Dargan, J. O. B., 50
Dawson, Joseph Martin, 143
Denominational reformers: centralizing desires of, 5; programmed piety of, 13; advocates of "intelligent worship," 78, 113, 258; conceptions of modernizing church life, 87–88, 157–58, 206–8; responding to Populism, 92–93; dealing with Holiness-Pentecostalism, 93–95; conceptions of revivals, 95–97; attempt to reform singing, 97–102; and fund-raising, 102–5; and lay power in churches, 118–20; advocate professionalized ministry, 138, 142–45, 157–58, 162–66, 258; decline of Calvinism among, 154; attitudes toward ministry, 157–58, 162–63; conceptions of manliness, 165–66; advocate scientific management of churches, 197–98, 258; business-mindedness of, 199–200; and corporate model for, 200; fears of commercialism, 200–201; and new vision of

church discipline, 206–7; critique modernist theology, 243–44
Denominations, 12, 22, 104–5, 113, 176–77, 199–201, 260
Dexter Avenue Baptist Church (Montgomery), 50, 58, 192
Disfranchisement, 58–59, 218–20, 230–32
Dixon, Thomas, Jr., 2, 4, 43, 169, 189, 220, 231, 234, 263 (n. 2). *See also* Racism: popular culture of
Doctrine, 83–84, 94, 152–53, 155–56, 206–10
Dodd, M. E., 224
Dorsey, Thomas Andrew, 111, 115, 129, 132, 250, 255
Dorsey, Thomas Madison, 111
Douglass, Frederick, 10, 64
Du Bois, W. E. B., 114, 123, 129, 169, 182, 229, 243, 235–36, 250, 253
Duke, Jesse, 58
Duncan, A. W., 142

Eason, James Henry, 133
Eason, John H., 192
Eaton, Thomas T., 147–48
Edgefield County, South Carolina, 18, 34, 35, 51, 52, 53
Edmonds, Richard, 214
Education: Spelman College, 2; decline of colleges, 22; opposition to interracial schools, 25; Selma University, 25; Baylor University, 37, 143; black theological institutions, 49; and trained ministry, 60, 62; support from northern Baptists, 63; black Baptists request more control over, 63–65; institutions supported by ABHMS, 65–69; racial conflicts in black schools, 68–70; musical education, 98–99, 129–32; importance for worship reform, 110–11; struggles of educational institutions in South, 143, 182–86; Mercer University, 144; Furman College, 145; Southern Baptist Theological Seminary, 145–52; effect of Civil War and Recon-

struction on, 146; Southwestern Baptist Theological Seminary, 151–52; black ministerial education, 180–86; Fortress Monroe agreement, 183–84; Benedict College, 190; Virginia Union University, 190; schools for mountaineers, 222; National Training School for Women and Girls, 242–43; history of black colleges, 277 (n. 42)

Edwards, Jonathan, 140
Elaw, Zilpha, 119
Ellison, John, 134
Emancipation, 31–34, 45, 107
Evangelicalism: centrality in South, 1; and individualism, 1; institutional expressions of, 1; concept of, 2; diverse varieties of, 2; in South, 4, 10, 13, 79–82, 93, 95–96, 152–53, 165–66, 199–201, 258, 265–66 (n. 15), 293 (n. 34); democratic forms of, 6; emotionalism in, 6, 94–97; black interpretation of, 9, 10, 257; as connected to modernism, 25, 31; domesticated forms of, 81, 152; theological conservatism of, 82, 93; Holiness-Pentecostal expressions of, 93–95; and revivalism, 95, 153–55; and hymnology, 97–101; intellectual history of, 152–53, 155–56; manliness in, 165
Evangelism, 40, 96–97, 163
Exodusters, 59

Farmer's Alliance, 92. See also Populism
Federal Council of Churches, 209, 223–24
First African Baptist Church, Richmond, 33, 48, 237
First African Baptist Church, Savannah, 9, 40, 48–49, 171, 173
First Baptist Church, Atlanta, 91
First Baptist Church, Columbus, Mississippi, 46
First Baptist Church, Jacksonville, Alabama, 36
First Baptist Church, Nashville, 48, 101
First Baptist Church, Natchez, Mississippi, 46

First Baptist Church, Richmond, Virginia, 33
First Bryan Baptist Church, 175. See also First African Baptist Church, Savannah
First Colored Baptist Church, Montgomery, 50
First Colored Baptist Church, Nashville, 67
Fisk University, 67, 116, 239, 250
Foner, Eric, 55
Footwashing, 78–79, 94
Foreign Mission Board (NBC), 188
Foreign Mission Board (SBC), 28
Fortress Monroe agreement, 183–84
Frazier, Garrison, 55
Freedmen's Bureau, 35, 49, 52, 55, 56, 64
Freedmen's Standard (Georgia), 57
Freedpeople: jubilation over freedom, 45, 107; suspicion of white Christians, 46; freedmen's conventions, 47, 53–56; assisted by whites, 48–51; establishing independent religious life, 50–52; harassed by whites, 52–54; political activity excited by ministers, 57–58; in plantation districts, 58, 111; social life of, 59, 124–25; seen as impulsive, 60; and CABMC, 62–64; religious culture of, 77–78, 107–8, 113–35; religious life ridiculed, 107–12; baptism of, 121–22; and ring shouts, 122–23; music of, 123; revivals and funerals of, 124–27; superstitions of, 126–27; musical preferences of, 128–30
Friendship Baptist Church (Atlanta), 49
Frost, James Marion, 29–30, 140, 148, 240, 244–45
Fuller, Thomas, 181, 188–89
Fundamentalism, 12, 91, 150, 152, 153, 154, 207, 225, 259, 260, 267 (n. 24)
Fund-raising, 25–28, 51–52, 68–70, 101–5, 129–30, 146–47, 159–62, 173
Furman College, 145

Savannah Tribune, 112
Segregation, 42–43
Selma University, 58
Seventy-Five Million Campaign, 105.
    See also Fund-raising; Southern
    Baptist Convention: fund-raising
    methods of
Shaw University, 65–67, 187, 188
Sherman, William Tecumseh, 56
Shiloh Baptist Church, Northumberland
    County, Virginia, 50
Simkins, Paris, 52
Simmons, William J., 58, 70, 190, 193,
    239
Simms, James, 56–57, 175
Singing: southern styles of, 12, 97–99;
    lining out hymns, 13, 77, 97–98, 100,
    110, 113, 128–29; choirs, 97, 98,
    101–2, 129–30; shape-note singing,
    97–98, 100–102, 127–28, 129; older
    styles of, 97–98, 113, 128–29; newer
    styles of, 98–102, 113, 130–32; with
    organs, 100–101, 129; worries about
    stylistic excesses, 101–2; black styles
    of, 110–11, 113, 122–24, 126, 127–32;
    of slaves, 123, 128–29; at revivals and
    funerals, 124–26; meaning of for black
    Baptists, 128–31; and demise of spiri-
    tuals, 129–31
Slavery, 6, 8, 9, 11, 23, 31, 32, 38, 45–47,
    55–57, 108, 109, 123, 128–29, 134,
    152
Smith, Hoke, 219
Smith, W. R. L., 153
Social Darwinism, 204
Social gospel, 1, 91–92, 151–52, 197–98,
    204–6, 206–16 passim, 224–25, 302
    (n. 2)
South: blacks advised to live in, 1; patri-
    archal authority in, 6; seen as having
    special role, 31; seen as primitive, 78,
    258; modernizing of, 113, 199–201,
    203–6; urbanization of, 199–201;
    immigration to, 203; preservation of
    purity of, 203; class society in, 204–6.
    See also Southern Baptists; Southern

evangelicalism; Southern religious
history
South Carolina, 18, 21, 31, 32, 51, 208
Southern Baptist Convention (SBC):
    formation of, 6, 18; legal structure of,
    6–7; constituency of, 8, 214; size of,
    17, 22, 30–31; policy toward reunion
    with northern Baptists, 23, 28, 38;
    conceptions of women's roles, 26–27,
    104; Home Mission Board of, 27–28;
    Sunday School Board of, 28–30, 70–
    71; and corporate methods of opera-
    tion, 30, 104–5, 200; policy toward
    black withdrawal from churches, 38,
    40; opposition to antimissionism,
    83–84; rural church surveys of, 86–88;
    attacked by antimissionists, 90–91;
    and Populism, 92–93; policy toward
    revivals, 96–97; hymnbooks of, 98–
    100; fund-raising methods of, 102–6;
    Seventy-Five Million Campaign of,
    104–5; promoting professionalized
    ministry, 140–41, 154–55; and Whit-
    sitt controversy, 149; assistance in
    black ministerial education, 182–86;
    opposition to interracial endeavors,
    184–85; conservative orthodoxy of,
    198; social gospel in, 198, 209–11; atti-
    tudes toward working class, 203–5;
    Social Service Commission of, 209–
    10; attitudes toward women's suffrage,
    211–12; women's role in meetings of,
    212; and Prohibition movement, 216–
    18; and work among mountaineers,
    220–22; support for World War I,
    223–24; relationship to Interchurch
    World Movement, 224; conservative
    coup in, 259–60. *See also* Southern
    Baptists
Southern Baptists: as part of mainstream
    of religious history, 3; drive for respect-
    ability, 3–5, 78–79, 94–97, 143–44;
    cultural captivity of, 4; localism of, 4;
    split from North, 6, 9; defending slav-
    ery, 9; responding to Civil War, 11, 18,
    20; congregationalism of, 12; theologi-

cal views of, 12, 147–48, 152–56; as
part of evangelical consensus, 13, 152;
marginalization from dominant culture, 13, 267 (n. 26); opposition to civil
rights, 21–23, 41–42; ministering to
blacks, 39–40, 182–84; and white and
black religious separation, 46–49; rural
constituency of, 80, 86–88; religious
culture of, 81–85; and doctrine, 83–84,
94–95; encouraged to support temperance, 84–85; Landmarkists, 88–90;
differences in Southeast and Southwest, 88–90, 145, 147–48, 152; and
Populism, 91–93; and Holiness-
Pentecostalism, 93–95, 134–35; and
hymnbooks, 98–101; and singing styles
of, 97–100; and fund-raising, 100–106;
and black worship, 108–12; and professionalization of clergy, 138, 144,
158–66; ministerial education among,
142–52; modernizing theology of,
153–56; as defenders of theological
conservatism, 154–56; changing pulpit
manner, 156–58; ministerial salaries of,
158–62; and conflict between ministers and laypeople, 160–65; rural ministers among, 165; as advocates of
social gospel, 198, 206–22 passim; fear
of immigrants among, 202–3; and
women's suffrage, 211; and women's
social activism, 211–14; and mountaineers, 220–22; responding to World
War I, 222–24; and Interchurch World
Movement, 224
Southern Baptist Theological Seminary,
Louisville, Kentucky, 18, 79, 90, 99,
144–54, 184, 208–10, 212–13, 231, 293
(n. 31)
Southern culture, 4, 22, 31, 77–78, 79–
80, 91–97, 108–9, 113–14, 199–201
Southern Education Board, 24, 231. See
also Curry, Jabez Lamar Monroe
Southern evangelicalism: emphasis on
experience, 4; moral failings of, 4;
varieties of, 4; responses to slavery,
8–9; national identity of, 31; paternal-

istic community of, 34; slave evangelization of, 38; evangelization of
among freedpeople, 40–41; folk cul-
ture of, 78–80; self-denial required in,
115; sects in, 116; effect of slavery on,
152; responding to urbanization, 199–
201; and social gospel, 206–22 passim,
301–2 (nn. 2, 3, 4); and response to
World War I, 222–25
Southern honor, 22, 200
Southern religious history, 1, 3, 177–78,
262–63 (n. 1)
Southern Tenant Farmer's Union, 117.
See also Cobb, Ned
Southwestern Baptist Theological Semi-
nary, 99, 151–52
Spanish-American War, 41, 250
Spelman College, 49, 65
Spencer, James H., 19, 20, 158, 221
Spilman, Bernard, 147, 217
Springfield Baptist Church, Augusta,
Georgia, 174
Stearns, Shubal, 5
Stetson, George, 122
Stevens, Thaddeus, 32
Stowe, Harriet Beecher, 172
Sunday School Board, Southern Baptist
Convention, 28–30, 71, 140, 244–45
Sunday schools, 29, 30, 35, 70–71, 83,
87, 129–30

Tabernacle Baptist Church, Raleigh,
218
Tardy, William Thomas, 164
Taylor, Frederick Winslow, 197
Temperance. See Prohibition
Tennessee, 19, 29, 88–91, 143, 145–46
Tennessee Baptist and Reflector, 89–90
Texas, 21, 37, 62, 69–70
Theology: literalism in, 1, 146; Calvinist
variations of, 4–5, 96, 145, 152–53,
154–55; proslavery views in, 8–9, 32;
struggle against modernism, 12, 13,
29, 39, 143, 146–48, 151, 154–55, 197;
southern evangelical varieties of, 12,
151–55; critique of liberal faith, 17,

23–25, 39, 89; explanations of war, 18–20; explanation of Reconstruction, 21, 23; explanation of role of South, 22; defense of conservatism in, 25, 30, 143–44, 148, 155; as expressed in publications, 29, 30; explanation of emancipation and black withdrawal, 33, 34–35; and church discipline, 82; on predestination, 83; southeastern and southwestern variations of, 89–91, 148, 151; Holiness-Pentecostal variations of, 93–94, 133–34; in hymnbooks, 97–101; of singing styles, 101–2; of black conceptions of salvation, 114–20; of dreams and visions, 117–20; of white conceptions of salvation, 140–42; in creed of seminaries, 145; in controversies in seminaries, 147–48; moderate versions of, 150, 154; revivalist varieties of, 152, 155; northern versus southern versions of, 152; millennialism in, 154–55, 209; of social gospel, 208–10; and conceptions of women's role, 211–12; feminist versions of, 241–42

Third African Baptist Church, Savannah, Georgia, 56
Thompson, Holland, 58
Tichenor, Isaac Taylor, 27, 39
Towne, Laura, 117, 122–23
Townsend, Arthur Melvin, 132
Toy, Crawford H., 147
Tucker, Henry Holcombe, 31, 41
Tupper, Henry M., 66–67
Turner, Frederick Jackson, 80
Turner, Henry McNeal, 228, 250
Turner, Nat, 9
Tyrell, Bernard, 236

Unionism, 35, 42, 47, 56–58, 188
Union Transportation Company, 248
University of Virginia, 143

Vaughan, Allen, 127
Veblen, Thorstein, 204
Vesey, Denmark, 9

Victorianism, 100, 152, 203, 209, 229, 258
Virginia, 70, 190
Virginia Baptists: support for Confederacy, 18; Baptist worship houses destroyed in, 19; attitude toward Redemption, 59; social life of, 59; organization of state convention in, 61; schism of black state convention, 70; support of cooperationism, 73; social service programs of, 87–88; and Landmarkism, 87–90, 149; and revivalism, 96; John Jasper as representative of, 109; and folk ministerial conceptions, 142; supporting W. H. Whitsitt, 149; fears of urbanization among, 200; and social gospel, 208; and World War I, 225, 254
Virginia Seminary, 70
Virginia Union University, Richmond, 70, 190

Waddell, Arthur, 53
Wake Forest Baptist Church, Winston-Salem, North Carolina, 34, 85, 103, 159, 162
Walker, Charles T. 171, 237
Walker, William ("Singing Billy"), 98
Walnut Street Baptist Church, Louisville, Kentucky, 147
Washington, Booker T., 2, 55, 178, 187, 193, 229, 231, 235–36, 243, 249
Waters Normal Institute, 65
Watson, Tom, 92
Watts, Isaac, 99, 131
Wayland, Francis, 145
Weaver, Rufus, 202
Wesley, Charles, 131
White, Charley, 116, 133–34, 170, 178
White, John E., 88, 211, 220
White, H. H., 63
White, William Jefferson, 55–56, 192, 248
White supremacy, 18, 22, 23, 24, 31, 37, 39, 42–43, 93, 219–20
Whitsitt, William H. 148–49